ISBN 978-1-331-18936-7
PIBN 10156085

FB &c Ltd, Dalton House, 60 Windsor Avenue, London, SW19 2RR.
Company number 08720141. Registered in England and Wales.

For support please visit www.forgottenbooks.com

A HISTORY OF WALES

FROM THE EARLIEST TIMES TO THE
EDWARDIAN CONQUEST

BY

JOHN EDWARD LLOYD, M.A.

PROFESSOR OF HISTORY IN THE UNIVERSITY COLLEGE OF NORTH WALES, BANGOR

IN TWO VOLUMES

VOL. I

LONGMANS, GREEN, AND CO.

39 PATERNOSTER ROW, LONDON

NEW YORK, BOMBAY, AND CALCUTTA

1911

ST. MICHAEL'S COLLEGE
LIBRARY

PREFACE.

In this work it has been my endeavour to bring together and to weave into a continuous narrative what may be fairly regarded as the ascertained facts of the history of Wales up to the fall of Llywelyn ap Gruffydd in 1282. In a field where so much is matter of conjecture, it has not been possible altogether to avoid speculation and hypothesis, but I can honestly say that I have not written in support of any special theory or to urge any preconceived opinion upon the reader. My purpose has been to map out, in this difficult region of study, what is already known and established, and thus to define more clearly the limits of that "terra incognita" which still awaits discovery. The task has not been attempted in English since Miss Jane Williams (Ysgafell) published her *History of Wales* in 1869, and it cannot be doubted, therefore, that it was time to undertake it anew.

The enterprise, it need scarcely be said, has been a laborious one, and, as the occupation of somewhat limited hours of leisure, has been spread over a considerable number of years. In some respects this may have been an advantage, but it has entailed certain drawbacks also. Had the earlier chapters been written more recently, they might have owed more than they do to the study of such works as Dr. Holmes' *Ancient Britain* and Professor Bury's *Life of St. Patrick.* For this and many other shortcomings I can but crave the indulgence of the reader.

It has been my endeavour to indicate, in the footnotes and elsewhere, my innumerable obligations to other workers in this field of study. But I should wish here to express my general indebtedness to Sir John Rhys, Mr. Egerton Phillimore, Mr. Alfred N. Palmer, and Dr. Hugh Williams for the pioneer work which has so greatly facilitated the scientific study of Welsh history. I owe to them what cannot be expressed in the debit of citation and reference, namely, outlook and method and inspiration.

For assistance given to me ungrudgingly during the progress of the work, I desire to thank Principal J. R. Ainsworth Davis, M.A., Professor T. F. Tout, M.A., Professor J. Morris Jones, M.A., Professor W. Lewis Jones, M.A., Mr. Edward Greenly, F.G.S., Mr. Percy G. Thomas, M.A., Mr. O. T. Williams, M.A., and the Rev. T. Shankland.

Most of the primary authorities used are discussed in some part or other of the book. The reader may notice, however, that nowhere is there any full and systematic discussion of the chronicles included in *Annales Cambriæ* and *Brut y Tywysogion.* I had originally intended to include a critical account of these authorities in the work, but afterwards came to the conclusion that the task was too ambitious for the present occasion and must be separately undertaken. Let it suffice here to say that I have throughout treated *Brut y Tywysogion* and *Brut* (or *Brenhinedd*) *y Saeson* as two independent translations of a Latin original partially (but by no means fully) represented in MSS. B. and C. of *Annales Cambriæ.*

The Map is intended to be of general service to

those who may use the book, and does not reproduce the political divisions of Wales at any definite point in its history. For North Wales, however, it is approximately correct for the year 1200. Cantrefs are usually indicated, but in Anglesey, Powys, Ceredigion and Morgannwg, commotes are shown as there the more important.

In the spelling of Welsh names, I have sought to observe the rules laid down in 1893 by the Orthographical Committee of the Society for Utilising the Welsh Language.

My thanks are due to Miss E. M. Samson for the compilation of the Index.

JOHN EDWARD LLOYD.

BANGOR, 1st *November*, 1910.

CONTENTS OF VOLUME I.

CHAPTER V.

THE AGE OF THE SAINTS.

CHAPTER VI.

STRUGGLE OF THE CYMRY AND THE ENGLISH.

CHAPTER VII.

THE AGE OF ISOLATION.

CHAPTER VIII.

THE TRIBAL DIVISIONS OF WALES.

CHAPTER IX.

EARLY WELSH INSTITUTIONS.

CHAPTER X.

THE AGE OF THE SEA-ROVERS.

CORRIGENDA.

Page	43, line	8.	*For* understand,		*read*	understood.
,,	129, ,,	17.	,, form,		,,	from.
,,	132, ,,	6.	,, Aurelius,		,,	Aurelianus.

INDEX OF AUTHORS, WORKS, MSS., ETC., CITED IN THE NOTES.

A. S. Chr. The Anglo-Saxon or English Chronicles are quoted by reference to the annal and sometimes to the MS. also. The text used is that of Earle and Plummer ("Two of the Saxon Chronicles parallel," revised text, Oxford, 1892); references to the introduction and notes of this edition are given as Plummer, ii.

Ang. Sac. Anglia Sacra [ed. Hen. Wharton]. Two vols. London, 1691.

Ann. ad 1298. Annals from A.D. 600-1298 written in Breviate of Domesday (K. R. miscellaneous books i.), ff. 29-35, and printed in Arch. Camb. III. viii. (1862), 273-283.

Ann. C. Annales Cambriæ. Ed. J. Williams Ab Ithel (Rolls Series). 1860.

Ann. Cest. Annales Cestrienses [Mostyn MS. 157]. Ed. R. C. Christie (Lancashire and Cheshire Record Society, vol. xiv.). London, 1887.

Ann. Dunst. Annales Prioratus de Dunstaplia in vol. iii. of Annales Monastici (Rolls Series). London, 1866.

Ann. Marg. Annales de Margan in vol. i. of Annales Monastici (Rolls Series). London, 1864.

Ann. Osen. Annales Monasterii de Oseneia in vol. iv. of Annales Monastici (Rolls Series). London, 1869.

Ann. S. Edm. Annales S. Edmundi [Bury St. Edmund's] printed by Liebermann in Ungedruckte Anglo-Normanische Geschichtsquellen from Harl. MS. 447. Strassburg, 1879.

Ann. Theokesb. Annales de Theokesberia in vol. i. of Annales Monastici (Rolls Series). London, 1864.

Ann. Ult. The Annals of Ulster or Annals of Senat. Issued by the Royal Irish Academy (Dublin).

Vol. i. 431-1056 (ed. W. M. Hennessy). 1887.
ii. 1057-1378 (ed. B. MacCarthy). 1893.
iii. 1379-1541 („ „). 1895.

Ann. Waverl. Annales Monasterii de Waverleia in vol. ii. of Annales Monastici (Rolls Series). London, 1865.

Ann. Wigorn. Annales Prioratus de Wigornia in vol. iv. of Annales Monastici (Rolls Series). London, 1869.

Ann. Wint. Annales Monasterii de Wintonia in vol. ii. of Annales Monastici (Rolls Series). London, 1865.

Antt. Legg. De Antiquis Legibus Liber; Cronica Maiorum et Vicecomitum Londoniarum. Ed. T. Stapleton (Camden Society). London, 1846.

App. Land Com. Bibliographical, Statistical, and other miscellaneous Memoranda, being appendices to the Report of the Royal Commission on Land in Wales and Monmouthshire [Compiled chiefly by the Secretary, D. Lleufer Thomas]. London, 1896.

Arch. Camb. Archæologia Cambrensis, the journal of the Cambrian Archæological Association. The capital Roman numeral denotes the series (I. 1846-9; II. 1850-4; III. 1855-69; IV. 1870-83; V. 1884-1900; VI. to date), the uncial letter the volume (to which the year is added in brackets), and the Arabic numeral the page.

Arth. Legend. Studies in the Arthurian Legend. By John Rhys. Oxford, 1891.

Asser. The Life of Alfred is quoted, by reference to the chapter, from the edition of W. H. Stevenson (Oxford, 1904). The notes, etc., of this edition are cited as Stev.

B. Saes. The Welsh chronicle in Cottonian MS. Cleopatra B. v. ff. 111-164*b*, there styled "Brenhined y Saesson," but by the Myvyrian editors "Brut y Saesson" (Myv. Arch. II. 468-582 [652-684]), is cited by reference to the annal.

B. T. Brut y Tywysogion. Ed. J. Williams Ab Ithel (Rolls Series). 1860.

B. Willis, Bangor. Survey of the Cathedral Church of Bangor, with an appendix of records. Collected by Browne Willis. London, 1721.

Bede, H. E. The "Historia Ecclesiastica Gentis Anglorum" is cited, by reference to book and chapter, from vol. i. of "Baedae Opera Historica," edited by C. Plummer (Oxford, 1896). References to the introduction, notes, etc., of this edition are given as Plummer's Bede, with no. of volume and page.

Bémont. Simon de Montfort, comte de Leicester. Par Ch. Bémont. Paris, 1884.

Ben. Abb. Gesta Regis Henrici Secundi Benedicti Abbatis. Two vols. Ed. W. Stubbs (Rolls Series). 1867.

Blk. Bk. The Black Book of Carmarthen (Peniarth MS. 1 = Hengwrt MS. 11) is cited from the facsimile edition issued by J. Gwenogvryn Evans (Oxford, 1888) and reproduced by the same editor in print (Pwllheli, 1906). Another printed text will be found in IV. Anc. Bks. ii. 3-61.

Blk. Bk of St. David's. The Black Book of St. David's [an extent of the lands and rents of the bishop in 1326 = Br. Mus. Add. MS. 34,125]. Ed. J. W. Willis-Bund (Cymmrodorion Society). London, 1902.

Breconsh. (2). A History of the County of Brecknock. By Theophilus Jones. Originally issued in two vols. (1805, 1809); reissued in one by Edwin Davies. Brecknock, 1898.

Britannia. By W. Camden. Cited from the edition of 1600. (George Bishop, London.)

Bruts. The text of the Bruts [Brut y Brenhinoedd, Brut y Tywysogion, etc.] from the Red Book of Hergest. Edited by John Rhys and J. Gwenogvryn Evans. Oxford, 1890.

Buch. Gr. ap C. "Buchedd Gruffydd ap Cynan" is cited (by page) from Arch. Camb. III. xii. (1866), 30-45, 112-128, with a further reference in brackets to the page of Myv. Arch., second edition.

Bye-Gones. Notes contributed to the "Bye-Gones" column of the (weekly) Oswestry Advertiser and separately published in yearly half-volumes.

C.I.L. Corpus Inscriptionum Latinarum. Vol. vii. (ed. Hübner, Berlin, 1873) deals with the Latin inscriptions of Britain of older date than 500 A.D.

Cal. Close R. Calendar of the Close Rolls, prepared under the superintendence of the Deputy Keeper of the Records.

Edward I.—vol. i. 1272-9. London, 1900.

Cal. Doc. Fr. Calendar of Documents preserved in France illustrative of the

History of Great Britain and Ireland [from 918 to 1206]. Ed. J. H. Round. London, 1899.

Cal. Pat. R. Calendar of the Patent Rolls, prepared under the superintendence of the Deputy Keeper of the Records.
Henry III.—vol. i. 1232-47. London, 1906.
ii. 1247-58. „ 1908.
Edward I.—vol. i. 1272-81. „ 1901.

Camb. Biog. The Cambrian Biography. By William Owen [W. O. Pughe]. London, 1803.

Camb. Qu. Mag. The Cambrian Quarterly Magazine. London, 1829-33.

Camb. Reg. The Cambrian Register [edited by W. O. Pughe]. London.
Vol. i. 1796.
ii. 1799.
iii. 1818.

Cambro-Br. SS. Lives of the Cambro-British Saints. Ed. W. J. Rees (Welsh MSS. Society.) Llandovery, 1853.
[For a long list of corrections to be made in Rees' text, see Cymr. xiii. 76-96 (Kuno Meyer).]

Card. Priory. Cardigan Priory in the Olden Days. By E. M. Pritchard. London, 1904.

Carlisle, Top. Dict. A Topographical Dictionary of the Dominion of Wales. By Nicholas Carlisle. London, 1811.

Carm. Cart. Cartularium S. Johannis Bapt. [corrige Evang.] de Caermarthen [Hengwrt MS. 440]. Privately printed for [Sir] T[homas] P[hillips]. Cheltenham, 1865.

Carnh. Hanes Cymru. Gan T. Price (Carnhuanawc). Crughywel, 1842.

Cart. Brec. See chapter xii. note 128.

Cart. Glouc. Historia et Cartularium Monasterii Sancti Petri Gloucestriae Ed. W. H. Hart (Rolls Series). London.
Vol. i. 1863.
ii. 1865.
iii. 1867.

Cart. Sax. Cartularium Saxonicum. Ed. W. de Gray Birch. London.
Vol. i. 1885.
ii. 1887.
iii. 1893.
index, 1899.

Cartae Glam. Cartae et alia munimenta quae ad Dominium de Glamorgan pertinent. Curante Geo. T. Clark.
Vol. i. Dowlais, 1885.
ii. Cardiff, 1890.
iii. 1891.
iv. 1893.

Celt. Br. Celtic Britain. By John Rhys. London. Usually cited from the (second) edition of 1884 (2), but sometimes from that of 1904 (3).

Celt. Folklore. Celtic Folklore. By John Rhys. Two vols. Oxford, 1901.

Celt. Heath. The Origin and Growth of Religion as illustrated by Celtic Heathendom (Hibbert Lectures for 1886). By John Rhys. London, 1888.

Celt. Remains. Celtic Remains. By Lewis Morris [1700-65]. Ed. D. Silvan Evans (Cambrian Archæological Association). London, 1878.

Charter Rolls. Calendar of the Charter Rolls, printed under the superintendence of the Deputy Keeper of the Records. London.
Vol. i. (1226-1257)—1903.
ii. (1257-1300)—1906.

Gir. Camb. Giraldi Cambrensis Opera (*continued*).
Particular works are referred to as follows:—
De Rebus. De Rebus a se Gestis.
Top. Hib. Topographica Hibernica.
Exp. Hib. Expugnatio Hibernica.
Invect. De Invectionibus.
Sym. El. Symbolum Electorum.
Gemma. Gemma Ecclesiastica.
Men. Eccl. De Jure et Statu Menevensis Ecclesiae.
Spec. Speculum Ecclesiae.
Princ. Instr. De Principis Instructione.

Godwin (2). De Praesulibus Angliae. By F. Godwin. Ed. W. Richardson. Cambridge, 1743.

Goss. Guide. The Gossiping Guide to Wales (North Wales and Aberystwyth). Traveller's edition, issued annually. London, Oswestry, and Wrexham. [Recent editions have been revised and amplified by Egerton Phillimore —see pref.]

Gr. Celt. (2). Grammatica Celtica. By I. C. Zeuss. Ed. H. Ebel. Berlin, 1871.

Gw. ap Rhys. Hanes y Brytaniaid a'r Cymry. Gan Gweirydd ap Rhys [ac eraill]. Llundain.
Cyf. i.—1872.
Cyf. ii.—1874.

Gw. Brut. The Gwentian Brut or "Brut Aberpergwm" is printed in Myv. Arch. II. 468-582 [685-715] from a MS. dated 1764.

Gwydir Fam. The History of the Gwydir Family. By Sir John Wynne [1553-1626]. Oswestry, 1878.

H. and St. Councils and Ecclesiastical Documents relating to Great Britain and Ireland. Ed. A. W. Haddan and W. Stubbs. Oxford.
Vol. i.—1869.
ii. pt. 1—1873; pt. 2—1878.
[For these two volumes, dealing with the Celtic churches, Mr. Haddan was responsible (see pref. to vol. i.), though the second appeared after his death.]

Harl. MS. 3859. See note appended to chap. v.

Hemingb. Chronicon Walteri de Hemingburgh. Ed. H. C. Hamilton (English Historical Society). Two vols. London, 1848-9.

Hen. Hunt. Henrici Archidiaconi Huntendunensis Historia Anglorum. Ed. T. Arnold (Rolls Series). London, 1879.

Hist. Britt. The "Historia Brittonum" usually coupled with the name of Nennius is cited from the same edition as Gildas (see above). For a brief account of the "Historia" and of "Nennius," see chap. vii. § 3.

Hist. Ch. York. The Historians of the Church of York and its Archbishops. Ed. James Raine (Rolls Series). London.
Vol. i.—1879.
ii.—1886.
iii.—1894.

Reg. The "Historia Regum Britanniae" of Geoffrey of Monmouth is usually cited from the edition of J. A. Giles (London, 1844), but references are occasionally made to the (unpublished) Berne MS. The readings of this MS. I give on the authority of Mr. G. B. Matthews, who collated it in 1898 and has kindly allowed me to make use of his notes.

Hoare, Itin. The Itinerary of Archbishop Baldwin through Wales. Translated by R. C. Hoare. Two vols. London, 1806.

Hoveden. Chronica Magistri Rogeri de Houedene. Ed. W. Stubbs (Rolls Series). Four vols. London, 1868-71.

Inq. p. mortem. Calendar of Inquisitions post mortem, prepared under the superintendence of the Deputy Keeper of the Records.
Vol. i. (Henry III.), London, 1904.
ii. (Edward I.), ,, 1906.

Inscr. Chr. Inscriptiones Britanniae Christianae. Ed. Hübner. Berlin and London, 1876.

Iolo MSS. Iolo Manuscripts. Ed. Taliesin Williams (Welsh MSS. Society). Llandovery, 1848. Reprinted by I. Foulkes, Liverpool, 1888.

Itin. Ant. Itinerarium Antonii Augusti. Ed. Parthey and Pinder. Berlin, 1848.

Jaffé (2). Regesta Pontificum Romanorum ad annum 1198. Ed. Ph. Jaffé. Second edition. Leipzig.
Vol. i.—1885.
ii.—1888.

Jones and Freem. The History and Antiquities of Saint David's. By W. Basil Jones and E. A. Freeman. London, 1856.

L. G. Cothi. Poetical Works of Lewis Glyn Cothi. Ed. John Jones (Tegid) and Walter Davies (Gwallter Mechain) (Cymmrodorion Society). Two vols. Oxford, 1837.

Land of Morgan. By G. T. Clark (Cambrian Archæological Association). London, 1883.

Lap. W. Lapidarium Walliae. By J. O. Westwood. Oxford, 1876-9.

Leland, Wales. The Itinerary in Wales of John Leland in or about 1536-9. Arranged and edited by Lucy Toulmin Smith. London, 1906.

Letters, Hen. III. Royal and other Letters illustrative of the reign of Henry III. Ed. W. W. Shirley (Rolls Series). London.
Vol. i.—1862.
ii.—1866.

Lewis, Top. Dict. A Topographical Dictionary of Wales. By Samuel Lewis. Two vols. Cited from the first edition (London, 1833).

Lib. Land. The Text of the Book of Llan Dâv, reproduced from the Gwysaney MS. by J. Gwenogvryn Evans. Oxford, 1893.

Lib. Nig. Liber Niger Scaccarii. Ed. T. Hearne. Second edition. London, 1774.

Lit. Eng. The History of Little England beyond Wales [= Pembrokeshire]. By Edward Laws. London, 1888.

Lit. Kym. (2). The Literature of the Kymry [during the period 1080-1322]. By Thomas Stephens. Ed. D. Silvan Evans. London, 1876.

LL. Ancient Laws and Institutes of Wales. Ed. Aneurin Owen (Record Commission). Two vols. London, 1841.
Ven. Dim. Gw. = Venedotian, Dimetian, and Gwentian codes of this edition (vol. i.).
Lat. A., B., C. = Peniarth MS. 28, Cott. MS. Vespasian E. xi., Harl. MS. 1796, as printed in vol. ii. 749-907.

Llyfr yr Ancr. The Elucidarium and other Tracts in Welsh, from Llyvyr Agkyr Llandewivrevi [Jesus Coll. MS. 119]. Ed. J. Morris Jones and John Rhys (Anecdota Oxoniensia). Oxford, 1894.

Lpool. W. Nat. Trans. Transactions of the Liverpool Welsh National Society. Issued annually since 1886.

R. de Torigini. The Chronicle of Robert of Torigni. Ed. R. Howlett in vol. iv. (London, 1889) of "Chronicles of the Reigns of Stephen, Henry II. and Richard II. (Rolls Series).

Radnorsh. (2). A General History of the County of Radnor. From the MS. of Jonathan Williams. Compiled by Edwin Davies. Brecknock, 1905.
[Williams's MS. was first printed in Arch. Camb. and was separately issued in 1859 (Tenby).]

Rec. Carn. Registrum vulgariter nuncupatum "The Record of Caernarvon" [Harleian MS. 696]. Ed. Henry Ellis (Record Commission). [London], 1838.

Reg. Conway. Register and Chronicle of Aberconway [Harl. MS. 3725]. Ed. Henry Ellis (Camden Miscellany, vol. i.). [London], 1847.

Reg. Sacr. (2). Registrum Sacrum Anglicanum. By W. Stubbs. Second edition. Oxford, 1897.

Rev. Celt. La Revue Celtique. Paris, 1870 to date.

Rot. Chart. Rotuli Chartarum in Turri Londinensi asservati. Ed. T. D. Hardy (Record Commission). [London], 1837.
Vol. i. pt. 1 (1199-1216).

Rot. Claus. Rotuli Litterarum Clausarum in Turri Londinensi asservati. Ed. T. D. Hardy (Record Commission). London.
Vol. i. (1204-1224)—1833.
ii. (1224-1227)—1844.

Rot. Fin. Excerpta e Rotulis Finium. . . Henrico Tertio rege. Ed. C. Roberts (Record Commission). London.
Vol. i. (1216-1246)—1835.
ii. (1246-1272)—1836.

Rot. Norm. Magni Rotuli Scaccarii Normanniae . . . ed. T. Stapleton (Society of Antiquaries). London.
Vol. i.—1840.
ii.—1844.

Rot. Pat. Rotuli Litterarum Patentium in Turri Londinensi asservati. Ed. T. D. Hardy (Record Commission). [London.]
Vol. i. pt. i. (1201-1216)—1835.
[An Itinerary of King John is appended to the introduction.]

Rot. regn. Joh. Rotuli de Liberate ac de Misis et Praestitis regnante Johanne. Ed. T. D. Hardy. London, 1844.

Round, Anc. Charters. Ancient Charters prior to A.D. 1200. Ed. J. H. Round. (Pipe Roll Society's vol. x.) London, 1888.

Royal Charters. Royal Charters and other documents relating to Carmarthen, Talley, and Ty Gwyn ar Daf. By J. R. Daniel-Tyssen and Alcwyn C. Evans. Carmarthen, 1878.

Rymer. Foedera, Conventiones, Litterae, etc. Ed. T. Rymer and R. Sanderson. Fourth edition, in four vols., by Clarke, Holbrooke, and Caley. London, 1816-69.

Sax. Gen. The "Saxon Genealogies," or chaps. 57-65 of Hist. Britt. See p. 116.

Sim. Dun. Symeonis Monachi Opera Omnia. Ed. T. Arnold (Rolls Series). London.
Vol. i.—1882.
ii.—1885.

Song of Dermot. The Song of Dermot and the Earl—from Carew MS. 596 (Lambeth). Ed. G. H. Orpen. Oxford, 1892.
V. refers to the lines of the poem, p. to the pages of this work.

Spurrell, Carm. Carmarthen and its Neighbourhood. By William Spurrell. Second edition. Carmarthen, 1879.

Stev. See Asser.

Str. Flor. The Cistercian Abbey of Strata Florida. By Stephen W. Williams. London, 1889.

Stubbs, Const. Hist. The Constitutional History of England. By William Stubbs. Third edition. Oxford.
Vol. i.—1880.
ii.—1883.

Sweetman. Calendar of Documents relating to Ireland in the Public Record Office. Ed. H. S. Sweetman. London.
Vol. i. (1171-1251)—1875.
ii. (1252-1284)—1887.

Tanner. Notitia Monastica. By Bishop Thomas Tanner of St. Asaph. Ed. J. Tanner. London, 1744.

Tax. Nich. Taxatio Ecclesiastica Angliae et Walliae auctoritate P. Nicholai IV., circa A.D. 1291. Record Commission, 1802.
References are to the page and column (*a* or *b*).

Testa de Nevill. Sive Liber Feodorum temp. Hen. III. et Edw. I. [London] 1807.

Thomas, S. Asaph. A History of the Diocese of St. Asaph. By D. R. Thomas. London, 1874.

Trans. Cymr. Transactions of the Honourable Society of Cymmrodorion. Issued sessionally from 1892-3 to date. London.

Trans. Roy. Hist. Soc. Transactions of the Royal Historical Society. London.

Trevet. Triveti Annales. Ed. T. Hog (English Historical Society). London, 1845.

Triads. Cited by reference to the three series (i. ii. iii.) printed in Myv. Arch. II. 1-22, 57-75 (388-411), the Arabic numeral giving the number of the triad. For some account of the Triads, see note to chap. iv.

Trib. System. The Tribal System in Wales. By Frederic Seebohm. London, 1895.
[App. refers to the documents printed as Appendices.]

Urk. Spr. Urkeltischer Sprachschatz. By Whitley Stokes and A. Bezzenberger. Göttingen, 1894.
This is pt. ii. of the fourth edition of A. Fick, Vergleichendes Wörterbuch der Indogermanischen Sprachen.]

V. S. Columb. Adamnan's Life of St. Columba is cited from the edition of J. T. Fowler. (Oxford, 1894.)

Valor Eccl. Valor Ecclesiasticus temp. Henr. VIII. Six vols. (Record Commission.) London, 1810-34.

W. People. The Welsh People. By John Rhŷs and David Brynmor-Jones. London, 1900.

W. Phil. (2). Lectures on Welsh Philology. By John Rhŷs. Second edition. London, 1879.

Walt. Cov. The Historical Collections of Walter of Coventry. Ed. W. Stubbs (Rolls Series). Two vols. London, 1872-3.

War of G. and G. The War of the Gaedhil with the Gaill. Ed. J. H. Todd (Rolls Series). London, 1867.

Welsh SS. Essay on the Welsh Saints. By Rice Rees. London, 1836.

Wendover. Rogeri de Wendover Chronica. Ed. H. O. Coxe (English Historical Society). Four vols. London, 1841-4.

Wht. Bk. See Mab.

Williams, Aberconwy. The History and Antiquities of the Town of Aberconwy. By Robert Williams. Denbigh, 1835.

Wm. Malm. The works of William of Malmesbury are cited as follows:—

G. R. = Gesta Regum } Ed. W. Stubbs (Rolls Series). London,
H. N. = Historia Novella } 1887-9.

References in brackets are to the edition of T. D. Hardy (English Historical Society, London, 1840).

G. P. = Gesta Pontificum. Ed. N. E. S. A. Hamilton (Rolls Series). London, 1870.

Wm. Newb. Historia Rerum Anglicarum. Ed. Richard Howlett in "Chronicles of the Reigns of Stephen, Henry II., and Richard I." (Rolls Series), vol. i. (bks. i.-iv.—1884) and vol. ii. (bk. v.—1885).

Woodward. The History of Wales. By B. B. Woodward. Two vols. London [1852].

Wotton. Cyfreithjeu Hywel Dda ac Eraill. Seu Leges Wallicae. Ed. Gul. Wottonus, adiuvante Mose Gulielmio [Moses Williams]. London, 1730.

Wykes. Chronicon Thomae Wykes. Ed. H. R. Luard in vol. iv. of Annales Monastici (Rolls Series). London, 1869.

Wynne. The History of Wales. By Dr. Powel. Newly arranged and improved by W. Wynne [ob. 1704]. London, 1697.

[A new edition of the "Historie" of Powel, with additional matter, taken mainly from the notes of Robert Vaughan of Hengwrt. See pref. 4*b*.]

Yorke (2). The Royal Tribes of Wales. By Philip Yorke of Erddig [1734-1804]. [Original edition, Wrexham, 1799.] Ed. R. Williams. Liverpool, 1887.

Zeit. Celt. Ph. Zeitschrift für Celtische Philologie. Issued at Halle from 1897 to date.

CHAPTER I.

THE PREHISTORIC EPOCHS.[1]

I. PALÆOLITHIC WALES.

CHAP. I.

THE region now known as Wales was inhabited by man in the earliest period during which science has clearly shown him to have dwelt in the British Isles.[2] In the Pleistocene Age of geology,[3] separated from our own by an interval which must be measured by tens of thousands of years, a rude race of hunters and fishers is proved by the discovery of its implements—roughly chipped flints, carved fragments of bone and horn—to have ranged the hills and valleys of Southern Britain and waged a not unequal struggle with great beasts of prey, of which many belonged to species now extinct. Our islands had then no separate existence; in the beds of what are now the North Sea and the English Channel mighty rivers flowed north and west to a coast-line far out in the Atlantic, which lay where the 100 fathom line now marks the beginning of the dip toward oceanic depths. The relics of pleistocene, or, as he is more commonly termed (from the primitive fashion of his stone weapons), palæolithic man are found both in the beds of ancient rivers, left high and dry as the stream has cut its way down, and in caves, those natural houses—cool in summer and

[1] In writing this chapter I have chiefly used the following: Boyd Dawkins, *Early Man in Britain*; Evans, *Ancient Stone Implements*; Beddoe, *Races of Britain*; Taylor, *Origin of the Aryans*; Munro, *Prehistoric Scotland*; Greenwell and Rolleston, *British Barrows*; Schrader, *Prehistoric Antiquities of the Aryan Peoples*; Sergi, *The Mediterranean Race*; Ripley, *The Races of Europe*; *British Museum Guides*—(i) The Stone Age, (ii) The Bronze Age, compiled by C. H. Read.

[2] It is assumed that *Eo*lithic man belongs as yet to the region of hypothesis.

[3] I follow the terminology of Prof. Boyd Dawkins, who makes the Pleistocene Age end with the beginning of the Neolithic.

warm in winter—of which man availed himself from the very first. In South-eastern Britain it is the river drift which supplies evidence of the conditions of life in palæolithic times; in Wales, on the other hand, our knowledge of the period is entirely derived from the caves which abound in the carboniferous limestone of the district.

The exploration of caves has yielded traces, indubitable however slight, of the presence of palæolithic man in four Welsh regions, namely, the Vale of Clwyd, South Pembrokeshire, Gower and the neighbourhood of Monmouth. In 1861, during the excavation of the Long Hole in Gower, flakes of flint which had been used for cutting were found amid the bones of extinct mammals of the Pleistocene Age. It was about the same time that the bone-bearing caves of the Tenby district were being opened up; here Mr. Laws discovered in the Coygan cave, not far from Laugharne, a bone awl and a worked flint lying under bones of the rhinoceros. In King Arthur's Cave, on Great Doward Hill, near Monmouth, Mr. Symonds found flint flakes among abundant remains of pleistocene mammals. Similar discoveries have also been made in the Denbighshire caves: in that of Pont Newydd, one of the famous caves of Cefn Meiriadog, palæolithic implements came to light in association with bones of the hippopotamus and the straight-tusked elephant, and the presence of man was made doubly certain by the finding of a human tooth. On the other side of the valley, Dr. Hicks explored the Ffynnon Feuno and the Cae Gwyn caves, near Tremeirchion, and in both discovered flint implements, with bones of the mammoth and the rhinoceros. There would seem to be no doubt, therefore, that palæolithic man ranged over the whole of Wales.[4]

The list of great mammals who disputed with him the possession of the country is an impressive one. It includes, in addition to the mammoth, the rhinoceros (of two varieties), the hippopotamus and the straight-tusked elephant, already mentioned, the cave lion, the cave bear, the hyæna, the bison, the reindeer, the Irish elk and the wild horse. When the author of the third series of the Triads described the first settlers of Britain as finding it full of "bears and wolves

[4] Evans, *Ancient Stone Implements*, second edition (1897), pp. 520-1.

and dragons and long-horned oxen" (eirth a bleiddiau ac efeinc ac ychain bannog),[5] he was no doubt giving rein to a lively imagination, but the truth revealed by science is a hundredfold stranger than his ingenuous fiction.

The palæolithic remains found in England and France have enabled students of the subject to trace a gradual improvement in civilisation, showing itself at last in a quite surprising degree of skill in carving and drawing. But the Welsh relics are too few to furnish much evidence of the kind, and, so far as they have been classified at all, appear to belong to a very primitive type. Nor can it be said that their relation has yet been finally determined to the glacial epoch of British geology, an epoch falling within the limits of the Pleistocene Age, when the greater part of Wales was wrapped in a curtain of ice and snow as inhospitable as that which now envelops Greenland. The high authority of Sir John Evans may be cited in support of the view that the palæolithic climate was not much colder than that of our own day and that palæolithic man was post-glacial;[6] Dr. Hicks, on the other hand, argues from the evidence furnished by the Welsh caves that the characteristic pleistocene mammals, with whose remains those of man are so often associated, lived before the age of the glaciers, and, with the palæolithic race, disappeared as it laid its icy hand on the soil.[7]

So far as Britain is concerned, the story of palæolithic man certainly ends abruptly. On the Continent, archæologists have met with some success in the effort to bridge over the gap which severs this from the succeeding, the Neolithic Age. In our own land this has not yet been done, and it must remain highly probable that, as the strange beasts around him disappeared from our valleys, so also did the cunning savage who watched and entrapped them, and this without leaving any of his posterity behind. Welshmen have inherited neolithic blood and the neolithic civilisation; in the palæolithic man of Britain it is probable they have no part.

[5] *Myv. Arch.* ii. 57 (400).

[6] Presidential Address at the Toronto Meeting (1897) of the British Association (*Report of the Association for the year*, p. 13).

[7] *Proceedings of the Geological Society*, May, 1898, ci.

CHAP. I.

II. Neolithic Wales.

With the opening of the Neolithic or New Stone Age begins, so far as is now known, the continuous history of man in Wales. That period, in which the use of metal for the practical purposes of life was unknown, was in time succeeded by the Age of Bronze, when the newly discovered alloy of copper and tin gave the hard cutting edge which folk needed for tools and weapons, and this in turn by the Age of Iron, which may be regarded as lasting to our own day. But no break separates these periods from each other ; the arts introduced by neolithic man into Britain—the management of domestic animals, the making of pottery, the grinding of stone implements—have never been forgotten ; the men who first practised them here are still, there is no reason to doubt, plentifully represented in the population of these islands. The beginning of each new period marks an advance in culture and, probably, the arrival of a new race, but the past has not been obliterated ; its influence is still potent in the new era.

In the neolithic period the contour of the British Isles presented the same general appearance as at present. Valleys and plains had sunk so as to form encircling seas, whose billows swept through the Straits of Dover and St. George's Channel. The process of depression was, however, not yet complete, for it has been shown by discoveries made in many parts of our coast-line, notably in Wales, that tracts of mud and sand now regularly washed by each tide were in neolithic times covered with a luxuriant forest growth, giving no hint of the neighbourhood of the sea. The blackened stumps of such a forest were laid bare in the winter of 1171-1172, to the no small perplexity of the wise men of Dyfed, by a great gale which swept over the sands of St. Bride's Bay,[8] and in recent years submerged areas of the kind have been examined at Whitesand Bay, near St. David's, at Barry,[9] and at Borth, near Aberystwyth, and have proved to be land surfaces of the Neolithic Age. It is clear, therefore, that during this period the Welsh coast-line was, speaking generally, much further out to sea than at present, and there may well have been a time within

[8] Gir. Camb. vi. 100 (*Itin.* i. 13) ; v. 284 (*Exp. Hib.* i. 36).

[9] *Quarterly Journal of the Geological Society*, Aug. 1896, pp. 474-89.

the memory of neolithic man when Anglesey was not an island and Cardigan Bay, which hardly anywhere exceeds twenty fathoms in depth, was dry land. One is tempted to inquire whether we may not have in the well-known Cantref y Gwaelod and Traeth Lafan legends, which are stories of the submergence of flourishing realms beneath the pitiless sea, reminiscences handed down through many generations of the effects—at times, perhaps, startling—of this gradual subsidence attested by geology. In the original story of the Lowland Hundred, as told in a poem in the Black Book of Carmarthen, there is no mention of the embankment, invested with such interest for lovers of literature by the sardonic humour of Peacock,[10] nor is it a drunken "Lord High Commissioner," but a mysterious maid, servant of a magic well, who is blamed for the catastrophe. Hence there can be no doubt that the tale is thoroughly primitive; it remains, however, for students of folk-lore to say whether this and kindred legends known to the Welsh people have any special features which show them to embody genuine traditional history, or whether they are merely specimens of a class of story known in all parts of the world.

At what time neolithic man first crossed the channel and the precise degree of civilisation he had attained at the time of his arrival here are matters of conjecture, hardly as yet of definite knowledge. The neolithic culture of Europe is believed to have slowly arisen within the continent itself, perhaps out of palæolithic germs, during a period which began not less than ten thousand years ago. Much progress had no doubt been made before the long canoes, fashioned out of single tree trunks, grated upon our shores and discharged their human burthen, the first ancestors of the British people; the Neolithic Age must have been far advanced ere such an immigration could have taken place. Probably the chief domestic animals—the dog, the ox, the sheep, the goat, the pig—had been tamed; a rude kind of pottery was made; skill had been acquired in the grinding of smooth stone axes, which were highly polished,

10 "That the embankment is old, I am free to confess; that it is somewhat rotten in parts, I will not altogether deny; that it is any the worse for that, I do most sturdily gainsay. It does its business; it works well; it keeps out the water from the land, and it lets in the wine upon the High Commission of Embankment" (*Misfortunes of Elphin*, chap. ii.).

CHAP. I.

furnished with sharp edges and hafted in wooden handles. Besides these weapons of polished stone, others were in use which had been chipped into shape with the utmost care. For shelter men betook themselves to caves, where the neolithic level of occupation is often to be found above that of palæolithic times, or they dug themselves pits in the ground, or with their stone axes cut timber and made square log huts. That they were given to the regular tillage of the soil there is nothing to show; primitive folk would seem to have had little taste for the toilsome pursuit of agriculture as long as an easier method of making a living was open to them. They clothed themselves in leathern garments, for the most part, though some use was also made of a coarse linen, woven in a primitive kind of loom. Their dead they laid to rest, in the crouching attitude of sleep, in a cave or a stone chamber which, though encased in a mound or a cairn, had an entrance which might be used for further burials. By their side they placed the implements which they took to be needful for the use of the departed in the spirit life just begun.

Many generations, no doubt, went by ere the civilisation just described reached the highlands of Wales. But there is no lack of evidence that it rooted itself thoroughly in Welsh soil. The limestone caves of Pembrokeshire and Denbighshire were occupied by neolithic as well as by palæolithic man, and show us the former race in the early stages of its development. In the Little Hoyle cave in Longbury Bank, near Tenby, bones of the ox, goat (or sheep), pig and dog were found with charcoal (the ashes of the primitive hearth), pottery, and implements of bone and flint. The greater pleistocene beasts had by this time entirely disappeared, but the brown bear, the wild horse and the red deer still provided big game for the neolithic hunter. In the exploration of this cave it was a matter of surprise to find human bones, representing no less than nine individuals, mingled in great confusion with the house rubbish above described; this, however, appears to have been due to an accident which had let fall through the roof of the cave the contents of the neolithic burying place above.[11] A group of four caves in the neighbourhood of Llanarmon in Yale, used partly

[11] *Lit. Eng.* pp. 15-16.

as dwelling-places and partly as tombs, illustrates the neolithic civilisation as found in North Wales. Remains of the same domestic and wild animals were found as in the Little Hoyle; there were also "fragments of rude black pottery, hand made, composed of clay worked up with small pieces of stone, to prevent fracture while it was being subjected to the fire". A few flint implements were discovered, but the most interesting find was "a beautiful polished axe made of greenstone, with the edge uninjured by use". The caves of the Cefn Meiriadog district were also inhabited in this age and have yielded remains of the same type.[12]

On the Pembrokeshire coast a neolithic settlement of a different kind, though probably of the same early stage, was recently explored by Mr. Laws. Under the blown sand on Giltar Head, near Tenby, a clay floor, hardened by fire and covered with charcoal, came to light; upon it lay flint and bone implements, but the most valuable evidence as to the life led by the men who had used it was derived from a large refuse heap or "kitchen midden," of the kind which has furnished Danish archæologists with data of the highest value for the early Neolithic Age. This contained the bones of domestic animals, but greatly in excess of these in quantity were the tons of shells of twenty-four varieties, which showed that the dwellers in this seaside camp—a place, perhaps, of summer resort—were great eaters of shell fish and by no means relied entirely upon their cattle and upon the chase for food.[13]

In other countries much information about the Neolithic Age has been gleaned from the vestiges of lake dwellings, built for safety on piles or artificial islands at some little distance from the shore. One such "crannog," to use the Irish name, has been discovered in Wales, namely, in Llangorse Lake, but the remains were too scanty to make it possible to fix the age of its construction and occupation, since the lake dwelling as such is not specially characteristic of any one of the great prehistoric periods.[14] There may also have been a lake dwelling in Llyn Llydaw at the foot of Snowdon, for a lowering of the water level of this lake some years ago exposed to

[12] *Cave Hunting* (1874), by Prof. Boyd Dawkins, chap. v.

[13] *Arch. Camb.* IV. xi. (1880), 244-5.

[14] *Arch. Camb.* IV. i. (1870), 192-8; iii. (1872), 146-8.

CHAP. I.

view a canoe of the early type known in Welsh as "cafn unpren," the hulk fashioned from a single tree, which is the most primitive known form of boat.[15]

Stone implements of neolithic pattern have been picked up in many parts of Wales,[16] but, while they testify to the occupation of the country for many centuries by neolithic man, they tell us little else when they are not found in company with other remains, domestic or sepulchral.

The neolithic burying places of Wales next claim attention. In the new Stone Age the practice of burning the dead was rarely followed, and it was also unusual to provide each corpse with a separate grave; instead, a vault or chamber was prepared, which was regarded as a house of the dead and opened from time to time to receive fresh burials. Sometimes this chamber was natural, a cave (as at Rhos Ddigre)[17] or a cleft in the rock; sometimes it was excavated; but, especially in the later Neolithic Age, as greater skill was acquired in the handling of large masses of stone, it was very commonly built of boulders and loose stones, with a great slab for roof and another to keep the entrance. The whole was covered with a mound of earth, for protection from the weather and from beasts of prey, and then formed a "barrow," the Welsh "tomen";[18] or, if the ribs of the earth were thereabouts but thinly coated with soil, small stones were used instead to form a "cairn" or "carnedd". Owing to the need of providing an entrance passage, the structure was usually rather long in proportion to its breadth, but this was an accidental, not an essential feature of it, and for this reason the term "chambered barrow" is to be preferred, as suggesting a truer classification, to the more familiar "long barrow". The chambered barrows and cairns of Wales have not yielded the abundant evidence with regard to the civilisation and physique of neolithic man which has been furnished by those of the South of England.

[15] *Arch. Camb.* IV. v. (1874), 147-51.

[16] See index to Evans, *Ancient Stone Implements.*

[17] *Cave Hunting*, chap. v.

[18] The simple form "tom" also occurs, as in Cwm Dom (where there is a tumulus), near Llanfyllin, Bon y Dom, the original name of Moel y don, Anglesey (Penn. iii. 16), and the line, attributed to Llywarch Hên,

Tom elwithan (=Elwyddan) neus gwlych glaw,

for which see *IV. Anc. Bks.* ii. p. 291.

Few of them remain in the cairn or barrow form, and of these many have been rifled of their contents and are only interesting to-day as structures. Such has been the fate of Carneddau Hengwm, near Barmouth, two huge cairns, of which the larger is 150 feet long; it is possible, however, that all the chambers have not yet been opened.[19] The mound near Plas Newydd, Anglesey, measuring about 150 by 100 feet and locally known as "Bryn yr hên bobl" (The old folks' hill) was opened about 1730, but there is no record of the exploration.[20] Not far off is another carnedd, that of Bryn Celli Ddu, which appears in the old one-inch Ordnance map as "Yr Ogof" (The Cave); here the chamber has been almost entirely stripped of its covering, but the entrance passage is still intact. Pennant records the discovery of human bones in a very friable condition in this chamber when it was first opened up; a broken flint knife was recently found there also, so that it was beyond any doubt a neolithic burying place.[21] Two of the chambered carneddi of Wales have been explored since the scientific study of such monuments began and accordingly have yielded some evidence, scanty though it be, as to the neolithic population of the country. That of Park Cwm in the parish of Penmaen, Gower, which measured about 60 by 50 feet in area, contained the remains of some twenty or thirty skeletons in such disorder as to show that the bodies must have been placed there in succession and at long intervals. Some pottery came to light, but there were no implements to indicate more precisely the stage of civilisation which had been reached by the builders of the carnedd. It may, nevertheless, be regarded as suggestive of some progress in ideas and in manual skill that the four chambers opened into a single corridor, instead of having each its own means of access from the open air; the feature is one which appears in some of the "long barrows" of the neighbouring English counties.[22] The carnedd at Tyddyn Bleiddyn, near St. Asaph, was of a simpler pattern; in its two separate

[19] *Arch. Camb.* IV. iv. (1873), 91-5.

[20] Penn. iii. 21; *Arch. Camb.* IV. i. (1870), 51-8 (W. O. Stanley); xi. (1880), 81-96 (E. L. Barnwell). For the name see vol. ii. of the *Cambrian Register* (1799), p. 289.

[21] Penn. iii. 53-4; *Arch. Camb.* I. ii. (1847), 1-6; III. xv. (1869), 140-7 (E. L. Barnwell); Griffith, *Cromlechs of Anglesey and Carnarvonshire* (1900).

[22] *Arch. Camb.* IV. ii. (1871), 168-72.

CHAP. I.

chambers human remains were found, so huddled together that the burials could not have been simultaneous; there were also bones of the domestic animals.[23]

Stripped of its casing of earth and stones, the neolithic grave chamber became a cromlech. The bleak Atlantic winds and rain storms of many a century and the misguided industry of farmers and road menders in recent times have reduced a great number of the chambered cairns and barrows of Wales to the bare stone skeleton, so that cromlechs are far commoner in the country than the structures just described. Their massive outlines, telling unmistakably of immense toil lavished upon some great purpose and yet giving scarcely a hint as to what this might be, have for ages whetted men's curiosity. Nothing, indeed, can serve better to show how completely their original use has been forgotten than the names which have been given to them by the country folk in historic times. The cromlech at Ashbury, in Berkshire, was known as early as the tenth century as "Wayland's smithy," where the great smith god of the Teutonic peoples plied his demon art.[24] So in Wales very many cromlechs bear the name of "Coeten Arthur" (Arthur's Quoit);[25] one is "Bwrdd Arthur" (Arthur's Table), also known as "Gwâl y Filast" (The Lair of the Greyhound Bitch);[26] another is "Llety 'r Filiast" (The Greyhound Bitch's Lodging);[27] another, "Barclodaid y Gawres" (The Giantess's Apronful);[28] another, "Llech y Drybedd" (The Tripod Stone),[29] another, "Ty Illtud" (Illtud's House).[30] Cromlech itself appears, in point of fact, to be a name of this description; on the analogy of "cromglwyd,"[31] a wattle roof, it should mean a covering or

[23] *Cave Hunting*, pp. 161-4.

[24] Kemble, *Codex Diplomaticus*, v. 332. For the legend see Elton, *Origins of English History*, second edition (1890), p. 127.

[25] *E.g.*, those at Llugwy, Anglesey (Penn. iii. 56), at Llanfair by Harlech (Gibson, 661), and at Cefn Amwlch, Lleyn (*Arch. Camb.* I. ii. 97). Inquiring for a "cromlech" at Rhoslan, near Cricieth, I was told that nothing of the kind was known there, but upon its appearing that what I wanted was to see "Coeten Arthur," I was taken at once to the spot. Mr. J. E. Griffith says the name is frequently given to "blocs perchés".

[26] At Dol Wilym in Carmarthenshire (Gibson, 628).

[27] On the Great Orme (Griffith's *Cromlechs*).

[28] At Trecastell, Anglesey (*ibid.*).

[29] Near Nevern, Pembrokeshire (Gibson, 638).

[30] At Llanamwlch, Brecknockshire (*ibid.* 593).

[31] For this form see *Mab.* 76 (cromglwyt).

sheltering stone, and in the Welsh version of the Bible this is the sole use: "cromlechydd y creigiau" stands for "clefts" or "holes of the rocks".[32] It is George Owen of Henllys who, writing in the same age as the translators of the Welsh Bible, first applies the term to a megalithic structure; the terms of his references, however, to "the stone called Maen y gromlegh vpon Pentre Jevan lande"[33] clearly show that he is quoting a popular description (The Shelter Stone), without the least intention of applying the name to this class of monument as a whole. But, just as in the region round Harlech "Coeten Arthur" was so common a name for these structures as to have almost become at one time their usual designation,[34] so in Anglesey at the beginning of the eighteenth century they were "vulgarly called by the name of cromlech,"[35] and, through the writings of Henry Rowlands and other Anglesey antiquaries, this came to be the term by which they were generally known among the English and Welsh writers who speculated as to their origin. Yet it would be a mistake to suppose that the name is of greater historical significance than the others which we dismiss at once as mere freaks of popular fancy: no light, in short, is cast upon the origin of the cromlech by any of the names it bears.

In the eighteenth century the theory was broached that cromlechs were Druidical altars, probably because they are especially common in Anglesey, which is known to have been a centre of Druidical worship. Beginning at the end of the seventeenth century with John Aubrey,[36] the view that these and other rude stone monuments were the handiwork of the Druids

[32] Isaiah vii. 19; lvii. 5. *Cf.* also Jeremiah xlix. 16.

[33] *Descr. Pemb.* i. 251.

[34] "Nid oedd yn eich amser chwi, Syr, ond bargeinion bol clawdd, a llêd llaw o scrifen am dyddyn canpunt, a chodi carnedd neu goeten *Arthur* yn goffadwriaeth o'r pryniant a'r terfyneu" (*Y Bardd Cwsg*, p. 62 of Prof. J. Morris Jones' edition). See also Lewis Morris, *Celtic Remains*, p. 96, "Coeten Arthur," *i.e.*, King Arthur's Quoit. By this name a great many of those ancient monuments in Wales are called, which by the moderns are supposed to have been the altars of the Druids; but in some places they are called "cromlech," pl. "cromlechau". "Dolmen," it may be remarked, is not a term known in Wales. It has been employed since about 1800 by French archæologists as the equivalent of the British cromlech, but there seems no reason why an English writer should use it, save that the French have confused matters by using "cromlech" in the sense of a stone circle.

[35] *Mon. Ant.* 47 (Lond. 47). *Cf.* Gibson, 676. [36] Gibson, 637.

CHAP. I. acquired a marvellous hold upon the minds of the learned and has only been driven from the field within the last thirty or forty years. In *Mona Antiqua* (1723) it appears fully grown—the Druids, says the confident author, "had their Altars or *Cromleche*, on which they perform'd the Solemnities of Sacrifice and their sacred Rites of *Aruspicy* and *Divination*".[37] It was useless to urge that local tradition knew nothing of any such august associations, that the ordinary cromlech capstone was of such a form and so poised that no priest could have sacrificed upon it with dignity, and that many cromlechs had apparently been until recently covered; little impression was made upon the fashionable creed until systematic research in the latter half of the nineteenth century showed that the cromlech only differed from the chambered sepulchral barrow in being the ruin of its former self—the hard kernel which had defied the hand of time and had only to fear what man could do.[38] In the prehistoric cemetery near Auray in Brittany, cromlechs, according to Mr. Romilly Allen, "are to be seen in every stage of decay," [39] and Wales is not without examples of the process of destruction. Of the chambered mounds of the country, that at Bryn Celli Ddu has been stripped almost, but not quite bare; the cromlechs of Llugwy in Anglesey, of St. David's Head, of St. Nicholas in Glamorganshire, and of Llanamwlch in Breconshire show traces of the vanished mound or cairn;[40] while the cromlechs themselves survive in every degree of dilapidation, from the complete chamber of "Cwt y Bugail" (Shepherd's Hut), near Y Ro Wen, Carnarvonshire, to the single supporter which is all that remains of "Yr Allor" (The Altar), near Rhos Colyn.[41]

Fascinating as they have always been to the inquirer, cromlechs cannot in the nature of things yield much evidence as to the men who built and used them. Human bones and pottery have in some cases been found within them, removing

[37] P. 69 (Lond. 69).

[38] A very full discussion of cromlech theories will be found in E. L. Barnwell's contributions on the subject to *Arch. Camb.* See III. vii. 49-55; xv. 118-131; IV. iii. 81-125; xi. 89; V. i. 129-36.

[39] *Arch. Camb.* V. xvii. 221.

[40] *Arch. Camb.* III. xiii. (1867), 137; IV. iii. (1872), 143; IV. v. (1874), 72.

[41] Both these cromlechs are included in Mr. J. E. Griffith's book. I am informed that "Cwt y Bugail" is not the local name of the cromlech, but of a neighbouring cottage.

all doubt as to their sepulchral character, but the only Welsh cromlech excavated to any purpose in recent times has been that of Pant y Saer, near Llanfair Mathafarn Eithaf, Anglesey. Here in 1874 the Rev. W. Wynn Williams found, under a large flat stone not previously disturbed, the remains of several bodies buried in a contracted posture; in the same cromlech were other human remains, bones of the ox and pig, sea shells, charcoal, and one bit of coarse pottery.[42] The arrangement of the bodies found underneath the slab makes it fairly certain that this was a neolithic interment, whatever doubt may attach to the remains found at a higher level, and, in general, it may be said that cromlechs are products of the Neolithic Age, though, when once erected, they may have been used for burial by the people of later epochs.

Cromlechs are often found in groups, as at Plas Newydd, at Ystum Cegid and at Carreg y Gof (Pembrokeshire), and the idea is thus suggested that the neolithic race dwelt together in little settlements, bound together for common defence. If it could be regarded as certain that the hill fortresses and the cliff castles, fenced with ditch and mound and dry stone wall, which are so frequently seen in Wales, had been planned and set in order for their wars by neolithic tribesmen, the question might be regarded as settled, and the New Stone Age might be treated as an era of village communities. But the frequent discovery of flint flakes and arrow heads in our primitive camps does not prove them neolithic; these smaller trifles were made in stone, it appears certain, long after the introduction of metal for the fashioning of the more substantial weapons of a warrior's equipment,[43] and it is beyond doubt that fortresses of this kind were in general use as late as the time of the Roman Conquest.[44] That some of them may be neolithic is all, then, that can with safety be asserted.

So far nothing has been said as to the physical type and race affinities of the neolithic dwellers in Wales. Yet if, as has been maintained, it is to this people the ancestry of the modern Welshman must in a large measure be traced, the

[42] *Arch. Camb.* IV. vi. (1875), 341-8.

[43] Munro, *Prehistoric Scotland* (1899), p. 203.

[44] This has been conclusively proved in the case of the great walled fortress of Tre'r Ceiri, Carnarvonshire, by excavations carried on in the summer of 1903.

CHAP. I. matter is clearly one of great interest. Investigations in the "long barrows" of England have furnished a fairly definite picture of the neolithic occupant of the Wiltshire and Yorkshire uplands. He was short of stature, averaging about five feet five inches in height (the women were under five feet), small featured and small limbed. A low, narrow forehead, a thin, shapely nose, eyebrows and lips which projected but slightly beyond the plane of the face, gave an impression of mildness, upon which it might not have been safe to presume. Most important character of all, from the point of view of the anthropologist, was the oval form of the head, as looked at from above, *i.e.*, the "long barrow" race were dolichocephalic or long-headed, as distinguished from the brachycephalic or round-headed races. Few communities, indeed, were more pronounced in their dolichocephaly, for the average proportion of the breadth of the skull to its length was as 71 or 72 to 100, a proportion expressed in scientific language by the statement that the "cephalic index" was 71 or 72.[45]

If a comparison be now instituted between the few skeletons of Neolithic Age discovered in Wales and this general description, it will appear that the Welsh remains are in respect of stature and the contour of the head of the same class as those of England, with the exception that the Welsh skulls are not so long, those from the Denbighshire and Flintshire caves having an average index, not of 71 or 72, but of 76 or 77.[46] This difference is not, however, important enough to warrant us in supposing that the neolithic population of Wales was not essentially the same as that of England.

No help is, of course, to be expected from neolithic tombs in determining the question of the colour of the hair and the complexion of the people of the New Stone Age. But the probabilities are much in favour of black, curly hair and a brunet rather than blond aspect. Later immigrations seem to have been predominantly of fair-haired folk, and the facts point to the dark element in the British population as the oldest. It is in harmony with this view that dark eyes and hair are found in the greatest preponderance in the western parts of the British

[45] For the "long barrow race" see *British Barrows*, pp. 645-60; *Prehistoric Scotland*, pp. 448-52.

[46] *Cave Hunting*, p. 171.

Isles and particularly in secluded spots, where there has been very little disturbance of the population. Thus the tables compiled by Dr. Beddoe show Wales, in company with Cornwall and the West of Ireland, as a land of dark folk, who nowhere muster in greater strength than in the two old-world centres of Rhayader and Beddgelert.[47]

When the neolithic inhabitants of Britain have been conceived of as a short, dark and long-headed people, it is not difficult to find relatives for them on the Continent. Tacitus long ago recorded the observation (doubtless) of Agricola, that the swarthy visages and twisted locks of the South-Welsh tribe of Silures pointed to their Iberian origin.[48] The Iberians, the oldest known inhabitants of the Spanish peninsula, are still the dominant element in this quarter of Europe; "the present population of Spain," says Ripley, "is closely typical of that of the earliest prehistoric period". He adds that "it is cranially not distinguishable either from the prehistoric Long Barrow type in the British Isles or from that which prevailed throughout France anterior to its present broad-headed population of Celtic derivation".[49] The early neolithic race type was, in fact, uniform throughout Northern Africa, Spain, France, Italy and the British Isles, to go no further afield; Western Europe was held by the race styled by some Iberian, and by others Mediterranean. Its features and build are represented in modern Britain by the short, dark Welshman of South Wales, possibly its very qualities of soul and mind in the typical collier and "eisteddfodwr," impulsive and wayward, but susceptible to the influences of music and religion. Theories of this kind, which offer a simple explanation of a great variety of facts, are eyed with much suspicion by students whose work has made them familiar with the real complexity of race problems. But no more satisfactory explanation has yet been put forward of the race affinities of neolithic man as he is seen in Britain; the Iberian or Mediterranean theory, indeed, has recently received from one quarter unexpected confirmation. It has long been

[47] *Races of Britain* (1885), pp. 185, 186. The results are conveniently mapped in Ripley's *Races of Europe*, p. 318.

[48] "Silurum colorati vultus torti plerumque crines et posita contra Hispania Hiberos veteres traiecisse easque sedes occupasse fidem faciunt" (*Agricola*, xi.).

[49] *Races of Europe*, p. 277.

CHAP. I. known that Irish and Welsh, though as Celtic tongues they draw the bulk of their vocabulary and inflexions from the great Aryan fountain-head, have a syntax which is entirely unlike that of the Aryan group of languages, and the conjecture was natural that this arose through the adoption of Aryan speech by a non-Aryan people, who perpetuated in the new tongue the idioms of the old, in the manner of modern Welshmen whose mastery of English is imperfect. To Prof. Morris Jones is due the credit, however, of pointing out that these anomalous idioms, for instance, the habit of beginning the sentence with the verb ("dywedodd Arthur" for "Arthur said") and the suffixing of pronominal endings to prepositions (ynddo = in him), are exactly paralleled in Egyptian and Berber, and that the pre-Aryan language involved must accordingly have been of the so-called Hamitic family.[50] This much, then, is certain—that before the advent of the first Celtic invaders, *i.e.*, as will shortly be seen, the beginning of the Bronze Age, at least one of the languages (perhaps the only one) spoken in Britain was nearly akin to that of the Berber or Lybian race of North Africa. Should the attempt be made to establish an African connection in other than linguistic matters, there is no insuperable difficulty. The modern Berber is spare in figure and averages five feet seven inches in stature; his skin is white and gives no suggestion of negro blood; his hair is usually dark and the blond type is rarely seen; though dolichocephalic, he is not more so than the men of the Denbighshire caves, with an average index of 76 or 75. "The Chawia," remark the authors of *Libyan Notes* (1901), "are, generally speaking, remarkably European in their appearance; many might have passed for Irishmen or Scotchmen. The boys in particular, when about the age of fifteen or sixteen, would, if put into similar dress, be almost indistinguishable from English lads of the same age." The race is hardy, industrious, intelligent, and of independent spirit; if due allowance be made for the effect of long centuries of growth and contact with civilisation, there seems no reason why it should not be taken as fairly representing the neolithic folk of Wales. Even the cromlechs are not wanting, and, though the art of building great stone chambers for the burial of the dead in course of

[50] See Appendix B. to *W. People.*

time spread so far afield that as a race criterion it is somewhat precarious, it is surely of some significance that the "dolmen" at Roknia in Algeria selected for illustration in *Libyan Notes* might very well have been taken, if left undescribed, for a typical cromlech from Anglesey or Pembrokeshire. CHAP. I.

III. The Bronze Age.

Three events are associated with the Bronze Age in Britain, *viz.*, the adoption of a new material for the making of weapons, the arrival of a new race, and the introduction of new burial customs. How far these three events are to be connected with each other, whether the new customs were those of the new race, whose victories were the natural outcome of their possession of the new weapons, is no doubt open to argument, but that bronze, the practice of cremation and a broad-headed people make their first appearance in these islands during the same epoch will hardly be denied. It will be convenient first to deal with the new element in the population.

While the investigation of the neolithic chambered tombs of England and Wales has never brought to light any but long skulls, the round barrows and cairns in which bodies, frequently, but not always, after a process of cremation, are placed without the protection of a chamber, have yielded great numbers of round or brachycephalic skulls as well as those of the older form. The contrast between the two races goes beyond the shape of the skull, and is indeed as complete as it well could be. In height the new-comer averaged five feet eight inches, being several inches taller than his neolithic opponent. Powerful of limb, with wide forehead, overhanging eyebrows, prominent cheek-bones and ample jaws, he was planned for immediate conquest, if we may not say for ultimate victory in the struggle of races.[51] In colouring he was most probably light; it is noteworthy in this connection that the hair and eyes of the eighty-two broad-headed men examined by Dr. Beddoe in Wales and the West of England were "very much lighter, generally speaking, than those of the rest of the local population".[52]

There is every reason to suppose that this round-headed

[51] *British Barrows*, pp. 637-45. [52] *Races of Britain*, p. 17.

CHAP. I. invader, who perhaps first crossed the channel about twelve centuries before the Christian era, was the man who introduced Aryan speech, in its Celtic form, into Britain. Within recent years the Aryan question has undergone great modifications. It is no longer considered necessary, in order to explain the phenomenon of a great Aryan group of languages, that a single Aryan race, living in a remote past in some definite region of the East, should be supposed to have broken up in course of time into Indo-Iranian, Celtic, Teutonic, Hellenic and other branches and have scattered itself over the whole of what is now the area of Aryan speech. Prehistoric archæology has shown that there is no evidence to support this theory of a great migration from east to west, that on the contrary the leading races of Europe have been settled in that continent from early neolithic times, and that Aryan languages are and have for ages been spoken by peoples of widely different physical type. What the philologist has now to explain, therefore, is not the extension of a race, but the diffusion of a language, which was, no doubt, the language at first of a particular race in some European or Asiatic district, but had the exceptional fortune to be adopted by other surrounding races, each of whom spoke it with its own accent and idiom, so that it became a group of dialects, instead of a uniform tongue. In view, then, of this altered aspect of the question, it is not necessary to contend that the Bronze Age invaders of Britain were of Aryan stock; it suffices to show that they were nearly akin to continental peoples who spoke an Aryan language.

At the close of the Neolithic Age a race of the same physical type as the men of the British round barrows is found in possession of the valleys of the Seine and Rhine, and even as far afield as Northern Italy and the upper valley of the Danube. Of this race it is clear that the round-barrow men formed an offshoot, attracted to Britain by causes which cannot now be ascertained. Now while the portion of this stock which was settled in the valley of the Po became the progenitor of the Umbrian people and the creator of Latin, the bulk of it undoubtedly went to make the great Celtic nation of history, speaking an Aryan language closely related to Latin, out of which Welsh and Irish have in course of time developed. The term Celtic is perhaps unfortunate, though there can be now no question, in the domain of philology at least, of substituting another for it. It has been often pointed out that the name Celt was never recognised as a national designation by the whole of the family of tribes to whom we nowadays apply it; in Britain, for instance, it was quite unknown, and, until the rise of comparative philology, no one would have dreamed of looking for a Celt in these islands. Historically, the name is that which the south-western wing of the Celtic-speaking community bore among themselves when they first touched the Mediterranean;[53] owing to the establishment in this region at an early date of a Greek colony at Marseilles, it became widely diffused as the Greek term for the whole race, nor was it until a later age that the name which the more northerly tribes gave themselves, *viz.*, Galatæ, became generally known, and, owing to its adoption by the Romans in the form Galli, finally ousted the other as a general designation. In choosing to speak, therefore, of the primitive Celtic race, philologists use a phrase which is far from exact, but, so long as the true position of the "Celts of history," the dwellers between the Seine and the Garonne, is kept in mind, no confusion can arise from the use of a term which has won for itself, as a symbol of what is common to Gael and Brython, a very secure position in the English language.

The primitive Celtic race was, however, not homogeneous. No fact in connection with this group of languages is better known than that it falls into two main divisions, the Goidelic (to use the convenient terms coined by Sir J. Rhys)[54] and the Brythonic. To the former belong the Celtic tongues spoken in Ireland, Scotland and the Isle of Man, to the latter those of Wales and of Brittany, together with the extinct Cornish. Within the two divisions the linguistic barriers are not formidable; the gap is widest between Welsh and Breton, though even in this case there is no reason why we should look back more than fifteen centuries for the point of separation. But the cleavage between the two divisions themselves goes deep and shows itself in matters of the first importance. One of the best-known points of divergence is the treatment of primitive QU; while Goidelic long retained the original sound (it

[53] See page 31 below.

[54] In the first edition of *Celtic Britain* (1882).

is still heard in Manx), only reducing it to C within historic times, Brythonic had in all words in which it occurred converted it into P, by the double process of dropping the guttural and modifying the labial, before the Brythonic peoples appeared on the historic stage. Thus early Celtic "*qu*etveres" (= four) becomes in Irish "*c*eathair," but in Welsh "*p*edwar" and in Breton "*p*evar"; old Welsh "ma*p*" answers to Irish "ma*c*," which in the Ogam inscriptions is found as "ma*qu*i" (in the genitive), with the primitive sound unaltered. The differences between Goidelic and Brythonic, of which one example has been given, are so numerous and fundamental that it must be supposed that the two peoples who spoke these two forms of the language were either long separated from each other or were not originally, despite the use of a common tongue, of the same stock. Which, then, it will be asked, was the branch which invaded Britain at the beginning of the Bronze Age? The answer can hardly be a matter of doubt if the relative position of Goidels and Brythons in our island group since the beginning of history be present to the mind. The Goidelic has always lain to the north-west of the Brythonic country, which has interposed between it and the Continent; before it was proper (if it is now) to speak of a "Celtic fringe," there was a Goidelic fringe, the remnant of an early Celtic migration driven over mountain and sea by the pressure of a newer.

It was at one time believed that the Goidelic migration to Britain was so complete as to leave no trace behind in the Celtic area of the Continent. But of late the view has been advanced that the historical Celts, the inhabitants of Central Gaul, were to a great extent Goidelic in speech and that herein lay the difference between them and their Galatic neighbours, whose language beyond question belonged to the Brythonic branch.[55]

The characteristic weapon of the Age of Bronze was the bronze axe. At first, it was of the simplest form, reproducing in metal the outlines of the neolithic celt; perfectly flat, it had no means of attachment to its wooden handle, which must accordingly have been cleft to receive it. As the art of the smith developed, more serviceable forms were devised; in the

[55] For the whole subject see *W. People*, chap. i., and Rhys, *Celtæ and Galli* (1905).

palstave type there are stop-ridges which prevent the head of the axe from slipping too far back into its handle and a loop which enables head and handle to be firmly fixed by means of a thong to each other. Last of all came the socketed axe, a shell of metal into which the wooden haft was inserted. Side by side with the development of the axe may be traced that of the sword. The neolithic knife was first reproduced in bronze in the form of a short squat dagger, secured by rivets to a wooden or horn handle; this grew in course of time into a long and graceful sword, of which the hilt as well as the blade might occasionally be of bronze. At the same time the dagger underwent another development and grew into a bronze spear head, having a hollow stock for the insertion of the wooden shaft. The flint arrow head of the Neolithic Age held its own undisturbed throughout this period, for no one seems to have thought it wise to waste good bronze in the making of a missile which the owner was quite likely to lose on the first occasion of using it.

It is not probable that many, if indeed any, of these developments were due to the ingenuity of British artificers. Like the discovery of bronze itself, the revelation to the neolithic craftsman of the happy effect upon his unmanageable copper of a moderate admixture of tin, they must be referred to the Continent, with which the insular Celts, through their kinsmen on the Rhine and Seine, no doubt maintained a connection. But if the ideas came from abroad, there is no lack of evidence that the workmanship was to a great extent domestic. The identity of the word for "smith" in all the Celtic languages suggests that the craft was known to the Bronze Age men at the time of their arrival here; [56] for later periods there is the still stronger proof afforded by the discovery of the tools employed, including the moulds in which the various weapons were cast. Many articles were no doubt imported, and this would especially be the case in the late Bronze Age, when work was being produced on the Continent in which beauty of design was considered no less than mere utility.

The custom of cremation made its appearance in Britain in

[56] See *Urk. Spr. s.v.* "gobân," 114 (Irish "goba" = Welsh and Cornish "gof").

CHAP. I.

the early part of the Bronze Age. Whatever its precise origin, it had no doubt a religious significance, and, far from implying contradiction of the neolithic idea, that the existence of the dead was a continuance in the spirit world of the life once lived in this, it may well have been designed for the purpose of giving that idea a more reasonable expression. In order that the human spirit might range freely in the new sphere of its being, it was right that it should be delivered from the incubus of the body. The corpse was first burnt to ashes on a funeral pyre. This rite was still remembered by the Welsh at the date of the composition of the so-called "historical" Triads, for in them it is told how a party rode on the back of one horse to see the smoking bier of the men of Gwenddoleu who had fallen in the fight of Arderydd.[57] The remains were then in most cases placed in a funeral urn, which was a roughly shaped crock about a foot or a foot and a half high, decorated with the characteristic patterns of the period.[58] As in neolithic times, implements and trinkets of various kinds were buried with the dead, though it is remarkable that hardly any bronze axes or swords or spear heads have been found so interred in these islands—they were perhaps too valuable to be spared. In the disposition of the urn, no set custom seems to have been observed; sometimes it was enclosed in a "cist" or small receptacle of flat stones, sometimes it rested mouth downward on a single slab, and sometimes it had no protection whatever. Over the whole a great barrow or cairn was raised, which, as no passage had to be provided to a permanent grave-chamber, was naturally round in figure. The true characteristic of the Bronze Age burial, as seen in the greater part of Britain, is not, however, the shape of the covering "crug" or "tomen," but the absence of an accessible chamber.

Though the fashion of burning the dead spread during this age to every corner of the British Isles, and even established itself in remote districts among people who long after the close of the neolithic period still built sepulchral chambers,[59] it did

[57] "Ar eil marchlwyth aduc coruann march meibon eliffer gosgorduawr . . . y edrych ar vygedorth llu gwendoleu yn arderyd" (Triad in *Mab.* 301).

[58] The art of the Bronze Age is the subject of chap. ii. in Mr. Romilly Allen's *Handbook to Celtic Art* (London, 1904).

[59] *Prehistoric Scotland*, p. 478.

not at once displace the older custom of simple burial. Bronze Age barrows contain unburnt skeletons as well as bones which have undergone cremation, and evidence which would otherwise be wanting is thus obtained as to the physical characteristics of the population during this period. The old race and the new are found lying side by side, so that, while there can be little doubt that the vigorous, athletic Celt was everywhere master and lord, he must in many parts of the country have spared for servile labour the older inhabitants of the soil. He would especially need their help, if, as there is good reason to think, he practised a primitive agriculture. The neolithic life was, probably, purely pastoral, but comparative philology shows that the peoples among whom the European form of Aryan speech was evolved were familiar with the tillage of the soil,[60] though their implements were of the rudest, and this conclusion is supported by the discovery of grain-crushers in the round barrows of the Yorkshire wolds.[61] In other respects, also, the civilisation which was the fruit of the union of the two races was an advance upon that of the Age of Stone; the pottery made was of a better kind and was stamped with geometrical patterns; ornaments were more elaborate, among them being handsome necklaces of jet, such as that of which the remains were found in 1828 in a Bronze Age grave at Pen y Bonc, near Holyhead;[62] while the occupation of hill fortresses with their round stone huts shows the existence of a tribal life, presided over by the tribal chieftain, the Celtic rix or "rhi".[63]

The sepulchral monument did not always in this age take the form of a cairn or barrow. Investigation of the stone circles of Great Britain and Ireland has led to the conclusion that very many of them are Bronze Age burying-places. Though the greater triumphs of the megalithic builder, such as Stonehenge and Avebury, can hardly be disposed of so lightly, and may very well have had some religious purpose, the ordinary circle as seen in Wales, for instance, on the hills above Penmaen Mawr or in the parish of Llanidan, Anglesey, was no doubt a place of burial. Barrows, both chambered and un-

[60] See part iv. chap. v. of Schrader's work.

[61] *British Barrows*, pp. 114-5.

[62] *Ancient Stone Implements*, p. 459.

[63] *Urk. Spr.* 230.

CHAP. I.

chambered, are often found to have a ring of standing stones around them, so that in the stone circle a part of the old form of monument survives, after the barrow itself has been abandoned as unnecessary. The simplest memorial of all is the single standing stone or "maen hir" (long stone), which may have had many purposes from time to time, but was certainly often used to mark the resting-place of the dead. As in the case of cromlechs, the traditional names of "meini hirion" are no safe guide to their early history: "Llech Idris" (The Stone of Idris),[64] "Carreg y Bwgi" (The Bogey Stone)[65] and "Maen Beuno" (The Stone of Beuno),[66] for instance, but preserve the speculations of a peasantry who knew nothing of the original design of the monument.

Abundant remains of the civilisation of the Bronze Age have been discovered in Wales, and this in all parts of the country, so that it is clear that the conquering race of Goidels in time made their influence felt in every corner of it. But each successive tide of culture which has washed the shores of Britain has made a belated appearance in Wales, and hence it need not be supposed that the new era began in these western highlands until long after it had obtained a firm foothold in the south-eastern plain. That the Bronze Age of Britain was far advanced ere its customs rooted themselves in Wales may, indeed, be inferred from the rarity in Welsh burials of the period of any other method of disposing of the dead than cremation,[67] and from the prevalence of highly developed forms among the bronze weapons which have been collected on Welsh soil. In the life of the little community whose home and burying-place under the brow of a limestone cliff were recently excavated by Prof Boyd Dawkins near Newmarket in Flintshire, the first contact with the new culture seems to be brought to light.[68] Charcoal, the remains of domestic animals and a polished flint flake; great numbers of human bones huddled together in a square sepulchral chamber—here was nothing which might not be neolithic. But the skulls,

[64] Near Trawsfynydd.
[65] Between Cellan and Llan y Crwys (*Arch. Camb.* IV. ix. 325).
[66] *Arch. Camb.* III. iii. (1857), 299-300.
[67] *British Barrows*, p. 21 (note 1).
[68] *Arch. Camb.* V. viii. (1891), 71-2; *Archæological Journal*, 1901, pp. 322-41.

though for the most part long, included some of which the breadth indicated the presence of the newer race, and, most convincing proof of all, the pottery was of unmistakable Bronze Age pattern. Like many conquering stocks, the Goidels who settled in Wales may have been a minority, a military aristocracy; it could hardly have fallen out otherwise that in a later age the Silures should have still vividly recalled in aspect and build their Iberian kinsmen. Nor is it likely, from what is known of the Welsh tribes in the time of Cæsar, that Aryan agriculture made much headway in the country. But the pottery, the weapons, and the burial usages of the Bronze Age became ultimately as common in Wales as in the rest of Britain. In Pembrokeshire, for instance, where the number of cromlechs shows that neolithic ideas survived in strength to a late period, as compared with the time of their disappearance from the rest of South Wales, over thirty round barrows, locally known as "tumps," have been excavated and in almost all the remains found have been those of cremated bodies.[69] In the mountain-locked glen, sloping seaward, where now stands the village of Penmaen Mawr, ensconced in what was, until the making of the Chester and Holyhead railway, one of the most secluded spots in North Wales, a Bronze Age burial was in 1889 accidentally brought to light.[70] The urns, shaped and decorated in the usual manner of the period, were found resting mouth downward on flat stones; they were full of calcined bones. Further, to put beyond all doubt the epoch to which they belonged, in each of two of them a small bronze pin was discovered.[71]

NOTE TO CHAPTER I. § ii.—*Cantref y Gwaelod.*

The story of the Submerged Hundred first makes its appearance in a poem in the Black Book of Carmarthen (53b, 54a), written in the last part of the book, and, therefore, about 1200. This poem has been often translated; there is, for instance, an English version in Meyrick's *History of Cardiganshire* (2), 153 and a modern Welsh one in *Cymru Fu* (p. 6). The best is, however, the most recent,

[69] *Lit. Eng.* p. 29.

[70] *Arch. Camb.* V. viii. (1891), 33.

[71] It should be observed that Dr. T. Rice Holmes, in his recently published *Ancient Britain and the Invasions of Cæsar* (Oxford, 1907), challenges many of the accepted views as to the prehistoric civilisation of these islands, and, in particular, the view that the Early Bronze Age invaders were Celts. The whole subject must be regarded as still under discussion.

CHAP. I.

that of Sir J. Rhys in the *Cymmrodorion Transactions for* 1892-3 (pp. 14-16), from which it appears that the Plain of Gwyddneu was overwhelmed by the sea by reason of the wickedness of its inhabitants, who had given themselves up to eating and drinking and insolent pride of heart. The person who let loose this judgment upon the land was a maiden, perhaps called Margâret ("Mererid"), who at a time of feasting suffered the waters of a magical well which was under her charge to escape and overflow the country round. What the share of "witless Seithennin" was in the catastrophe is not apparent; he survives it, however, and is called upon to survey the melancholy scene. Such was the primitive story; it is supplemented in one point by the compiler of the earliest form of the *Pedigrees of the Saints* (also dating from about 1200), who speaks of five "Saints" as sons of *King* Seithennin of the Plain of Gwyddno, whose realm was swallowed up by the sea (*Myv. Arch.* II. 24 [416]). For the germ of the modern legend, which is in many ways a very different one, we have to look to the third series of Triads, belonging to the sixteenth century; the third of the Three Arrant Drunkards of Britain (a festive group unknown to the older triadic literature) is there said to be Seithinyn the Drunken, King of Dyfed, who in his cups let the sea loose over the Lowland Hundred, a region of fair cities and the patrimony of Gwyddno Garanhir, King of Ceredigion (*Myv.* II. 64 [404]). The well maiden has now disappeared, Seithennin has become the author of the mischief, and the drowned kingdom is no longer his, but that of his neighbour Gwyddno. But the famous embankment has still to be introduced into the story. It was to the antiquary Robert Vaughan of Hengwrt (1592-1667) that the idea first occurred of connecting the story of the Lowland Hundred with the natural causeway near Harlech called by the peasantry, in that age as in this, "Sarn Badrig" or St. Patrick's Causeway. The popular explanation no doubt was that this was the saint's private road home to his beloved Ireland, but for Vaughan it is "a great stone wall made as a fence against the sea," which he has no difficulty in supposing to have once been a rampart of the buried realm. Lewis Morris, in the next century, took the same view, and, remembering the poem in the Black Book, added a suggestion of his own, "that by drunkenness the flood-gates were left open" (*Celtic Remains*, p. 73; *cf.* p. 390). But one more touch was needed to give the narrative its modern form; the business of the flood-gates must be specially laid at the door of Seithennin, who must play the part of the drunken lockman. This is done in Owen's *Cambrian Biography* (1803); under the patronage of so influential a student of Welsh antiquities, the story as thus rounded off won great popularity and furnished an attractive theme for literary treatment. Englishmen were made familiar with it by the fascinating pages of *The Misfortunes of Elphin*; for Welshmen it was vigorously told in the verse of Hiraethog and Ieuan Glan Geirionydd.

CHAPTER II.

THE HISTORIC DAWN.

(Use has been made of Elton, *Origins of English History*; Evans, *Coins of the Ancient Britons*; Rhys, *Celtic Britain*; Rhys and Brynmor-Jones, *Welsh People*; A. J. Evans, *Rhind Lectures*, as well as of the original authorities, Cæsar, Diodorus Siculus, Strabo and Ptolemy.)

I. FIRST CONTACT WITH CIVILISATION.

CHAP. II.

AS the Bronze Age draws to its close, there is more and more evidence of trade intercourse between Britain and the outer world. The first civilised visitor to these shores would seem to have been the Phœnician trader, who sailed from Southern Spain to the south-western corner of Britain:—

> There, where down cloudy cliffs, through sheets of foam,
> Shy traffickers, the dark Iberians come,
> And on the beach undid his corded bales.

It is true that the Cassiterides, the "Isles of Tin," whence the Phœnicians obtained great quantities of this metal, so much in request for the making of bronze, are no longer identified with the Scilly Isles, but it is suggested with much probability that they were the British Isles themselves.[1] The Phœnicians were careful to conceal their situation from the knowledge of the rest of the world, so much so that Herodotus in the fifth century B.C. doubted their very existence,[2] and thus it came about that when they finally came to light, as the result of the voyage of Pytheas, under another name, geographers still continued to locate the Isles of Tin off the north coast of Spain and distinguished them from the isles of Albion and Ierne. Side by

[1] The question of the situation of the Cassiterides is fully discussed in Elton's *Origins of English History*, chap. i. But the view there put forward is now abandoned in favour of that of Müllenhoff, for which see *W. People*, p. 61 (note); Arbois de Jubainville, *Cours de Littérature Celtique*, xii. (1902), pp. 4-11; *Eng. Hist. Rev.* xix. (1904), p. 140 (note).

[2] Οὔτε νήσους οἶδα Κασσιτερίδας ἐούσας (iii. 115).

side with this intercourse with Phœnician civilisation, which seems to have had little or no effect upon the inner life of Britain, there was communication, too, with the Celtic peoples of the mainland. About six or seven centuries before Christ the Celts of the Continent had attained a high degree of skill in the designing and fashioning of weapons and ornaments; it was the era of what is known, from one of its important seats in the Noric Alps, as the Hallstatt culture,[3] and the importation into Britain in the late Bronze Age of bronze articles of the Hallstatt type shows that there was at this time a trade route which carried such articles across the Straits of Dover. Britain was gradually being drawn into contact with the organised communities which, clustering around the Middle Sea, formed the civilised world of the day.

In the middle of the fourth century B.C. the Greeks, wide as was their geographical knowledge, had no certain knowledge of the islands in the Ocean beyond the region of the Celts. But commercial rivalry came to the aid of geography. The adventurous traders of the Greek colony of Massalia (Marseilles) in Southern Gaul, having vainly sought to obtain access to the regions beyond the Pillars of Hercules—our Straits of Gibraltar—whence their Carthaginian competitors drew such abundant stores of tin, resolved to send out into the unknown Ocean an expedition which should either open up for them this market or find a new one in the mysterious North-west. A learned citizen of the place, one Pytheas,[4] an astronomer, was placed in charge, and under his guidance a voyage was made which not only achieved the immediate commercial purpose, but also added vast regions to the known world of Greek geographical science. Having sailed right round the Spanish coast, the expedition directed its course to Brittany and thence to the Straits of Dover; Pytheas not only landed in Britain, but spent a considerable time in the island, making himself fully acquainted with at least the south-eastern portion and ascertain-

[3] There is a concise account of the discoveries at Hallstatt and of their significance in the second edition (1900) of Munro's *Rambles and Studies in Bosnia and Herzegovina*, chap. xi.

[4] The works of Pytheas have long been lost, and our knowledge of his doings is entirely derived from the incidental references of later (and often hostile) writers. Full justice is meted out to him in Elton's *Origins of English History*, chaps. i. and ii.

ing that there would be no difficulty in obtaining from the mines of the Cornish peninsula an ample supply of tin for the purposes of his employers in Marseilles. With good reason is he regarded as the discoverer of Britain, its Columbus, who first made it known to learning and civilisation.

The Brythonic Celts had not yet, so far as can be gathered, made any settlements on the northern side of the channel.[5] They held the opposite coast, from the estuary of the Rhine to that of the Seine, but were still a purely continental people. Yet it is probable that the two great islands which Pytheas brought within the ken of Greek merchants and scholars were even then known as the Pretanic Isles (*αἱ Πρεττανικαὶ νῆσοι*), a form preserved for many centuries by writers on geography.[6] The truth is, this term has in origin no connection with Britain or the Britons; it is, on the other hand, closely related to the Ynys Prydain of the Welsh, who never, save under the influence of a misguided purism, speak of Ynys *B*rydain. Prydyn, the mediæval Welsh name of Scotland, is clearly the same word, and so too, Celtic philologists assure us, the Irish name for the Picts, *viz.*, Cruithni.[7] Thus the Pretanic Isles may mean the Pictish Islands and, as the form (with its *p* for the Goidelic *qu*) is Brythonic, it receives the most natural explanation if we suppose it to be a name given to the group by the Brythonic or Galatic dwellers on the northern coast of Gaul (who perhaps learnt it from Goidelic predecessors), on account of the large "Iberian" or Pictish element in its population.

When it was desired to distinguish the two islands, the one was called Albion, the other Ierne. According to the elder Pliny, Albion was known to be a more ancient name than Britannia,[8] and this is confirmed by the fact that, in the forms Alba, Alban (whence the Welsh "yr Alban" for Scotland), it has long been used by the Goidelic peoples to denote either

[5] This, the former opinion of Sir John Rhys (*W. People*, p. 75), is now abandoned by him (*Celt. Br.* (3), p. 4).

[6] Müller believes Πρεττανική to be the true reading throughout Strabo's *Geography* (Firmin-Didot edition, 965). It is also the form regularly used by Marcian of Heraclea (see Müller's edition of the *Minor Greek Geographers*, Paris, 1882, vol. i. pp. 516-7).

[7] *Urk. Spr.* 63; *W. People*, pp. 76, 79.

[8] "Albion ipsi nomen fuit, cum Britanniae vocarentur omnes" (*Nat. Hist.* iv. 102).

CHAP. II. the whole or a substantial part of Britain. Albion was the "white land,"[9] whose gleaming cliffs were the constant wonder of the continental Celts as they gazed across the blue waters of the Channel, and thus the mediæval Welsh scribe, though he knew nothing of Celtic philology and was thinking only of the Latin "albus," was happily inspired when he rendered it "Y Wen Ynys" (The White Island).[10]

II. The Brythonic Settlement.

It was, perhaps, about the middle of the third century B.C. that the Brythons began to settle in Britain.[11] Their arrival marks the appearance in the island of the third and last of the three considerable race elements which have gone to the making of the Welsh people. If it be contended that the first of these, the Neolithic, was the most important in respect of its contribution to the national physique and character, and that the second, the Goidelic, was the source of the early political and social institutions of the Welsh, it cannot be denied that it is to the third we owe the Welsh language. Notwithstanding the alien idioms to which reference was made in the last chapter as traceable to an African origin, Welsh is historically an Aryan and a Celtic tongue, the lineal descendant of the speech of the men who, as Cæsar says,[12] first came hither, on hostile and plunderous errands, in the age immediately preceding his own.

In the well-known exordium to the "Gallic War," Cæsar gives this people the general name of Belgæ. But it may be doubted whether this was really an ancient race-name which they recognised among themselves. Cæsar elsewhere[13] states that most of the Belgic settlers in Britain retained as colonists the tribal names which they had borne at home, and this is known in some instances to have been the case; there were,

[9] *Urk. Spr.* 21; *W. People*, p. 77.

[10] "Ar amser hwnnw y gelwit hi y wen ynys" (Brut y Brenhinoedd in Bruts, 58; *cf.* also 40).

[11] So Dr. A. J. Evans in his *Rhind Lectures*. *Cf. W. People*, p. 5. As a result of the Aylesford finds (*Archæologia*, lii. 317-88), archæologists are now disposed to regard the Belgic settlement as a late Brythonic invasion of about 150 B.C.

[12] *Bell. Gall.* v. 12: "Iis qui praedae ac belli inferendi causa ex Belgio transierant . . . et bello illato ibi permanserunt atque agros colere coeperunt".

[13] *Ibid.*: "Qui omnes fere iis nominibus civitatum appellantur quibus orti ex civitatibus eo pervenerunt".

for instance, Parisi to the north of the Humber as well as Parisii on the banks of the Seine, Atrebatii south of the Thames as well as Atrebates where Arras now stands.[14] But, strangely enough, while there was in Britain a tribe of Belgæ occupying what may be called the Bath and Winchester region,[15] no corresponding tribe appears in Gaul, the name being applied instead to a great tribal group, by no means closely knit together. It would almost seem, therefore, as if the original Belgæ had, as Sir J. Rhys suggests,[16] transferred themselves lock, stock and barrel to Britain, but had left behind them in Northern Gaul, in the wide extension of their tribal name, a lasting memorial of the military supremacy which they had once exercised in the region.

If any general name was current among the Brythonic or Belgic tribes of Northern Gaul, it was probably Galat, or, if the Latin be preferred to the Greek form, Galli. Diodorus of Sicily, writing in the first century B.C., essays to correct the popular misuse of the terms Celt and Gaul.[17] The Celts (*Κελτούς*), he says, are those who inhabit the "hinterland" of Marseilles and the regions adjacent to the Alps and the Pyrenees; the country bordering on the Ocean and the Hercynian Forest and away east to Scythia belongs to the Gauls (*Γαλάτας*). It is the Romans who have caused confusion by massing all together as Gauls (*Γαλάτας* for Gallos). So wide, in fact, had the application of the name now become in Latin usage that Cæsar could find no better distinctive name for these northerners than Belgæ.

The vogue of the Galatic name was the result of the career of world-wide conquest upon which the Galatæ embarked about the beginning of the fourth century B.C. Celtic scholars derive the word from a root which in Irish has yielded "gal," valour, and in Welsh "gallu," to be strong, and thus explain it as signifying "strong men," "braves".[18] Few races of fighters, indeed, have left a more definite impression of themselves in the pages of antiquity. For the invasion and settlement of South-eastern Britain was but one of their achievements; the

[14] All four tribes are mentioned by Ptolemy (II. iii. 10, 12; viii. 10; ix. 4).

[15] Βέλγαι καὶ πόλεις· Ἴσκαλις, Ὕδατα Θερμά, Οὐέντα (Ptol. II. iii. 13).

[16] *W. People*, p. 6.

[17] Diod. Sic. v. 32.

[18] *Urk. Spr.* 107; *Celt. Br.* (2), 267, 298. Whitley Stokes appears to regard Gallus as a word of different origin (*Urk. Spr.* 108).

CHAP. II. sack of Rome in 390 B.C. was their work and the attack upon Delphi in 278 B.C., while the name Galatia preserves to all time a record of their great settlement in the heart of Asia Minor. In some of these movements the Celts strictly so called may have borne a part, but the originating impulse was Galatic, spreading in every direction from the valley of the Rhine. Thus the figure of the Galatic warrior looms large in classical literature, and there is little difficulty in forming a mental picture of the kind of man who came over in the Brythonic host of invasion.[19] He was of commanding height; Strabo testifies to seeing at Rome British lads who were six inches taller than the tallest men in the city. The women, inured to the same perils and even sharing the rough fortune of battle, were built on the same scale, and possessed all the spirit and daring of their spouses. The limbs of the Galat were long and vigorous, but he was not well put together; his great, unwieldy frame, formidable by reason of its weight, had not the compact agility of the more resourceful southerner. He had the clear red and white complexion of the true blond; his hair was yellow or yellowish-brown, and so proud was he of its golden tint that, in Gaul, at least, he was in the habit of heightening the colour by means of a dye. His ample locks were bound together in a mass above and behind the head; his chin was bare, but long moustaches drooped over the mouth. His under-garment was a sleeved tunic, while on his legs he wore the characteristic Gallic breeches, fitting loosely round the ankle; on his shoulders was a thick woollen cloak, fastened in front by a brooch of delicate workmanship. Such was the outer man; in disposition the Galat was impetuous, boastful, self-indulgent, a shedder of much blood, but brave, hospitable, true to his honourable ideals and at bottom of childlike simplicity. He was lavish in expense upon his own adornment and that of his arms and warlike accoutrements, but no money could buy from him the embalmed heads which had been handed down to him as the grim trophies of his ancestors' valour.

This portrait reveals to us, as was intended by the polished,

[19] The account which follows is based upon Diod. Sic. v. 26-31, and Strabo, IV. iv., the Firmin-Didot edition having been used in each case.

self-restrained observers to whom we owe it, the lineaments of a barbarian, but the race was nevertheless one, as these writers themselves allow, of great capacity. In several important respects, it had already made great advances in culture. Of these the chief was perhaps the adoption of iron instead of bronze for the manufacture of weapons and cutting implements. The age of the Hallstatt culture, though it coincided with the late Bronze Age of Britain and is only represented in this country by bronze objects, was one in which considerable progress was made in Central Europe in the adaptation of iron to warlike and domestic uses, and thus, when the time came for the Galatic tribes to play their part in the history of the West, they were fully equipped in this respect. Sword, lance-head and javelin were of iron; so too, in many cases, the metal fittings of the long shield which protected the warrior's whole body and the metal brooch which pinned his cloak around him. It is most probable that the use of iron was introduced into Britain by the Brythonic invader, and that the beginning of the British Iron Age thus coincides with the era of the Brythonic settlement.

This is certainly the conclusion suggested by the small number of barrows which can be assigned to the period between the introduction of iron and the arrival of the Romans and by the entire absence of barrows of the kind in Scotland and Ireland, districts only slightly affected by the incoming of the Brythons. But it was not the use of a new material alone which distinguished the Galatic peoples as a progressive community; their skill in the working of metals, of bronze, of silver, and of gold, no less than of iron, furnished them with numberless articles of ornament, of which the artistic beauty of design was every whit as remarkable as the excellence of the workmanship. Nothing more free and graceful can be imagined than the best decorative work of this age, known sometimes as the Late Celtic, but on the Continent associated with the name of La Tène, a Galatic fortress on Lake Neuchâtel in Switzerland which has yielded abundant remains of the period. Though they lived in roughly timbered huts of wattle-work and sat down to their meals on littered straw covered with rugs of wolf- or dog-skin, the Galatic chiefs had torques of gold about their necks, golden bracelets

CHAP. II.

on their arms, and arms of offence and defence which, whether of bronze or of iron, were richly moulded and incised by artists of genuine ability.[20]

Two other evidences there are of the progress in civilisation which the race had achieved at the time of its settlement in our island—its mastery of horsemanship and charioteering and its possession of a coinage. Strabo bears emphatic witness to the former point; the Gauls, he says, fight best on horseback and supply Rome with its most efficient cavalry. He speaks, too, as does Diodorus, of their use of chariots in war, and it will be remembered how Cæsar, when he came into contact with this kind of fighting in Kent, was struck by the ease with which his enemies managed their horses and by the reckless daring of their movements.[21] Nor is archæological evidence wanting of the important place occupied in Galatic life by the horse and the wheeled vehicle. Horse trappings, and in particular bridle bits, are among the commonest objects found among Late Celtic remains, and at La Tène an entire chariot wheel was discovered. The series of Gaulish coins begins about 300 B.C., and is altogether derived by imitation from a gold coin issued about the middle of the previous century by Philip II. of Macedon;[22] yet, though in this direction little artistic originality was displayed, the mere existence of a coinage shows that the multiplying needs of a community advancing towards civilisation were making the old methods of barter obsolete.

There is little difficulty in understanding how a race thus equipped overbore the opposition of the earlier inhabitants of Britain and established flourishing colonies in the most attractive parts of the island. Nor need there be much hesitation as to the region where they first found a foothold. They would naturally direct their skiffs in the first instance to Kent, and, in conformity with this, Cæsar states that Kent was

[20] The questions connected with the introduction of iron into Britain and the development of the Late Celtic style of decoration are discussed by Dr. Munro in *Prehistoric Scotland*, chap. vii., and *Rambles and Studies in Bosnia and Herzegovina*, second edition, chap. xi. See also A. J. Evans, *Rhind Lectures*, and J. Romilly Allen, *Celtic Art in Pagan and Christian Times.*

[21] *Bell. Gall.* iv. 33.

[22] Evans, *Coins of the Ancient Britons*, 1864 (Supplement published in 1890), pp. 23-5.

much the most civilised part of Britain and in its customs differed little from Gaul.[23] This being the case, it is somewhat remarkable that the inhabitants of this district were not known by any tribal name connecting them with a Belgic tribe on the other side of the water. They were simply termed Cantii, from the place name Cantion, which is said, like Albion, to signify "white land"[24] This anomaly has led to the ingenious conjecture that the true name for them was Brittones, that as the van of the Belgic invasion they migrated bodily from their first homes at the mouth of the Somme (where there is still a village called Bretagne) and that this was how their continental kinsmen came to apply the British name to all inhabitants of our island. It must be remembered that the Brythonic-speaking members of the Celtic family have always dubbed themselves Brython, representing an old Brittones, while the Goidelic-speaking members have in like manner agreed to call them Bretain, for an older Brittani, so that, whether the Kentishmen be the original Britons or not, the term is properly confined to the Belgic or Galatic immigrants of the Iron Age, who may henceforth be spoken of as Brythons. Why both the Greeks and the Romans should have preferred the Goidelic to the Brythonic form of the name (Greek *Βρεττανοί*, Latin Brittani and, less correctly, Britanni) has not yet been satisfactorily explained.[25]

The descriptions which Diodorus and Strabo give of Galatic life and manners both on the Continent and in Britain are believed to owe much to the travels of Posidonius, the Stoic philosopher who traversed Spain, Gaul, and probably Britain at the beginning of the first century B.C. These travels, however, are not extant, and thus the first authentic account of the Brythons in their island home is furnished by Julius Cæsar. When he made his famous expeditions in 55 and 54 B.C., they were firmly established in the south-eastern region. In this, termed by him the "maritime part" of Britain, population was dense, agriculture flourished, sheep and cattle were

[23] "Ex his omnibus longe sunt humanissimi qui Cantium incolunt neque multum a Gallica differunt consuetudine" (*Bell. Gall.* v. 14).

[24] *W. People*, pp. 77, 78.

[25] See for the whole question *Celt. Br.* (2), pp. 205-13, with the modifications in *W. People*, pp. 6, 75-7.

CHAP. II.

to be seen in great abundance.[26] Arriving at the season of harvest, his troops were able on the first expedition to supply themselves with corn at the expense of the British farmer.[27] Nor was the art of war neglected; the progress of the Roman general was seriously opposed by men who were skilful in the use of chariots and of horses and in the fortifying of positions of natural strength; some amount of political combination there was also, for a number of the tribes had united to resist the Romans under the leadership of Cassivellaunus, the first dweller in these islands whose name has been handed down by history. Much, no doubt, remained to show that the Brythons were but a partially civilised race, for instance, the habit of staining the body blue, indulged in by the Brythonic "braves" when they went forth to battle,[28] and certain singular marriage customs. Yet the general view presented by Cæsar's narrative is undoubtedly that of a thriving and busy people, whom there is no difficulty in imagining as the makers and buyers of the beautiful creations of Late Celtic art.

Behind this prosperous Brythonic foreground, Cæsar reveals to us, in dim and shadowy tints, a background of savage life of which, in all probability, he knew nothing from actual observation. "The men of the interior," he says (distinguishing them from those of the coastwise lands), "for the most part sow no corn, but live on milk and flesh and clothe themselves in skins."[29] They are, in short, a pastoral and not an agricultural people, alike in their food, their clothing and their habits. Thus is briefly described the condition at this epoch of the older inhabitants of Britain, those who, according to their own traditions, were the autochthonous children of the island, sprung from its very soil,[30] but whom history recognises as Iberians and Goidels, descended from prehistoric immigrants. It is true that the Goidelic race, whatever may be said as to

[26] "Hominum est infinita multitudo creberrimaque aedificia . . . pecorum magnus numerus" (*Bell. Gall.* v. 12).

[27] See especially *Bell. Gall.* iv. 32 ("frumentatum missa") and v. 17 ("pabulandi causa").

[28] "*Omnes* vero se Britanni vitro inficiunt" (v. 14) makes it clear that the Brythons are included.

[29] *Bell. Gall.* v. 14.

[30] "Pars interior ab iis incolitur quos natos in insula ipsi memoria proditum dicunt" (v. 12).

the Iberian, practised agriculture, but, apart from the very summary character of Cæsar's account and his qualification "plerumque," one must remember that the seizure by the Brythons of the best of the corn-growing regions would tend to discourage the tillage of the soil among a race thrown back upon the great pasture lands of the North and West. The history of Wales shows clearly that a people familiar with agriculture may be led by the physical conditions to relegate it to a secondary place in the tribal economy and to give its main strength to the rearing of sheep and cattle.

III. Wales at the Christian Era.

During the century which followed Cæsar's attacks upon Britain, the Brythons continued to advance in civilisation and to encroach more and more upon their Goidelic and Iberian neighbours. It was during this period that they developed an inscribed coinage,[31] and the range of Brythonic influence is well shown by the wide extent of country over which specimens of this coinage have been found. South-east of a line drawn from the Wash to the Bristol Channel it was apparently (save in the western peninsula) in general use, while occasional coins strayed as far as the Tyne and the west of Cornwall.[32] But no British inscribed coin has yet been found within the limits of modern Wales, and the impression is thus created, which is in the main confirmed by other considerations, that this district remained little affected by the Brythonic immigration and the culture associated with it down to the very eve of the Roman conquest. It was part of Cæsar's "interior," a stronghold of primitive ideas, of barbarous customs and of simple modes of life.

Using the information to be derived from the geographer Ptolemy and other writers who dealt with Britain after its occupation by the Romans, one may without much hazard attempt an outline of the tribal divisions of pre-Roman Wales. Along the northern shores of the Bristol Channel dwelt the Silures, already referred to as an Iberian people. The only place which is certainly known to lie within the ancient limits

[31] "The introduction of a legend on British coins does not appear to have taken place until about the period of the accession of his (*i.e.* Commios's) sons" (Evans, *Coins*, p. 156).

[32] See map in Evans, *Coins*, suppl.

CHAP. II.

of this tribe is Caerwent in Monmouthshire,[33] but, in view of the important part which they played in the resistance to the Romans, no narrower theatre can be assigned to them than the modern counties of Monmouth, Glamorgan and Brecknock. Celtic scholars have so far been baffled in the attempt to explain the name from Brythonic or Goidelic sources,[34] and to this extent the theory that the race was predominantly non-Aryan finds confirmation. Yet traces of Celtic influence are not wanting also; one of the principal rivers of the district bore the Celtic name of Isca, represented by the modern Usk, and, whatever the meaning of the name Venta by which the tribal centre was distinguished, its occurrence elsewhere leaves little doubt as to its Celtic origin. It may be inferred, too, from their willingness to accept, in the great struggle with Ostorius Scapula, the leadership of the Brython Caratâcus, of the Catuvellaunian royal house, that the Silures set no impassable barrier between themselves and the Celtic tribes of the South-east. Yet, when all is said, they appear as a race apart, confronting their foes with that stubborn spirit, incapable of being melted by kindness or quelled by severity, which there are good grounds for regarding as a specially Iberian characteristic.[35] Hemmed in by the Forest of Dean on the east and thus parted from the Dobuni, separated from the Belgæ and the Dumnonii by the Severn Sea, they held a position of great natural strength and made full use of its military advantages.

To the west of the Silures came the Demetæ. Ptolemy alone of ancient writers mentions them, but their existence is placed beyond doubt and their situation indicated by the persistence of the name Dyfed, which is derived from the old form through the early Welsh Demet. Dyfed has had various

33 "Venta Silurum" is found both in the *Itinerary* of Antoine and the Geographer of Ravenna. I know of no ancient authority for the form "Isca Silurum," and indeed the tribal name appears to have been added in such cases, not for the purpose of distinguishing places of the same name, but in order to indicate the tribal centre. Ptolemy only assigns to the Silures the town of Βούλλαιον, which is reasonably, but not certainly, identified with the Burrium (=Usk) of the *Itinerary*.

34 *Celt. Br.* (2), p. 306.

35 Strabo points out (IV. iv. 2) that the Romans found the Iberians much more difficult to conquer than the Gauls. They husbanded their forces and fought in small detachments, ληστρικῶς πολεμοῦντες.

meanings at various epochs in Welsh history, but it has never ceased to stand for a considerable region in South-western Wales. In conformity with this, Ptolemy[36] assigns to this tribe the station of Maridunum, which can be none other than our Carmarthen. As his Luentinum is further supposed to be Llanio in Cardiganshire, it would appear safe to locate the Demetæ in the three modern counties of Carmarthen, Cardigan and Pembroke. The tribe seems to have been reckoned for all purposes, save those of precise geography, as a section of the Silures, who probably held them in a kind of subjection; thus, according to the elder Pliny,[37] the shortest passage from Britain to Ireland, for which he gives the very low estimate of thirty Roman miles, was "a Silurum gente". If this be so, it is right to extend to the Demetæ the description given by Tacitus of the dark-haired Silures and to regard them also as a race of Iberian origin, as indeed is suggested by the figures of Dr. Beddoe, who found as dark a population at Carmarthen as at almost any Welsh centre at which he made his observations.[38] Celtic influences had no doubt been brought hither, as further to the east, by the victorious Goidels; a Celtic name, Maridunum, was given to the fortress which stood at the head of the tidal portion of the Towy; but there is nothing to show that the Brythons had made their way into this region before the Romans appeared upon the scene.

It is not easy to say what people inhabited the north-western corner of Wales, the district which was in later times the stronghold of Welsh independence. Ptolemy here fails us, for, though it has until recently been taken for granted that he assigned to the Ordovices the whole of North Wales, the places mentioned by him as belonging to this tribe lie to the east, near what is now the English border, and in reality this part of his map, save for the name of a cape and that of a river, is blank.[39] Of Segontium and Conovium, stations in the district

[36] II. iii. 12. [37] *Nat. Hist.* iv. 102. [38] *Races of Britain*, p. 185.

[39] This does not appear from the map of Ptolemy's Britain contributed by Dr. Henry Bradley to *Archæologia* (xlviii. 379). But in this the Toisobios River is made to precede the cape of the Gangam and to belong to the north coast of Wales, whereas the better reading adopted by Müller reverses this order and so puts the mouth of this river somewhere near Portmadoc, an arrangement which has the further advantage of bringing Ptolemy's Μόνα νῆσος into closer connection with his North Wales.

CHAP. II.

of which mention is made elsewhere, he had apparently not heard. The same impression, that Anglesey and Snowdonia were not in the occupation of the Ordovices, is conveyed by the passage in the *Agricola* of Tacitus[40] which tells of the subjugation of the latter; they were all but annihilated in the first campaign of the new general, who then, the narrative continues, mindful of the necessity of pressing home his advantage and of not allowing the first impression of terror to wear off, set himself seriously to the task of reducing Anglesey. Only one clue is obtainable as to the condition of affairs at this time in the Snowdon region, and this is furnished by the Welsh name of the district, *viz.*, Gwynedd. This is undoubtedly ancient, appearing, as it does, in the form "Venedotis" (a genitive, presupposing some such nominative as "Venedas"), in an inscription at Penmachno, Carnarvonshire, of the sixth or seventh century.[41] The meaning is indicated by the cognate Irish word, "fine," a tribe or sept, and Gwynedd would thus denote a group or confederacy of tribes. If this interpretation be correct, it will not be matter for wonder that no general tribal name can be found which covers the whole district; the task of the investigator will rather be to distinguish the individual tribes included in the group. Nor is it out of the question to achieve something in this direction. Ptolemy himself, when he gives the title of "Cape of the Gangani"[42] to the extreme point of the Lleyn peninsula, supplies the name of one tribe and suggests its Goidelic (or Iberian) origin, for there were Gangani in the West of Ireland. The chronicler who speaks of Degannwy as "arx Decantorum"[43] furnishes another, and again a parallel form, "Decantæ," is forthcoming, this time from the Pictish North. The "Decangi" of Tacitus, dwelling not far from "the sea which looks towards Ireland,"[44] may be regarded as a third Venedotian tribe, and, if the view of Sir J. Rhys should be accepted, that the true form is "Deceangli,"[45]

[40] Cap. 18.

[41] *Arch. Camb.* IV. ii. (1871), 257-8. See *Celt. Br.* (2), p. 311; *Urk. Spr.* 270. The inscription is No. 135 in Hübner's *Inscriptiones Britanniæ Christianæ.*

[42] II. iii. 2. Γαγγανῶν is the reading of most of the MSS. and is much to be preferred to Müller's fanciful Καιαγγανῶν.

[43] Harl. MS. 3859, printed in *Y Cymmrodor*, ix. (1888), p. 163. "Arx" is supplied from other sources.

[44] *Annals*, xii. 32.

[45] *W. People*, p. 94.

would naturally be assigned to Tegeingl or Northern Flintshire. Llanfihangel Din Silwy and Llanfair yng Nghornwy may suggest that there were Selgovæ and Cornavii in Anglesey, while Porth aethwy and Din daethwy appear to be the "creek" and the "stronghold" of another of the tribes of the island. Of the whole group, no less than of the Silures and the Demetæ, it may be said that the primitive Iberian element was prominent in it, tempered, no doubt, by a Goidelic admixture;[46] here was the peculiar home of Druidism, hither fled those to whom the civilisation of the Roman province was irksome; under the shadow of the venerable oaks of Mona the very air was redolent of tradition and ancestral calm.

The fourth region of Wales, corresponding roughly to the modern counties of Montgomery and Radnor with the adjacent portions of Merioneth and Denbigh, was occupied by the Ordovices, who, strong in the difficult nature of their country, offered as fierce a resistance to the invader as did the Silures, and were among the last tribes in Southern Britain to lay down their arms. But, unlike the Silures, they represented not the older but the newer elements in the population of the island. Celts they undoubtedly were, for the tribal name is derived from the Celtic root ord-, meaning "mallet" or hammer;[47] they were the "hammer-men," wielding in battle the axe-hammers of stone which were in common use during the Bronze Age and probably much later. But more than this; they are also believed to have been Brythons, leaders of that Brythonic forward movement which in the first century of our era was making rapid progress, the people, in short, from whom the rest of Wales learnt the Welsh language.[48] That the tribe which held the land to the east, the Cornavii of our Cheshire, Shropshire and Staffordshire, were of the Brythonic race is known from the name of one of the places within their bounds, *viz.*, Pennocrucium (now Penkridge), which is pure Brythonic for "the head of the mound" or "the place of the chief of the mound".[49] Testimony of the same direct kind

[46] The discoveries made in 1903 in the Venedotian stronghold of "Tre'r Ceiri," crowning the eastern spur of the Rivals in Carnarvonshire, show that the productions of Late Celtic, and even of Roman art, were making their way into this region during the first century of our era (*Arch. Camb.* VI. iv. (1904), 1-16).

[47] *Celt. Br.* (2), p. 303.

[48] *Ibid.*, pp. 87, 217-8.

[49] Rhys, *Hibbert Lectures*, publ. 1888, pp. 202-4; *W. People*, p. 7.

is not forthcoming in the case of the Ordovices, but two facts make it highly probable that this was the centre from which Brythonic influences radiated into North and South Wales; the district is entirely free from those evidences of a late Goidelic occupation which occur throughout the rest of Wales, and tradition knows nothing of any conquest of it in post-Roman times such as elsewhere is attributed to the prowess of the Brython. The men of Powys, to give the district its mediæval name, were of ancient standing in the land and must have been already in possession when the Romans appeared on the banks of the Severn and the Dee.

Of the degree of civilisation attained by the Ordovices before their subjection to the Roman yoke a fair notion may be formed from the remains discovered on the site of the Glastonbury lake village in 1892 and subsequent years.[50] The date at which the history of this settlement comes to an end is shown by the fact that no trace of Roman influence has yet been observed by the explorers who have examined the site, while on the other hand the culture to which the remains bear witness is unmistakably Late Celtic in character. No coins have yet come to light, so that the lake dwellers appear to have resembled the Ordovices in making little or no use of money; in other respects, their civilisation has a thoroughly Brythonic aspect and may well represent the normal state of things all along the Brythonic frontier.

The site of the village, lying a little north of Glastonbury, is now dry, but in former days the Mear Pool, of which a remnant survived in the sixteenth century, no doubt spread over the whole of the low-lying region between the Hartlake and the Brue. Sixty to seventy low mounds mark the position of as many round or oval houses, which once rose out of the water, resting on foundations of timber and brushwood which were secured in their places by rows of wooden piles driven into the peat of the lake bottom. The floors of the huts were of clay and in the centre of each was the hearth. In diameter they varied from 20 to 35 feet. The walls were of timber,

[50] For the account I give of the Glastonbury lake village I am indebted to Mr. Arthur Bulleid's paper in the *Proceedings of the Somerset Natural History and Archæological Society* for 1894, and to the reports made to the British Association from 1893 to 1899 by the special committee appointed to superintend the excavations.

filled in with wattle and daub; in one case a doorstep and threshold were found intact. The dwellers in these huts are shown to have been tillers of the soil by the discovery of an iron reaping-hook and of a sickle of the same material, each having its wooden handle attached; the bones of their domestic animals—ox, goat, sheep, pig, horse, dog, fowl—bear witness to a fully developed system of rural economy. An iron horse-bit and parts of a wheel show that they understand horsemanship and the use of wheeled vehicles; appliances for weaving have also been brought to light. Among the objects of domestic use mention should be made of the querns or hand mills for grinding corn, the staved buckets and the Late Celtic pottery. Bronze ornaments for the person, together with a fragment of a bronze mirror, illustrate the lighter side of this Brythonic culture, and are in keeping with that love of adornment which the grave Strabo notes [51] as a Galatic weakness. Finally, the very boats and ladders by means of which this islanded community kept up communication with the outer world have been preserved, so that the picture lacks nothing to make it complete.

IV. DRUIDISM.

In dealing with the subject of this section, one is confronted on the threshold, with the difficulty of reducing to sober proportions a theme upon which more misguided ingenuity has been expended than, perhaps, any other within the range of Welsh history. Edward Davies's treatise of six hundred pages upon *The Mythology and Rites of the British Druids* [52] is but one of many works in which the creed, rites, institutions and monuments of the Druids are described with a particularity for which nothing in the ancient authorities gives any warrant, and which is, in truth, only attained by the unrestrained exercise of the imagination. History has little to tell of the Druids of Gaul, still less of those of Britain; except for some three chapters in the *Gallic War* of Cæsar, what is known of the order is derived from the scanty incidental notices of writers who do not seem to have had any first-hand knowledge of the facts.

Undoubtedly, the Druidic system was one which deeply

[51] IV. iv. 5. [52] London, 1809.

CHAP. II.

impressed itself upon the imagination of the Roman world; otherwise (so slight was the interest taken in barbarian religions) no account whatever of its features would probably have been preserved. Its ruthless immolation of human victims startled a society which was learning to be humane; the curious in matters of philosophy were attracted by the Druidic doctrine, recalling that of the Greek Pythagoras, as to the transmigration of souls; while statesmen took note of the completeness of the Druidic organisation, its hold upon the mass of the people, the thoroughness of its educational discipline. As a whole, the system was to the Roman mind strange and uncanny; a fact which lends support to the view[53] that it was not of Celtic origin, in spite of its prevalence in the Celtic lands, but had been taken over from some more primitive race (such as the Iberian) which practised rites and observed customs long since discarded by the Aryan peoples. According to Cæsar, its real home was Britain, whither accordingly inquirers went who desired to drink at the undefiled fountain-head. In Britain, its stronghold—indeed, the only district with which it is expressly associated—is found to be the island of Mona, where the Iberian element is on other grounds believed to have been important, and thus another reason is furnished for regarding Druidism as an importation into the Celtic world. The difficulty of explaining the word "druid" from Celtic sources points in the same direction.[54]

If this view be accepted, it follows, as indeed is suggested by Cæsar, that the comparatively enlightened and philosophical form of Druidism described at length in the sixth book of the *Gallic War* is a modification of the true and unadulterated Druidism, as depicted for us, with brief but vivid touches, by Tacitus in his account of the attack of Suetonius upon Anglesey.[55] It may well be suspected that the highly developed organisation which enabled the whole Gallic order to meet annually, in the country of the Carnutes (the district of

[53] *Celt. Br.* (2), p. 69; *W. People*, p. 83.

[54] According to Dr. Whitley Stokes (*Urk. Spr.* 157), the etymology of "druid" is still quite uncertain. No connection can be established with "derva," the Celtic original of "derw" (oak), or its congeners "dari," "darik," "daru," of the same meaning.

[55] *Annals*, xiv. 30.

Chartres), under the presidency of an elective Arch-druid, for the trial and determination of causes from all parts of Gaul, had been devised not long before Cæsar's day in the interests of some political movement. The account given of Druidism in the *Gallic War* is believed to have been based to a great extent on information supplied to Cæsar by his friend Diviciacus the Æduan, himself a prominent member of the order and yet an admirer of Roman civilisation.[56] With such a man it would be a point of honour to put the very best face upon the Druidic system, and, while he would recognise that it was useless to strive to conceal the darker aspects of its ritual, the merits of the Druids as teachers, judges, philosophers and peacemakers would be emphasised by him in the fullest manner.

The Druids of Britain were men of a grim and forbidding aspect, skilful in the use of the terrors of religion, and needing no association with inhuman rites to appear awful in the eyes of Roman soldiers. The gods to whom they appealed with uplifted hands were fierce powers whose wrath could oftentimes only be appeased by the shedding of human blood and whose will was declared by the movements of tortured human victims. No temples were raised for the worship of these deities, but they were served in forest sanctuaries, where the thick leafage and undergrowth shut out the gaze of the vulgar and cast a gloom over the savage altars. Such is the picture handed down by Tacitus, and little can be added to it save by way of conjecture. It may be surmised that in Britain, as in Gaul, the Druidic order included a guild of "bardi" or professional minstrels, for this is the readiest explanation of the fact that when "beirdd" first make their appearance in Welsh history, in the Laws of Hywel the Good, they are found to be united in a regular organisation. Another character assumed by the British Druid was certainly that of diviner and

[56] Diviciacus (a form which is to be preferred to the Divitiacus of the ordinary editions of Cæsar; see *Celt. Br.* (2) p. 292) was an Æduan noble in constant attendance upon Cæsar and high in his confidence during his wars in Gaul. He had shown himself a friend of Rome for many years and had visited the city to seek the help of the Senate against a neighbouring tribe (*Bell. Gall.* vi. 12). That he was a Druid and professed knowledge of the future we know from a reference in Cicero's *De Divinatione* (i. 41).

CHAP. II.

magician; this is the ordinary sense of the word "derwydd" in early Welsh literature, as in the lines of Cynddelw—[57]

Nis gwyr namyn Duw a dewinion byd
A diwyd Derwydon
O eurdorf eurdorchogion
Ein rif yn Riweirth afon

("None knoweth, save God and the world's diviners and Druids assiduous, how many were of us, that golden torqued host, at the river of Rhiweirth.")

But it will not do to assume, without trustworthy evidence and against historic probability, that the Druids worshipped one God, that they sacrificed on cromlechs, that their lore was cast into the triadic form, and that it is represented in spirit and scope by the documents put forward in their name by the bards of Glamorgan in comparatively recent times.[58] The idea that Druidism was a British variety of the religion of the patriarchs, presided over by dignified and benevolent sages, was begotten by the political philosophy of the eighteenth century, which in its superficial knowledge of savage life idealised the "state of nature" and endowed with all the virtues the rude denizen of steppe and forest. "What may be considered as the foundation of the Order was the doctrine of *Universal Peace* and *Good Will*". When William Owen Pughe writes thus in his *Sketch of British Bardism*,[59] he is under the influence of the idea to which Locke gives expression in the words—"the woods and forests, where the irrational untaught inhabitants keep right by following Nature, are fitter to give us rules than cities and palaces"[60] All ancient testimony is against him; Druidism, in short, represents, not the high-water mark of early British civilisation, but a survival from the less civilised past.

[57] *Myv. Arch.* I. 212 (155). The modern form "Rhiwarth" obscures the derivation of the name from that of the Eirth, which here falls into the Tanat.

[58] These documents have been thoroughly examined and their true history elucidated by Prof. J. Morris Jones in *Cymru*, vol. x. (1896).

[59] *Heroic Elegies of Llywarch Hen* (London, 1792), xxv.

[60] *Civil Government*, bk. i. chap. vi.

CHAPTER III.

WALES UNDER ROMAN RULE.

I. THE ROMAN CONQUEST.

(The chief authority for the events narrated in section i. of this chapter is Tacitus; to the editions of the *Annals* and the *Agricola* by Mr. Furneaux I am accordingly much indebted. Among other works used mention may be made of Mommsen's *Provinces*, Rhys's *Celtic Britain*, Evans's *Coins of the Ancient Britons*, Henderson's *Life and Principate of Nero* (1903).)

CÆSAR attacked Britain, he tells us, because he wished to cut off from the tribes of Northern Gaul the assistance which in their struggles against the power of Rome they constantly received from this island.[1] This reason may well have been the real one, for though he does not record many instances of British support afforded to the Gauls,[2] there was between the Brythonic settlers and the Belgæ of the Continent so close a connection in point of race and civilisation as to make joint action in war and politics easy and, in fact, inevitable. The Straits of Dover formed at this time no race frontier, but flowed between two sections of the Belgic or Galatic world. No doubt, in the course of the preparations for this somewhat hazardous enterprise, other considerations were put forward, fitted to recommend it to the rank and file of the army; the wealth of Britain, its mines of silver, the pearls of its coasts, were not allowed to be forgotten;[3] but, so far as the general

[1] "Quod omnibus fere Gallicis bellis hostibus nostris inde subministrata auxilia intellegebat" (*Bell. Gall.* iv. 20).

[2] Certain chiefs of the Bellovaci, having failed in a movement against Rome, fled to Britain (*ibid.* ii. 14). The Veneti sought aid from Britain in 56 B.C. (*ibid.* iii. 9).

[3] Evidence of the disappointment which naturally followed is furnished by the letters of Cicero, whose brother Quintus served in the second expedition. Writing to Atticus, he says (Ad. Att. iv. 16): "etiam illud iam cognitum est, neque argenti scripulum esse ullum in illa insula neque ullam spem praedae nisi ex mancipiis"; *cf.* "nulla praeda" in iv. 17. In a letter written to Quintus

CHAP. III.

was concerned, the main object of the two expeditions was probably that which he achieved, namely, to convince the British tribes that Rome was a dangerous power with which to meddle, and that their safety lay in abstention from interference with the affairs of Gaul.

It is, of course, not unlikely that, if Cæsar had found the British resistance less formidable than it proved to be, he might have brought at least a portion of the island under the sway of Rome, but there is nothing to show that the idea of a permanent conquest had in any way taken possession of him. When he withdrew from Britain in 54 B.C., he did indeed stipulate for the payment of a fixed annual tribute to the Roman people, but the unreality of this arrangement must have been patent to him, and it was made, not in order that a new province might be added to the Roman Empire, but with the view of furnishing an excuse, should necessity arise, for a fresh attack upon the island.

Whatever schemes may have floated in the minds of Cæsar and those who followed him as heads of the Roman state, it is certain that after 54 B.C. no serious attempt was made to conquer Britain for almost a hundred years. On two occasions Augustus planned an invasion of the island,[4] raising high the hopes of his admirers; Virgil saw distant Thule enter his service[5] and Horace exclaimed that this new triumph would raise him forthwith to the rank of a god.[6] But more urgent business drew him aside from his purpose and he was content, when his power became firmly established, to extend a benevolent patronage to fugitive British princes, grounding his inaction on the plea that the Empire was growing too big to be manageable.[7] Tiberius very readily fell in with this idea

(ii. 16) when news had just arrived of the landing, he says that the enterprise "plus habet tamen spei quam timoris, magisque sum sollicitus exspectatione quam metu," but after the receipt of another letter from Britain "de Britannicis rebus cognovi," he writes (iii. 1), "ex tuis litteris nihil esse nec quod metuamus *nec quod gaudeamus*".

[4] Dio Cassius, xlix. 38; liii. 22, 25.

[5] "Tibi serviat ultima Thule" (*Georgics*, i. 30). *Cf.* Horace, *Epodes*, vii. 7, and *Georgics*, iii. 25. All three references belong to the period 35-30 B.C.

[6] "Præsens divus habebitur
Augustus adiectis Britannis
Imperio."
(Horace, *Odes*, III. v. 3. *Cf.* I. xxxv. 29. The year is 27 B.C.)

[7] *Agricola*, 13.

and left Britain alone; Gaius, familiarly known as Caligula, revived the notion of a conquest of the island, only to make it ridiculous by his madcap tricks; hence it was not until 43 A.D., in the early years of Claudius, that the Britons found arrayed against them, with formidable intent and real purpose, those legions which had tamed the rest of the Western world.

The opportunity for the expedition was probably afforded by the death of Cunobelinus. This prince is shown by the evidence of his coinage to have borne sway in the South-east of Britain for a long period at the beginning of the first century of our era. His capital was at Camulodunum, the modern Colchester, as appears not only from the story of the Roman conquest, but also from the inscriptions upon his coins.[8] That he belonged, however, to the Catuvellauni of mid-England and not to the Trinovantes of Essex, is clear from the fact that his father Tasciovanus coined at Verlamium (St. Albans)[9] and that his sons are said by Dio Cassius to be Catuvellauni.[10] It is not too much to suppose, therefore, that he was of the family of Cassivellaunus, the doughty antagonist of Cæsar, and that he carried on his dynastic traditions, having perhaps shifted the seat of government for convenience of access to the sea. Everything goes to show that he was a powerful, wealthy ruler, with abundant resources and means to enforce his will. He is last mentioned in A.D. 40, as having expelled from Britain his son Amminius, whom Gaius ostentatiously received but in no way helped to recover his own;[11] when the Roman army in another three years attacks the island, it is confronted, not by the old king, but by two of his sons. It is obvious that the removal of so conspicuous a figure in the political life of Britain must have led to great confusion and change; depressed parties would regain their courage, dynastic and tribal

[8] Evans, *Coins of the Ancient Britons*, pp. 284-348, 555-73.

[9] *Ibid.*, p. 225.

[10] This point was overlooked by Mommsen (*Provinces*, i. 171). The view taken in the text is that of Rhys (*Celt. Br.* (2), pp. 26-8).

[11] Suetonius, *Gaius*, 44. The "Adminio Cynobellini Britannorum regis filio" of this author was copied by Paulus Orosius (about 416) in the form "Minocynobelinum Britannorum regis filium" (*Hist.* vii. 5, ed. Zangemeister). This produced, in the pages of Nennius, a "Bellinus" son of "Minocanni" (cap. 19), who figures conspicuously in later Welsh legend as Beli Fawr ap Manogan (*Mab.* 26, 88, 93). To Prof. Zimmer is due the credit of having worked out the true pedigree of this mythological impostor (*Nennius Vindicatus*, 271-3).

CHAP. III. ambitions would revive; this was, it can hardly be doubted, the moment chosen by the Romans as the most suitable for their enterprise.

The expedition was planned on a large scale. Four legions, the Second (Augusta), the Ninth, the Fourteenth and the Twentieth,[12] were detached from the Rhine and the Danube frontiers (where two new legions took their place), and formed, with a very large body of auxiliary troops, an army of invasion of not less than 50,000 men. At its head was set a capable general, Aulus Plautius Silvanus, who had been for many years in the service of the state and who proved himself on this occasion fully worthy of the charge laid upon his shoulders. He had under him able lieutenants, notably Flavius Vespasianus, commander of the Second Legion, who was in later life to wear the imperial purple. Claudius himself crossed the Channel when the campaign was well advanced and took part in the storming of Camulodunum, but, though he thus earned the title of Britannicus and had other distinctions bestowed upon him by the senate, the sixteen days he spent in the island [13] can have had little effect upon the course of the campaign, and too much honour is done him when reference is made to the "Claudian" conquest. Important as the enterprise was, there is but one extant account of it, that of Dio Cassius, the no doubt full narrative of Tacitus being in one of the lost books of the *Annals*, and from Dio's pages it is difficult to construct a story of the struggle which will suit the geography of South-eastern Britain. It remains beyond doubt, however, that the invaders were opposed by two of the sons of Cunobelinus, Caratâcus and Togodumnus, the latter of whom died in the course of the war, and the inference is a safe one, that the tribe specially singled out for attack was the Catuvellauni, whose power was shattered and whose rule over other tribes came to an end. The seat of their authority, Camulodunum, became the centre of the Roman province, where in a few years a temple was set up in honour of the deified Claudius and a colony of veterans was established. Among the tribes

[12] A full discussion of the difficult problems connected with the movements of these four legions during the era of conquest will be found in *Engl. Hist. Rev.* xviii. (1903), pp. 1-23.

[13] Dio Cassius, lx. 23.

who were led by jealousy of the Catuvellauni to espouse the Roman cause and who were thus included in the new province without having been first humbled by defeat were the Eceni of our Norfolk and Suffolk,[14] the "Boduni" of uncertain situation,[15] and the subjects of a certain Cogidumnus,[16] probably the Regni of Sussex. The subjugation of the south-west of the island appears to have been the work of Vespasian, who is expressly said to have conquered the Isle of Wight[17] and whose legion (the Second) is ultimately found at Isca in the country of the Silures.

Plautius returned to Rome in A.D. 47 and was voted the exceptional honour of an ovation, being the last private citizen who received it under the Empire. With the accession to office of the new legate of the province, Publius Ostorius Scapula, the war enters upon a new phase and the Roman forces are marshalled against the less civilised inhabitants of Britain, the tribes of the North and the West. They had so far had to deal only with the Brythonic or Galatic settlers of the South-east, who had offered a stout resistance, but, when once thoroughly defeated, were not unwilling to become subjects of the great Roman Empire. An agricultural people, they could not carry on the struggle indefinitely without risk of starvation; a partly civilised people, they were not insensible to the attractions of Roman culture. With the wild pastoral tribes of the hills, half Goidelic and half Iberian, it was otherwise. As in later ages, the fact that they had no stake in the soil, no rich crops to rot in the ground, no well-built houses and barns which an enemy might burn, gave them infinite mobility; nothing was gained by an inroad on their homes; they must themselves be hunted out and brought to bay. Moreover, Rome could not tempt them; in the barbaric simplicity of their life their one fierce desire was for independence. Hence, it is not at all surprising that this second stage of conquest proved much more tedious and harassing than the first, and that the slow progress made by the Romans in the

[14] "Valida gens nec proeliis contusi, quia societatem nostram volentes accesserant" (*Annals*, xii. 31).

[15] Dio, lx. 20.

[16] "Quaedam civitates Cogidumno regi donatae: is ad nostram usque memoriam fidissimus mansit" (*Agricola*, 14).

[17] Suetonius, *Vespasianus*, 4.

CHAP. III. subjugation of the more backward tribes even encouraged the dwellers in the settled South-east to rise in revolt against their new rulers.

When Ostorius assumed command, he found Britain south of the Humber and east of the Severn nominally subject to Roman rule, the Brigantes who dwelt north of the former river in alliance with Rome, but the tribes of what is now Wales, from the mouth of the Dee to that of the Wye, in a state of active hostility, which showed itself in raids upon the recently conquered districts. His first step was to make sure of the uneasy allegiance of the province itself, the lands bounded by the Severn and the Trent,[18] and this he did not accomplish without ruffling the susceptibilities of the friendly Eceni, who then first learnt that, though never subjugated, they were a subject people. Next, he attacked the Decangi, who had probably been among the principal raiders of the border, and penetrated so far into their country as almost to reach the shores of the Irish Sea; he repaid with interest their ravages, but they, true to their highland methods, would not be enticed into the open field, so that their strength was not really laid low. At this stage, troubles among the Brigantes showed Ostorius the insecurity of his position in this part of Britain; having composed them, he retired southward, and, if the narrative of Tacitus gives a correct impression, henceforth devoted his energies to the conquest of the Silures.

The strength of this tribe lay in their untamable, resolute spirit and the rugged character of the country they occupied. But they had at this moment the additional advantage of the leadership of Caratâcus, who, when all had been lost in the East, had thrown in his lot with the rough hill-folk of the West, strangers to him in speech and in manners, but his comrades in love of liberty. He seems to have spent some three years among the Silures and their neighbours, the Ordovices, organising the resistance to the Romans and rendering infinitely difficult the task which Ostorius had set himself. Of the details of the struggle nothing is known, though it may be that some faint tradition of it is preserved in the name "Caer Caradog"

[18] I follow the suggestion of Bradley: "cunctaque cis Trisantonam et Sabrinam fluvios cohibere parat". See Furneaux, *Annals of Tacitus*, vol. ii. p. 252, and *Celt. Br.* (2), p. 80.

borne by more than one hill-fortress in Southern Shropshire.[19] It ended in A.D. 51 in the signal defeat of Caratâcus, at a spot which it is now impossible to identify, since the description of Tacitus carries the reader no further than this, that it was a hill-fortress in the country of the Ordovices, protected on one side by a river not easy to ford.[20] Though the capacity of the Silures for resistance was not seriously diminished, they now lost their leader, who fled for safety to the Brigantes and by them was handed over to his foes.

In the opinion of the authorities, the capture of this famous chieftain, who had for so many years bidden defiance to the Roman arms, afforded the proper opportunity for celebrating in the capital with due ceremony the victories won in Britain. Caratâcus was led in triumph, with his kinsmen and dependants, through the streets of Rome; Claudius set up a triumphal arch to commemorate the submission of eleven kings and the first extension of Roman rule beyond the Ocean. But the course of events soon showed that, so far as the tribes of the West were concerned, the struggle was but just begun. Ostorius thought it requisite to establish in the Silurian country a permanent camp, which was no doubt fixed at Isca, the home in later times of the Second Legion, but he found the utmost difficulty in carrying out his design. The enemy set upon the soldiers to whom the work had been entrusted, cut off foraging parties, put the auxiliary forces to flight, and, by the system of guerilla warfare afterwards so well known in Wales, even shook the stability of the legions. In the midst of this obstinate warfare Ostorius died, overpowered, as was generally supposed, by the weight of the difficulties with which he had to contend. Immediate advantage was taken by the Silures of

[19] There is a Caer Caradoc near Church Stretton (Penn. iii. 271-3), as well as one near Clun (Gibson, 541, 551), which is also known as Gaer Ditches. The "cair caratauc" of the *Civitates* of Nennius (p. 211 of Mommsen's edition) must, on the other hand, have been, like other "caerau" in the list, a Roman city or station: it is mentioned in the Book of Taliesin ("O gaer glut hyt gaer garadawc," *IV. Anc. Bks.* ii. p. 194), and by Geoffrey of Monmouth (*Hist. Reg.* vi. 15; viii. 9) and "Brut y Brenhinoedd" (*Bruts*, 140, 165) is arbitrarily fixed at Salisbury.

[20] Notwithstanding the paucity of data, the question of the site of this battle has been hotly debated among antiquaries. The favourite suggestions have been the Gaer Ditches (Humphrey Llwyd, Camden), Coxwall Knoll in the same district (Hoare, Roy), Cefn Carnedd, near Llanidloes (Hartshorne), and the Breiddin near Welshpool (*Arch.* C. II. ii. (1851), 122-43; IV. x. (1879), 272-83).

CHAP. III. the withdrawal of the strong hand of the governor; before his successor could arrive, the Second Legion had suffered a grave reverse, and the first business of Aulus Didius Gallus was to determine the lines of his frontier policy. He resolved to abandon the attempt to subjugate the Silures; during the five years of his governorship (A.D. 52-57) the limits of the province remained practically unaltered.[21] Old age and satisfied ambition are said to have had not a little to do with the adoption of this conservative attitude, but the total failure of the persistent activity of Ostorius shows that it was not an unreasonable one.

With the arrival of Quintus Veranius, the fourth of the governors of Britain (A.D. 58), the policy of extension is resumed and the Silures are again attacked. But death cut short the schemes of this governor before the end of his first year of office, and the idle boast of his will, that in two years more he would have reduced the whole country to subjection, suggests that he had taken no true measure of the task before him. He was followed by a soldier of the first rank, Caius Suetonius Paulinus, who had won a great reputation by his achievements in Mauretania and whose appointment to Britain signified that the war was to be vigorously carried on. For a while he was remarkably successful; leaving the Silures, it would appear, to themselves for the time being, he directed his attention specially to the north-western side of the province, which was exposed to the attacks of the Ordovices, of the Decangi and, as the result of a change in tribal policy, of the Brigantes. It was during this period, if not earlier, that strong camps were established at Lindum (Lincoln), Dêva (Chester) and Viroconium (Wroxeter), which became the head-quarters of the Ninth, the Twentieth and the Fourteenth Legions respectively; the second and the third of these stations were connected with each other and with the Kentish coast by the great military road known to later ages as Watling Street. Having thus firmly established his position at the mouth of the Dee, Suetonius resolved to

[21] "Didius Gallus parta a prioribus continuit, paucis admodum castellis (*i.e.*, forts, not legionary camps) in ulteriora promotis" (*Agr.* c. 14). *Cf. Ann.* xii. 40: "arcere hostem satis habebat". With this testimony before one, it is difficult to believe that "Didius seized the occasion to advance the head-quarters of the Fourteenth and Twentieth Legions from Viroconium to Deva" (Henderson's *Nero*, p. 205).

undertake the conquest of Mona, where the fertility of the soil and the protection given by the great mountain barrier of Snowdonia enabled a large population to defy the arms of the invader and where the rites of Druidism were still practised undisturbed. He rightly judged that a blow struck here would have a moral effect quite out of proportion to the actual injury inflicted on the foe. In A.D. 60 or 61 [22] the island was accordingly attacked; flat-bottomed ships were specially constructed in order to carry the legionaries across the shallows of the Menai Straits, while the auxiliary cavalry, accustomed probably to crossing tidal waters in their own homes, contrived to make the passage on the backs of their horses. Tacitus, as his manner is, gives hardly any clue as to the spot at which the crossing took place; the sands between Aber and Beaumaris, where a good deal of the traffic for Ireland formerly entered Anglesey, may be as confidently suggested as the narrower reaches near Port Dinorwic favoured by many antiquaries.[23] For the moment, the expedition was entirely successful; startled and awe-struck as the Roman soldiers were for a few brief moments at the grim and forbidding spectacle which awaited them on their landing, their practised valour soon won the day; the Druids and their attendant host were overwhelmed, the sacred groves were cut down, and measures were at once taken for holding the island by means of a permanent camp and garrison.

But once again the forward policy received a severe check. At the moment of his triumph Suetonius received the news of the great rebellion of the south-eastern tribes, led by the Eceni and their heroic mistress, Boudica.[24] The struggle which

[22] A.D. 61 is the date implied in the narrative of Tacitus, but good grounds have been advanced for believing that the rebellion really belongs to the previous year. (See Henderson's *Nero*, pp. 477-8.)

[23] The Rev. John Davies, rector of Newborough (d. 1695), first suggested the neighbourhood of Llanidan (Gibson, 675) and was followed by Rowlands in *Mona Antiqua*, 98 (99), who cites "Pant yr Yscraphie" as a place name in point.

[24] "Boadicea" is not found in any MS. and must, therefore, in any case be rejected. Of the various forms actually recorded, Boudica is most favoured by Celtic scholars, as a likely derivative of the root "boudi," victory, seen in Welsh "budd" and "buddugol" (*Urk. Spr.* 176; *Celt. Br.* (2), p. 282). Thus it was a fortunate hit of Theophilus Evans when in his "Drych y Prif Oesoedd" (1716) he styled the queen "Buddug". His other renderings of the old names, *e.g.*, "Ploccyn" for Plautius, are less felicitous.

CHAP. III.

followed was a decisive one in the history of these islands, had the insurgents defeated Suetonius, Roman rule must have come to an end in Britain. But even the signal victory which the general won, over a force vastly outnumbering his own and flushed by its early successes, left the situation greatly modified. He fought with the Fourteenth Legion, together with a detachment of the Twentieth and some auxiliaries; hence, the main body of the Twentieth was no doubt left to hold Dêva, while the Second (from which Suetonius, through the inaction of the prefect of the camp, then in temporary command, derived no assistance) remained stationed at Isca. But, though the borders of the Western tribes were thus firmly held, there could be now no question of any aggressive movement against them, when the whole province required from the government the most anxious supervision and the most skilful treatment, lest the wounds left by the great encounter should become open sores. Suetonius, fit instrument as he was of the policy of aggression and conquest, was now out of place in a post which called for the exercise of powers of diplomacy and pacification. He was recalled, and Publius Petronius Turpilianus was sent in his stead to govern Britain, with instructions to show clemency to the subject peoples and to embark on no new enterprise against the still unconquered tribes. When after a year or two he returned to Rome, his place was filled by the appointment of another man of peace, Lucius Trebellius Maximus, who was so little of a soldier as not to be able even to earn the respect of his troops; they scorned the miser whose chief purpose seemed to be to amass wealth at the expense of the province, and under him and his no less weak, though more amiable, successor, Marcus Vettius Bolanus, the legions of Britain were idle and disorderly; the purpose of completing the conquest of the island might seem to have been finally abandoned.

It was reserved for a new imperial dynasty, the Flavian, to extend the province to its natural limits by the subjugation of all the tribes of the island save those of the extreme North. Vespasian was first and foremost a soldier; though his latest honours had been won in the East, he had fought with distinction in Britain under Aulus Plautius, and thus it was natural that his accession to the supreme power should mark a new epoch in the attitude of the government towards the British question. Energetic measures are once more in favour, as is seen in the appointment as governor in A.D. 71 of the emperor's friend, Quintus Petilius Cerialis, who had crushed a formidable rebellion in Gaul and held a high position as a soldier. Petilius justified his appointment by breaking the power of the Brigantes, the leading tribe of the island, whose independence had been a menace to the peace of the province for twenty years. On his return (A.D. 74), another man of mark was sent here by Vespasian, namely, Sextus Julius Frontinus, the author of extant works on the art of war and the construction of aqueducts, a man who happily combined literary with practical ability. He was, too, of a noble simplicity of character; while careful in the evil days of the tyrant Domitian to give no reasonable ground of offence, he refrained from flattery, and the words deserve to be recorded in which he declined the honour of a monument to his memory: "The expense is unnecessary; our memory will endure if we have deserved it by our life".[25] Such was the general who now grappled successfully with the task which had proved too thorny for his predecessors, the conquest of the Silures; two or three lines in the *Agricola*, as ill luck will have it, are the sole record handed down of what must have been a very important series of campaigns, ending about A.D. 78 in the complete occupation of our South Wales. Of the work of Frontinus all that can be said is that it was never necessary to repeat it.

The third of the distinguished soldiers appointed by Vespasian to the governorship of Britain was the most famous of all. Julius Agricola had already seen a good deal of service in the island. At the beginning of his official career he had been here as a military tribune, when he enjoyed the special confidence of the governor, Suetonius Paulinus; he had gone through the great rebellion, and it may be surmised that the moderation and justice of his rule as a governor were due in no small degree to his experience in that year of the fatal effects of rapine and oppression. After filling the usual public offices in Rome, he had returned to take the command of the Twentieth Legion, stationed at Dêva, and had proved a loyal subordinate to two commanders of such diverse types as Bolanus

[25] Pliny, *Letters*, ix. 19.

CHAP. III.

and Cerialis. In A.D. 78, after some experience as governor of Aquitaine and a subsequent nomination to the consulship, he was chosen to complete the conquest of Southern Britain. His admiring son-in-law dwells with filial pride upon the vigour with which he entered upon the duties of his office. The Ordovices were on the warpath and had just annihilated almost the whole of a detachment of auxiliary cavalry which had been stationed within their limits; the summer was drawing to its close, and it was, in the opinion of all, too late for measures of reprisal. Nevertheless, Agricola resolved, immediately upon his arrival, to attack the offending tribe and moreover to inflict upon them so severe a chastisement as finally to deprive them of their power to injure the province. With a force composed of picked men from the legions under his charge, he breasted the hills which cluster round the Upper Severn and the Dee and utterly defeated in their mountain fastnesses this race who were not to be tempted into the open country. Determined to press to the uttermost the advantage he had won, he pushed on for Mona,[26] which he had seen slip from the hands of Suetonius in the moment of victory. This time there were no boats in readiness for such an enterprise, undreamed of alike by friend and foe, but the auxiliary cavalry made short work of the passage, and the suddenness of the attack placed the island at Agricola's mercy. Thus at the beginning of the year 79 the whole of our Wales had been reduced and the general was free to devote himself to those more ambitious schemes of conquest in the North which engrossed the remaining six years of his governorship. He probably spent the winter of 78-79 at Dêva, and it may be that we have a concrete memorial of his activity there in the lead piping now in the Grosvenor Museum at Chester which bears his name as "Legatus Augusti pro prætore," *i.e.*, governor of the province, and a date equivalent to A.D. 79.[27]

[26] Pennant is responsible (ii. 27) for the view that the general passed on his westward march through a gap in the Clwydian range which he calls "Bwlch Agricla," but which locally seems to be known as "Bwlch criglas" and "Bwlch saeth cricaeth" (*Arch. Camb.* II. i. 89). The name Agricola could not have come down unaltered in such a connection; it yields Aircol in old Welsh (*Celt. Br.* (2), p. 256) and in modern Welsh would have been still further modified.

[27] The piping was found in 1899 on the north side of Eastgate Street, Chester. The inscription, in its perfect form, runs "IMP VESP VIIII T IMP VII COS

After an obstinate struggle of rather more than thirty years, the Western tribes thus came under the direct rule of Rome. No more is to be learnt from written records as to their fortunes until they emerge to view once again at the beginning of the fifth century. But, if their history is in this sense a blank during the three centuries of Roman occupation, much light has nevertheless been thrown upon this period by the labours of archæologists who have studied its remains, and with the aid of their researches it is possible to form some idea of the leading features of the Roman occupation of Wales.

II. THE ROMAN OCCUPATION.

(In all matters relating to the Roman occupation of Britain, Prof. Haverfield's authority is paramount, and I have accordingly based much of what I have to say upon his writings, only regretting for my own sake and that of other students that he has never been prevailed upon to embody his unrivalled knowledge of the subject in the form of a textbook. The sections contributed by him to the illustrated edition of *Social England* (vol. i. 1901) have been of great service, as also the chapter on Roman Britain in *Authority and Archæology* (ed. Hogarth, 1899). I have, of course, made use of the seventh volume of the Berlin *Corpus Inscriptionum* (ed. Hübner, 1873), of Westwood's *Lapidarium Walliæ* (Oxford, 1876-9), and of the papers in *Archæologia Cambrensis* and the *Antiquary* dealing with Roman sites in Wales and Monmouthshire.)

While the Roman Empire may be regarded from some points of view as a military despotism, its headship the prize of the successful soldier, its basis military force, it was by no means the case that throughout its whole extent it presented a military aspect. Broad regions lying at its heart—Gaul, Italy, Greece, Asia—were without any garrison, the loyalty of the inhabitants being sufficiently assured, and it was only in the frontier provinces, such as Syria, Pannonia and the two Germanies, which were newly conquered and exposed to barbarian attack, that Rome showed herself as the true mother of armies. The legions which maintained her power were disposed in a circle around the peaceful, well-governed provinces of the centre; they were the watch-dogs which kept the portals.

Of the provinces in which, as the result of their position on the border, the military element predominated, Britain was

CN IVLIO AGRICOLA LEG AVG PR PR". See Haverfield's *Catalogue of Roman Stones in the Grosvenor Museum* (1900), pp. 86, 87, 127.

CHAP. III.

one of the most important. Not only the fierce and stubborn valour of the conquered peoples, but also the presence in Caledonia and Hibernia of barbarians yet unconquered, made it necessary to maintain a large force in the island; during the period of conquest, four legions, after the governorship of Agricola, three, were stationed here, together with a large number of auxiliary troops, so that the army of occupation rarely fell below a tenth of the whole Roman force. But the distinction between garrisoned and ungarrisoned districts which is so marked in the Empire as a whole reappears within the bounds of Britain itself. The troops were concentrated in those parts of the province which lay open to barbarian invasion; one legion at York, with a great force of auxiliaries on or about the Wall, opposed a firm front to the Caledonians, one at Dêva and one at Isca, with other auxiliary troops, guarded the Western coast against Irish irruptions. Meanwhile, to quote Mr. Haverfield, the highest authority on the subject, "the Midlands and the South-east of Britain were almost as empty of soldiery as Italy itself They contained a peaceful population which was not unacquainted with Roman speech and culture."[28] Though Britain was a poor province, which could show nothing to compare with the rich and busy life of Antioch, Lyons or Alexandria, it was not, in the settled South-east, without civil life of a kind, and it is only of the North and West that one can say without reserve that the occupation was that of a garrison in an unfriendly country, holding itself in constant readiness for defence.

One region in the West had, indeed, an exceptional history. So far as the available evidence goes, it would appear that the Romans, during the second and third centuries, left the peninsula of Devon and Cornwall to itself. There is no trace of any military occupation of the district, no proof, on the other hand, that its dwellers quietly accepted Roman civilisation. While it is probable enough that Vespasian fought in this region, his successors apparently left the Dumnonii to their own devices, finding, it may be supposed, that they were not likely to disturb the peace of the province. The tin mines had for some reason ceased to yield their ancient tribute of

[28] *Social England*, illustrated ed., i. p. 83.

ore, and thus what might otherwise have been a strong motive for conquest was taken away.[29]

North of the Severn Sea it was very different. With the exception of the neighbourhood of the Wall of Hadrian, there is no part of Britain which affords such ample evidence of the presence of the Romans as an army in possession as Wales and the Welsh border. The spade brings constantly to light traces of the activity of the conquerors in this district, and they are almost invariably traces of military occupation. A survey of the country, dealing with the remains of the Roman period, will make it clear how thorough that occupation was, and will suggest the inquiry what the special dangers were against which the province needed to be in this quarter so carefully protected.

At the point where the river Dee, emerging from the sandstone bluffs through which it has urged its rapid course, swings round into what is now the great Roodee meadow, but was once a broad stretch of sand and the head of the river's extensive estuary, the lines were early laid down of the military station of Dêva.[30] Paulinus, it has already been suggested,[31] had fortified the spot before he advanced on Mona, and one of the tombstones preserved in the Grosvenor Museum, that of a centurion who ended a long military career in the Twentieth Legion, is believed to belong to this period.[32] It is not likely that the Cornavii, in whose territory the new station stood, had previously any important settlement on the spot, for it seems to have had no British name, and the Roman name, as in so many other cases, was adopted from that of the river on which the camp stood, the Dêva or the "divinity," if we may accept the explanation of Sir John Rhys.[33] From the first it was the permanent seat of the Twentieth Legion, Victorious, Valerian, of which the name appears on countless titles which have been

[29] For the history of Devon and Cornwall during the Roman occupation see the *Archæological Journal*, xlix. (1892), pp. 176-81, and the *Edinburgh Review*, April, 1899, p. 389.

[30] The best handbook to Roman Chester is Haverfield's *Catalogue of the Roman Inscribed and Sculptured Stones in the Grosvenor Museum* (Chester, 1900).

[31] See p. 54. [32] *Catalogue*, No. 54.

[33] *Celt. Br.* (2), pp. 291-2. Whitley Stokes appears to question this etymology (*Urk. Spr.* 145).

CHAP. III.

discovered on the spot. Another legion, the second "Adiutrix," has indeed left many signs of its presence in Dêva, but its stay in the island is known to have been short, hardly more than fifteen years, and during this period the camp may have had a double garrison.[34] It was the Twentieth which, remaining in occupation until the end of the Roman period, gave the place its British name of "Caer Lleon," the "fort of the legion": [35] twenty-five tombstones of its officers and men have at various times come to light, and fragments of roof ornament show that many a building in the settlement displayed the boar which was the badge of this celebrated corps.[36] Its members were drawn, citizens of the Roman state though they all were, from the most diverse parts of the Empire; Syria, Spain, Gaul, Germany, and Noricum were represented in its ranks, though the Western element, as was but natural, largely predominated. Twenty years' service on the banks of the Dee would tend to make them all men of Dêva, the place where their life-work was done and their comrades and kinsfolk were buried.

It is not possible to say with precision what part of the modern city of Chester was occupied by the original fortress. Its centre probably lay not far from St. Peter's Church, where the four ancient streets of the city met at right angles, for it is in this neighbourhood that the foundations have been discovered of the more important buildings of the settlement. The four streets may themselves be the direct successors of the principal ways of the camp, as originally laid down in conformity with Roman practice. What is now, however, certain, as the result of discoveries made in 1887 and subsequent years, is that the existing walls, from Morgan's Mount on the north side to Newgate on the east, represent the defences of Dêva in that direction, as erected (either by way of extension or on old foundations) about the end of the second century of our era, the lower courses being in point of fact the original Roman work. The special value of these discoveries was that they brought to

[34] *Catalogue*, Introd. pp. 9-10.

[35] The earliest occurrence is in Bede (*H.E.* ii. 2: "Carlegion"), who, however, wrongly explains it as "ciuitatem legion*um*". See also the list of cities in *Hist. Britt.* 211 (c. 66a "Cair Legion"). Leon in Spain was similarly so styled as the head-quarters of the legion VII. Gemina (*Eng. Hist. Rev.* ii. (1887), p. 645).

[36] *Catalogue*, No. 200.

light a great number of Roman tombstones which, on the occasion of this rebuilding of the wall, had been taken from an adjacent cemetery and used as rough material to form a backing for the well-worked masonry of the surface. Much new material thus became available for the study of Roman Chester, while at the same time, as the work of excavation proceeded, no room was left for doubt as to the genuinely Roman character of the walling. The northern and eastern limits of Dêva during the third and the fourth century are therefore well ascertained; it is still a matter of conjecture how its western and southern walls ran, though most antiquaries agree that the Castle heights were not included.

As a military station of the first class, Dêva had an important position in the system of roads which, in this country as elsewhere in the Empire, was a conspicuous feature of Roman civilisation.[37] The earliest road laid down was no doubt that by which the fortress was approached from the south, known in later times as Watling Street and connecting the station with Viroconium, Londinium, and the ports of embarkation for Gaul. This road crossed the Dee, probably by a ford, not far from the old bridge, which is mediæval, and thence ran southward to Aldford, where there was another ford, across which the traveller made his way to the unidentified station of Bovium and on to Wroxeter. The course of the road from Chester to Aldford is well ascertained, and portions of the original paving have been discovered, made of the red sandstone of the district. Another road, leaving the fort by the East Gate, ran by way of Condate, which is perhaps Kinderton, near Middlewich, to Manchester, and thus supplied the means of communicating with another great military centre, Eborâcum, the seat of the Sixth Legion. The North Gate was the starting-point of a road which led to the fort at Wilderspool on the Mersey, and thence to the stations which guarded the western shores of the country of the Brigantes. From the road-book known as the *Itinerary of Antonine* it appears that a western road also left Dêva, passing through the station of Varæ, not yet identified, to Caerhun and Carnarvon. This in all probability branched off from the

[37] For an account of the Roman roads running out of Chester see Watkin, *Roman Cheshire* (1886), chap. iii.

Wroxeter road some little distance to the south of the fortress, for direct access to the west was blocked by the wide spreading sands and marshes of the estuary of the Dee.

Strongly posted, with a great river defending its southern and western sides, protected by massive stone walls, garrisoned by a strictly Roman force of over 5,000 heavy armed infantry, Dêva was above all else a place of arms, where everything was subordinated to military considerations. It was a standing camp, within the walls of which none but soldiers might dwell, and though it had, no doubt, like other fortresses of the kind, its outlying civilian settlements in the suburbs, there is nothing to show that these were of special importance. Such trade as was carried on was probably conducted in the interests of the garrison; the place was not, so far as we know, a colony, with citizen rights, like the legionary fortress at Eborâcum—it was a great stronghold and nothing more.

On the western side of the Dee estuary lay the country of the Decangi. Little has been found in this district in the way of direct testimony to the Roman military occupation, and even the course of the road to Caerhun has not yet been made out, for the identification of Varae with Botffaru, the "bod" or dwelling of Tyfarru, has no philological and scarcely any other basis.[38] But evidence is not wanting to show that, as might be expected in a region so close to Dêva, the Romans were in full possession of the country and that their enterprise turned its natural resources to practical use. Great quantities of slag, of half-melted lead and of lead ore have been found along the coast in the neighbourhood of Flint, and with them Roman coins and trinkets, showing that the smelting of lead drawn from the neighbouring hills was in Roman times a regular industry in this district.[39] It was here that the pigs of lead bearing the legend "Deceangi" (often in a curtailed form)

[38] Camden (*Britannia*, 602) was the first to argue that "Bod Vari" must be the "Var(ae)" of the *Itinerary* (p. 231), which is said to be 32 miles from Dêva and 18 from Conovium. The old forms are, however, "Boteuuarul" in Domesday (*Cheshire*, i. 269a1), "(B)ottyfarru" (*Myv. Arch.* II. 25 (416)), "Buttanari" (*Monasticon*, ii. 387), "Bottewarrn" (*Mont. Coll.* xxi. 332), and "Bottervarrn" (*Tax. Nich.* 287), all implying some such form as Bod Tyfarru. Traces of Roman occupation are said to have been found at Pont Ruffydd, somewhat to the west of the church (*Arch. Camb.* III. v. (1859), 128).

[39] Penn. i. 71-2, 93-9.

which have been found in various parts of Britain were made up and stamped so as to show the date and place of origin. None have so far come to light in Flintshire itself, but two, now preserved in the Grosvenor Museum, have been found in the vicinity of Chester.[40] All the known specimens are of early date and show that lead mining was being briskly carried on in the country of the Decangi within a few years after the supposed date of the foundation of Dêva.[41]

The wild North-west of Wales, known to later ages as Gwynedd and inhabited in the Roman period by a mixed Iberian and Goidelic population of primitive habits, was held for the Empire by a group of forts, similar in plan and purpose to those which clustered round the great Wall in the North of Britain. Forts of this type reproduced, on a much smaller scale, the features of the legionary fortresses; like them they were of rectangular form, with rounded corners, and were enclosed by a substantial stone wall. They were permanently garrisoned, either by a detachment of the nearest legion, or, more often, by a body of those auxiliary troops raised by the Romans from among the subjects of their Empire who were not citizens. At least five such forts are known to have been built in the old Principality of North Wales represented by the modern counties of Anglesey, Carnarvon and Merioneth, *viz.*, at Caerhun, Carnarvon, Tomen y Mur, Caer Gai and Pennal, and the roads which secured their communications are still in a large measure traceable.[42]

The first named of these forts protected the passage of the Conway and accordingly took its name of Conovium from that of the river. Though Caerhun must be compounded from the personal name Rhun, and cannot be, as Camden[43] and even Edward Llwyd[44] supposed, a corruption of "Caer hên," the ancient city, its identity with the "Conovio" of the *Itinerary* has never been questioned, and the discovery of the name on a milestone in the district has lately set the matter beyond possible doubt. The fort itself occupies rising ground a little

[40] *Catalogue*, Nos. 196, 197. [41] *C.I.L.* vii. Nos. 1204-6.

[42] Few of the Roman forts of Wales have as yet been scientifically excavated, and accordingly it may seem rash to assume that they were all occupied in the same age and formed part of one system. The evidence at present available seems, however, on the whole to favour this conclusion.

[43] *Britannia*, 597. [44] Gibson, 670.

CHAP. III.

distance from the western bank of the river, which is here tidal and easily navigable by small craft; it forms a square of about one hundred yards, in the centre of which now stands the parish church of St. Mary. The principal discoveries appear to have been made in "Erw Gaer," or the Castle acre, which lies between the fort and the river. Here the foundations of a building were laid bare; it contained the usual arrangements for heating by means of a hypocaust or cellar furnace, and tiles bearing the stamp of the Twentieth Legion afforded evidence that it was meant for the use of that legion. Pottery of the Roman period was found in abundance, together with a great cake of copper, weighing over forty pounds, upon which was a Latin inscription, showing that it was private property and probably on its way to Rome.[45]

Caerhun stands in an amphitheatre of mountains, among the loftiest in Eryri, which seem to forbid all progress to the west. Through these the road from Dêva to Segontium threaded its way by the pass of Bwlch y Ddeufaen, rising as it did so to a height of nearly 1,400 feet above the sea-level. Passing over desolate moors which have never known the plough, it is in this portion of its course easily recognised; the raised "sarn" or causeway marks it out at once from the ordinary British or mediæval trackway. It descended to the coast between Aber and Llanfair Fechan, and here was found in 1883, on the farm of Rhiwiau Uchaf, the milestone already referred to which marked the eighth (Roman) mile "*a Kanovio*".[46] The stone was erected in the time of the Emperor Hadrian (between A.D. 119 and A.D. 138), but there is no need to suppose that this was the age in which the road itself was laid down; such monuments were of necessity renewed from time to time, and a second milestone was, in fact, discovered in the immediate neighbourhood of the first which had been set up about A.D. 200, under Septimius Severus.[47] From Aber to Carnarvon the line taken by the road has not been ascertained, but its general direction may be inferred from the discovery of a milestone of Caracalla (A.D. 211-217), near Ty

[45] Penn. i. 87-8, iii. 136-7; *Archæologia*, xvi. 127-34; *C.I.L.* vii. No. 1200; Watkin, *Roman Cheshire*, p. 122.

[46] *Arch. Camb.* IV. xiv. (1883), 170-1; *Mont. Coll.* xvii. 282-91.

[47] *Ibid.* xvii. 291-6. Both stones are now in the British Museum.

Coch, Bangor,[48] and one of Decius (A.D. 249-251), near Llanddeiniolen.[49]

The fort of Segontium bore a Celtic name and was perhaps so called from the river Saint,[50] which here makes a great curve to the south ere it falls into the Menai Straits. It did not occupy the same position as the modern town of Carnarvon, but was placed on the higher ground within this curve, where the parish church of Llanbeblig now stands. It was of considerable size, covering about 6 acres, and had, no doubt, some importance as the terminus of the North Welsh road and one of the ports giving access to Ireland. The coins found on the spot range from the time of Vespasian to that of the Constantines, so that it may be assumed it was held from the end of the first century, when Agricola, perhaps, built the fort, until at least the middle of the fourth. One inscription has come to light, recording that about A.D. 200 the first cohort of Sunici repaired the conduit which supplied the place with water. As this auxiliary force, drawn in the first instance from a people who dwelt around the lower reaches of the Meuse, is known to have been in Britain in the age of Hadrian, at the beginning of the first century, the suggestion may be hazarded that it formed the permanent garrison of Segontium.[51]

A passing reference should be made to the Roman occupation of Anglesey. No inscription or other clear witness to the presence of Roman soldiery has been found in the island, but it does not admit of doubt that Agricola's conquest of Mona was permanent, and at least three sites are with some probability pointed out as those of Roman military works The very name of Caergybi (Holyhead), recalling as it does Caerhun, Caergai, Caersws, Caerfyrddin and many others, carries with it this suggestion, and serious consideration has been given to the view of Pennant that the churchyard walls

[48] *Cambrian Quarterly Magazine*, iv. (1832), p. 515; *Arch. Camb.* I. ii. (1847), 50-2; *Lap. W.* 183; *C.I.L.* vii. No. 1164.

[49] *Camb. Quart. Mag.* iv. p. 515; *Lap. W.* 173-4; *C.I.L.* vii. No. 1163.

[50] Saint represents the old Welsh Segeint, seen in the "Cair Segeint" (which may or may not be Carnarvon) of *Hist. Britt.* 166 (*c.* 25) and 211 (*c.* 66a), and this again goes back to Segontion (*Celt. Heath.* pp. 272-3).

[51] Penn. ii. 412-4; *Lap. W.* 172-3; *C.I.L.* vii. No. 142; *Arch. Camb.* I. i. (1846), 75-9, 177-82, 284-9; iii. (1848), 362-3; iv. (1849), 150; II. iv. (1853), 71-2; VI. v. (1905), 73-6. For the Sunici see Tac. *Hist.* iv. 66, and Pliny, *Nat. Hist.* iv. 31.

CHAP. III.

were originally those of a small Roman fort which protected the harbour.[52] At Rhuddgaer, too, the "red fort" opposite Segontium, Roman coins and pottery have come to light,[53] while similar finds at Caerleb, in the parish of Llanidan, lend support to the view that this was also a Roman station.[54]

From Segontium a road no doubt ran to the next fort to be mentioned, which was situated not far from Trawsfynydd in Merionethshire and was known in the Middle Ages as Mur y Castell,[55] but nowadays bears the name of Castell Tomen y Mur. This line of communication is, however, no longer traceable;[56] only the northern and southern approaches to this fort, each known by the traditional name of Sarn Helen, *i.e.*, "Helen's Causeway,"[57] have been satisfactorily made out. The former, starting, no doubt, from Conovium, is a well-marked track over the hills between Dolwyddelan and Festiniog, passing through Bwlch Carreg y Frân and giving its name to the ford of Rhyd yr *Halen*. The latter, running due south, is visible at Pen y Stryd (Street End) and for many miles along the ridge which separates the valley of the Eden from that of the Cain. What name was borne by the station which was thus linked with the rest of the Roman world it is useless to conjecture; those who imagine it is to be found in the *Heriri Mons* of "Richard of Cirencester" overlook the certainty that this form was taken by Bertram, the forger of that work, straight out of Nennius, who uses it for the Snowdonian region.[58] Tomen y Mur[59] is placed on the south-western slope of a hill

[52] Penn. iii. 75; *Arch. Camb.* IV. i. (1870), 359.

[53] *Arch. Camb.* III. ii. (1856), 326-8; iii. (1857), 218-9; vii. (1861), 37.

[54] *Ibid.* xii. (1866), 209-14; IV. ii. (1871), 63-4. It should be added that there is evidence of the working of the Parys Mountain copper mines in Roman times (*C.I.L.* vii. No. 1199).

[55] *Mab.* 74; *Bruts*, 293; *Myv. Arch.* II. 547 (672), 603 (733).

[56] There seems to be a bit of genuine Roman paving on the moors above Bwlch Gwernog.

[57] The northern road was known by this name in the time of Camden (*Britannia*, 593), while Edward Llwyd called attention to its occurrence also in the parish of Llanbadarn Odwyn, Cardiganshire, and between Brecon and Neath (Gibson, 661). The association of this form with ancient lines of communication is certainly very remarkable; Llwybr Hilyn and Moel Hilyn (not "Heilyn," as in the maps), near Llanfyllin, Pen Ffordd Elen, near Penygroes, and Sarn Hwlcyn, near Newmarket, may be cited as cases in point.

[58] *Hist. Britt.* c. 40, where "in montibus heriri" is the reading of many MSS.

[59] Penn. ii. 258; *Arch. Camb.* IV. ii. (1871), 190-202; *C.I.L.* vii. Nos. 143, 144, 145; *Lap. W.* 155.

which commands a wide view of the surrounding country; its situation proclaims its character as a post of observation. It was a small fort, of not more than half a acre in extent, but very carefully built of non-local stone of the requisite hardness, laid in unmortared but closely fitting courses. There is nothing to show what body of troops was stationed here, but a number of centurial stones have been discovered, recording the names of Julius Mansuetus and of Perpetuus, two centurions whose men had charge of certain sections of the building work. A portion of the eastern gateway is still intact, testifying to the care with which this work was done. The purpose of the "tomen" or "mound" which occupies an angle of the walls is obscure; probably it is no part of the original fortress, but was added in the Middle Ages, when the place was a residence of the chieftains of Ardudwy.

Caergai,[60] the next of the forts of this district to claim attention, crowns a slight rise at the head of Bala Lake and probably marks the point, though the Roman roads of the district have not been satisfactorily traced, where the road from Chester to Tomen y Mur branched off from that which led to Pennal and the country of the Demetæ. Camden [61] regarded the place as so called because built by a Roman Caius, but the Cai with which tradition connects it is Cai Hir ap Cynyr, the "Sir Kay the Steward" of the Arthurian romances, of whom Spenser says, referring to Caergai,

> His dwelling is low in a valley greene,
> Under the foot of Rauran mossy hore. [62]

The name is thus post-Roman in origin, like Caerhun and Caergybi, and the history of the fort can only be deduced from the remains found on the spot. Until 1885 these were limited to coins, tiles and pottery, but in that year the lower part of a monument of some description, which was possibly sepulchral and contained a complete inscription, came to light. It gives the name of Julius, son of Gavero, a soldier of the first cohort of Nervii.[63] This detachment of auxiliary troops, drawn

[60] Penn. ii. 220; *Camb. Reg.* i. 191; *Arch. Camb.* V. ii. (1885), 196-204.

[61] *Britannia*, 593.

[62] *Faery Queene*, bk. i. canto 9. "Rauran" comes from Saxton's map of Merionethshire (1578), which places "Rarau uaure Hill" (Yr Aran Fawr) where Arenig should be.

[63] *Chester Catalogue*, No. 210.

CHAP. III.

from the North of Gaul and recorded as serving in Britain in the time of Trajan,[64] may well have formed the garrison of Caergai.

The fort at Cefn Caer,[65] a little to the south-east of the village of Pennal, has so far yielded no inscriptions, but the quadrangular form of the defences, the coins and other small objects discovered, and, last of all, the remains of a hypocaust uncovered in 1866, are unmistakable evidence of its character. Like Tomen y Mur, it was built of stone conveyed from a distance. Its purpose was clearly to protect the passage of the Dovey; a pitched way or "sarn" leads to the bank of the river, which affords ready access for light vessels to the sea and at the same time is fordable at low water. Of this fort also the Roman name is unknown, for Camden's suggestion that the name of the neighbouring town of Machynlleth points to its being the "Maglona" (really Maglo*v*a) where a garrison was kept in the last years of the Roman occupation, will not hold water for a moment. The two names can have no connection, since Machynlleth is easily explained as the Plain of Cynllaith, and wherever Maglova was, the context in which the name occurs makes it necessary to look for it in the North of England.[66]

There is, therefore, good evidence that the Romans were in permanent military possession of Gwynedd during the greater part of their stay in this island. The case is not otherwise if we turn to the country of the Ordovices, which became the Powys of a later age. Four forts in this district, *viz.*, at Caergwrle, Y Gaer, near Montgomery, Caersws and Castell Collen bear witness to the thoroughness of the Roman conquest. It should at once be said that there seems no prospect at present of the two towns assigned by Ptolemy to the Ordovices being identified; no one has yet ventured to locate Brannogenium, and, though in the case of Mediolanium there is the additional evidence of the *Itinerary* and the help of the name itself, which denotes "the place in the midst of the plain," [67] antiquaries have, from the days of Camden to our own, propounded so many solutions of the problem that it is

[64] *C.I.L.* vii. No. 1194.
[65] Camden, *Britannia*, 589; Gibson, 651; *Arch. Camb.* III. xii. (1866), 542.
[66] *Not. Dig.*, 209.
[67] *Urk. Spr.* 207, 236.

not unreasonable to regard it as in the light of present knowledge insoluble. Only modern names can therefore be given to the four forts now to be described; yet their Roman origin is none the less certain. Caergwrle,[68] on the banks of the Alun, was an outpost of Dêva; the tiles found on the spot show that it was built by a detachment of the Twentieth Legion. Here, as in the Flint district, the smelting of ore was apparently carried on, and the remains dug up at Bryn Iorcyn, a little to the south of Caergwrle itself, seem to suggest a fairly flourishing settlement. A wide gap separates this from the two Montgomeryshire forts, and none of the efforts made to bridge it by conjectures as to the road system can be pronounced quite satisfactory. It would no doubt go a long way to clear up the topography of this district if Mediolanium could with any confidence be identified. Of the two forts which secured the upper valley of the Severn the eastern stands on the English bank of the river, a little below the historic ford of Montgomery. Locally, it is known as "Y Gaer," [69] which probably stands for some longer form like Caerhun or Caergwrle, but for "Caer Flos," a name by which it is sometimes distinguished, there appears to be no older authority than the Ordnance Survey map published in 1836. It is of considerable extent, occupying about 5 acres, but no remains of any kind have so far been unearthed, so that it is possible that it was not a standing camp, but merely served for the purposes of a single campaign. Of greater interest is the western fort, stationed at the meeting-place of three valleys which give access to the heart of the Plynlimmon mountain region. Caersws,[70] which there is reason to think is a shortened form of some such name as Caerswyswen, was built of red sandstone on a low-lying site washed on the southern side by the Carno and the Severn. It was almost a square, with rounded angles and an area of about 7 acres. The Cambrian railway station now occupies its south-west corner and the farm-house of Pendre its centre. The inscrip-

[68] Camden, *Britannia*, 605; Penn. ii. 46; *C.I.L.* vii. No. 1225; Lewis, *Top. Dict. s.v.* Hope; *Arch. Camb.* IV. ii. (1871), 97-8.

[69] Penn. iii. 199; *Mont. Coll.* xvii. (1884), 105-8.

[70] Gibson, 653; Penn. iii. 192; *Arch. Camb.* I. iii. (1848), 91-6; *Mont. Coll.* ii. (1869), 46-65; *C.I.L.* vii. Nos. 1243, 1336 (533). For the name see L. G. Cothi, i. 12; *Camb. Quart. Mag.* i. p. 34.

CHAP. III.

tions which have come to light from time to time are so elliptic as to afford no information as to the character of the garrison, but, as in the case of Caerhun, the remains have been discovered between the fort and the river of a building which was probably a bath-house, and which is shown by the coins found in its ruins to have been occupied as late as the second half of the third century. The roads leading out of Caersws have been partially traced, and one in particular is well preserved, namely, that which strikes westward, along the valley of Tarannon. This can hardly have been a line of communication with any other fort, and is most naturally explained as the road to the lead mines which it is believed the Romans worked in the district of Dylife.

The southward road from Caersws led to Castell Collen,[71] a fort on the banks of the Ieithon, not far from Llandrindod Wells, which held in subjection the inhabitants of our Radnorshire. It is of the usual rectangular form, with rounded angles, and covers about 4 acres. At present, the defences have the appearance of having been roughly thrown together and no stone walling is to be seen; but this is not surprising when it is borne in mind that the ruins have for years been used as a quarry, from which the farmers of the district have supplied themselves with building stone. No inscriptions have been found at Castell Collen itself, but it is most likely that the centurial stone, recording the name of a centurion Valerius Flavinus, which was found in pulling down the walls of the neighbouring church of Llanbadarn Fawr, was originally from this place. Coins, pottery and tiles have been found, and the course of the road which runs south to the fort near Brecon is well marked across the common at Howey and Llandrindod.

It may be of advantage, in order to give more definite outlines to this survey of Roman Wales, to cast a brief glance at the condition during this period of what is now the Welsh border. Its northern end was occupied, it has been shown, by a strong military post, and it will shortly appear that the same may be said of the southern extremity. But the intervening region is remarkably free from traces of military occupation. In Herefordshire there is no Roman fortress, unless there be

[71] Hoare's *Giraldus Cambrensis* (1806), I. clvi.; *Radnorsh.* (2), pp. 119, 359; *Lap. W.* 240.

one at Leintwardine, which is pretty certainly the "Bravonium" of the *Itinerary*.[72] The same is true of Shropshire and South Cheshire. The type of settlement found in these regions is one which is common in South-eastern Britain, but of which no example occurs within the limits of the twelve counties of modern Wales, namely, the Romano-British town, inhabited by a civil population, in which the British element was large, while the civilisation was Roman. Shropshire furnishes an excellent instance of this type in Wroxeter,[73] the Viroconium of the Romans, once the most important centre of the district, though long superseded by Shrewsbury. Among the inscriptions yielded by Wroxeter are two which commemorate soldiers of the Fourteenth Twin Legion,[74] and it has therefore been supposed that in the early days of the occupation it was the permanent station of that corps. While this may well have been the case, the withdrawal of the legion from Britain about A.D. 70 must have put an early end to the military importance of Viroconium, which henceforward is a purely civil centre. A British settlement had existed here before the conquest, in connection, no doubt, with the ford across the Severn, and had apparently been the tribal centre of the Cornavii.[75] In Roman times the place was a straggling town, spreading over 170 acres of undulating land, which in the later days of the occupation were enclosed within roughly built walls for protection against barbarian attack. In its centre were public buildings of some pretensions, including a large town hall and a complete set of bath-houses. The multitude of small objects discovered during the process of excavation, lamps, earthen and glass vessels, finger rings, brooches, statuettes, door keys and workmen's tools, bears ample witness to the busy and many-sided life of this half Roman, half British community. Moreover, it was a life which underwent no eclipse until the end of the period of Roman occupation, as is proved by the discovery, in association with its remains, of coins of the second half of the

CHAP. III.

[72] *Archæological Survey of Herefordshire* (Westminster, 1896), p. 4.

[73] The remains at Wroxeter have been described by J. Corbet Anderson (London, 1867), Thomas Wright (London, 1872), and G. E. Fox (*Archæological Journal*, liv. (1897), pp. 123-73).

[74] *C.I.L.* vii. Nos. 154, 155.

[75] I infer this from the form "U(t)riconion Cornoviorum" handed down by the Geographer of Ravenna.

CHAP. III.

fourth century. Wroxeter, in short, supplies abundant material for those who would argue that the Britons were, within the limits of the province, thoroughly Romanised.

Returning, however, to our survey of Wales, we are once more on military ground. In the country of the Demetæ no certain traces of Roman settlement are to be found save the vestiges of two, perhaps three, forts which, with their connecting roads, served to maintain order in the district. A road ran south from Cefn Caer into our Cardiganshire [76] which, from the Wyre onwards, is clearly traceable and bears the significant name of Sarn Helen.[77] At the passage of the Teifi it was guarded by the fort of Llanio,[78] which may be the Luentinum (or Luentium) of the geographer Ptolemy, though the philological connection is not at all obvious. The ground is now partly occupied by the farm-house and buildings of Llanio Isaf and the lines of the original fortress are difficult to trace. But four inscriptions which have been dug out of the ruins point to the site as a military one, and one mentions (as also does the inscription in the wall of Llanddewi Brefi church, which is not far off) the second cohort of Astures, a body of Spanish auxiliaries which is more closely connected with the fort of Aesica (Great Chesters) on the wall of Hadrian,[79] but may well have occupied Llanio at one period of its history. The other undoubted fort of this district was situated at Carmarthen,[80] at the head of the tidal portion of the Towy, in a strategic position which has many times proved of crucial importance in the history of Wales. It was a hill-fort of the Demetæ, known by the Celtic name of Maridunum; under the Romans it became a centre of roads which branched out to the north, the east and the south-east. In the days of Giraldus

[76] The fort placed by Haverfield (map in *Social England*, vol. i.) near "Llanbadarn Vawr," Aberystwyth, owes its existence to confusion with Castell Collen, which is near Llanbadarn Fawr, Radnorshire.

[77] Gibson, 661.

[78] *Ibid.* 645; *C.I.L.* vii. Nos. 148-50; *Lap. W.* 141, 142, 143; *Ephemeris Epigraphica*, vii. p. 285; *Arch. Camb.* IV. ix. (1878), 353; V. v. (1888), 297-317; vi. (1889), 180-1.

[79] *C.I.L.* vii. Nos. 732, 1228. The cohort was in Germany in the first century A.D., but appears in Britain as early as A.D. 105 (*C.I.L.* vii. No. 1194).

[80] Gir. Camb. vi. 80 (*Itin.* i. 10); Charter of Henry II. in *Carm. Cart.* No. 78; Camden, *Britannia*, 578; *Lap. W.* 98-9; *Ephemeris Epigraphica*, iii. 139 *Antiquary*, 1897, p. 231.

Cambrensis the walls were still standing and their circuit was known as "the old city"; but the bustling civic life of seven centuries has obliterated all traces of them, and it is now only possible to conjecture that Maridunum lay to the east of mediæval Carmarthen, St. Peter's Church and the Priory, but not the Castle, being within its limits and the Parade representing its river front. Remains of the usual description have been found from time to time, but little of the history of the place can be inferred from them, save that it was still occupied at the beginning of the fourth century.

West of Maridunum the Romans do not seem to have ordinarily travelled. The coast road to Isca is made to start here in the *Itinerary*, as though no one who used a road-book would be likely to have any business further west. Nor have judicious antiquaries been able to find either Roman settlements or Roman roads in Pembrokeshire.[81] The Dimetian peninsula seems, like the Cornish, to have been left to itself But, in addition to the north road to Llanio, two lines of communication connected Carmarthen with the east. One of these led to the forts on the Loughor and the Neath, in the Silurian country; the other took the line of the Towy and, passing not far from Llandeilo, as is shown by the milestone of the Emperor Tacitus (275-276) found in the neighbourhood,[82] kept the course of the river until it reached the hillock near Llandovery, now crowned by the church of Llanfair ar y Bryn. Here there is some evidence of the existence of a third Dimetian fort.[83] From this point the road, joined no doubt by a branch from Llanio which can be clearly traced thence as far as the ancient mines of Gogofau on the Cothi,[84] struck eastward across the watershed. Not far from the highest point, near the old Black Cock Inn, a milestone has been discovered bearing the name of Postumus (258-268).[85] Thence the valley of the Usk was followed to the fort at Y Gaer, near Brecon.

The character and extent of the Roman occupation of the country of the Silures can best be understood by beginning

[81] *Lit. Eng.* pp. 37-48. A Roman site has lately been discovered at Cwm Brwyn, near Laugharne (*Arch. Camb.* VI. vii. 175).

[82] *Arch. Camb.* III. iv. (1858), 346; *Lap. W.* 98; *Eph. Epigraphica*, iii. 139.

[83] Hoare's *Giraldus*, I. cl.

[84] Lewis, *Top. Dict. s.v.* Cayo.

[85] Hoare's *Giraldus*, I. cl.; *Breconsh.* (2), p. 493; *C.I.L.* vii. No. 1161.

CHAP. III. with the great military centre of the district, the legionary fortress of Isca.[86] Here, as in the case of Dêva, it is unlikely that a British settlement preceded that of the Romans, since the latter had recourse, for the purpose of naming the site, to the name of the river, the Usk, in Welsh the Ŵysg, which winds majestically past it to the sea. It has already been suggested that the station was first established by Ostorius[87] and that it remained in Roman hands during the long struggle with the Silures. To this period, perhaps, belongs the building discovered in 1877, in which were found four coins of Vespasian.[88] But the substantial evidence of the importance of Isca is mainly of the second and the third century, when it was beyond any doubt the standing camp of the second Augustan Legion and a sister fortress to Dêva, and thus acquired its Welsh name of Caerllion,[89] which English tongues have turned into Caerleon. A large number of inscriptions have come to light, bringing out clearly, on the one hand, the purely military character of the settlement, and, on the other, the manifold interests represented in the head-quarters of a legion. Flavius Postumius, legate of the legion or of the province, restores the temple of Diana. The barracks of the seventh cohort of the legion are rebuilt from the foundations about A.D. 255 by order of the governor of Britain and the local commander. One prefect of the camp raises a votive altar to Fortune; another joins his two sons in a dedication which has in view the weal of the emperor Septimius Severus and his sons, Caracalla and Geta. A standard bearer of the Second Legion, whose native place is Lyons, is buried by his heir. Tadia Exuperata raises, beside her father's grave, a monument to her mother and also to her brother, who died on an expedition to Germany. These inscriptions have been found, not only at Caerleon itself, but also at various places in the immediate neighbourhood, such as Bulmore, Kemeys Inferior and St. Julian's, showing that the life of the fortress overflowed into the surrounding country and made the settlement one of the busiest in Roman Britain.

[86] Hen. Hunt. p. 7; Gir. Camb. vi. 55-6 (*Itin.* i. 5); J. E. Lee, *Isca Silurum*, London, 1862 (Supplement, Newport, 1868); *C.I.L.* vii. 36-42; *Lap. W.* 211-34.

[87] P. 53.

[88] *Arch. Camb.* IV. viii. (1877), 161.

[89] Gildas (c. 10) is responsible for the incorrect form, "Legion*um* urbs".

The outline of the walls can still be traced, though there are few traces of the magnificence which Giraldus Cambrensis saw, with the eye, possibly, of the historic imagination, and not that of sight, for the duller Henry of Huntingdon asserts, half a century earlier, that hardly anything of the walls is to be seen. They enclosed a square of about fifty acres, in the midst of which now stand the church and village of Caerleon; each side was pierced by a gateway, the position of which can still be determined. The Castle Mound, situated without the walls at their eastern angle, has been proved to be a mediæval work; it partially covers the ruins of Roman buildings. The circular earthwork which lies between the south-western wall and the river has, on the other hand, been very generally regarded as a place assigned to the sports and exercises of the soldiery; it occupies a plot of ground which, hemmed in as it is by the river, must have been secluded and well suited for such a purpose. Roads led from Isca in at least three directions, eastward to Venta, northward to Burrium, and westward to the forts of our Glamorganshire. A brief account of the stations thus connected with the legionary centre will bring this survey to a close.

Two of the forts which may be regarded as western outposts of Isca have recently been excavated with interesting results. It had long been suspected from the situation, the name and the visible remains of the ancient stronghold of Cardiff that it had commenced its history as a Roman station, and this has now been proved by the spade-work set on foot by the late Marquis of Bute, the owner of the Castle.[90] The Roman wall, over 10 feet thick, was found embedded in the great earthen rampart which had been thrown over it by later defenders of the spot to the extent of nearly two-thirds of its length. At regular intervals along it appeared polygonal bastions, and the north gateway, with its guard chambers, was found to be in exceptionally good preservation. It had been, apparently, long occupied and had been altered by the addition of the bastions at the close of the period of Roman occupation. The Cardiff fort was of some size, covering about 10 acres; in the hills to the north was a smaller station, of

[90] *Archæologia*, lvii. (1901), 335-52 (J. Ward).

CHAP. III.

some 3½ acres, near the church of Gelligaer,[91] of which the walls and gateways have also been remarkably well preserved. "The raised sill of one of the portals is to all appearances," to quote an account of the excavations of 1900, "as fresh to-day as when the camp was abandoned sixteen or seventeen centuries ago. It shows the hollows worn by the chariot wheels, the sockets in which the pivots of the great doors turned, and the square hole into which the great bolt shot to make all fast for the night, or when danger approached."[92] Close by a road, known as Heol Adda (Adam's Street), runs along the ridge in the direction of the fort near Brecon.[93]

Forts, no doubt, guarded at intervals the road which ran west from Cardiff to Carmarthen, but their sites have not yet been ascertained, and all that can safely be said of them is that the Nidum and Leucarum of the *Itinerary* must have stood on the banks of the rivers so called, the Nedd and the Llwchwr of to-day. The portion of the road between the Ogwr and the Nedd has been specially productive of mile-stones; one found near Pyle was inscribed with the name of the usurper Victorinus (about 267),[94] the two from the neighbourhood of Aberavon belonged to the age of Diocletian (284-313),[95] while the fourth, recently discovered at Melin Crythan, also bore the name of this emperor.[96]

From the mouth of the Nedd a road struck across the hills to the north-east, which is still clearly traceable for a large part of its course under the name "Sarn Helen"[97] Its destination was the fort in the valley of the Usk, two or three miles above Brecon, which has more than once been mentioned

[91] Gelligaer was excavated with scientific precision by the Cardiff Naturalists' Society in 1899-1901. A full account of the discoveries, compiled by Mr. John Ward, was issued in 1903 (*The Roman Fort of Gellygaer*, London). The fort, though very complete in its details, is not believed to have been held for any long period.

[92] *Arch. Camb.* VI. i. (1901), 59.

[93] At Penydarren, Merthyr Tydfil, which lies upon the line of this road, traces of an important Roman settlement have lately been discovered, though its character has not yet been determined. See *Arch. Camb.* VI. vi. (1906), 193-208.

[94] *C.I.L.* vii. No. 1160; *Lap. W.* 40.

[95] *C.I.L.* vii. Nos. 1158, 1159; *Lap. W.* 38, 41; *Academy*, 1st Aug., 1896 (p. 86).

[96] *Antiquary*, 1894, i. p. 245.

[97] Gibson, 661.

as the goal of Roman roads in Mid Wales. "Y Gaer,"[98] as it is locally known, had once a longer Welsh name, which it does not seem possible to restore; its Roman name, too, is unknown. It was a large fort of 6 acres, with walls 7½ feet thick, and occupied a pleasant site near the confluence of the Ysgir and the Usk. Tiles inscribed with the name of the second Augustan legion furnish evidence that it was an outpost of Caerleon, while the military character of the settlement further appears from two tombstones from the immediate vicinity. The one,[99] known for centuries as "Maen y Morynion" ("The Maidens' Stone"), stands on the line of the Roman road which runs east and west a little to the north of Y Gaer, and, though sadly weather-beaten, still shows the sculptured outlines of a Roman soldier and his wife. The other [100] was discovered in 1877 in a field about a mile away, and is interesting as the gravestone of an officer or soldier of the cavalry troop of Vettones, Spanish auxiliaries known to have been in Britain from about A.D. 100,[101] the approximate date of the inscription. It is possible that the troop may in the first century A.D. have formed the garrison of the station, though later on it is found in the neighbourhood of the Wall of Hadrian.[102]

The eastward road from this fort followed the course of the Usk, in a line still easy to trace, to another, also known as "Y Gaer," in the vale of the Rhiangoll, not far from Tretower.[103] Theophilus Jones was the first to point this out as a Roman site and to show how it broke the long stretch of road from the Ysgir to the Gefenni. The ramparts, of the usual rectangular form, are well marked, and tiles, coins and fragments of building material supply the evidence of Roman occupation. Nor can there be much doubt that the two stones found at Tretower and bearing the names of the centurions Valens and Peregrinus were taken from the ruins of Y Gaer. At Abergavenny few Roman remains have come to light, and it is

[98] *Breconsh.* (2), p. 218; *C.I.L.* vii. No. 1222; *Arch. Camb.* II. ii. (1851), 167; IV. ix. (1878), 235; VI. iii. (1903), 12.

[99] Gibson, 593; *C.I.L.* vii. No. 152; *Lap. W.* 57.

[100] *Lap. W.* 75-6; *Ephemeris Epigraphica*, iv. (1881), 198

[101] *C.I.L.* vii. No. 1193.

[102] *Ibid.* No. 273; *Ephemeris Epigraphica*, vii. Nos. 979, 980.

[103] *Breconsh.* (2), pp. 416-7; *C.I.L.* vii. Nos. 146, 147; *Lap. W.* 54.

CHAP. III.

therefore not certain that a fort here guarded the pass which leads to the Herefordshire plains. At the same time the existence at this spot of a station of some kind or other, styled Gobannium from its position on the Gefenni, is clear, not only from the *Itinerary*, but also from the direction of Stone Street, the Roman road which runs south from Kenchester (Magna) and has been traced as far as Abbey Dore.[104] At Usk,[105] the Burrium of the *Itinerary*, there was certainly a fort, in the neighbourhood of the present county gaol, where Roman tiles and pottery have been found, together with fragmentary inscriptions which tell of the activity at this spot of the ever-busy Second Legion.

West and north of Caerleon, therefore, the military necessities to which it owed its existence had everywhere to be recognised, to the all but absolute exclusion of Roman civil life. It was only necessary to travel a few miles eastward to enter a different atmosphere. Caerwent, it may be inferred from its name of Venta Silurum, was a tribal centre before it fell under Roman sway;[106] its ruins have hitherto furnished no evidence of the presence of a garrison in the Roman period, but, so far as they have been excavated, suggest that it retained its importance as a place of peaceful resort and habitation, where luxury was not unknown. True, it was girt with massive walls, but it can hardly have been necessary to build a fortress of 40 acres in extent within 10 miles of Caerleon, and the explanation of these defences no doubt is that, as in the case of Wroxeter, they were raised at a late period of the Roman occupation, when the old military system could no longer give proper protection from barbarian attack, and each city had to transform itself into a camp of refuge. From Caerwent it was no long journey to Bath, the Aquae Sulis of the Romans, then as now famous for its medicinal waters and frequented by visitors from all parts of the province; Gloucester, too, was not far off, one of the few British towns which had Roman civic rights—the whole region had been not merely

[104] *Archæological Survey of Herefordshire*, p. 14.

[105] Camden, *Britannia*, 568; *Arch. Camb.* I. i. (1846), 188; *Ephemeris Epigraphia*, iv. (1881), 198, 206.

[106] Proof of this has of late been afforded by the discovery of an inscription (*Athenæum*, 26th Sept., 1903).

subdued by Rome but had become an integral part of her Empire. CHAP. III.

III. The Subject Tribes.

A question has now to be considered which thus far has been only indirectly touched upon, but which must be answered ere any wide view can be taken of the course of development of Welsh history. What was the relation of the subject population of Wales, the conquered Silures, Demetæ, Ordovices and men of Gwynedd to this Roman civilisation which established itself at so many points in the country? Were they Romanised as well as subdued, accepting, as other provincials did in Western Europe, Roman institutions, learning the Latin tongue and merging their distinctive tribal features in the general life of the Empire? Or did they live in tribal isolation, retaining their Celtic speech and institutions and learning little from the soldiers who moved in and out among them? These are questions which will not be answered for us by any contemporary record; for, save for some geographical particulars, nothing is to be gleaned from the literature of the day as to the internal history of Wales from the age of Tacitus to that of Gildas. Only the evidence supplied by archæology, by philology, and by the later history of the country is at our service in this inquiry, and this is in many ways so precarious that it is not surprising that upon it widely different views should be founded.

It is desirable, however, at the outset to separate entirely the question here under discussion, namely, the extent of Roman influence upon Wales, from another and much more complicated issue, namely, the extent of that influence upon the province of Britain. Enough has been said in the previous section to show that the Roman occupation of Wales differed essentially in character from that of the rest of Southern Britain and only found a parallel in what is now the North of England. The presence of troops throughout the country inevitably suggests a state of things very unlike that which must have prevailed in the districts where it was not necessary to brandish the sword. Moreover, the fact that Wales to this day speaks a Celtic language and long retained an archaic system of laws and institutions raises a presumption as to what must have happened here which cannot be extended to the

CHAP. III.

south-east, for it is only matter of conjecture what language and what institutions were there overwhelmed by the tide of Teutonic invasion in the fifth and sixth centuries. It would, indeed, be not at all wonderful, but in conformity with the earlier and the later history of Britain, if it should ultimately appear that during the Roman period the corn-lands of the East went a different way from the rough hill-pastures of the West.

The first point, then, which has a bearing on the question of the relations of conquerors and conquered in Wales is the military purpose of the two standing camps of Isca and Dêva, with their network of dependent forts. No one who knows anything of the Roman army under the Empire will need to be told that two legions were not quartered for at least a couple of centuries on what is now the Welsh border without very good military reasons. There were but three in Britain and not many more than thirty in the whole Empire. It is a natural suggestion that, as the Sixth Legion at York, with its auxiliary forces, protected the north of the province from the barbarians of Caledonia, so the Second and the Twentieth were responsible for the defence of the west against possible attacks from Ireland. But, though they no doubt performed this function, it is difficult to think of it as their sole duty. While the northern peril was real and instant, calling for unceasing vigilance and for fresh measures of defence under each successive emperor, the western is not once mentioned in any record of the time, and its existence is purely a matter of inference. It was surely for more potent reasons that these fortresses were maintained on so large a scale and at so great a cost to the Empire. Just as the northern force had to reckon, not only with attacks from without, but also with the disaffection of the Brigantes, who in the time of Hadrian annihilated the legion quartered at York and for many years afterwards were restless and defiant,[107] so the legions of Chester and Caerleon were stationed there quite as much to keep in subjection the Ordovices and the Silures, whom it had taken so many years to subdue, as to guard the coasts from piratical incursions.

But a people whom it was necessary thus to overawe can hardly have been ordinary peaceable subjects of the Empire. That they enjoyed political independence it is, of course, absurd

[107] *C.I.L.* vii. 64; Pausanias, *Græc. Descr.* viii. 43.

to imagine; they no doubt bore the burdens of Empire, paid tribute, worked mines, and furnished recruits for the auxiliary part of the army. But they so far held aloof from Roman civilisation as to be a possible source of danger to the province, and the very thorough way in which their country was covered with military stations, while it allowed no room for tribal leadership and tribal warfare, shows that they could not be left to themselves, to work out their own destiny, so strong was the old tribal feeling and so easy the return to the conditions which obtained before the conquest.

CHAP. III.

The positive evidence supplied by the character of the Roman remains in Wales may be supplemented by the negative evidence afforded by what is not to be found there. It has already been stated that no Romano-British town of the type so common in England, no Silchester or Wroxeter or Bath, has yet been discovered in Wales strictly so called, though Monmouthshire furnishes an instance in Caerwent. It has now to be added that another feature of the orderly, peaceable south-east, namely, the "villa" or Roman country house, is also notable by its absence, save in the district nearest Caerleon. At the end of the eighteenth century the foundations of a building were unearthed at Llanfrynach,[108] Brecknockshire, about half-way between the two "Gaers" of the county, which have since been destroyed, but appear to have been the remains of a "villa". The discovery of a villa at Llantwit Major was also recorded in 1888.[109] Elsewhere nothing has come to light to show that it was usual for wealthy civilians, unconnected with the army, to live at their ease in Wales as they did in the districts nearer Gaul. Here, again, the analogy of the North of England suggests itself, for in the country of the Brigantes no "villa" has been found much to the north of York.[110] So far as the evidence goes, the Romans had only one interest in Wales beyond the military, namely, the mines which native labour made profitable to the imperial exchequer. But for these they might have been content to make the line

[108] *Breconsh.* (2), pp. 19, 462.

[109] *Transactions of the Cardiff Naturalists' Society*, vol. xx. (1888), pp. 49-61. The remains discovered at Ely, near Cardiff, in 1893 are now held to mark the site of a small fort (*Archæologia*, lvii. (1901), 335).

[110] *Edinburgh Review*, April, 1899, p. 386. The article is now understood to be from the pen of Mr. Haverfield (*Eng. Hist. Rev.* xix. (1904), p. 629, note 10).

CHAP. III.

from Isca to Dêva the western frontier of the province and to justify the abandonment of Wales in the same terms as were used by Appian[111] to defend the withdrawal from Caledonia—"we have the really valuable part of the island, and stand in no need of the rest"

The existence, again, of the Welsh language is a fact of the first importance in its bearing on the question of Roman influence in Wales. If, when the light of history once more discloses, at the beginning of the Middle Ages, the peoples of Cornwall, Wales and Strathclyde, they are found speaking not a Romance but a Celtic language, the conclusion seems inevitable that they had never ceased to do so, having escaped the influences which elsewhere in Western Europe made Latin universal. Efforts have been made to explain Welsh as a language introduced at the close of the Roman period by Brythonic invaders from the region of the two Walls,[112] but though this invasion undoubtedly took place and materially aided the Brythonic form of the Celtic speech in its struggle with the Goidelic, it is made to assume undue proportions when it is deemed capable of wiping out Latin throughout the whole of Wales and introducing Welsh in its place. It must, therefore, be concluded that the inhabitants of Wales were so far divorced from the main current of Roman life as to speak a separate language, which linked them with the customs and traditions of the past.

But, though they retained their Celtic speech, the Welsh tribes were far from being unaffected by the influence of the Latin which must have overflowed their country with the coming of the soldiers. Welsh contains a very large number of Latin loan-words, of which some, no doubt, came in with the acceptance of Christianity and a few as learned book-words, but most as the result of contact with Roman civilisation during the three centuries of military occupation.[113] They entered into the language in the same way as the English loan-words which abound in modern spoken Welsh, and which,

[111] *Hist. Rom.*, *prooem.* 5. [112] *W. People*, p. 503.

[113] For the material employed in the following paragraphs I am chiefly indebted to *Les Mots Latins dans les Langues Brittoniques*, by M. Loth (Paris, 1892). The lists on pages 42-45 I found especially useful. In the matter of the Celtic roots I followed, of course, the *Urkeltischer Sprachschatz* of Dr. Whitley Stokes (Göttingen, 1894).

despite the wrath of the purist in such matters, are steadily working themselves into an assured position in the language. Now it is obvious that these loan-words do more than bear a general testimony to intercourse between the Welsh and their conquerors; they indicate the points of contact. From them it may be inferred in what regions of life and thought there was borrowing from the richer civilisation of the conquering people, while their absence in certain other spheres may be taken as evidence that in these foreign influence did not tell. It has, of course, to be premised that, on the assumption made in these pages, namely, that the native speech of most of the Welsh tribes was Goidelic, evidence drawn from the Latin element in modern Welsh can only hold good for the tribe who spoke Brythonic, to wit, the Ordovices of Mid-Wales. But this need not in any way baulk us; since there is no reason to think that there was anything exceptional in the relations between this tribe and the Roman power.

The first domain in which there is evidence of extensive borrowing is the military. In the names of arms of offence and defence there was no great change; the sword (cleddyf), the shield (ysgwyd), the javelin (gwaew) retained their Celtic names,[114] and only in the name of the arrow (saeth from sagitta) is there any indication of the adoption of a new weapon. What probably happened in this particular case was the substitution of an iron tip for the old arrow-head of stone or horn.[115] But in military engineering and the like the old race had everything to learn from the new. "Mur" (wall), "magwyr" (the same), "ffos" (trench), "castell" (castle), "pont" (bridge), "pabell" (tent) are loan-words which show how considerable was the borrowing in this direction. For two of the most characteristic products of Roman military activity the Brython, indeed, used native names; the fort which held him to obedience he called "caer,"[116] the paved road which made his mountains passable he termed "sarn,"[117] or causeway.

[114] *Urk. Spr.* 82, 309, 281.

[115] Schrader, *Prehistoric Antiquities of the Aryan Peoples*, tr. Jevons (London, 1890), p. 233.

[116] Even this may be from "castrum," though Stokes (*Urk. Spr.* 74) gives a native "kastro-". Prof. Morris Jones considers that the problem has not as yet been solved.

[117] *Ibid.* 313.

CHAP. III.

But in general it may be said that the evidence of language supports the conclusion, to which on other grounds it is natural to come, that in all that concerned warfare the tribesmen of Wales were highly susceptible to Roman influence. One remembers that there is no gift at the disposal of European civilisation which is better appreciated by a primitive race than the modern rifle.

Another sphere in which the influence of the conquerors was paramount was that of letters. The Celts had no native alphabet or system of writing; in Gaul, Cæsar states, their men of learning, the Druids, used Greek characters (no doubt borrowed from Marseilles) for business purposes, and thought it wrong to commit their professional lore to writing in any form.[118] When the Brythons began to make use of an inscribed coinage they adopted the Roman alphabet, and it will be seen in a later chapter that, after the withdrawal of Roman troops from the country, the inhabitants of Wales used in their sepulchral inscriptions not only the Roman letters, but also the Latin tongue. It is not surprising, therefore, to find in Welsh a large number of loan-words which have to do with reading and writing; such are "llyfr" (book), "llythyr" (letter), "ysgrif" (script), "ysgrifennu" (to write), "llên" (what is read), and "awdwr" (author). Be it observed that it is the absence of literature in the strict sense, of written compositions, to which these words bear witness; the Welsh tribesmen had beyond a doubt their skilled poets and musicians, whose flights of song were independent of literary aid, for the leading terms connected with these two arts, such as "bardd" (poet), "prydydd" (maker), "cerddor" (musician), "crwth" (crowd), "telyn" (harp), "cathl" (song), "tant" (string),[119] are of purely Celtic origin, being, for the most part, common to Brythons and Goidels. But the songs and tales and sayings of these minstrels, with whom were deposited the remnants of Druidic tradition, were handed down orally, and it was only from the foreigner that any knowledge of letters was to be obtained.

A third class of important loan-words is connected with the home and its material civilisation, and witnesses unmistakably

[118] *Bell. Gall.* vi. 14.

[119] *Urk. Spr.* 162, 60, 80, 99, 69, 128. For "telyn" see *W. Ph.* (2), 184.

to the higher standard of comfort which was brought in by the Romans. The primitive Celt had his "ty" (house), with its "to" (roof), its "aelwyd" (hearth), and its "drws" (door) secured by a "clo" (bolt).[120] But "ffenestr" (window), "pared" (partition), "ystafell" (chamber), "post" and "colofn" (pillar), "trawst" (beam), and "ceibr" (rafter) are all of Latin origin, so that it must be concluded that familiarity with Roman methods of building led to greater solidity of construction among the Welsh in the domestic as in the military sphere. It was much the same with the household furniture and utensils. The bronze or iron cauldron (pair), in which the meat of the household was boiled, was, with its attendant spit (bêr),[121] an ancient feature of Celtic civilisation, which enters into many of the early legends of the race; of primitive origin, too, were the earthen pot (crochan) and the spoon or ladle (llwy).[122] But the knife (cyllell), the dish (dysgl), the metal pan (padell), the gridiron (cradell), the bowl (ffiol), the chest (cist, arch), the candle (cannwyll), the three-legged stool (trybedd), the couch (lleithig) and the chair of state (cadair) were all gifts of Roman culture to the Welsh tribes. How the old influences blended with the new is well seen in the bronze strainer found at Cyngadel, near Laugharne, in the early part of the last century.[123] The vessel is of a familiar Roman type, and, in view of the fact that it contained coins of Carausius, must have been made for an owner accustomed to Roman ways at the end of the third century of our era. But in its design it reveals the hand of a native artificer, whose models were not those in vogue among the metal workers of the Empire, but the graceful creations of Late Celtic art—an art by this time extinct in the Romanised portion of Britain but still vigorous among the independent tribes of Caledonia and Hibernia.

Significant as these groups of loan-words are, they are not more so than the absence of important borrowing from the Latin in other spheres in which the ruling people might have been expected to dominate their half-civilised subjects. Hardly any of the technical terms of Welsh law and politics, as they emerge in the Middle Ages, are derived from Latin sources;

[120] *Urk. Spr.* 126, 127, 7, 158, 103.
[121] *Ibid.* 61, 170.
[122] *Ibid.* 99, 241.
[123] *Arch. Camb.* VI. i. (1901), 24-38.

CHAP. III.

popular speech may employ such words as "ciwdod" (folk), "pobl" (people), "estron" (foreigner), and "gwig" (village), but the language of the courts and of the text-books knows (with the exception of "tyst," a witness, and a few others) no such alien terms; its "gwlad" (country), "tref" (settlement), "alltud" (stranger), "cenedl" (kindred), "aillt" (serf), "brenhin" (chieftain), and "brawdwr" (judge),[124] in short, the names of the cardinal features of the Welsh system of law and society, are of undoubtedly native origin. The impression thus created, that Roman law, so potent a force in every country in which Roman influence really made itself felt, found no permanent foothold in Wales, will be deepened upon examination of the substance of the Welsh codes. Though it is possible to discern, especially if comparison be made with Irish legal ideas and methods, the effect of intercourse with a people among whom the central authority was strong, the main ideas reflected in these codes are the primitive and tribal, and it is, in particular, difficult to imagine any race which had gone through the mill of Roman jurisprudence retaining the blood-feud and the composition for manslaughter.

A few other indications there are which show the extent of Roman influence in Wales. Certain personal names, such as Ambrosius (Emrys), Æternus (Edern), Agricola (Aergol), Tacitus (Tegid), and Donatus (Dunod), became popular among the tribes, but this was chiefly, no doubt, as the result of the introduction of Christianity and therefore at the close of the period of Roman occupation. Two or three Roman sites, such as Caerwent and Caerfyrddin, are also known to have retained, after the withdrawal of the troops, the names which they had previously borne, but against these must be set a much larger number, such as Caerhun, Caerlleon, Caerllion, Caergybi, and Mur y Castell, of which the names are recent, or at any rate have not come from Roman lips. Lastly, it has to be added that, while excavation has not as yet done much in Wales to bring to light actual vestiges of the British settlements of the Roman period, the scanty evidence which is afforded in no way runs counter to the view of the matter which has been put forward above. In 1849 Mr. W. Wynne

[124] *Urk. Spr.* 262, 137, 22, 77, 21 (see corrigenda), 169. For "brenin" see *Celt. Br.* (2), p. 282.

Foulkes conducted a systematic exploration of the hill-fortresses which crown the long mountain rampart to the east of the Vale of Clwyd. There was clear evidence that they had been occupied both during and after the Roman period. On Moel Fenlli, Romano-British pottery was found in association with a stone knife; a hoard of coins, ranging in date over the whole of the period of occupation, had also been exposed by a chance fire on the heathy hillside.[125] Moel y Gaer, too, yielded Roman pottery, which lay beneath the defences upon the original surface of the rock;[126] pottery of the same type, with flint arrow-heads and vestiges of iron, came to light on Moel Arthur.[127] Roman coins and fragments of "Samian" ware were also found during the excavation of the ancient dwellings on Holyhead Island, which appear to have been inhabited by a mining population in a very rudimentary stage of culture.[128] CHAP. III.

Roman civilisation, then, while it imported many new influences into the old Celtic society, did not break up its essential structure or sever its connection with the past. It left Wales richer in many respects, its parting gift of a new religion (to be dealt with in the next chapter) being the greatest of all it bestowed, but the land remained a home of primitive ways and ideas, the dwelling-place of a people who, taken as a whole, had scarcely attained the level of culture of the Britons of the south-east at the time of the Roman conquest.[129]

Note to Chapter III. § i. *Caratâcus.*

The popular form, Caractacus, comes from the early editions of Tacitus, in which the value of the Medicean MS., as the only independent authority for the text of *Annals*, xi.-xvi., was not properly recognised. In this MS. the name appears almost always as Caratac(us), and this is the form which, according to the rules of Celtic philology, would yield the Welsh "Caradog". The name is to be connected with "car-u," to love; in Irish it is found as "Carthach," whence the modern McCarthy (*Celt. Br.* p. 284; *Urk. Spr.* 71).

Welsh tradition knows nothing of a Caradog ap Cynfelyn [130] and has handed

[125] *Arch. Camb.* II. i. (1850), 82-7. [126] *Ibid.* 174-81. [127] *Ibid.* 181-5.

[128] *Cyttiau'r Gwyddelod*, by the Hon. W. O. Stanley (London, 1871).

[129] Vinogradoff, in his *Growth of the Manor* (London, 1905), takes very definitely the view that the Romans did not attempt to uproot Celtic customs and institutions in Western Britain, and that even in the rest of the country Celtic speech and tradition survived. See bk. i. chap. 2.

[130] There is a "Caratauc map Cinbelin" in one of the pedigrees in Harl. MS. 3859 (*Cymr.* ix. 176), but nothing seems to connect him in any way with the Caradog under discussion.

CHAP. III.

down no recollection of the gallant deeds of the Catuvellaunian prince. Its silence on this subject and on the no less stirring theme of the exploits of Boudica is clear proof that it does not really carry us beyond the period of the Roman occupation; the so-called Historical Triads, while they may throw some gleams of light on the sixth and the seventh centuries, can do nothing to enlighten the darkness of the first. Even Geoffrey of Monmouth, ignorant as he was of the writings of Tacitus, is silent as to the fame of Caratâcus, whose eventful career, had he known of it, would have provided him with the material for several eloquent chapters. Two Caradogs are commemorated in the Welsh mediæval writings, but neither can be identified with the opponent of Ostorius. The one is Caradog ap Brân Fendigaid, a figure in the mythological group of which the doings are rehearsed in the Four Branches of the *Mabinogi*. When his father Brân the Blessed led an expedition to Ireland, he was left in charge of Britain as the chief of seven ministers or guardians ("kynweissat"); his father's cousin, Caswallon ap Beli, then came upon him, slew the other six under cover of a magic veil which concealed everything save the death-dealing weapon, and took the kingdom from him, so that he died of a broken heart (*Mab.* 35, 41; *cf. W. People*, pp. 40-1). In accordance with this, Caradog ap Brân appears in the Triads (though not in the oldest form of the triad—see *Mab.* 302 and *Myv. Arch.* II. 12 (397)) as one of the Three Chief Ministers of the Isle of Britain (*Myv. Arch.* II. 4 (389), and *IV. Anc. Bks.* ii. 458). The other Caradog known to Welsh tradition is Caradog of the Stout Arm (Freichfras), a figure of the Arthurian cycle. He is represented as the son of Llyr Merini (*Mab.* 150, 261), as chief counsellor to Arthur, as a friend of St. Padarn (*Cambro-Br. SS.* 193) and as ancestor of the rulers of Brycheiniog (*Breconsh.* (2), pp. 28, 35) and of Morgannwg (*Cymr.* viii. 85). In spite of what is said by Camden (*Britannia*, 524) and Rhys (*Arth. Legend*, p. 172), he appears to be clearly distinguished both from the Caradog of the *Mabinogi* and the Caratâcus of history.

CHAPTER IV.

THE FIFTH CENTURY.

I. BRITAIN LOST TO THE EMPIRE.

(In this section I owe much to the guidance afforded by Dr. Hodgkin in *Italy and her Invaders.*)

CHAP. IV.

THE fifth century beheld the overthrow of that marvellous imperial system which had lasted so long that men had almost come to regard it as immortal. Unable to resist any longer the pressure of barbarian invasion, Rome bent her head to the storm, and, though Constantinople carried on for centuries the imperial traditions, the Teutonic flood submerged Western Europe and swept away for ever the symbols of Roman greatness. Yet it must not be supposed that the causes of this great catastrophe were purely external. The barbarians of the North had for ages threatened the borders of the Empire and had occasionally broken through them in wild forays, but until the beginning of the fifth century they had won hardly any lasting successes; some great captain or other had always arisen to vindicate the honour of Rome and drive them back into their forests. If they now succeeded, it was because the Empire had lost, through internal decay, its power of effective resistance. There was a general collapse of the arrangements for imperial defence, and this, it has been pointed out,[1] was the result of the economic situation. The ill-advised measures of the govern ment had reduced to misery and almost extinguished the middle class of the provinces, the smaller landowners who bore the main burden of taxation and whose industry and frugality made them the backbone of the Empire. Wealth

[1] Dill, *Roman Society in the Last Century of the Empire* (1898), pp. 204-34. According to Vinogradoff, *Growth of the Manor*, undue stress has been laid on this element in the problem, which still remains unsolved (pp. 67-8, 73-4).

CHAP. IV.

there was still in abundance, but it was in the hands of a few, whose lands were tilled by servile labour and who contrived in a great measure to evade their obligations to the state. Thus the Empire fell as much, if not more, through its own weakness than through the might of the assailants.

Britain, as an outlying member of the Roman State, was one of the first to feel the effects of this lowered vitality. At the end of the third century it had been for a time cut off from the rest of the Roman State through the achievements of Carausius, the Belgic adventurer[2] who first showed the insular strength of Britain and the ease with which an invader could be held at arm's length, when once the control of the Channel had been secured. The connection with Rome was, however, restored by Constantius, the father of Constantine the Great, and thenceforth maintained until the last quarter of the fourth century; it is not until the age of Gratian and Theodosius I. is reached that plain signs appear of the coming dissolution. Maximus, a Spanish soldier of humble origin, who had held a minor post in the household of Theodosius when that emperor was with his father in Britain,[3] was stirred up by his late master's sudden rise to make a desperate bid for greatness himself He found the troops which guarded Britain profoundly discontented with the rule of Gratian and had no difficulty in organising a movement for his own election as emperor.[4] Crossing at the head of his army to Gaul he soon came face to face with Gratian, whom he caused to be slain on 25th August, 383. Gaul, Spain and Britain were now his, and for

[2] He was, according to Sextus Aurelius Victor, who flourished in the middle of the next century, "Menapiae civis" (*De Cæsaribus*, 39). As the contemporary panegyrist of Constantine calls Maximus an "alumnus" of Batavia (*Panegyrici Latini*, ed. Baehrens, p. 163), I see no reason why we should look further for his origin than the tribe of Menapii who dwelt in the region between the mouths of the Scheldt and the Meuse. See, on the other hand, *W. People*, p. 99. The name became popular in Britain and was borne by a contemporary of the usurper Constantine who issued a coin found not long ago at Richborough (A. J. Evans in *Arch. Camb.* V. v. pp. 138-63) and by a Christian who was buried in a cairn near Penmachno (Carnarvonshire) somewhat later in the fifth century (*Lap. W.* 175-6; *Inscr. Chr.* No. 136).

[3] The abuse of Ausonius (Ordo Urbium Nobilium, v. 70) and of Pacatus (*Panegyrici Latini*, ed. Baehrens, pp. 298-9) must rest on some fact of this kind.

[4] "*Invitus*. . . imperator creatus," says Orosius (*Adversum Paganos*, vii. 34). But this was the emperor's standing excuse; see the life of St. Martin by Sulpicius Severus, c. 20. The form *Clemens* Maximus is due to a misreading of a passage (ii. 49, ed. Halm) in the *Chronicle* of Sulpicius.

several years he ruled them not unjustly, winning the favour of St. Martin of Tours, whose prejudice against a usurper he contrived to overcome. But his ambition was not yet sated; in 387 he attacked Italy, having collected for the purpose a great army of natives of Britain and Gaul.[5] At first successful, he was in 388 overthrown at Aquileia by Theodosius, who thus regained Western Europe for its legitimate rulers, Valentinian II. and himself. Such was the true career of the "Macsen Wledig" (Prince Maxen) of Welsh romance; in the mediæval accounts he is an emperor who has thirty-two crowned kings as his vassals, who journeys from Rome to Carnarvon to wed Elen, the daughter of a Welsh chief, and who recaptures the imperial city, taken by his enemies during his absence, with the aid of his wife's brave kinsmen.[6] The story, fantastic though it be, bears witness to the abiding impression made upon the people of Britain by the personality and the exploits of Maximus; it is, moreover, noteworthy that history and fable alike speak of him as one who enlisted the youth of Britain in his military enterprises, thus weakening the province in its struggle against its barbarian foes. Gildas perhaps puts the matter too strongly when he alleges that Maximus despoiled the country of all its soldiers and military supplies,[7] but there can be no doubt that the strength of the garrison was reduced to carry out his ambitious schemes and that the way was thus prepared for the final separation of Britain from the Empire.

A few years after the death of Maximus there was a temporary strengthening of the army of occupation, as the result of the energy and vigilance of Stilicho, the great general and minister of the Emperor Honorius.[8] But in 402 Stilicho seems to have withdrawn, for service against Alaric and the host of Goths who were invading Italy, the legion (probably the sixth) which was specially charged with the defence of the

[5] Sozomen, *Ecclesiastical History*, vii. 13. Pacatus refers to the "satellitum Britannorum" of Maximus, who did his rough work in Gaul (*Pan. Lat.* p. 297).

[6] "Breuddwyd Macsen Wledig" (Prince Maxen's Dream) is one of the stories included in the *Mabinogion*. For the Red Book text see *Mab.* 82-92.

[7] "Exin Britannia omni armato milite, militaribus copiis, rectoribus licet immanibus, ingenti iuventute spoliata, quae comitata vestigiis supra dicti tyranni (*i.e.*, Maximi) domum nusquam ultra rediit" (c. 14).

[8] Claudian, *On the First Consulship of Stilicho*, ii. vv. 250-5.

northern frontier of Britain.[9] It was then, in all probability, a sadly diminished body of soldiery which in 406 found its communications with Rome cut by the Teutonic occupation of a large part of Gaul, and in its alarm began to cast about for the means of ensuring its own safety. Three emperors, Marcus, Gratian and Constantine, were chosen in the space of a few months; the first two lost life and office in quick succession, the third, although only a common soldier at the time of his elevation, was more fortunate—he led his troops across the Channel and made for himself a position in Gaul which he maintained until 411. But the army which he carried off was the last which held the province for Rome; when the inhabitants learnt that it was henceforth no part of Constantine's policy to defend Britain from barbarian attack, they ceased to look to the Empire for protection, made their own military arrangements and dismissed such civil officers of Rome as still remained in the island.[10] No doubt they still regarded themselves as in theory members of the Empire, and the letter in which Honorius in 410 exhorted them to strenuous self-defence[11] should by no means be taken as a grant of independence; yet for all practical purposes Roman rule in Britain was at an end.

II. The British Defence of Britain.

By the withdrawal of the military protection of Rome, the province was left at the mercy of three groups of barbarian freebooters. The Saxons, a general name for the Low German plunderers who came from beyond the Frisian country, had menaced the south-eastern coast of Britain for more than a century, for they were among the foes with whom it was the special business of Carausius to deal when he took advantage of

[9] Claudian, *Gothic War*, vv. 416-8. Hodgkin (*Italy and her Invaders*, vol. i. (2), 716) understands this passage of the Twentieth Legion, which is nowhere mentioned in the "Notitia," and was, he suggests, in transit when that document was compiled.

[10] Zosimus (vi. 5) is very explicit as to the steps taken by the Britons and is probably following here the earlier narrative of Olympiodorus. Coulanges takes the view that the "Roman officers" dislodged were merely those appointed by the usurper Constantine and that this was a preliminary to a return to loyalty. There is no hint in the narrative of anything of the kind. See *L'Invasion Germanique*, Paris, 1891, pp. 6-7.

[11] Zosimus, vi. 10.

the possession of a fleet to make himself supreme in the island. In order to check their piratical onslaughts, new military arrangements had been made in this quarter of Britain; forts had been built and garrisoned on the threatened coast-line and a new officer, styled Count of the Saxon Shore in Britain, had been placed in command of the troops detailed for this service. The Picts first appear under this name in the years following the overthrow of Carausius and his successor, Allectus; the term soon gained favour as a convenient general description of the unconquered tribes of Northern Britain, whose hostile attitude was the chief military problem which had to be faced by the governors of the province from the time of Agricola to that of the usurper Constantine. "Painted folk" they certainly were, tattooing their faces and bodies with the figures of birds and beasts, but it is not certain that this was the real origin of the name.[12] Against the inroads of the Picts the province had been fortified with especial care. Two great barriers had been raised at different times to keep them at arm's length; the first, running from the Tyne to the Solway Firth, had been constructed in the time of the Emperor Hadrian; the second, connecting the Forth and the Clyde, under his successor, Antoninus Pius. It had not been found practicable to hold the northern line of defence for more than a few years,[13] but the southern, of which the remains are still to be seen in great abundance, was one of the most important links in the imperial frontier system and was guarded at all times by a very considerable force.

The third quarter from which the province suffered attack was Ireland. It has already been suggested [14] that the danger of Irish invasion was one against which provision was made from the start, that this was, in fact, one reason for the establishment of strong legionary stations at Chester and at Caerleon. But it is only at the end of the period of Roman occupation that evidence actually occurs of Irish inroads; in 360 is found the first mention of the "Scotti," as acting with the Picts in certain raids in the region of the northern barriers.[15] The

[12] For another explanation see *W. People*, p. 79.

[13] This is the view of Prof. Haverfield (*Social England*, illustrated edition, i. p. 92). *Cf.* also *Edinburgh Review*, April, 1899, p. 376.

[14] P. 82.

[15] Ammianus Marcellinus, xx. 1.

CHAP. IV.

Scots, who were not for many ages to give to the land in which they afterwards settled its modern name of Scotland, were dwellers in the North of Ireland, and thus their association with the Picts was natural, for the passage from Ulster to Galloway, which is known to have been a Pictish country, was easily accomplished. So Gildas speaks of their attacking Britain from the north-west, while the Picts hailed from the north.[16] Partly, no doubt, they came by land, in which case the obstacle set in their path was the Wall of Hadrian; but many crossed the Irish Sea in the rude skiffs they termed coracles, whose dark hulls, says Gildas, might be seen creeping across the glassy surface of the main like so many insects awakened from torpor by the heat of the noonday sun and making with one accord for some familiar haunt.[17] How the western coast was defended at this time is not at all certain; the document which forms the chief authority for the organisation of the Empire at the beginning of the fifth century, the "Notitia Dignitatum," shows no legion at Chester or Caerleon, the Twentieth having disappeared and the Second being stationed at Rutupiae, our Richborough, at this time the chief British port on the Straits of Dover.[18] On the whole, it seems likely that the western system of frontier defence had been kept up to a comparatively late period, but had broken down about the time of Maximus.

A theory has, indeed, been put forward that during the third and the fourth centuries of our era the western regions of Britain were not only constantly ravaged, but to a large extent settled by Irish sea-rovers.[19] In this way is explained the presence in Wales and the Cornish peninsula of a substantial Goidelic-speaking element in the population, as unmistakably evidenced by the inscriptions on their tombstones. A different explanation has, however, been adopted in the foregoing chapters, so far as Wales, at least, is concerned, namely, that

[16] "Scottorum a circione, Pictorum ab aquilone" (c. 14).

[17] C. 19. For Gildas see chap. v. [18] *Not. Dig.* 181.

[19] See a paper by Prof. Kuno Meyer in the *Transactions of the Cymmrodorion Society for* 1895-6 (pp. 55-86). The view there expressed is endorsed by Prof. Zimmer (*The Celtic Church in Britain and Ireland*, Eng. tr., 1902, p. 17) and M. Arbois de Jubainville (*Rev. Celt.* xviii. p. 355). Sir John Rhys replies briefly in *W. People*, pp. 82-3.

the Irish thus commemorated by inscriptions in their own tongue were the ancient inhabitants of the land, who had not been dislodged by the advancing tide of Brythonic invasion when the " Roman peace " put an end to tribal warfare. This explanation, though not without its difficulties, certainly gains force when regarded in the light of what is known as to the Roman occupation of Wales. It has already been shown that the road which led from Caerleon to Carmarthen was in regular use in the age of Diocletian (284-313),[20] and, if evidence of the activity of the Romans in South Wales in the fourth century is of the scantiest, this is equally true of the province of Britain generally. There is, in short, no indication that the conquerors so far relaxed their hold upon the west in the last two centuries of their occupation of the island as to leave room for a real settlement, carried out on a large scale by Goidelic invaders.

At the same time, it is not only possible, but likely that between the Goidels of Wales and those of the opposite coast there was regular intercourse. Roman coins have been found in great abundance on the east coast of Ireland,[21] bearing witness to a certain amount of commerce between the two countries. Along with trade there may well have been a certain amount of peaceful colonisation, leading to the formation of ties of kindred between the subject and the independent Goidels. Wherever and whenever the Romans relaxed their hold, these ties would become important and would serve as a basis for the building up of native dynasties. It is thus one can most readily explain the interesting facts brought out by the upholders of the invasion theory—that some of the Goidels of South Wales were known by the same tribal name (" Kin of Letan ") as the Ui Liathain, an Irish tribe settled between Cork and Lismore,[22] and that in the eighth century Tewdos ap Rhain, king of Dyfed, was claimed by the Deisi of our county Waterford as a descendant of one of their chieftains,

[20] P. 78.

[21] G. T. Stokes, *Ireland and the Celtic Church*, second edition (1888), p. 16.

[22] " Filii autem Liethan obtinuerunt in regione Demetorum et in aliis regionibus id est Guir (et) Cetgueli " (*Hist. Britt.* c. 14). Cormac in his Glossary also places a " Dind map Letani " among the Cornish Britons (*s.v. mugeime*).

CHAP. IV.

Eochaid Allmuir, whose surname points him out as one who had sought his fortune beyond the sea.[23]

The task thrown upon the inhabitants of Britain by the withdrawal of the Roman forces was, it will be seen, one of grave difficulty. Nor is there anything to show that it was not manfully entered upon and vigorously carried out. The popular notion that, as soon as the legions departed, the Britons weakly resigned themselves to their fate and offered no serious opposition to their foes, rests entirely upon the language of Gildas, whose object it undoubtedly was to convey this impression. But Gildas writes more than a century after the departure of the Roman army and in such dense ignorance of the history of the island as to suppose that the Wall of Hadrian and the forts of the Saxon Shore were only built on the eve of the withdrawal, in order to help the distressed provincials in the performance of their new duties. Moreover, he writes with a purpose, which is to convict the British nation (Briton though he is himself) of unfaithfulness to God, and to show that its calamities flow directly from its vices. In the earlier chapters of his work, misunderstanding a passage in the history of his chief authority, Paulus Orosius, he makes the truly astonishing statement that the conquest of Britain by the Romans was a bloodless one, threats and judgments serving instead of fire and sword, and the usual engines of war![24] Having thus begun by painting the Britons as shifty cowards, he continues to represent them in that light as long as he can, until he reaches victories of which the memory is so vivid that he must perforce alter his tone. Little importance, therefore, attaches to the general outlines of Gildas's picture, though it is

[23] See the Irish tale edited by Prof. Kuno Meyer for vol. xiv. of the *Cymmrodor*. The Welsh form of the pedigree is to be found in Harl. MS. 3859 (*Cymr.* ix. 171) and Jesus College (Oxford) MS. 20 (*Cymr.* viii. 86).

[24] Orosius, following Suetonius (*Claudius*, 17), says (*Adv. Pag.* vii. 6) that the emperor Claudius "sine ullo proelio ac sanguine intra paucissimos dies plurimam insulae partem in deditionem recipit". The ground had been so well prepared by Aulus Plautius that the emperor himself, when he came over, had nothing to do but receive the submission of foes already conquered. Gildas takes the passage as meaning that at no stage were the Romans resisted: "imbellemque populum . . . non tam ferro igne machinis, ut alias gentes, quam solis minis vel iudiciorum concussionibus . . . subiugavit" (c. 5). The "Parthorum pacem" mentioned earlier in the chapter is, of course, that in the time of Augustus (20 B.C.), to which Orosius so often recurs (*Adv. Pag.* i. 1; iii. 8; vi. 21).

likely enough that it preserves for us some valuable details, such as the appeal for help in 446 (or soon afterwards) to Aetius, ruler of Northern Gaul in the name of Valentinian III.[25] The facts are, that the Picts and the Scots were kept almost entirely out of the province and that the Saxons only effected a lodgment in it after a long struggle; obscure as is the history of the period, it may be regarded as certain that the place of the Roman legions was taken by a fairly efficient fighting organisation.

In its main features the new system was, no doubt, a continuation of the old. The existing walls and forts gave the starting-point that was needed, and it was a simple matter to appoint new officers in place of those who had left. According to the "Notitia Dignitatum,"[26] there were in Britain three important military officials in the closing years of the Roman occupation. The Count of Britain commanded forces which were not assigned to the defence of any particular district, but were available to meet any unexpected danger. The Count of the Saxon Shore had under him the Second Legion and the other troops which garrisoned the nine forts of the south-eastern coast. The Duke of the Britains was in charge of Hadrian's Wall, with the Sixth Legion and the garrisons of thirty-six forts at his command. No clear trace has yet come to light of a successor to the Count of Britain, though Sir John Rhys suggests that this was the real part played by Arthur, who is commonly termed "emperor" by Welsh tradition.[27] But the duties of the other two officers appear to have been carried on by certain Britons who were dignified with the title of "gwledig". Derived from a Celtic root signifying "authority, lordship,"[28] this term in itself means no more than "prince, ruler," and is so employed in mediæval Welsh literature.[29] It does not seem, however, to be applied to any historical figure of later

[25] Aetius might be addressed as "ter consul" not only in 446, but in any year thereafter until his fourth consulship and death in 454.

[26] Pp. 180, 182, 209.

[27] *W. People*, p. 105.

[28] *Celt. Br.* (2), p. 67; *Urk. Spr.* 262.

[29] See, for instance, the proverb from the Red Book of Hergest printed by Dr. Gwenogvryn Evans in the *Transactions of the Liverpool Eisteddfod of* 1884: "Gnawd gwin yn llaw wledig," *i.e.*, "One expects wine in the hand of a prince". *Cf.* also *Myv. Arch.* I. 192 (142), where the Deity is called "gwledig gwlad orfod," "lord of the realm of fate".

CHAP. IV.

date than the middle of the sixth century, and thus the conjecture of Sir John Rhys, that it is, in the names in which it occurs, a Brythonic rendering of "dux" and "comes," has much to recommend it.[30] Of the four best-known wearers of the title, Macsen Wledig belongs, of course, to the Roman period; Cunedda Wledig and Ceredig Wledig are connected with the North and appear to be guardians of the wall, while Emrys Wledig, the Ambrosius Aurelianus of Gildas, is the antagonist of the Saxons. Thus Cunedda and Ceredig may be regarded as Dukes of the Britains, while Emrys is a British Count of the Saxon Shore.[31]

It was inevitable that in the altered state of things the military element should outweigh and reduce to insignificance the civil. Rome had governed the province with the aid of two distinct sets of officers; and her civil functionaries, responsible as they were for justice and finance, were no less important than the captains of her troops. But, in ceasing to form part of a great imperial system, Britain lost the impulse which gave life and vigour to her civil institutions, and it was but natural that power should now fall entirely into the hands of the men who rendered the country the first and most necessary service by freeing it from its foes. One sign of this shifting of the centre of gravity is the disappearance of the cities as a political force in the island. City life, it would appear, was at no time very highly developed in Roman Britain;[32] yet it was to the cities Honorius wrote when he bade the Britons defend themselves, and they might have been expected to play some part in the struggle with the barbarians. There is no evidence that they did so; Gildas speaks in the next century of their past glories, the solid walls, the lofty towers,

[30] This view is expounded in *Celt. Br.* (2), p. 104 and *W. People*, pp. 105-8. Skene had previously suggested that "gwledig" was the Welsh equivalent of "imperator" (*IV. Anc. Bks.* i. p. 48). Geoffrey of Monmouth seems to have been puzzled by the title in the case of Macsen, whom he styles "Maximianum *senatorem*" (*Hist. Reg.* v. 9).

[31] A number of chiefs are styled "gwledig" in the *Mabinogion* (see *Mab.* 342), but the only one of them (save Macsen) of whom anything is known is Amlodd Wledig, who is represented as the maternal grandfather of several notable figures in British fable and history, including Arthur and Illtud. See *Mab.* 100; *Myv. Arch.* II. 25 (416); *Cambro-Br. SS.* 158, and *Myv. Arch.* II. 289 (461).

[32] *Social England*, illustrated ed., i. p. 83 (F. Haverfield).

the well-built houses,[33] but in the ruin which marked the barbarians' progress they fell, according to him, without recovery, and in his own age still lay in hideous overthrow, desolate and untenanted.[34] Calpurnius, the father of St. Patrick, was a "decurio" or town councillor of some British city, but this did not prevent a band of pirate Scots from plundering his country estate and carrying off his young son into degrading captivity.[35] The case is typical and makes it easy to understand how in this crisis the cities lost such authority and prestige as they had, and how those who could command military force became the supreme arbiters of the destinies of the island.

Of what origin the men were who now stepped to the front in Britain it is not very easy to say. Ambrosius Aurelianus, says Gildas, was the son of one who had worn the imperial purple, having, no doubt, been made emperor by the Britons; he appears in the narrative as the only man of "Roman" race left in the island.[36] He belonged, it is likely, to a family founded by some Roman official. For Rome still exercised her majestic sway over the minds of the Britons, though she had ceased to command their obedience. St. Patrick, in the middle of this fifth century, and Gildas, a hundred years later, claim to be regarded as "cives," heirs and custodians of Roman civilisation, in opposition to the untamed barbarians. [37] Germanus of Auxerre, visiting Britain in 429, makes the acquaintance of a great man who wields "tribunician power".[38] Even a thoroughly Celtic king like Voteporix, ruler of Dyfed in the days of Gildas, has graven on

[33] C. 3. In this chapter Gildas has, I believe, used an old description of the province, no longer applicable in respect of its account of the twenty-eight cities.

[34] "Sed ne nunc quidem, ut antea, civitates patriæ inhabitantur; sed desertæ dirutæque hactenus squalent" (c. 26). Mommsen must have overlooked this passage when he hazarded the suggestion that the cities still survived, though ruinous, in the age of Gildas, and were centres, in the sixth century, of Latin speech (preface to Gildas, p. 10).

[35] See § iii. of this chapter. [36] C. 25.

[37] For St. Patrick, see his letter to the subjects of Coroticus (Ceredig Wledig of Strathclyde), addressed "non dico ciuibus meis atque ciuibus sanctorum Romanorum, sed ciuibus daemoniorum ob mala opera ipsorum, qui barbarorum ritu hostili in morte vivunt" (H. and St. ii. 314). For Gildas, see especially the end of c. 26: "Quippe quid celabunt cives, quæ non solum norunt sed exprobrant iam in circuitu nationes?"

[38] Bede, *H.E.* i. 18.

CHAP. IV.

his tombstone no Celtic title, but the high-sounding style of "protector".[39] These are facts which show that, when it was possible, the new rulers were glad to establish a connection with the old order of things and to represent themselves as lawful successors of the former officials.

But it is fairly certain that it was not so much the official class as the wealthy landowners of Britain who supplied the new leaders of the British people. In Gaul the old landed families of the country, proud of their descent and tilling vast estates by the labour of a peasantry little better than slaves, form at this period the most prominent feature of provincial society,[40] and the conditions in the settled parts of Britain were probably much the same. Wealth and the habit of command would give members of this class the advantage necessary to raise them to power in the general struggle for ascendancy, and from it no doubt sprang the "tyranni" of the fifth century, men like Cunedda Wledig and Vortigern, who, whatever titles they may have assumed, were in point of fact the founders of Celtic dynasties.

III. THE BEGINNINGS OF CHRISTIANITY.

(On the subject of the early British Church there is a considerable literature. Nearly all the documentary evidence is given, in a most convenient form, in the first and second volumes of *Councils and Ecclesiastical Documents*, for which Mr. Haddan was responsible. The following works, dealing generally with the subject, have also been used: Usher, *Britannicarum Ecclesiarum Antiquitates* (Dublin, 1639); Warren, *Liturgy and Ritual of the Celtic Church* (Oxford, 1881); Loofs, *Antiquæ Britonum Scotorumque Ecclesiæ quales fuerint mores*, etc., (Leipzig and London, 1882); Romilly Allen, *Monumental History of the Early British Church* (London, 1889). More recently, the whole ground has been traversed and new questions raised by Hugh Williams in the "Christian Church in Wales" (*Transactions of Cymmrodorion Society* for 1893-4), by Haverfield in the *English Historical Review* for July, 1896 (vol. xi. pp. 417 *et seq.*), and by Zimmer in his article on the Celtic Church in the *Realencyclopädie für protestantische Theologie und Kirche* (vol. x.), separately issued in an English translation in 1902 (London). For a searching review of the last named by Prof. Williams see the *Zeitschrift für Celtische Philologie*, iv. pp. 527-74 (Halle, 1903).)

No one has yet succeeded in penetrating the darkness which hangs around the first preaching of Christianity in Britain. Such was the fascination of the subject that legends were certain to grow up around it, and mediæval writers do

[39] See pp. 115 and 132.

[40] Dill, *Roman Society*, p. 167; *Edinburgh Review*, April, 1899, p. 386.

not fail to bring hither apostles and other New Testament figures, such as Joseph of Arimathæa, as the first Christian missionaries.[41] Welshmen have been taught to believe that the father of the great Caratâcus accompanied his son to Rome, there became a convert to the new faith, and, returning as a missionary to his native land, won immortal renown as "Brân the Blessed".[42] A very old story, which gained credit at Rome as early as the end of the seventh century, tells how a pope of the second century was asked by one "Lucius, King of the Britains," to send a mission to this country, which became in consequence a Christian land.[43] Upon examination, these and similar stories vanish into thin air, and all that is certain is that at the beginning of the fourth century, when Christianity secured the protection and patronage of the Emperor Constantine the Great, it had already obtained a footing and made some progress in Britain. That the British martyrs honoured in later ages, Albanus of Verulamium, Aaron and Julius of Isca,[44] suffered in the great persecution which preceded this sudden change of fortune, may be reasonably supposed, though Gildas, who had heard something of their story, is not able to say so with certainty.[45] The first ascertained fact in the history of British Christianity is that in 314 the bishops of three British churches, those of York, London and (probably)

[41] H. and St. i. 22-4.

[42] The Brân story is only found in the Third and latest series of Triads (*Myv. Arch.* II. 61, 63 (402, 404)), and the related Iolo MSS. (100, 115, 135, 147). It was unknown even to Theophilus Evans, as late as the appearance in 1740 of the second edition of *Drych y Prif Oesoedd.* Rees (*Welsh SS.* 77-81) showed that it could not be reconciled with what is known of Caratâcus and his family. No doubt Rhys is right in supposing (*Arth. Legend*, pp. 172-3) that the mischief began with a misunderstanding of the name Brân *Fendigaid* (the Blessed).

[43] The Lucius story, in itself incredible, was not known, it would seem, to Gildas, Augustine of Canterbury or Aldhelm. It first appears in this country in the works of Bede (*H.E.* i. 4 and v. 24; see also De Temporum Ratione in Opp. vi. 305), who, however, drew his information from a Roman source, the Liber Pontificalis. See H. and St. i. 25; *Nenn. V.* 140-6; *Cymr. Trans.* 1893 4, 62-4 (Hugh Williams). Harnack has recently shown how the story originated; see *Eng. Hist. Rev.* xxii. 767-70.

[44] "Legionum (for legionis) urbis cives," says Gildas (c. 10). This might refer either to Dêva (Caerlleon) or Isca (Caerllion), but the local tradition (see *Lib. Land.* 225, "territorium sanctorum martirum iulii et aaron") must be allowed some weight.

[45] "Ut conicimus" is the true reading (p. 31 of Mommsen's edition), "cognoscimus" occurring only in the inferior (Cambridge) MS. Ff. I. 27.

CHAP. IV.

Lincoln,[46] attended a council summoned to Arles in Southern Gaul to determine controversies which had arisen among the churches of Africa. It was as the result of the expansion of the new religion in an Empire in which communications were good and ideas rapidly circulated, and not in consequence of any notable missionary campaign, that the Christian faith was first planted in this island.

During the next century, the last of the Roman occupation, the area covered by Christianity, which was now the imperial creed, was no doubt greatly extended, so that at the time of the severance from the Empire the whole province, so far as it was really Roman, may be regarded as Christian. Maximus, for instance, was not only a Christian, but took pains to put himself forward as a special champion of orthodoxy. It is true that archæology furnishes very little evidence of the presence of Christians in the island during the Roman period, but it has been already remarked that it tells us little of any aspect of fourth-century life in Britain; moreover, one very important bit of evidence has recently been unearthed at Silchester. Here, on the site of the little town of Calleva, a Roman settlement which was built within the circuit of the tribal fort of the Atrebates, the foundations were laid bare in 1892 of a building generally recognised to be a fourth-century Christian church. It measured 27 feet by 42, was approached at the eastern end by a porch, and had within the apse which rounded off the western end a mosaic panel which probably marked the position of a movable altar. In its design the structure closely resembles the early basilicas of Africa and Italy, and, as the earliest known place of Christian worship in Britain, it is of altogether unique interest.[47] Further light on the advance made by Christianity in this century is to be obtained from the accounts of the Council of Rimini (359), at which British bishops were present in such force as to make the action of three of their number who took a line of their own appear as that of an inconsiderable minority.[48]

[46] The Corbey MS. has "colonia Londinensium" (H. and St. i. 7). This has been variously corrected, but the suggestion of Lingard, that it is an error for "Lindensium," appears the most reasonable. See *Eng. Hist. Rev.* xi. p. 419 (Haverfield).

[47] *Ibid.* xi. p. 424; *Encyclopædia Britannica*, 10th edition, vol. xxxii. p. 627.

[48] Zimmer (*Celtic Church*, p. 4) shows how this is involved in the language of Sulpicius Severus (*Chron.* ii. 41, ed. Halm: "tres tantum ex Britannia")

The question whether this growth of the new religion extended in the fourth century beyond the bounds of the area of which Roman civilisation was in full possession is a more difficult one, and has given rise to widely divergent views. "It is difficult to believe," says Prof. Hugh Williams, "that there were Christian churches in Wales before the beginning of the fifth century." [49] Prof. Zimmer, on the other hand, thinks it likely that "Christianity was gradually spread throughout Ireland in the fourth century by Irish-speaking Britons".[50] On the whole, the balance of evidence seems to favour the former view. The army, it is said, was the part of the imperial system which longest retained the leaven of paganism; nowhere was Christianity weaker than at the military centres.[51] Hence it is not surprising that scarcely a trace of it is to be found at Isca or Dêva or in the region of the Walls, and it will also follow that the Welsh tribes and those of the North were not likely to have heard much of the new creed from their nearest Roman neighbours. Testimony, at any rate, is so far wanting that any of the more primitive communities of the island had accepted Christianity before the closing years of the fourth century.

About this time, however, a powerful impetus was given to missionary work by the extension to Britain of the monastic movement. Beginning in the deserts of Egypt, this passion for a life of bodily mortification and freedom from common joys and cares had travelled steadily westwards, and, in an age of violence and self-indulgence, had thrown its potent charm over many of the truest representatives of the Christian spirit. At the end of the fourth century the monastic idea had been popularised in Northern Gaul by St. Martin of Tours, and it is probable that before his death, which is placed about 400, disciples of his had reached Britain. One of their number, a Briton called Nyniaw, is said, indeed, to have undertaken about this time a mission to the Southern Picts and to have been buried in their midst, at Whithern in Galloway, in a stone church which he had dedicated to the memory of his revered master. The story, which has been accidentally preserved in the pages of Bede,[52] may be regarded as typical of the way in which the

[49] *Cymr. Trans.* 1893-4, 68.

[50] *Celtic Church*, p. 26.

[51] So Prof. Haverfield in *Eng. Hist. Rev.* xi. pp. 419 (note 5), 423-4, 427.

[52] *H.E.* iii. 4. It is not expressly stated, but is a fair inference, that Nyniaw was a disciple of St. Martin's.

CHAP. IV.

new monastic enthusiasm proved a spur to missionary effort; no doubt it was by men who had been trained in the same ascetic school, though not of necessity by the same teacher, that the gospel was now preached in the wilds of Cornwall, Wales and the North, and perhaps carried across the sea to some of the tribes of Southern Ireland.[53]

A vivid glimpse of British Christianity, as it appeared some thirty years later, is afforded by the narrative of the first visit of Germanus.[54] Pelagius, a British monk,[55] adopted at Rome about 400 the views as to original sin, free will, and Divine grace ever since connected with his name; their promulgation gave rise to a furious controversy throughout the Christian Church, St. Augustine and St. Jerome being the leading champions of the orthodox or predestinarian theology. In 418 Pelagianism was finally condemned, so far as the Western Empire was concerned, but the isolated position of Britain enabled it to find an asylum there, after it had been banished from Italy and Gaul. In 429 a synod of the bishops of Gaul resolved to send across the Channel two of the most distinguished of their number, Germanus of Auxerre and Lupus of Troyes, in order to uproot this dreaded heresy. They spent several months in the island, and, according to the account of Constantius, who wrote a life of Germanus about forty or fifty years later, were entirely successful in their mission, in spite of the influential support which the Pelagians were able to command. Christianity had by this time clearly won, in some form or other, the allegiance of the whole country, for heathenism makes no appearance in the story; the conflict lies solely between heresy and the orthodox faith. The two envoys do not confine their activity to the churches; everywhere, in town

[53] This seems to be involved in the reference of Prosper to "Scottos in Christum credentes," *s.a.* 431.

[54] Bede in this part of the *Ecclesiastical History* (i. 17-20) is simply a transcriber, the original source being the Life of Germanus by Constantius, a presbyter of Lyons, written about A.D. 480.

[55] For the British origin of Pelagius see H. and St. i. 15. The attempt of Zimmer (*Pelagius in Irland*, Berlin, 1901, pp. 18-21) to prove him an Irishman cannot be said to have been very successful (see Williams' review in the *Zeitschrift für Celtische Philologie*, iv. pp. 531-34). As the name was widely diffused in the Empire, it is not probable it was a translation from the British; but if so, the modern Welsh equivalent would be Morien (*cf. Iolo MSS.* 42, 43) and not Morgan, as in the Welsh version of the Thirty-nine Articles (*Celt. Heath.* p. 229, note).

and country alike, where they can find audience, they deliver themselves of their message. The disputation between them and their adversaries is a public ceremony, of which men, women and children in great multitudes are spectators. News arriving during the bishops' stay of a barbarian invasion of the province, they enter the British camp and infuse a new spirit of confidence into the soldiery, so that the invaders, having been drawn into a narrow valley which is hemmed in by lofty hills, are scattered by the mere noise of the shouts of "Alleluia" sent ringing down from the o'erhanging rocks. The whole narrative is suggestive of a Christian atmosphere, nor does the statement that very many of the British soldiers sought baptism from Germanus and Lupus seriously affect this impression, for baptism was often deferred in this age by adherents of Christianity until a late period of life.

Something may be further learned of the British Christianity of this period from the early life of St. Patrick. Into the many vexed questions which cluster round the name of the so-called apostle of Ireland it is not necessary here to enter, since their bearing on the history of Wales is slight. But it is common ground among the investigators who have busied themselves with his career that the "Confession" and the "Letter to Coroticus" are two genuine works of his, which may be safely used as guides in threading the mazes of his history.[56] They bear, indeed, manifestly upon them, in their rough, uncouth Latinity, their abrupt transitions, and their passionate earnestness, the marks of their origin as the work, not of a scholar aiming at literary effect, but of a busy, zealous missionary whose purposes are all of the practical order. It would appear from them that the young Patricius came of a clerical family; his father was a deacon, his grandfather (or great grandfather) a priest. Thus his ancestors had been Christians for several generations; their names also suggest that they represented the Roman and not the Celtic element in the province. Patrick's father was, indeed, a "decurio"[57] or member of the "curia"

[56] See H. and St. (whose text I have used), ii. 296; Whitley Stokes, *Tripartite Life of St. Patrick* (London, 1887), pref. xciii, c; Zimmer, *Celtic Church*, pp. 27, 28; *Eng. Hist. Rev.* xvii. (1902), p. 235 (J. B. Bury).

[57] "Ingenuus sum secundum carnem, nam decurione patre nascor" (H. and St. ii. 316).

CHAP. IV.

or town council of some British city; he belonged to the class of smaller landholders and had an estate, worked by slaves, not far from the village or posting-house of Bannaventa,[58] which stood on Watling Street, about 12 miles north of Towcester. Yet it would appear that the home language was not Latin, for in the "Confession" Patrick says that he could not write as others, who from earliest childhood had spoken the same language; he was compelled to translate his utterances into a foreign tongue.[59] It is a reasonable supposition that he had been brought up to speak Brythonic. At the age of sixteen or thereabouts, he was carried off by a band of ravaging Scots to Ireland—a fate, he says, which befell great numbers at that time. For six years he served a master whose home has been generally supposed to lie in the modern county of Antrim, not far from Slemish mountain. There, drinking the bitter cup of servitude and ignominy, he was deeply impressed by the religious truths to which he had paid little heed in the days of his boyish freedom and prosperity; as he tended the cattle of Miliuc, he spent long hours in prayer, until at last a vision by night told him that the time of his deliverance had come. He escaped from captivity, made a journey of 200 miles to a certain port, and there found a ship to take him to Britain. After many privations and strange adventures, he at last reached his home, little expecting to see Ireland again. The purpose of preaching the gospel to the people of that country, who were still almost entirely heathen,[60] seems to have gradually formed itself in his mind; the claim of the benighted race upon one who had learnt their language and was familiar with their customs grew more and more insistent and, as was natural in one so impressionable and highly strung, took the shape of visions in which he heard the voices of those who dwelt beside the western sea calling him to their aid. Many years passed by ere he found means to obey the

[58] This explanation of the "Bannauem taberniae" of the Book of Armagh (H. and St. ii. 296) was first put forward by Mr. E. W. B. Nicholson in the *Academy* for 11th May, 1895. It is accepted by Dr. Zimmer (*Celtic Church*, p. 43). For Bannaventa see *Itin. Ant.* 224, 229.

[59] H. and St. ii. 298.

[60] "Hiberione, qui numquam notitiam (Dei) habuerunt, nissi idola et inmunda vsque semper coluerunt, quomodo nuper facta est plebs Domini" (H. and St. ii. 308).

summons, and in the meantime he did not repair the defects of his early education. Thus, when at the age of forty-five or so, having been for some time a deacon, he pressed upon the church authorities of Britain the question of his consecration as bishop for Ireland, the opposition was considerable. In the "Confession" he bitterly complains of the treachery of one of his most intimate friends, who revealed in full council, when this matter was under discussion, an incident of the saint's boyhood which Patrick had confided to him, in penitential anguish of spirit, before entering on the diaconate. The affair was all the more discreditable, in that this very friend had a few days previously warmly congratulated Patrick upon his expected promotion. The root of the opposition was in all probability the question of training; throughout the "Confession" Patrick writes as though he had to justify his mission in the eyes of men who doubted his fitness for the work, themselves masters of rhetoric, full of wisdom and knowledge and learned in the law. The same attitude is taken up in the "Letter to Coroticus"; "if my own people recognise me not, a prophet, be it remembered, has no honour in his own country".[61] There were also many to whom missionary effort made no appeal, such as the men whom Patrick describes in so lively a manner as jeering at him behind his back—"Why should that fellow go and endanger his life among godless barbarians?"[62]

British Christianity in the first half of the fifth century was, therefore, well organised, cultured, and in close touch with the churches of Gaul. Patrick himself expresses the wish, could he safely leave the great work he is doing in Ireland, to visit the brethren in Gaul and meet the saints of that country face to face.[63] The conversion of the heathen was, perhaps, not being officially undertaken with the zeal that might have been expected, but the contagion of monasticism was seizing hold of individuals and they, like Patrick and Nyniaw, were breaking through all obstacles and carrying unaided the torch of the new

[61] H. and St. ii. 316.

[62] "Iste quare se mittit in periculum inter hostes, qui Deum non nouerunt?" (H. and St. ii. 310).

[63] H. and St. ii. 308-9. For the semicolon in the first line of p. 309, substitute a note of interrogation. The passage, as Prof. Williams points out (*Zeitschrift für Celtische Philologie*, iv. p. 555), affords no help towards determining the question whether St. Patrick ever actually visited Gaul.

CHAP. IV.

faith into the darkness of barbarian lands. Such was the aspect of affairs when the success of the Saxon marauders in effecting a settlement in South-eastern Britain interposed a heathen barrier between the British churches and those of the nearest part of the Continent. Communication with Europe was not, indeed, rendered wholly impossible; at the western end of the English Channel it was soon to grow more active than ever through the British settlement of the Armorican peninsula. But henceforward relations between British and continental Christianity were casual and unauthoritative, as is sufficiently shown by the fact that, when it is proposed by Augustine of Canterbury, a hundred and fifty years later, to re-establish them, the Celts are found to be still following rules for the computation of Easter which had been abandoned by Gaul about the time of the conquest of Kent.[64]

IV. The Brythonic Conquest of Wales.

(This is a subject which Sir John Rhys has made peculiarly his own and treated fully in *Celtic Britain*, *Celtic Folklore* (Oxford, 1901), *The Welsh People*, and *Arch. Camb.* V. xii. 18-39, 264-302. The inscriptions, both Ogam and Latin, may be studied in Hübner, *Inscriptiones Britanniae Christianae* (Berlin and London, 1876); Westwood, *Lapidarium Walliæ* (Oxford, 1876-9); Rhys, *Lectures on Welsh Philology*, second edition (London, 1879); and the numerous notices in *Archæologia Cambrensis*, which has always extended to epigraphic studies a very liberal patronage.)

The division of the responsibility for the defence of Britain between a Northern and a Southern "gwledig," the one dealing with the Picts and Scots, the other with the Saxons (whom it will henceforth be more convenient to call the English), had momentous consequences for the island. It led to the division of the Britons themselves into two sections, each with its own battle to fight and with little interest in that carried on by its neighbour. It has often been confidently stated that the natives of South-eastern Britain, when driven from their homes by the English invaders, found a refuge in large numbers in the mountains of Wales and thus became the ancestors of the Welsh people.[65] But for migration into Wales at this

[64] H. and St. i. 152.

[65] Early exponents of this view are Geoffrey of Monmouth (*Hist. Reg.* xi. 10: "secesserunt itaque Britonum reliquiæ in occidentales regni partes, Cornubiam videlicet in Wallias,") and William of Newburgh (*Hist. Angl.* ii. 5: "qui evadere potuerunt refugerunt in Wallias").

period from the East or from the South there is no evidence whatever; it is, on the contrary, remarkable how little genuine Welsh tradition has to tell of the great duel in the South-east between Celt and Saxon, while on the other hand it is circumstantial in its account of the varying fortunes of the Britons of the North. The story of Vortigern is, of course, known in the West and the fame of Arthur penetrates there, but, save for a few great names like these, it would seem that the dwellers in Wales knew little of the course of the struggle which was gradually making Britain England. Even their comrades on the southern side of the Bristol Channel, the men of Devon and Cornwall, they regarded as so divorced from them in interests as not to include them with themselves in the name of "Cymry" or "fellow-countrymen"[66] which they willingly extended to the Britons of the Solway and the Clyde. Thus the historian of Wales is not concerned with the progress of the English conquest until it has reached an advanced stage; for him the importance of the fifth century lies in quite another direction.

It was in this age that the Brythonic race secured a lasting supremacy throughout Wales, winning over the Goidelic tribes such victories as in time led to the total extinction of Goidelic speech on this side of St. George's Channel. Different opinions are held, as has already been pointed out, with regard to the origin of the Goidelic element in the population of fifth-century Wales, but there is no room for doubt as to its existence. Welsh popular tradition has always maintained that the "Gwyddelod" (Irish) preceded the Welsh in many parts of the country and has ascribed to them, under the name of "Cytiau Gwyddelod" (Irishmen's huts), the round stone dwellings of which the ruins were once so common on the bare slopes of the Welsh hills.[67] "Gryniau Gwyddelod" (Irishmen's ridges) are also shown, the supposed vestiges of a primitive agriculture. The tradition has left its mark in Welsh literature; it appears

[66] For the history of this name see p. 164.

[67] Camden, in his account of Anglesey, refers to the fact that certain remains in the island were known as "Hibernicorum casulae". Llwyd (Gibson, 677) and Rowlands (*Mon. Ant.* 27) were both familiar with the popular term "Cytiau Gwyddelod," though they deemed it a misnomer. Cytiau may still be seen near the South Stack, at Tre'r Ceiri, at Muriau'r Dre in Nant Gwynen, near Beddau Gwyr Ardudwy, and above Bwlch Gwernog in Nanmor.

CHAP. IV.

in the lives of Welsh saints,[68] in the Triads,[69] and in the memoranda included in the "Iolo MSS".[70] Accordingly Dr. Basil Jones (afterwards bishop of St. David's) was able in 1850 to put forward in his *Vestiges of the Gael in Gwynedd* (published in 1851) a considerable amount of evidence in support of the view that the Gael, or as he is now more conveniently styled, the Goidel, was in possession of North Wales at the time of the collapse of Roman rule. But the decisive evidence of Goidelic occupation (applying, however, rather to South than to North Wales) came to light after the publication of this book. It had long been known that in Ireland a mysterious system of writing, known as Ogam and consisting of groups of notches, had been in use in early times, but, the key to it having escaped the notice of scholars, ogam inscriptions remained undecipherable, until in 1848 Dr. Graves unfolded the mystery and showed how the alphabet was constructed. It was then discovered that a very large number of these inscriptions still survived, particularly in the counties of Kerry, Cork and Waterford; the language was invariably Irish, in an early stage of its history; the purpose of the inscription was in each case to mark a burying-place. Some of the inscriptions appeared to commemorate Christians, though this could not be positively stated of the ogams as a whole. The ogam question took a new and interesting turn when inscriptions in this character began to be discovered in Wales. The careful scrutiny of Edward Llwyd had in 1693 noted the ogams on a drawing of the Pool Park stone, but he offered no conjecture as to their purpose; "as for ye stroaks on ye edges, I met with them on other tombstones, and I make not ye least question but this is also a tombstone".[71] Prof Westwood in 1846 recognised as ogams the marks on the edges of the Kenfig stone.[72] It was not, however, until 1859, when a reading of the ogams on the St. Dogmael's stone was submitted to the Cardigan meeting of the Cambrian Archæological Association,[73] that the Welsh inscriptions of this class began to be systematically studied and the facts ascertained which show how firmly the Goidelic race was rooted in Wales at the epoch now under consideration.

68 *Cambro-Br. SS.* 97, 101, 124.

69 Third series, Nos. 8, 12 (*Myv. Arch.* II. 58, 59 (401)).

70 Pp. 69, 71, 78-9, 81-2, 196-7.

71 *Arch. Camb.* I. iii. (1848), 310.

72 *Ibid.* I. i. (1846), 182.

73 *Ibid.* III. v. (1859), 345.

Some thirty ogam inscriptions have come to light in various parts of Wales. Of these two only, the Pool Park stone, which formerly stood on Bryn y Beddau, near Clocaenog and the stone lately discovered near Brynkir, Carnarvonshire,[74] belong to North Wales, a circumstance which has its importance, though it does not mean that this part of the country had no Goidelic inhabitants. The rest are distributed as follows—Brecknockshire, four; Glamorganshire, two; Cardiganshire, one; Carmarthenshire, six; Pembrokeshire, fifteen. In every case in which the inscription is still legible, it is found to be sepulchral, giving the name of the deceased with (commonly) some indication of the parentage, while the occurrence of the words "maqui" (son), "inigena" (daughter), "avi"[75] (grandson, descendant) makes it absolutely certain that the language in which they are written is Goidelic or old Irish. At the same time it is important to observe that twenty-two out of the thirty Welsh ogams are accompanied by inscriptions in Latin capitals and in the Latin language, which appear in almost every case to be a reproduction of the Goidelic epitaph in the more familiar tongue. In this respect the ogam inscriptions of Wales present as a group a great contrast to those of Ireland, for the Latin rendering is there a thing almost entirely unknown. While, therefore, the wide area over which these monuments are scattered makes it clear that Goidelic was a familiar tongue at the time they were erected throughout a large part of South Wales, it is equally certain that Latin had so far established itself as the literary language as to be used concurrently with the other in most of the ogam sepulchral inscriptions.

CHAP. IV.

These ogams, however, form only a small proportion of the inscribed stones found in Wales which are assigned to the period between the end of the Roman occupation and the beginning of the ninth century. No less than seventy Latin inscriptions of this age have at various times come to light, without reckon-

[74] Gibson, 686; *Arch. Camb.* VI. vii. (1907), 96.

[75] "Inigena" (in modern Irish, "inghean") appears as the equivalent of "filia" in the Eglwys Cymun inscription (*Arch. Camb.* V. vi. (1889), 224-32; x. (1893), 285). "Avi," genitive of "avias, descendant, occurs, in the form "avvi," on the Llanwinio stone (now at Middleton Hall, Llanarthney). See *Inscr. Chr.* No. 89; *Lap. W.* 91; *W. Phil.* 2), 280. "Maqui," genitive of "maquas," is fairly common.

CHAP. IV.

ing the bilingual epitaphs mentioned above, and it becomes necessary to discuss their relation to the Goidelic question. The first point which claims notice is that the monoglot inscriptions in Latin capitals are not separated from the Latin ones on bilingual stones by any well-marked characteristics, but appear to be of the same age and carved by the hands of the same race. At the east end of the ruined church of Llandeilo, near Maenclochog, was discovered in 1889 a bilingual inscription to the memory of "Andagelli fili Caveti," but this man's brother (presumably), named "Coimagni fili Caveti" was commemorated by a Latin inscription only, which came to light at the same time, after having been long built up into the churchyard stile.[76] A third stone, now in the churchyard of Cenarth, but originally found in the same neighbourhood, records, in Latin capitals only, the name of a third member of this family, one "Curcagni fili Andagelli".[77] Moreover, it is quite usual to find names which from their occurrence in ogams are known to be Goidelic also figuring in monoglot Latin epitaphs. Anglesey, where no ogams have as yet been discovered, furnishes two good instances in the "Cunogusi" of the Bodfeddan stone[78] and the "Maccudecceti" of that at Penrhos Lligwy.[79]

Hence, while the ogam inscriptions furnish incontestable evidence of the existence of a Goidelic population in the districts in which they are found, they afford no reason for limiting it to these parts of Wales. A comparison with Ireland will show that the fashion of using the ogam alphabet did not extend to every region settled by Goidels; the character was in common use only in the south of the island, and north of Kildare a few sporadic specimens are all that have come to light. It was in some part of Munster, no doubt, that this kind of writing obtained its first foothold in Ireland, and for some reason or other it had no great vogue outside that province. Similarly in Wales, the ogam stronghold is the region

[76] *Arch. Camb.* V. vi. (1889), 304-13.

[77] Westw. 86; *W. Phil.* (2), 388. For the situation of the stone in 1743 see *Arch. Camb.* V. xiii. (1896), 134.

[78] *W. Phil.* (2), 363; *Lap. W.* 192.

[79] *Inscr. Chr.* No. 154; *Lap. W.* 189; *W. Phil.* (2), 361; *Mon. Ant.* 156; *Celt. Br.* (2), p. 230.

of Dyfed, where, no doubt, the character made its first appearance in Britain, and the fact that elsewhere, and particularly in North Wales, it is sparsely represented only means that the Goidels of these districts did not take kindly to it. It would, in fact, appear that the really significant distinction is not that between the ogam-yielding districts and the rest of the country, but that which marks off the regions producing inscribed stones with rude Latin capitals from those where they are practically unknown. A line drawn along the course of the Clwyd, of the upper Dee and of the Mawddach would in North Wales mark off the district to the north-west in which these inscriptions are fairly common from that to the south-east in which they hardly ever occur. The corresponding line in South Wales would run from the mouth of the Aeron to the great bend of the Wye at Glasbury. In the angle between these two lines lies the region known as Powys, the country of the Ordovices, which has been treated above as a Brythonic region; the conclusion, therefore, seems irresistible that, as suggested by Sir John Rhys,[80] the custom of erecting over the grave of a notable man or woman a standing stone with the name of the deceased inscribed upon it was characteristically Goidelic and had little or no currency among the Brythonic tribes. Inscribed stones which commemorate Brythons are no doubt to be found, such as the well-known Porius stone at Penystryd near Trawsfynydd, but in the genuinely Brythonic parts of Wales their erection was not a customary way of paying honour to the dead.

It should be said that no serious question can arise as to the date of these inscriptions. While the earlier of them are shown by the comparatively pure style of lettering to be very little later than the end of the Roman occupation, there is from this period onward a gradual deflection from the severity of Latin capitals until a stage is reached, about the beginning of the ninth century, when the whole inscription is in "minuscules" or small letters of the Hiberno-Saxon type. At least two of the stones bear the names of historical persons who can be identified, namely, of King Voteporix of Dyfed [81] and

[80] *Celt. Br.* (2), pp. 248-50.

[81] *Arch. Camb.* V. xii. (1895), 303-13; xiii. (1896), 107; xv. (1898), 274. See also the *Academy* for 11th January, 1896 (p. 35), and *W. People*, p. 503.

CHAP. IV.

King Cadfan of Gwynedd,[82] who flourished in the sixth and the seventh century respectively. As a class they belong undoubtedly to Christian times. The majority of them have been found on or near ecclesiastical sites; very many have a cross incised on the stone, in addition to the inscription. At Cefn Amwlch in Lleyn two priests are commemorated, one being the Hynog ("Senacus" on the stone) whose name is still preserved in that of the neighbouring hill called "Bryn Hynog".[83] Even as regards the ogams, which it is not unnatural to regard as of pagan origin, the connection with Christianity is perfectly clear. More than half the Welsh ogams have been found in close association with churches or ancient chapels; several have incised crosses, though in one or two cases these may be the work of later hands.

During the fifth and sixth centuries the process was going on which gradually drove Goidelic speech altogether out of Wales and made the country what it has remained, save for the progress of English, to this day, a Brythonic-speaking land. Unfortunately, the story of the change has not been recorded by any contemporary writer; such details as have survived are embedded in traditional narratives, of which the authority is not too high. Nevertheless, it does not seem impossible to construct with their aid a fairly consistent account of the Brythonic conquest. The primary authority is the portion of the "Historia Brittonum," usually ascribed to Nennius, which, occurring in two MSS. only, is known as the "Saxon Genealogies" and is now recognised by scholars as a little Northumbrian or Cumbrian tract written at the end of the seventh century and tacked on to the "Historia" proper.[84] In this it is said that the great-grandfather of Maelgwn Gwynedd was "Cunedag," who with his eight sons came from the North, from Manaw Gododin, and drove out the Scots from Gwynedd with very great slaughter, so that they never returned.[85] This

[82] *Mon. Ant.* 156; *Inscr. Chr.* No. 149; *Lap. W.* 190-1; *W. Phil.* (2), 364; *Celt. Br.* (2), pp. 127-8.

[83] *Inscr. Chr.* Nos. 144 and 145; *Lap. W.* 177-8; *W. Phil.* (2), 365-6. The stones came from the site of an ancient chapel (*Arch. Camb.* V. xiii. 138).

[84] *Cymr.* xi. 134-8 (E. Phillimore); *Nenn. V.* 74-81; Mommsen, Pref. to *Hist. Britt.* (p. 117). Mommsen holds that the whole "Historia" may be of this date.

[85] *Hist. Britt.* 205 (c. 62).

was 146 years before the reign of Maelgwn, a chronological indication which is at once precise and vague, but which, taken in conjunction with the statement that Cunedda was Maelgwn's great-grandfather, may be regarded as assigning him to the beginning of the fifth century and the earliest years of the period of British independence. The genealogies of Welsh princes in Harleian MS. 3859, which were put together not later than the middle of the tenth century, supply the links which connect Maelgwn and Cunedda and furnish the latter with a long pedigree.[86] Maelgwn was the son of Cadwallon Lawhir (the Long-handed), the son of Einion Yrth (the Impetuous?),[87] the son of Cunedda; as to the ancestors ascribed to Cunedda, most of them may be disregarded, but the names of his father, grandfather and great-grandfather, namely, Edeyrn, Padarn Beisrudd (of the Red Robe), and Tegid, wear a historical aspect. In the same MS. is to be found an interesting account of the sons of Cunedda. Their names are given, in tenth-century orthography, as Osmail, Rumaun, Dunaut, Ceretic, Abloyc, Enniaun Girt, Docmail, and Etern; a ninth is added, called Typiaun, who is said to have died in Manaw Gododin before the great expedition and to have been represented in the division of the Brythonic spoils by his son Meriaun. The boundary of the nine, it is stated, was on the one hand the Dyfrdwy (Dee) and on the other the Teifi, and they held very many regions in Western Britain.[88] Which these regions were, though the MS. does not expressly mention them, may be inferred from the bounds given and from certain pedigrees which it contains, pedigrees of princes who traced their descent to sons of Cunedda and were clearly rulers of cantrefs or larger districts in North-west Wales. They were the districts which still preserved the names of Cunedda's sons and grandson, "Osmeliaun," which has not so far been identified, Rhufoniog, Dunoding,[89] Ceredigion, Aflogion (a cymwd of Lleyn),[90] Dog-

[86] *Cymr.* ix. 170. For the date of the MS. see Mr. Phillimore's introduction.

[87] Dafydd ap Gwilym speaks of "Brychan Yrth, breichiau nerthawg" (*Works*, ed. Cynddelw, 1873, 108). *Cf. Myv Arch.* I. 259 (187): "A gwyr gyrth am byrth yn burthyaw gorwlad".

[88] *Cymr.* ix. 182. [89] *Mab.* 73.

[90] This appears in the various lists as Gaualogion, Ganelogyon, Is Clogyon, etc. But the true form seems to be preserved in Jesus Coll. MS. 20, *viz.*, "aphlocyawn" (*Cymr.* viii. 85).

CHAP. IV.

feiling (the cantref of Dyffryn Clwyd),[91] Edeyrnion and Meirionydd. Other authorities add nothing of value to the story of the Brythonic conquest; the statement of the "Historia Brittonum" that Cunedda and his sons drove the Ui Liathain out of South-west Wales appears to be, as Prof. Zimmer holds,[92] an unwarranted extension of the original narrative, though, strangely enough, it is only in the region of Cydweli (expressly mentioned in the "Historia") that the name of the Brythonic leader survives in "Allt Cunedda" (Cunedda's Hill). As to the poem in the "Book of Taliesin" which deals with Cunedda,[93] it probably contains, as Sir John Rhys has pointed out,[94] some remnants of the primitive legend, but the use of the false form "Cunedda*f*," which restores a final "f" (= v) which never existed, shows that the writer is a bard of the Middle Ages, handling material of which he has not entire mastery.

Cunedda, it may safely be inferred from the names of his immediate ancestors, Eternus, Paternus and Tacitus, came of a family which, whatever its origin, had been for some time Roman and not Celtic in its manner of life and its traditions. Very probably the "red robe" of his grandfather Paternus was a robe of state, marking out its wearer as a high Roman official. Cunedda himself bore a Celtic name, which may indicate that about A.D. 400 the Celtic element in the province was beginning to earn for itself a quite unusual recognition, as the power of Rome visibly declined. Yet, if we may trust the account given above, he gave Latin names to three of his sons, Romanus (Rhufon), Donatus (Dunod) and Eternus (Edeyrn), and there was also a Marianus (Meirion) among his grandsons. His home lay near the Firth of Forth, for Manaw Gododin, so called to distinguish it from Ynys Manaw or the Isle of Man, was on the northern border of the country of the Votadini, where Slamannan in Stirlingshire still keeps the name alive. His title of "gwledig," it has already been suggested, points to him as the successor of some Roman general, and, if he really hailed from the North, no office would seem to be more appropriate to his position than that

[91] Owen, *Pemb.* i. 201, note by E. Phillimore.

[92] *Nenn. V.* 92-3.

[93] *IV. Anc. Bks.* ii. pp. 200-2; *Myv. Arch.* I. 71 (60-1).

[94] *Celt. Br.* (2), pp. 118-9.

of defender of the northern or the southern wall. It is fairly certain that he was a Christian, for not only does tradition connect him and his family with important missionary work in Wales, but the names Donatus and Marianus are of distinctively Christian origin.

Whether the men who gave their names to the districts lying between the Teifi and the Dee were really the sons of Cunedda and not rather his followers and lieutenants may be open to doubt, but that they were the actual founders of Brythonic chieftainships in this region can hardly be questioned. Names like Ceredigion (Caraticiana), Rhufoniog (Romaniaca), Meirionydd (Mariania), require a Ceredig, a Rhufon, a Meirion to make them intelligible and the Cunedda legend supplies the simplest and most reasonable explanation of their origin. Moreover, the legend in its oldest form establishes the sons of Cunedda in the precise part of Wales where history is prepared to find them. None are assigned to the isle of Anglesey or the opposite coast of Carnarvonshire, the Môn and Arfon of Welsh writers, and this harmonises with the tradition that it was in a later age that the Goidels were overcome in these, their latest strongholds. On the other hand, none are alleged to have made any conquests in Powys, which is thoroughly consistent with the view that the men of this region were already Brythons and not likely, therefore, to have had anything to do with Cunedda's enterprise save as allies.

An interesting question is raised by this last consideration, namely, how far Cunedda drew support from the Brythonic element in Wales itself. Tradition is silent on the point, but Sir John Rhys has adduced several reasons for thinking that the Ordovices of Powys were sharers in his undertaking and benefited largely by it.[95] Rhyd Orddwy, near Rhyl, Cantref Orddwyf, an old name of Meirionydd, and Dinorwig, which is found as Dinor*dd*wig, seem to mark their progress into Goidelic country, while at Penbryn, in Cardiganshire, is an inscribed stone of the fifth century set up in memory of "Corbalengi Ordous," an Ordovician settler, it may well be believed, who came into this district in the train of Ceredig.[96] A Brythonic immigration on a large scale is indeed required by the

95 *Celt. Br.* (2), p. 302.

96 Gibson, 648; *Inscr. Chr.* No. 115; *Lap. W.* 146; *W. Phil.* (2), 379.

CHAP. IV.

facts of the case, for it is not at all likely, despite the talk of "expulsion" in the traditional accounts, that there was any great displacement of the older population, and thus only the arrival of a very numerous Brythonic colony would establish that balance in favour of the language which enabled it ere long to sweep Goidelic from the field.

According to tradition, the reduction of the Goidels of Gwynedd was not completed by Cunedda and his sons. One of the eight, Einion Yrth, did not, it may be noticed, give his name to any cantref or cymwd, and the history of his descendants suggests that this was because he remained in the fighting line, waging war until the end of his life against the Goidels of Môn and Arfon. Be this as it may, it is to his son, Cadwallon the Long-handed, that the credit is given by tradition of finally securing Brythonic ascendancy in North Wales by defeating the Irish in a great battle fought at Cerryg y Gwyddyl, near Trefdraeth in Anglesey. This fight is first mentioned in the Triad which speaks of the Three Fettered Warbands of the Isle of Britain; one of their number was the warband of Cadwallon Lawhir, who, when fighting with "Serygei" the Irishman at Cerryg y Gwyddyl in Anglesey, tied to their feet the fetterlocks of their horses and so made flight impossible, leaving victory and death as sole alternatives.[97] Other accounts speak of the battle as fought at Llan y Gwyddyl,[98] but this was probably another name for the same place.[99] Henceforth, the Brythons were supreme in North Wales; Cadwallon's son Maelgwn seems to have had no difficulty with the newly conquered Goidels—on the contrary, Gwynedd was the centre of his power. How long Goidelic speech lingered on in this district it is not easy to say, but it is not probable that it disappeared at once. The

[97] Triads, first series, No. 49 = second series, No. 40 (*Myv. Arch.* II. 12, 16 (391, 397); *Cymr.* vii. 129; *Mab.* 305). Geoffrey of Monmouth makes "Caduallo Leuirh rex Venedotorum" one of the vassal princes of Arthur (*Hist. Reg.* ix. 12). *Cf. Bruts*, 200. Caswallon is only found in late authorities, *e.g.*, *Iolo MSS.* 81-2.

[98] *Iolo MSS.* 78-9.

[99] So *Iolo MSS.* 123. A stone circle in the parish of Towyn is (or was) known by the name of "Eglwys y Gwyddel" (*Arch. Camb.* IV. v. (1874), 242). Hence "Llan y Gwyddyl" and "Cerrig y Gwyddyl" are probably both popular descriptions of some monument of the kind.

"Maccudecceti" inscription, for instance, belongs to the sixth rather than to the fifth century.[100]

Even less is known of the progress of the Brythons in the South than in the North. Save for the occupation of Ceredigion, the activity of the house of Cunedda appears to have been confined to North Wales, and it is only possible to conjecture how the Brython gradually edged out the Goidel in the Vale of Towy, in Dyfed and in the land of the Silures. The Brythonic colonisers of the South were probably the Ordovices of our Radnorshire, whence they pressed up the vale of the Irfon into the region of Llandovery, Llandeilo and Llanelly. A movement such as this might explain the undoubted fact that few Latin inscriptions of this period have been discovered between the Towy and the Tawe, and also the story as to the conquests of Cunedda in Gower and Kidwelly. The Goidels of South Wales would thus be split up into two divisions, those of Dyfed and those of the Silurian country, and in each of these two districts there is evidence that the ancient language lingered for many generations. In Dyfed it was in use in the middle of the sixth century, as is shown by the tombstone of Voteporix which stood in Castell Dwyran churchyard, on the borders of Pembrokeshire and Carmarthenshire.[101] St. David, if we may believe his legend, found about the same time a "Scottus," that is, a Goidel, named Baia or Boia in possession of the land on which was afterwards established the saint's famous monastery of Mynyw.[102] In the other region, that of Morgannwg, evidence is likewise forthcoming of the late survival of Goidelic; in a rude Latin inscription at Merthyr Mawr, which is shown by its lettering to be not earlier than the seventh century, reference is made by the man who set up the memorial to his "scitlivissi," a word which Sir John Rhys regards as without doubt Goidelic for "scout, newsbearer". [103]

Thus it is likely that the older Celtic tongue, ever threatened by the victorious progress of Brythonic, nevertheless maintained a precarious hold upon certain parts of Wales until the eve of the Danish invasions. When it finally went, it left several

[100] Hübner places it in his second class (sixth and seventh centuries). See Pref. to *Inscr. Chr.* xx.

[101] See pp. 115, 132.

[102] *Cambro-Br. SS.* 124.

[103] *Inscr. Chr.* No. 67; *Lap. W.* 15-7; *Arch. Camb.* V. xvi. (1899), 158-63.

CHAP. IV.

legacies behind it. The syntax of the old language, which was itself an inheritance from pre-Aryan times, profoundly modified that of the new, giving modern Welsh those syntactical peculiarities which distinguish it so sharply from most other languages of the Aryan family. Goidelic loan-words remained in the Brythonic vocabulary, and many place-names, such as Cenarth (= Brythonic Pennarth) and Cwm Llwch (from Goidelic "loch," a lake), continued to wear their Irish dress. The folk-lore and legends of the conquered race also lived on, and thus it was that Welsh children came to hear of the great lawgiver, Dyfnwal Moelmud, of the wizard pilot and merchant, Manawyddan son of Llyr, and of the wily enchanter, Gwydion son of Dôn.

Note to Chapter IV. § iv. *The Historical Triads.*

The form of expression known as the Triad, in which objects are grouped together in threes, with a heading indicating the point of likeness (*e.g.*, "Three things not easily restrained, the flow of a torrent, the flight of an arrow, and the tongue of a fool") is characteristically Welsh and is found in the earliest Welsh literature. It has been supposed to be of Druidic origin, and passages from Pomponius Mela and Diogenes Laertius have been quoted as containing triads which were current in the Druidic schools (Edw. Davies, *Celtic Researches*, London, 1804, pp. 150-1). But the passage cited from Mela (iii. 2, "ut forent . . . manes") is not a triad at all; it simply states the Druidic doctrine of the transmigration of souls. That from Diogenes (prooem. 5) is triadic in arrangement; it does not, however, record an actual saying of the Druids, but is a summary of teaching common to this order and to the gymnosophists of India. The triad may more reasonably be connected with that reverence for the Trinity to which Giraldus bears testimony (vi. 203; *Descr.* i. 18) and which, according to him, was the source of the Welsh custom of sitting to a meal in groups of three. Whatever may have been its origin, it was a rhetorical form which flourished exceedingly in Welsh soil. Triads are found in the oldest Welsh MS., the Black Book of Carmarthen (fo. 14 *a*, *b*), and in the ancient versions of the Welsh Laws (see the "Three Stays of Blood" in LL. i. 456, 784; ii. 768, 890). References to well-known triads occur also in the "four branches" of the *Mabinogion* (42, 43, 44, 49, 80, 94) and in the poems of the mediæval bards; see, for instance, the reference to the "Three Open-handed Chiefs" in *Myv. Arch.* I. 293 (208). As time went on, the mass of triadic literature grew more and more bulky, and it ultimately became substantial enough to occupy a considerable proportion of the third volume of the *Myvyrian Archaiology*.

The so-called "Historical" Triads, or Triads of the Isle of Britain, have to do with the personages of early British history, of whom they tell a good deal which is not to be found in other sources. The question of their historical value is, therefore, of some importance. Two mistakes have commonly been made by those who have drawn upon the Triads for historical material; the worthless third series has been treated as of equal value with the first and the second, and it has been forgotten that the triad, as we have it, is not a literary record, but merely preserves an oral tradition at a certain stage in its transmission. The three series referred to are the three printed in the second volume of the *Myvyrian*

Archaiology; it will be seen, if they are carefully examined, that their compilers had in the main the same triads before them, but each collection represents the work of a separate editor. Series i. (II. 1-19, upper text (388-394)) contains ninety-two triads; it is not clearly shown by the Myvyrian editors how they arrived at their text, but the fact that Peniarth MS. 45, formerly Hengwrt MS. 536, a MS. of the end of the thirteenth century (Evans, *Rep.* i. pp. 379-80), contains Nos. 7-45 of this series in the Myvyrian order (printed in *IV. Anc. Bks.* ii. pp. 456-64) makes it fairly certain that it represents in the main an old collection. Stephens boldly assigned it to the fifteenth or sixteenth century (*Lit. Kym.* (2), 494), but the reference to "ystoria y Greal" (No. 61) on which he relied is probably a late addition. Series ii. (II. 1-22, lower text (395-399)) is taken from the Red Book of Hergest; a more accurate text will be found in *Mab.* 297-308. The Red Book was written about the year 1400 (Evans, *Rep.* ii. p. 1), but there is evidence which carries this second series somewhat further back, for Nos. 13-60 appear in Peniarth MS. 12, formerly Hengwrt MS. 202, of the fourteenth century, and it would seem that the MS., when complete, contained the whole series and that it was from this source that the series was copied by the scribe who included it in the Red Book (*Cymr.* vii. 89-90, 95-100; Evans, *Rep.* i. pp. 305, 324). It should be added that Stephens, when he sought (*Lit. Kym.* (2), 494) to date this series with the aid of a supposed reference to Owain Gwynedd (ob. 1170), overlooked the obvious fact that "owein gwyned" (*Mab.* 302) is a misreading of "o vein gwyned" (*Cymr.* vii. 98).

Considerable use has been made in these pages of the triads of the first and second series, in the belief that they have handed down genuine old traditions and thus contain historically valuable matter, though with a mythical admixture. The third series (*Myv. Arch.* II. 57-75 (400-11)) is of an entirely different character. Nothing at all resembling it is to be found in any ancient MS., and the history of the Myvyrian copy does not seem to go much further back than 1601. This is much the fullest of the three series, not only in the number of triads (126) which it contains, but also in its explanatory detail. The added matter is, however, of a very suspicious kind; it introduces a number of personages, such as Hu the Mighty, Dyfnwal Moelmud, and Plenydd, who are not mentioned in the other two series and of whom some are certainly mythical. An examination of this series, which has been largely used by writers on Welsh history from the time of Dr. Owen Pughe, leaves little doubt that it is the product of the unhappy activity of the Glamorgan school of bards and antiquaries of the sixteenth century (*Cymr.* xi. 126). For the historian it is almost wholly useless.

CHAPTER V.

THE AGE OF THE SAINTS.

I. Maelgwn Gwynedd and his Contemporaries.

(The material for this section has been chiefly derived from Gildas, for whom see the next section, with the appended note.)

CHAP. V.

Between the first settlement of the English in Britain and the mission of Augustine lie 150 years which are not a whit less important in the early history of Wales than in that of England. During this period the Welsh tribes cast off all traces of heathenism and of political subjection and, in common with the more civilised Britons of the East, become well organised Christian communities, ruled by powerful monarchs, ministered to by a learned clergy, led to battle by champions whose renown has not yet faded. This is the age of Maelgwn Gwynedd, of Gildas and David, above all, of Arthur and his knights of the Round Table. Did we know the true story of these years, it would beyond a doubt be found to be no less stirring and romantic than that which the deft hand of fable has woven around the dim figures of that far distant day. But the period is one for which we have, with one important exception, no contemporary evidence; were it not for Gildas, it would be involved in all but total darkness. There is, indeed, a mass of traditionary material, embodied in the Triads, the lives of the Welsh saints, the *Mabinogion*, the narrative of Geoffrey of Monmouth, and the works of the older poets, which probably has, to a far greater extent than is usually supposed, a substantial historical basis. But the clue to the interpretation of this evidence, the touchstone which will enable the inquirer to distinguish fact from fiction, history from legend, in this wonderful medley has not yet been discovered, and accordingly but sparing use has been made in these pages of tradition, in spite of the temptations which it spreads in the path of him who would write a connected history of the Welsh people. CHAP. V.

In the South and in the East the great struggle was going on which had as its final issue the making of England, the creation of a group of Teutonic states in which hardly a trace remained of the language, the religion, and the institutions of fifth-century Britain. It has been already remarked[1] that the interest of the Welsh tribes in this struggle seems to have been but languid and that they handed down few traditions of it. The fame of Arthur, who vindicated the honour of the British arms against the heathen invader in many victories, stood high among them, but they seem to have had little detailed knowledge of his achievements; he was "the Emperor Arthur," leader of a puissant band of warriors, but in the Welsh romances which recount his great doings and those of his men, the "Saeson," strangely enough, are not even mentioned.[2] One is not disposed, on this account merely, to banish him to the realm of myth, for there are many circumstances which tend to establish his real historical existence. The name, it has been pointed out, is probably of Roman origin and derived from that of the Artorian clan;[3] moreover, Gildas expressly says that the battle of Badon Hill, fought about the year 500, was a decisive victory for the Britons, giving them immunity from hostile attack for a generation,[4] and such a victory could surely only have been won under the leadership of a great captain. If Gildas refrains from giving the name of the victorious commander, that is of a piece with the reticence shown in this respect throughout his book; it is with him the exception to introduce a name, even where the narrative obviously calls for it.[5] But, while there can be little doubt

[1] P. 111. [2] See the index to *Mab.*

[3] *Celt. Br.* (2), p. 237. For the name of Artorius see Tacitus, *Annals*, xv. 71; Juvenal, iii. 29; *Social England*, illustrated edition, i. p. 98. Many members of the *gens* are included in Pauly-Wissowa.

[4] Cap. 26. "Mons Badonicus" is still unidentified. The view of Guest (*Origines Celticæ*, ii. pp. 187-9) that it was Badbury in Dorset has been very generally accepted, but Stevenson has shown (*Eng. Hist. Rev.* xvii. (1902), pp. 633-4) that the names are not, as was supposed, identical.

[5] See c. 23, where Vortigern is merely called "superbo" and "infausto tyranno"; c. 28, "immundae leanae Damnoniae," "sancti abbatis," and "legitima uxore"; c. 31, "propria coniuge"; c. 33, "avunclum regem"; c. 36, "magistrum elegantem".

CHAP. V.

that a great warrior named Arthur led the Britons to victory about the beginning of the sixth century, the vagueness of Welsh tradition[6] leaves the historian with no means of pinning him down to any particular part of the country and furnishes only negative evidence, for it may fairly be inferred from it that Wales, at any rate, was not the theatre of his deeds of prowess. On the whole, it is most likely that his wars were waged in the South and East of the island, and it may be of some significance in this connection that, according to the notice in the *Historia Brittonum*, four of his battles were fought on the river "Dubglas" in the region of "Linnuis," *i.e.*, Lindsey.[7]

The districts which were under the sway of the "gwledig" of the North-west do not seem to have tasted the bitterness of this strife until far on in the sixth century. In the old age of St. Patrick, about the year 450, a glimpse is afforded of the doings of Ceredig Wledig, the "Coroticus" of his letter of denunciation, who bore rule, it would seem, in the valley of the Clyde.[8] He is a powerful prince, who not only successfully raids the Irish coast and carries the natives off as slaves, but is also on good terms with his neighbours, the Picts and the Scots, to whom he is able advantageously to dispose of his ill-gotten gains. He is also a Christian ruler, having holy men about him and rendering alms to the Church; in his attack upon him for shameless disregard of the rights of Irish converts, St.

[6] The *Historia Brittonum*, in which appears the oldest account of Arthur, gives the names of twelve battles which he fought, winding up with "bellum in monte Badonis" (c. 56). So far as the places can be identified, they belong to the North and thus lend support to the theory of a Northern Arthur. But, to judge from the inclusion of "in urbe legionis" (the battle of Chester, fought about 615), the list is a miscellaneous one of famous battles of the period and furnishes no clue to the real field of Arthur's operations. Some of the Welsh romances give him a court at Caerleon (*Mab.* 162, 215, 244); older traditions connect him with Celli Wig in Cornwall (*Mab.* 133, 135, 141, 301).

[7] Lindens-es would yield Linnuis in old Welsh.

[8] For the letter to Coroticus see H. and St. ii. 314-9. This prince was long supposed to be Ceredig ap Cunedda, lord of Ceredigion (*Welsh SS.* p. 135; Todd, *St. Patrick*, p. 352; H. and St. ii. 314). But attention was called to the fact that Muirchu Maccu-Machtheni, a seventh-century writer on the life of St. Patrick, speaks of Coroticus as "Coirthech regem Aloo," *i.e.*, Ail Clúade or Dumbarton (Stokes, *Tripartite Life*, pp. 271, 498), which is a much more likely home than South Wales for an associate of Picts and Scots. "Ceretic guletic" appears in the pedigree of the princes of Strathclyde at a point consistent with the *floruit* here suggested, *viz.*, A.D. 450 (*Cymr.* ix. 173). The phrase "quem ego ex infantia docui" in the letter appears to point to the end of St. Patrick's career as the time of its composition.

Patrick can appeal to the Christian sentiment of his court and remind the warriors of Coroticus, whose conduct has put them outside the pale of Roman citizenship and made them the comrades of demons and fellow to the Pict and the Scot, that the glory of an earthly realm may vanish as a cloud, or as smoke that is scattered by the wind. The vices of Coroticus and his followers are those of the prosperous and strong, of men who hold a responsible position, but despise restraint; there is no hint that the British community had anything to fear from without, or that heathen peoples not so well in hand as the Picts and the Scots were surging at the gates.

A like impression of masterful strength, unbridled and undismayed, is conveyed by the picture painted by Gildas of the British rulers of his day. No doubt, the barbarian ravages, with their sequel, the heathen occupation of a large part of Britain, fill a large place in his narrative, and it is from him that modern historians have chiefly derived their conception of the conquest as a process of savage extermination. But, lurid as is the landscape when he sets himself to depict the devouring tide of conquest, it is, it should be remembered, a story of the past, of what befell Britain before he was born. That siege of Badon Hill, which happened in the year of his birth (and he wrote at the age of forty-three), saw the last and decisive victory of the British arms; wars with external foes have now, he says, ceased; the time is one of prosperity and skies are serene.[9] Unless we are entirely to discard the evidence supplied by Gildas, it must be believed that the first stage of the English conquest and occupation came to an end about the beginning of the sixth century, to be followed by a truce of half a century, and that it was not until 550 or thereabouts that a second onward movement began, threatening this time the Britons of the North and West and reducing them ere long within very narrow limits. The rulers whom Gildas ad-

[9] C. 26. I follow Zimmer (*Nenn. V.* 100) and Mommsen (pref. to Gildas, 8) in understanding Gildas to say that the year of Badon Hill and that of his own birth was the forty-fourth, reckoning backwards, from that in which he wrote. As he wrote before the death of Maelgwn in or about 547, the year referred to cannot have been much later than 504, while the fact that Gildas lived until about 570 makes it probable it was not much earlier. The entry in the chronicle in Harl. MS. 3859 ascribing "bellum badonis" to the year 516 (*Cymr.* xi. 154) is of no particular authority, and with it goes the common ascription of Gildas's work to the year 560.

CHAP. V.

dresses are men of assured position, harassed by no external difficulties. Law and order are maintained in their territories; criminals are brought before the seat of judgment, thieves hunted out and imprisoned, judicial oaths administered.[10] They have their troops, with which they wage war against each other, their bards who celebrate their praises and clergy who are much dependent on their favour.

Of the princes specially named and singled out for attack by Gildas, the most notable is Maglocunus,[11] in whom it is easy to recognise the Maelgwn Gwynedd of Welsh tradition. Had our knowledge of this vigorous ruler been drawn solely from this latter source, he would, without a doubt, have been treated, like Arthur, as a purely mythical figure and perhaps would have been refined into a solar deity. But in the pages of the *De Excidio* he is unmistakable flesh and blood. Taller in stature than most of the chieftains of Britain and therefore well deserving his title of "Maelgwn Hir" (the Tall),[12] he overtops them also in power. This position he has won by deeds of violence; many a neighbouring prince has been sacrificed to his ambition, and his reign began, when he was but a raw youth, with the overthrow of his maternal uncle,[13] whose brave troops he defeated and whose crown he usurped. His later years have been stained by crimes no less heinous, the murder of his wife and of a nephew, whose faithless spouse he was thus enabled to marry. Yet, heavy as is the catalogue of misdeeds laid to his charge, he is not without a certain tincture of nobleness. He is a liberal giver, and no common tyrant would, in the heyday of his greatness, have laid aside his royal dignity and have withdrawn, as Maelgwn did, to the austere seclusion of a monastic cell. All Christians must, it is true, deplore his sad relapse into a life no less worldly and sin-ridden than before, but the very making of the experiment proves him a prince of no ordinary mould.

[10] C. 27.

[11] Cc. 33-6. The mediæval form is always Maelg*wn*, not Maelg*wyn*. Maelgwn is nowhere styled "gwledig," yet it is reasonable to assume that his power rested on the continuance of some office of the kind.

[12] *Myv. Arch.* I. 476 (318).

[13] As the name of Maelgwn's mother is unknown, his "avunculus" cannot be identified. Some have thought he might be Arthur (Sharon Turner, *History of the Anglo-Saxons*, bk. iii. c. 3; *Arth. Legend*, 8).

Such was Maelgwn as he appeared to a contemporary who lashed his vices with no friendly hand, yet did not allow himself, as he did in attacking others, to sink into the language of contempt. The details of his career which have been handed down by tradition seem to harmonise well with the picture drawn by Gildas. He was the son of Cadwallon Lawhir, who finally overcame the Goidels of North Wales.[14] With this people, therefore, he is not represented as fighting; on the contrary, Gwynedd, in its Latinised form Venedotia, is the centre and stronghold of his power,[15] and his designation of "island dragon" is naturally explained with reference to his secure possession of Anglesey.[16] His especial home seems to have been the Creuddyn peninsula, where on the rock of Degannwy, the ancient hold of the Decanti, was the "court of Rhos" in which, according to the popular saying, he slept to awake no more.[17] His name is still preserved in the neighbourhood in that of Bryn Maelgwn, a height not far form Degannwy.[18] Tradition agrees with Gildas in explaining Maelgwn's advent to power as the result of a competition, but describes it as one not of arms, but of constructive skill; the contest came off, we are told, on the sands in the estuary of the Dovey, since known as "Traeth Maelgwn" (Maelgwn's Strand), and Maelgwn owed his victory to the cunning artificer who provided him with a floating chair, since he alone was able to hold his ground against the incoming tide, before which his rivals had to flee.[19] What the germ of truth may be in this story it is hard to tell, but it would seem, at any rate, to embody the view that the son of Cadwallon was a masterful man and one of many resources.

[14] See the pedigrees in Harl. MS. 3859 (*Cymr.* ix. 170).

[15] "Mailcunus magnus rex apud Brittones regnabat, id est in regione Guenedotae" (*Hist. Britt.* c. 62).

[16] "Insularis draco" (Gildas, c. 33). This is the view of Zimmer (*Nenn. V.* 101); Rhys takes the island to be Great Britain (*W. People*, p. 106).

[17] The passages which connect Maelgwn with Degannwy are mostly late (*Bruts*, 234; *Myv. Arch.* II. 359 (547); *ibid.* (597); "Hanes Taliesin," as printed in Lady Charlotte Guest's edition of the *Mabinogion*). But the place was an "arx" of some consequence as early as the beginning of the ninth century (*Cymr.* ix. 163, 164), so that the connection is a likely one. For the original form of the proverb about Maelgwn's long sleep see *Ann. C. s.a.* 547.

[18] The name is at least as old as Pennant's time (iii. 145).

[19] *LL.* ii. 48-50 (Peniarth MS. 32, of about 1380, and another). *Cf. Iolo MSS.* 73-4.

CHAP. V.

Tradition has something to say of the relations of Maelgwn both with the Christianity and the bardism of his time. He plays a prominent part in several of the lives of the saints, which exhibit him as in frequent conflict with the religious of his day, but as invariably brought to reason and repentance. St. Brynach in Dyfed, St. Cadog in Gwynllwg, St. Cybi in Anglesey, St. Padarn in Ceredigion,[20] and St. Tydecho in Powys[21] all had encounters with Maelgwn, which ended in their obtaining from him substantial privileges for their monastic foundations. St. Cybi received from him the royal "caer" or "castellum" in Holyhead Island, which has ever since borne the name of Caer Gybi, and had the legend of St. Deiniol, the founder of Bangor in Arfon, survived, some similar statement would doubtless be found in it explaining how the name of Maelgwn Gwynedd came to be connected with the origin of that monastery also.[22] All is in keeping with the "largior in dando, profusior in peccato" of Gildas, save that in the stories told by the writers of the legends, the order of the epithets is reversed and the almsgiving is the atonement offered for the crimes. Gildas and tradition are, again, in accord in representing Maelgwn as surrounded by a troop of sycophant bards. In the passage which describes,[23] with relentless invective, the king's return from the pure life of a monk to his former dignity and his ancient sins, it is said that he no longer hears the sweet strains of ecclesiastical melody and the praises of God sung by the tuneful voices of His servants, but worthless laudation of himself, as the rascally, lying quacks who serve him spit out their bacchanalian ravings. Though the fact is not expressly stated, the nature of the antithesis makes it very likely that the praises of Maelgwn were, like those of the Most High, set to music, and that the men so scornfully treated by Gildas were the bards of the royal court. Tradition has a good deal to say of these bards, who to the number of twenty-four surrounded Maelgwn on state occasions at Degannwy, but were confounded by the superior skill, in magic no less than in the more legiti-

[20] *Cambro-Br. SS.* 10-12, 50-6, 186-7, 191-2. [21] *Camb. Reg.* ii. 376.

[22] That Maelgwn founded Bangor appears to rest at present on the authority of the C.C.C.C. MS. of John Ross (Joannis Rossi, *Historia Regum Angliæ*, Oxoniæ, 1716, p. 65). Ross had visited Anglesey and Carnarvonshire in search of material (*ibid.* p. 54).

[23] C. 34 (end).

mate aspects of the poet's art, of the great Taliesin, who delivered his master Elphin from the prison of thirteen locks in which Maelgwn had immured him.[24] Whatever view may be taken as to the real nature of the conflict so described, it is clear that Maelgwn was traditionally regarded as a patron of native poesy and music.

This busy, restless career was cut short by the plague which devastated Europe in the middle of the sixth century.[25] According to the chronicle preserved in Harleian MS. 3859, the year was 547,[26] but better authority is needed ere so precise a date can be without question accepted; it is enough to say that probably it is not far wrong. The ancient proverb already referred to, *viz.*, "Hir hun Faelgwn yn Llys Rhos" (the long sleep of Maelgwn in the court of Rhos), suggests that he died at Degannwy, but a more picturesque account says that, when the Yellow Plague was roaming through the land in the guise of a loathly monster, he took refuge from it in a church not far from his court. "And Maelgwn Gwynedd beheld the Yellow Plague through the keyhole in the church door and forthwith died." [27] As to what it looked like, authorities are not agreed; in the *Story of Taliesin*, it is described as a strange beast, with yellow eyes, teeth and hair; but in the life of St. Teilo contained in the *Liber Landavensis* [28] it is a column of vapour rising from earth to heaven and sweeping along the ground as a shower of rain sweeps along the low-lying valleys. Terror gave it many shapes, and it was none the less mysterious that it had laid low the mighty prince who feared no face of man.

Four other British princes are attacked by name in the *De Excidio*.[29] Constantine [30] is called "the tyrannical

[24] "Hanes Taliesin;" Iolo MSS. 73.

[25] Bury, *History of the Later Roman Empire*, i. p. 401. [26] *Cymr.* ix. 155.

[27] *Iolo MSS.* 78, where the church is said to be Eglwys Rhos. Other accounts (*Bruts*, 234; *Myv. Arch.* II. 359 (547); *ibid.* (597)) merely say it was near Degannwy. The "eglwys y brodyr" of Jesus Coll. MS. 19 (*Myv. Arch.* II. 359 (471)) is perhaps explained by the appropriation of Eglwys Rhos to the Cistercian abbey of Conway (after 1284, Maenan).

[28] *Lib. Land.* 107.

[29] For various views as to the five kings of Gildas see Usher, *Antiquitates* (1639), 536-47; *Celt. Br.* (2), pp. 122-5; *Nenn. V.* 306-7; *Gildas*, ed. Hugh Williams (1899), pp. 69-83. The four beasts (leo, pardus, ursus, draco) appear to be taken from the Apocalypse (xiii. 2), where the dragon is supreme.

[30] C. 28.

CHAP. V.

whelp of the unclean lioness of Damnonia," so that it is probable he bore rule in the Devonian peninsula. "Aurelius Caninus,"[31] left solitary by the death of all his kin, is not connected with any particular British region, but it is very likely that we have in him the degenerate offspring, elsewhere referred to by Gildas,[32] of the great Ambrosius Aurelius or Emrys Wledig, and in this case his kingdom must be looked for in the neighbourhood of the English settlements rather than in Wales. The two remaining kings may be confidently placed on Welsh soil. "Vortiporius"[33] is described as the tyrant of the Demetæ, or men of Dyfed, the bad son of a good father, a man who has grown grey in the devil's service and who shows no sign of repentance as he draws near his end. The pedigree of the royal line of Dyfed as recorded in the eighth century included a "Guortepir," who was the son of "Aircol," or Agricola, the Long-handed,[34] and it is remarkable that, while in the *Liber Landavensis* several gifts of land to St. Teilo are associated with Aircol Lawhir,[35] none such are credited to his son. Even more interesting is the fact that in 1895 the tombstone of the object of Gildas's invective was discovered in the heart of his kingdom of Dyfed.[36] It is a rude standing-stone or "maenhir," with an inscription in Latin capitals running across horizontally and another in ogam characters along one of the edges. In the former, which is headed by a wheel cross betokening that the dead man was a Christian, the legend runs "Memoria Voteporigis protictoris"; the latter has nothing but the name, in its Goidelic form, "Votecorigas". The stone has latterly stood in the grounds of Gwarmacwydd House, but it originally came from the churchyard of Castell Dwyran, which may have been a chapel attached to a manor of the rulers of Dyfed. It will be observed

[31] C. 30. "Canine" is the reading of the Cottonian MS. Yet the name may really have been "Cuna(g)nus" (Cynan), as suggested by the Avranches MS. (see p. 43 of Mommsen's *Gildas*), and the other form have been coined by the author as a grim joke at the expense of Aurelius. *Cf.* his treatment of the name of "Cuneglasus".

[32] C. 25 (end). [33] C. 31.

[34] Harl. MS. 3859 (*Cymr.* ix. 171); Jesus Coll. MS. 20 (*Cymr.* viii. 86); see also the Irish forms in *Cymr.* xiv. 112.

[35] *Lib. Land.* 125-30.

[36] For references see p. 115. There is a good illustration of the stone in *Social England*, vol. i. (1901), p. 173.

that the stone, in addition to giving this prince the title of "protector," bestowed by the Romans in the declining years of their Empire upon notable barbarian leaders and no doubt borne by Voteporix hereditarily, is at variance with Gildas as to the spelling of the name; in this matter its authority is more weighty than that of the man of letters, who may easily have been misled by the idea of an analogy with such forms as Vortigernus and the like.

"Cuneglasus"[37] was also, no doubt, one of the rulers of Wales, for the pedigrees[38] include a certain "Cinglas," in modern Welsh Cynlas, who was a son of Owain the White-toothed, son of Einion, son of Cunedda, and therefore belonged to the same generation as Maelgwn. There is nowhere any indication of the seat of his power, but the probabilities are in favour of some part of North Wales lying between Powys and the region directly ruled over by Maelgwn. The ancient vill of Cynlas[39] in Penllyn may commemorate his name; his brothers Engan and Seiriol founded churches in North-west Wales,[40] and the Caradog King of Gwynedd who died in 798 appears to have been his descendant.[41] For Cynlas, Gildas has a special hatred and contempt, explained, it may be, by the fact that this king alone of the five is accused of active hostility to the Church, being not only a contemner of God, but also an oppressor of His clergy.[42] His Celtic name is held up to scorn and parodied in Latin as "Grey Butcher". He has transgressed, not only after the fashion of his fellow-kings, by warring against his Christian neighbours and by violating the sanctity of the marriage tie, but also by direct attacks upon the "saints" (*i.e.*, monks), whose sighs and groans will one day recoil upon him to his undoing.

[37] C. 32.

[38] Harl. MS. 3859 (*Cymr.* ix. 172).

[39] Until lately a township of the parish of Llandderfel, Merionethshire, now in that of Llanfor in the same county.

[40] At Llanengan in Lleyn and Penmon in Anglesey (*Myv.* II. 23 (415)).

[41] *Cf.* the entry under the year 798 in Harl. MS. 3859 with pedigree No. iii. in the same MS. (*Cymr.* ix. 163, 172).

[42] "Dei contemptor *sortisque* eius depressor" (c. 32).

CHAP. V.

II. Gildas.

(The authorities mentioned in connection with Chapter IV. § iii. continue to be important for the sixth century, and to them must be added Mommsen's edition of *Gildas*, my obligations to which are very great. I have also used with profit Williams's edition of the same author. Other sources, such as Rees's *Welsh Saints*, are mentioned in the notes.)

It is now time to turn to the one figure of sixth-century Wales who, revealed by his writings, stands out clearly among the somewhat elusive shapes of that romantic age. Gildas did not (save as an author) greatly impress his British contemporaries, if one may judge from the neglect of his name and achievements by the voice of Welsh tradition,[43] but he has the advantage of men who in his own day far outshone him in renown in that his "little homily,"[44] as he modestly calls it, is the only literary effort of his age and country which has come down to us, and thus while Arthur, Dewi, Illtud, Dyfrig and, to a less degree, Maelgwn are but shadows, Gildas is a man of whom it may be said that we have seen his face and heard him speak.

Little, indeed, is known of him outside his own work. Two lives have been handed down which profess to tell his history,[45] but so widely do they differ from each other in the tale they unfold that many of the older school of critics imagined there must have been two men of the name, *viz.*, the author of the *De Excidio*, born in the early part of the sixth century, and a Gildas of the North, who belonged to an older generation and had dealings with the great Arthur.[46] It is now recognised that "Gildas Albanius," as portrayed in the life ascribed to Caradog of Llancarfan, is a figment of the monks of Glastonbury, who desired to connect so famous a Briton with the early history of their house and had a life written to order for the

[43] No Welsh church is dedicated to Gildas. His name occurs several times in the *Mabinogion* (107, 160, 258), but no legend is told of him. In the older "Bonedd y Saint" he appears only as the father of saints (*Myv. Arch.* II. 25 (416)).

[44] "Admonitiuncula" (c. 1).

[45] For an account of the lives, MSS. and editions of Gildas see note appended to this chapter.

[46] This view was adopted from Bale and Pits by Usher (*Antiquitates*, 1639, 441-2), and subsequently by Stevenson (Pref. to ed. of *Gildas*, vi.). Schoell (de ecclesiasticae Britonum Scotorumque historiae fontibus, Berlin, 1851) showed how baseless it was.

purpose.[47] Caradog's work (if it be really his)[48] contains some interesting Arthurian matter, put together before all stories about the British king were made to match the portrait painted by Geoffrey of Monmouth, but of the true history of Gildas it hardly preserves a trace. The other life, written by a monk of Rhuis in Southern Brittany, is far less open to suspicion; its historical setting is not, for the most part, inconsistent with what is known of Gildas, and it is from some such foundation as Rhuis, traditionally connected with his name, that genuine records of his life and work might be expected to make their appearance. Still, its evidence, as that of a late source, can only be received after careful scrutiny and by way of supplement to the knowledge afforded by the *De Excidio* itself.

Gildas[49] was a native of Britain. Though he nowhere expressly calls himself a Briton,[50] the whole spirit of his treatise is that of one who was addressing his fellow-countrymen. In his preface he apologises for the uncompromising severity of his tone; let no one think him a misanthropist or a self-righteous despiser of his kind; he has a true pity for the woes and misfortunes of the country and would rejoice to see them remedied.[51] He descants with genuine pleasure upon the natural beauties of Britain, where, to quote familiar lines,

> Every prospect pleases
> And only man is vile.[52]

He claims a share in the martyrs of Britain, "lamps of exceeding brightness set alight for us, lest Britain should be involved in the thick darkness of pitchy night".[53] According to the Rhuis life, he came from the fertile land of "Arecluta," which lay (as its name implies) along the river Clyde; this is a statement there is no ground for disputing, and "Arecluta," in

[47] Williams, *Gildas*, pp. 390-1.

[48] Some doubt is raised by expressions which suggest that the author was not a Welshman, *e.g.*, "balnea . . . quod diligebatur a *sua* gente maxime" (c. 3) and "Walenses indigenae" (c. 8).

[49] The name is not of Latin origin and is not otherwise known among the Brythonic peoples. It appears in the forms Gilda (*Mab.*), Gildus (Bede), Gillas (Tighernach) and Giltas (Columbanus). Possibly it is Goidelic; *cf. Mab.* 110, where mention is made of a "Gilla goes hyd" (Gilla with the shanks of a hart) who was the best jumper in Ireland.

[50] According to Mommsen (pp. 9-10), Gildas's "patria" (cc. 1, 2, 18, etc.) means no more than "provincia". "Mea patria" is certainly not found.

[51] C. 1. [52] C. 2. [53] C. 10.

CHAP. V.

later Welsh Arglud, has been very reasonably identified with the rich alluvial tract to the south of the Clyde between Greenock and Glasgow.[54] Thus Gildas was a North Briton, but when it is further stated that his father "Caunus" was king of this region, one is inclined to pause and remember how many of the saints of this age are alleged to have been of royal blood. Addicted as Gildas was to rhetorical depreciation of himself and his merits, he would scarcely, in addressing Maelgwn, have conceded that he was "of the meanest rank,"[55] had his birth been as good as that of the redoubtable lord of Gwynedd himself. Nor does his attitude towards the British chieftains who built up their power on the ruins of the Roman state, men whom he calls tyrants and kings not anointed of God,[56] favour the suggestion that he drew his own origin from this class.

He was born, on his own testimony, in the year of the battle of Badon Hill, *i.e.*, in or about A.D. 500.[57] Christianity had by this time firmly rooted itself in the valley of the Clyde, for Ceredig Wledig, who had ruled over this region some fifty years earlier, was a professed, if a somewhat rudimentary Christian. Gildas, it is to be noted, knows nothing of any survival of paganism among those whom he recognises as his fellow-countrymen: he has seen in the ruins of the deserted temples monstrous effigies of gods worshipped aforetime; he has heard that mountains, hills and rivers were once invoked as divine; but all this is ancient history, which he will not, he says, rake up against the men of Britain.[58] He was brought up, it is clear, in a purely Christian atmosphere.

No one will doubt that he received an excellent education. Chafe as we may at the endless intricacies and involutions of his style, insipid as we may find his sugared rhetoric, he was beyond question a master of the Latin language, and the gulf

[54] *IV. Anc. Bks.* i. pp. 173-4; *Cymr.* xi. 75. Ar*e*cluta, with the connecting vowel (*cf.* "Aremoricis gentibus" in Orosius, *Adv. Pag.* vi. 11), must come from an almost contemporary source. The district is still known for its heavy crops of wheat.

[55] "Licet vilissimae qualitatis simus" (c. 36).

[56] "Ungebantur reges non per deum, sed qui ceteris crudeliores exstarent" (c. 21).

[57] See p. 125 and note 9.

[58] C. 4. The argument at the end of c. 38 implies that the men attacked by Gildas were not open to the charge of idolatry.

which separates him, as a writer of Latin, from later British historians such as "Nennius" is immense. He commands a wide vocabulary, is entirely at home in Latin syntax, and is familiar with the Latin poets, notably Vergil.[59] Of the Scriptures he had made an exhaustive study, and every reader of the *De Excidio* remembers how large a part of that work is made up of quotations, carefully marshalled, from holy writ. The school in which Gildas acquired this knowledge was, according to the Rhuis life, that of "Hildutus," the St. Illtud of Welsh tradition, under whose care, it is said, were many lads of good family, receiving a training not only in divine but also in secular learning.[60] Something will be said in a later section of the work and influence of Illtud; here it is enough to note that Gildas received an education which linked him closely with the past, and that, while in effect one of the pioneers of a new era, he drew his inspiration from the waning civilisation of Rome and by temper and disposition was always of the old order and not of the new. The literary culture of Rome, ere it faded from Britain, cast over the young Gildas a spell which bound him firmly to the end.

It was, no doubt, in the school of Illtud that he came under another spell, that of monasticism. He became not only a cleric, but also a monk,[61] full of pride in his order and of confidence in it as the sole salvation of the world. The monks are in his pages the true "saints" of God;[62] their convents are cool caverns and safe hiding-places where the good may find shelter from the attacks of the Evil One. As yet, the monastic element in the British Church is not in the ascendant; the men whom Gildas singles out for praise are "very few,"[63] a minority in the Church, whom he leaves out of account, save for one or two apologetic allusions,[64] in his comprehensive indictment of the British nation. The Church is not governed by monks; one reference there is to an abbot,[65] but the ecclesiastics who fill

[59] Pref. to Mommsen's ed., p. 6.

[60] Ed. Mommsen, p. 92.

[61] "Clericorum in nostro quoque ordine" (c. 65) is so interpreted by Williams (p. 160).

[62] See cc. 28 (sanctorum choris), 34 (sanctorum speluncas).

[63] "Paucis et valde paucis" (c. 26). *Cf.* "paucissimos bonos pastores" of c. 110.

[64] See c. 65 (ab his veniam impertiri, etc.).

[65] "Sub sancti abbatis amphibalo" (c. 28).

CHAP. V.

the scene are bishops and priests, whose power arises out of their office and has nothing monastic about it. Thus the party to which Gildas attached himself, though it threw its subtle charm for a time over the great Maelgwn, was not the dominant one in the island, and it was from no vantage-ground, save that of sincerity and zeal, that he hurled at his contemporaries the ringing challenge of the *De Excidio.*

The work had been long in preparation when at the age of forty-three he gave it to the world. Ten years had gone by from the time when its design had first taken shape in his mind and still he shrank from its publication, until at last he was overcome by the entreaties of his brother-monks and a sense of what was due from him as a witness for God's truth. He had not the official standing of a bishop [66] or the authority of a teacher of wide renown; [67] Britain, he pleads, has its recognised watchmen and rulers, and it scarce becomes the mere hand and foot, the humble instruments, to usurp the office of the warning lips and the vigilant eye. But the need of a clear testimony was too great to allow of any further postponement; that very year [68] deeds had been done which must be exposed in their true villainy; and thus, as Gildas puts it, the long-standing debt was finally paid.[69]

No hint is given in the *De Excidio* as to the place of its composition. The view that Gildas was at the time in Brittany and launched it across the Channel [70] rests on no better authority than the Rhuis life,[71] where it was almost inevitable that such a statement should be found, and it is rendered very unlikely by the use of the word "transmarine" to describe the continental sources used by the author in default of native authorities.[72] If the work, as seems most probable, was written in Britain, it surely made its appearance in a British state of which the ruler had not the honour to figure in its pages, for it can scarcely be believed that, as Zimmer has suggested,[73]

[66] The *Annals of Inisfallen* seem to style Gildas "episcopus," but in the Stowe Missal he appears, with St. Columba, among the "sacerdotes" and not the "episcopi" (Warren, *Liturgy and Ritual of the Celtic Church*, p. 240), and this is doubtless the sounder tradition.

[67] He says he is not "conspicuo ac summo doctori" (c. 1).

[68] "Hoc anno" (c. 28).

[69] C. 1.

[70] *Mon. Hist. Br.*, pref., 60, note 2.

[71] Ed. Mommsen, p. 97.

[72] "Transmarina relatione" (c. 4, end).

[73] *Nenn. V.* 308.

it was composed by Gildas in some monastery in the heart of that south-western corner of the island of which the great men are all held up to public reprobation. It has been pointed out that, so far as can be seen, not one of the five kings pilloried by Gildas belongs to the British country which at that time stretched from Chester to Dumbarton, a country on which the English invader had as yet made little impression.[74] May not his work have been written here, under the protection of a king who, while too bad for a formal blessing, was too good for cursing in the heroic vein which was thought necessary to meet the case of the hardened sinners of the South?

It was no part of the purpose of Gildas to write a history of Britain. His aim is that of the preacher and reformer, and the whole of his treatise, which he occasionally styles a "letter,"[75] is meant, in its narrative no less than its admonitory portions, to subserve the one moral end. If a good deal of history is introduced, this is because history, as handled by Gildas, has its lessons to teach. He is a disciple of Paulus Orosius, the Spanish presbyter who rather more than a century before had set the fashion of writing history with a homiletic purpose, and, like Orosius, he has for his theme "the lusts and the retributions of sinful men, the conflicts of the world and the judgments of God".[76] He would have it understood that the miseries of Britain in bygone days, miseries which he paints in the darkest colours, were the direct result of the wickedness and perversity of the natives of the island, and that, though a season of prosperity and peace has now succeeded, continuance in evil-doing will bring back the old calamities. Thus Gildas is of the order of prophets and not of historians, and what he says must be viewed in relation to the ethical purpose which constantly swayed him.

In one respect he was ill fitted to do justice to the new world which was being formed around him. It was a world in which the barbarian, the Celtic element, was daily growing more powerful, and Gildas was Roman to the finger-tips. His favourite name for his fellow-countrymen is "cives," citizens;[77]

[74] *Nenn. V.* 308.

[75] See cc. 1 (in hac epistola), 93 (huic epistolae). In c. 37 the Cottonian MS. has "flebilis haec querulaque malorum huius aevi *historia*"

[76] *Adv. Pag.* vii. 43.

[77] See cc. 4, 19, 26, 28, 32.

with them he contrasts the nations round about, the Saxon foe, the fierce hordes of Picts and Scots, shaggy-haired and of indecent nakedness,[78] barbarians, in short, with whom he recognises no bond of union. The Latin language is his tongue;[79] for Celtic names he has nothing but contempt. Throughout the story of Rome's dealings with the island—a story often grotesquely remote from the real facts—the men of Rome are the powerful lords and protectors, the men of Britain cowardly slaves who rebel when their masters' backs are turned, but who cannot stand in their own strength. No one is praised by name after the departure of the Romans save Ambrosius Aurelianus (Emrys Wledig), sole survivor in the catastrophes of the fifth century of the Roman and imperial race.[80]

Gildas cannot have had many who sympathised with him in this attitude and, as an upholder of legitimism against the ever-thickening growth of British chieftaincies, must have been indeed a voice crying in the wilderness. Was he isolated, too, in his onslaught upon the lives of the men who ruled at this time in Church and State? That there were men of influence who did not share his passionate conviction that Britain was rushing headlong to ruin seems open to no doubt. He blames such for their indifference to the immorality of the age, though he has no charge to make against them personally.[81] There are false prophets abroad, he intimates, doctors filled with a spirit of contrariness, whose words are smoother than butter and who cry "Peace, peace!" when there is no peace.[82] They were opportunists and friends of compromise, who condoned the vices of monarchs and gladly accepted their gifts to the Church—gifts which, in the opinion of Gildas, were no substitute for repentance and reform.[83] The British Church was by this time a well-developed organisation. Its bishops and priests were numerous; their offices were valuable and worth taking much trouble to secure.[84] In such a society there would be many, even among the reputable and diligent members, who would place loyalty to the institution before fidelity to a lofty

[78] C. 19.

[79] "Tribus, ut lingua eius exprimitur, cyulis, *nostra* longis navibus" (c. 23). The Avranches MS. reads "Latina," which is, no doubt, the right interpretation, for, if Gildas had meant to use the Brythonic loan-word "longa" (Welsh "llong"), he would not have added "navibus".

[80] C. 25. [81] Cc. 69, 110. [82] C. 40. [83] C. 42. [84] Cc. 66, 67.

and perhaps unattainable standard; Gildas the iconoclast would be in their eyes a dangerous fanatic and they would do their utmost to counteract his influence.

But it is not at all likely that they succeeded. The evils against which he so strenuously inveighed were real evils, the natural result of a long period of wealth and abundance in the history of a little community cut off from the rest of Europe. As to the crimes so definitely laid to the charge of the five princes there could, at any rate, be no doubt, and there is every reason to suppose that the earnest and fiery eloquence of the *De Excidio* did arouse an echo in many hearts. This may be inferred from the esteem in which "Gildas the Wise"[85] was held by later generations and from the remarkable progress of monasticism in the second half of the sixth century. He was, in fact, justified by the event. He foretold calamities as the inevitable issue of the licence and presumption of his age, and two calamities of the first magnitude ere long befell the British race—the yellow plague, spreading terror and ruin as it went, and the renewal of barbarian aggression, putting an end to the long truce between Briton and Saxon and reopening the conflict for the mastery of the island. Though the evidence for the progress of this conflict comes chiefly from traditional sources and is, therefore, a somewhat uncertain guide, it seems possible to trace, in the Saxon Chronicle, for instance, the rise of a forward movement on the part of the English about the year 550[86] which would afford a vivid contrast to the "present security" described by Gildas, and, coupled with the devastations of a great pestilence, would not fail to turn men's minds to thoughts of repentance and atonement. In the general humiliation Gildas would be recognised as a true seer, and the party to which he was attached, the monastic and ascetic one, would gain the upper hand in the British Church.

If it may be assumed that the *De Excidio* was written not long after 540, Gildas lived for a quarter of a century afterwards to wield great influence in the Celtic Church. The date of his death cannot be precisely given, but it was not far from

[85] The title "Sapiens" is given to Gildas by *Ann.* C. MS. C., the Cambridge MS. Ff. i. 27, and the Book of Leinster (Stokes, *Tripartite Life of St. Patrick*, p. 514).

[86] *Mak. Eng.* pp. 91-2.

CHAP. V.

the year 570.[87] He spent this closing period of his life, it would seem, in organising and directing the powerful monastic movement which had now laid hold upon the Celtic communities. In Wales and Cornwall, it is true, there is little evidence of influence directly exercised by him ; the offence given by his attacks upon the monarchs of those regions was not so easily forgotten. But elsewhere, his authority was high. In the North, his account of the English settlement was used in the next century by the author of the *Saxon Genealogies* and in the eighth by the Venerable Bede. Both lives, discordant though they are in most other respects, agree that he undertook a mission tour to Ireland, which the Rhuis life connects with the reign of Ainmire mac Setna, king of Erin about 568.[88] Here monasticism had already found a congenial soil ; Clonmacnois had been founded by St. Ciaran, Clonard by the elder Finnian, and Clonfert by the elder Brendan. But the advent of so notable a champion of the " perfect way " must have been a source of much encouragement to those of the same school of thought, and it is this, no doubt, which lies behind the somewhat mysterious statement made in an eighth-century Irish tract that the second order of Irish "saints," belonging to the latter half of the sixth century, received their ritual from Bishop David and Gildas and a third Briton.[89] That Gildas was held in high esteem in his lifetime among the monks of Ireland is made certain by the fact, recorded by Columbanus before the sixth century was out, that "Vennianus," probably Finnian of Moville, consulted the famous author as to the treatment of those inmates of monasteries who left their abbots without permission to take up the life of the anchorite.[90] Gildas, it is said, replied in a very charming letter, and some of the fragments bearing his name which have been preserved in Irish collections refer, in fact, to this very subject. These fragments show, not only how the words of the British reformer were valued, but also that, like many another reformer, he spent the evening of his days in checking and keeping with-

[87] This is the date implied in the entry in Harl. MS. 3859 (*Cymr.* ix. 155). *Cf.* the *Annals of Tighernach* (*Rev. Celt.* xvii. (1896), p. 149), *Ann. Ult. s.a.* 569 (repeated *s.a.* 576), *Ann. Inisf. s.a.* 570.

[88] Ed. Mommsen, p. 94.

[89] H. and St. ii. pt. 2, 293.

[90] *Gildas*, ed. Mommsen, p. 21 ; ed. Williams, pp. 256-7, 415.

in bounds the tendency and spirit which he had done so much to rouse by the eloquent outpourings of his youth. He has to deal, no longer with sloth and indifference, but with misplaced energy and misguided zeal.[91]

There need be no hesitation about accepting the statement of the Rhuis life that he died in Brittany. It is confirmed by the existence of monasteries at Rhuis and elsewhere claiming him as their founder and patron,[92] by the occurrence of his name in an early Breton litany,[93] and by the Breton origin of one of the two old MSS. of the *De Excidio.*[94] Thus Gildas ended his days in a species of exile, dwelling among the descendants of those harassed Britons whom he had described as seeking homes across the sea with loud lamentations, and chanting beneath the bellying sails their piteous refrain: "Thou hast given us as sheep appointed for meat and hast scattered us among the heathen". With some reason might he have anticipated another champion of righteousness in the well-known words: "I have loved the law of God and hated iniquity; therefore I die in exile".

III. Monastic Founders of the Welsh Church.

Gildas does not mention the name of a single ecclesiastic of his own time, and even leaves in obscurity the "very few" whom alone he regards as true sons of the Church. It is necessary, therefore, to turn to other sources in order to learn who were in this century the leading figures in the British Church, and this later evidence, dealing as it does with men who have been for ages the theme of religious legend, has to be used with great circumspection.

In the early part of the century the figure of Illtud[95] seems

[91] For the fragments of Gildas see H. and St. i. 108-12; Mommsen, pp. 12, 86-8; Williams, pp. 255-71.

[92] A cape at the mouth of the Loire is known by his name.

[93] H. and St. ii. pt. 1, 82.

[94] The Avranches MS. formerly belonged to the abbey of Mont St. Michel (Mommsen, p. 14).

[95] The life of Illtud printed in *Cambro-Br. SS.* 158-82 (from Cott. MS. Vesp. A. xiv.), though put together about 1100, at Llanilltud Fawr itself, is not consistent with the old authorities, making the saint die, for instance, at Dol in Brittany. Possibly, as Prof. Hugh Williams has suggested (*Cymr. Trans.* 1893-4, 110), two men of the same name have been confused, the one an Armorican, the other a denizen of Greater Britain.

CHAP. V.

to stand out with some distinctness. The earliest extant life of a British saint, that of Samson of Dol, which belongs in all probability to the seventh century,[96] represents "Eltutus"[97] as the head of a great monastery, which was also a school of the highest reputation, for the abbot was "of all the Britons best skilled in Holy Scripture, both the Old Testament and the New, as well as in every kind of learning, such as geometry, rhetoric, grammar, arithmetic and the knowledge of all arts; in divination, too, he was well proven and he had foreknowledge of the future". To this school young Samson was sent that he might be trained for a position in the Church; according to later accounts, he had as fellow-pupils Gildas, Paul Aurelian, and even Dewi, though the evidence for the last of these three names is not convincing.[98] The situation of Illtud's monastery is not indicated (though the writer of Samson's life had been there in quest of material),[99] but it seems certain it was in South Wales, and no site has better claims than Llanilltud Fawr, the Lantwit Major of to-day.[100] Wherever it stood, the school seems to have wielded

[96] Printed by Mabillon in *Acta sanctorum ordinis S. Benedicti*, i. 165 (Paris. 1668) and by Sollerius (to whose text my references are made) in the great *Acta Sanctorum*, July (28), vi. 573-91 (Venice. 1749). The internal evidence points unmistakably to a date in the century following Samson's death (*Cymr.* xi. 127; *Liverpool W. Nat. Trans.* 1896-7, 100), which is also suggested by such a form as "Tigerinomale," occurring in the dedication, pp. 573*a*, 587*b*. All the other lives are, as Sollerius says, derived from this, and I cannot except that printed by Plaine, from Andeg. MS. 719, in *Analecta Bollandiana*, vi. (1887), 77-150, which appears to me in many passages to introduce confusion into the Bollandist text. The reference to Germanus (d. 448) as Illtud's teacher (p. 575*b*) I regard as an early interpolation; it raises insurmountable difficulties of chronology.

[97] P. 575*b*. "Eltutus" yields the Elltud of Llanelltud, Merionethshire. The Illtud of the South seems to have been a Goidelic form (*Urk. Spr.* 41).

[98] Life of Paul Aurelian (founder of S. Pol de Léon in Brittany), as printed by Plaine in *Analecta Bollandiana*, i. (1882), 209-58 and Cuissard in *Rev. Celt.* v. pp. 417-58; Rhuis life of Gildas. The former bears date 884. For Dewi, see below.

[99] "In cujus magnifico monasterio ego fui" (575*b*).

[100] The later writers have confused two places which the author of the life of Samson keeps quite distinct, *viz.*, the "monasterium" of Illtud and the "insula" (also a monastery; *cf. Cymr. Trans.* 1893-4, 113), founded "non longe ab hoc monasterio" by the priest-monk Piro (578*b*). The latter may well have been Caldy Island (the "Enis Pir" of Gir. Camb. vi. 92 (*Itin.* i. 12)), where remains have been found of an early settlement of the kind (*Lap. W.* 106-8; *Arch. Camb.* V. xiii. (1896), 98-103); the former might be Llanilltud Fawr, if "non longe" were taken loosely as a traveller's casual estimate. In the life of Paul, Illtud's school is represented as being at the place "quem nunc Iltuti monasterium

great influence upon British society. It trained not only Gildas, but, as has been indicated above, other young men of energy and ability who took up the monastic idea; nay, even Maelgwn Gwynedd himself, according to a likely interpretation of a passage in the *De Excidio*,[101] was one of Illtud's pupils, a fact which would help to explain his brief divergence into the life of the cloister. This was, in fact, the permanent part of the great abbot's work; he gave new life and vigour to monasticism, but he founded no British school of learning. Tales of his austere seclusion at Oystermouth[102] and at Llanamwlch[103] were reverently heard by later generations, but his fame as a scholar almost entirely perished. He spent his whole life in Britain and probably died about 540.[104]

Of the men of the next generation, the contemporaries of Gildas, none has so well attested a history as Samson.[105] He was not of royal birth, though later ages connected him with Uthr Bendragon and Emyr Llydaw,[106] but belonged to the class which stood next in order, the royal courtiers and servants whose pride and boast it was to be the foster fathers of kings.[107] His father, Ammon, was a man of Dyfed (Demetiana patria), his mother, Anna, came from another South Welsh district, *viz.*, Gwent (de Ventia). It was not at first intended to make him a cleric, for his father held the order in no little contempt,[108] but the mother's influence was used on the side of the Church and at the age of five Samson entered the school of Illtud. Here he made great progress in

dicunt" and *also* on an island "Pyrus nomine Demetarum patriae in finibus sita". The Rhuis life of Gildas does not mention Piro, but he says that Illtud and his flock dwelt in a barren island, "quae insula usque in hodiernum diem Lanna Hilduti vocitatur" (ed. Mommsen, p. 93).

101 "Habueris praeceptorem paene totius Britanniae magistrum elegantem" (c. 36.) See *Cymr. Trans.* 1893-4, 109.

102 Nennius, c. 71 (Mirabilia). For the identification with Oystermouth see *Arch. Camb.* IV. xi. (1880), 155.

103 Gir. Camb. vi. 28 (*Itin.* i. 2); *Breconsh.* (2), 452.

104 For the Illtud dedications, which are chiefly in Glamorganshire, and for modern accretions to his legend, see *Welsh SS.* pp. 178-81.

105 For the Bollandist and other lives see note 96.

106 *Iolo MSS.* 107, 111, 132. The "annun du" (= Antonius the Black) of *Myv. Arch.* II. 24 (415) was probably a different person from Samson's father.

107 "Altrices regum" (574*a*). For the custom see *LL.* i. 788; Gir. Camb. vi. 211, 225 (*Descr.* ii. 4, 9); *Bruts*, 279.

108 "Utpote qui semper minister terreni regis fuisset" (575*a*).

CHAP. V.

learning, was ordained deacon and afterwards priest by Bishop Dubricius, and seemed to be marked out by his ability and sanctity as Illtud's successor. But Illtud had a nephew, advanced to the priesthood, who looked upon the abbacy as family property and his lawful inheritance, and with the aid of his brother, who was at the time cook, sought to rid himself of his rival by means of poison. The attempt failed, but it convinced Samson that the monastery could no longer be his home. He therefore transferred himself to the abbey of Piro, where by the favour of Dubricius he became, first, cook or steward (pistor) and then, on the death of Piro, abbot. During his tenure of the latter office he visited Ireland, having been persuaded to undertake the journey by certain Irish scholars of distinction who were passing through the country on their way back from a pilgrimage to Rome.[109] A true son of his age, Samson found his hunger for the things of the spirit only partially satisfied by life in a monastic community; after ruling the house for a year and a half, he resolved to quit it for the solitude of a hermitage. Taking with him three companions, he finds a spot to his mind on the banks of the Severn; the three live in a deserted fort, where they build a church to which Samson resorts on Sundays, but he himself withdraws to a cave in the trackless forest and his hiding-place is long unknown. He is, however, discovered and against his will made abbot of one of the famous houses of Britain. The day comes round when the bishops of Britain annually meet in synod to raise, according to their custom, three of their clergy to the episcopal dignity. Two candidates are in readiness, but who the third is to be remains uncertain, until Dubricius designates Samson for the honour. It is now revealed to the new bishop that he must become "peregrinus," must leave his native country and spend the rest of his life in service across the seas. With the journey through Cornwall and the voyage to Brittany, Samson's career in Britain closes; on the other side of the channel he appears as the founder of Dol and other monasteries and the successful champion of one Breton count against another. The life brings him into association with Childebert, king of Paris from 511

[109] "Quidam peritissimi Scoti de Roma venientes" (582*a*). That they had acquired their learning (didicisse) in Rome is an embellishment of the later writer (*Anal. Boll.* vi. 101).

to 558, and, in harmony with this, he is found signing, as "Samson peccator episcopus," the decrees of the council held at Paris in 555 or 557.[110] CHAP. V.

A prominent part was played in the early history of Samson by Dubricius. He moves mysteriously, indeed, across the stage, appearing with the authority of a bishop or overseer in various South Welsh monasteries, but with no hint furnished of the place from which or the sphere within which he exercised his sway. Yet he is clearly a genuine sixth-century ecclesiastic and may not be dismissed as one of the many unsubstantial shapes which were drawn into the vortex of the great Arthurian legend. He is in that company by the deliberate design of Geoffrey of Monmouth, who also invented for him his archbishopric of Caerleon on Usk, so that there might be a fitting dignitary to preside over the crowning of the puissant king.[111] The purely native tradition knows nothing of Dyfrig in this connection; the tales it has to tell are of his marvellous birth, of the fame of his school at "Henllan on the Wye," moved after seven years to "Mochros" in the same region, and of his retreat at the end of his life as an anchorite to that favourite haunt of British saints and goal of British pilgrims, Bardsey Island.[112] An attempt was made in the twelfth century to connect Dubricius with the see of Llandaff; his relics were translated from Bardsey in May, 1120, by Bishop Urban, and installed with much ceremony in the South Welsh cathedral.[113] But the chief churches dedicated to him[114] are to be found

[110] H. and St. ii. 75. There are no Welsh dedications to Samson, but he is commemorated in Cornwall (Southill), Guernsey and the Scilly Isles. His archbishopric of York is due to Geoffrey of Monmouth (*Hist. Reg.* viii. 12); in the pages of Giraldus Cambrensis, also, he plays an impossible part (H. and St. i. 149).

[111] *Hist. Reg.* viii. 12; ix. 1, 4, 12, 13, 15. The mention in ix. 12 of the "trium metropolitanarum sedium archipraesules, Londiniensis videlicet, Eboracensis, necnon ex urbe Legionum Dubricius" suggests that Geoffrey had seen somewhere the names of the British bishops present at the Council of Arles (H. and St. i. 7) and anticipated the conjecture of Stillingfleet (*Origines Britannicæ*, ed. Pantin, 1842, i. p. 115).

[112] Life in *Lib. Land.* 78-84. The life by Benedict, a monk of St. Peter's, Gloucester (printed in *Anglia Sacra*, ii. 654-61), is later and adopts the fables of Geoffrey.

[113] *Lib. Land.* 84-6.

[114] Llanfrother (now extinct), with its chapels of Hentland and Ballingham; Whitchurch by Monmouth.

CHAP. V.

within the limits of Archenfield in Herefordshire, the Welsh Erging, making it likely that this, rather than any other district in South Wales, was the special scene of his activity. What is certainly known of Dyfrig is that he was a bishop who used his influence on behalf of monasticism, and must therefore have been, in sympathy and aims, of the party of Gildas.[115]

Leaving the little group of men associated with the career of Samson, the student finds himself with scarcely any sure guide to the history of the great mass of Welsh "saints," [116] the founders in the sixth and seventh centuries of the principal parish churches of Wales. As to nearly all of them, it may be said that nothing has been handed down by tradition save their parentage, the names of the churches dedicated to their memory and presumed to have been founded by them, and the dates of their festivals, the feast day marking in each case the anniversary of the saint's happy translation to a better world.[117] Thus, to take an instance, Tydecho is said to have been the son of Anhun Ddu, son of Emyr of Brittany, to have founded the churches of Llanymawddwy (with its chapels of Mallwyd and Garthbeibio) and Cemais and to be commemorated on December 17th.[118] There is no reason why particulars of this kind should

[115] The obit given in Harl. MS. 3859, which is equivalent to A.D. 612 (*Cymr.* ix. 156), is pretty certainly fifty or sixty years too late.

[116] Of the "saints" of Wales, St. David is the only one canonised (about 1120) by the Roman Church. The term was used by the Celtic Church in the sense of Gildas (see note 62 above), *i.e.*, monk.

[117] The oldest form of "Bonedd y Saint" (Genealogies of the Saints) is that printed (from a Hafod MS.) in *Myv. Arch.* II. 23-5 (415-6). This is found in various MSS. of the thirteenth and fourteenth centuries, such as Peniarth MSS. 16 and 45 (Evans, *Rep.* i. pp. 339, 379). The documents printed in *Iolo MSS.* 100-153 are greatly inferior in value, having been compiled at a much later period by ignorant and reckless antiquaries (see the criticisms of Phillimore in *Bye-Gones*, 1890, pp. 448-9, 482-5, 532-6). In his *Essay on the Welsh Saints* (London, 1836), Rice Rees makes the fullest use of the material supplied by the "Bonedd" MSS., the dedications and the feast days of Welsh churches and similar data, and though the conclusions adopted (*e.g.*, as to the archbishopric of Caerleon, p. 173) will in many cases not stand the test of modern criticism, the book still remains most useful for purposes of reference. The ground is now being worked afresh in the admirably full and judicious *Lives of the British Saints* (S. Baring-Gould and J. Fisher), of which two volumes (A-E) have been issued.

[118] *Myv. Arch.* II. 24 (415); *Welsh SS.* 218. There was a legend or life of St. Tydecho, now lost, which brought him into conflict with Maelgwn Gwynedd; it is only known from a metrical version of it by Dafydd Llwyd of Mathafarn (fl. 1480), printed in *Camb. Reg.* ii. 375-7.

not be in the main authentic, for it is certain that they were kept on record from a very early period. "Many times," says the author of the life of Samson, "have I heard read at St. Samson's altar, when mass was sung, the names of both his parents."[119] The founding of monasteries and churches appears in the same life as an ordinary incident in the career of a monastic devotee,[120] and it would seem extremely probable that the memory of the "saint" who set apart the site of a monastery for religious uses, perhaps after a severe course of fasting such as is described by Bede,[121] would be carefully preserved on the spot. Thus a form like "Llandysilio" would be explained as "Tysilio's monastery,"[122] and its extension over the whole of Wales would create no difficulty, when it was borne in mind that the sixth-century "saint" was habitually a migrant, regarding the call to pilgrimage and travel in distant lands as a high spiritual distinction. The solemn observance of the day of a holy man's death, also, was a custom inherited by the Celtic Church from primitive times,[123] and there is every reason to think that the dates connected with the names of the patron saints of Welsh churches are, for the most part, genuine anniversaries.

But, though these brief notices are no doubt trustworthy in the main, they are embodied in documents so recent that it is not safe to use them for the purpose of detailed historical reconstruction. Many errors there must be, the result of a careless transcription, of confusion between persons of the same or of similar names, of attempts to give a favourite saint a little added height and dignity. As long as means do not exist of

[119] P. 574*a*.

[120] "Confirmatis itaque in bonis operibus his omnibus atque ad monasteria fundanda suggestis" (580*b*); Samson's mother expresses the hope that very soon he will be able, as bishop, to consecrate "monasteria quae nobis suggeris fundanda et ecclesias construendas".

[121] *H.E.* iii. 23.

[122] The original meaning of "llan" (Celtic "landa") is an open space or cleared enclosure, as in "gwinllan," "ydlan" (*Urk. Spr.* 239). It acquired in British speech the specialised sense of "monastery" (*Life of Gildas*, ed. Mommsen, c. 27; *Life of S. Pol de Léon*, *Rev. Celt.* v. p. 440), and, in Wales, owing to the prevalence of churches founded by monks, came at last to mean "church" simply.

[123] The custom is referred to in the early life of Samson, "magnifica illa ac sancta annualis solennitas . . . imminet" (587*b*-588*a*); indeed from this point the life is really a saint's day homily. *Cf.* Adamnan's *Life of St. Columba*, ii. 45.

CHAP. V.

tracking these errors, it is best to regard this whole group of facts as bearing abundant witness to the vigour and activity of the British monastic movement of the age of Gildas, and not to seek to erect upon it any more elaborate historical superstructure.

It might have been expected that the history of some at least of these notable pioneers of the faith would have been illustrated by the inscriptions of the period, which is fruitful in monuments of the kind and these of a distinctively Christian order. But, in point of fact, only a few fitful gleams of light are to be derived from that quarter. In one case only has time unearthed what would seem to be the original tombstone of a founder in the spot which still bears his name. The stone which records the burial of "beatus Saturninus" and "sua sa(ncta) coniux," who had no doubt also embraced the monastic life, was found in Llansadwrn churchyard, not far from Beaumaris, in the early part of the eighteenth century,[124] and, as it is certainly not later than 550, may be taken to belong to the "Sadwrn" to whom the foundation of the church is ascribed.[125] In another case, the saint's tombstone came to light some miles away from the church which bears his name, but this need cause no difficulty, even if it were certain that the stone was in its original position. The "Vendesetli" of this Llannor inscription undoubtedly represents the form which Gwynhoedl would assume in the fifth and sixth centuries, and there is no difficulty in supposing it to have been meant to commemorate the founder of Llangwynodl, an ancient church in the same region of Lleyn.[126] In like manner, it may be presumed that the stone found at Tyddyn Holland, near Llandudno, which is now read "Sanctanus sacerdus," marked the grave of Sannan, the founder of Llansannan in Denbighshire.[127] It remains to

[124] *Inscr. Chr.* No. 153; *Lap. W.* 188; *W. Phil.* (2), 363; *Arch. Camb.* V. xiii. (1896), 139.

[125] Rhys calls attention (*Cymr.* xviii. 32-3) to the difference between Sadwrn (Saturnus) and Sadyrnin (Saturninus). But, according to Carlisle, *Top. Dict.*, the annual fair of Llansadwrn, Carmarthenshire, was held on the same day (Oct. 5) as that of Llansadyrnin, which suggests that the two names were used interchangeably. The longer was perhaps an affectionate diminutive.

[126] *Inscr. Chr.* No. 139; *Lap. W.* 180; *W. Phil.* (2), 366-7; *Arch. Camb.* I. ii. (1847), 201-3; IV. viii. (1877), 141-4; *Urk. Spr.* 265.

[127] *Lap. W.* 182; *W. Phil.* (2), 370-2; *Arch. Camb.* V. xiii. (1896), 138; xiv. (1897), 140-2. Rees (*Welsh SS.* 240) confounds Sannan, whose day was

mention the case of Paulinus, which is by no means so clear. In the life of St. David by Rhygyfarch it is said that the saint received instruction for many years from "Paulinus scriba," who led a holy life in a certain unnamed "insula" and had around him many disciples.[128] Paulinus, in short, was head of a monastic school of the same type as Illtud's. No hint, however, is given as to where it stood. That it was situated at Whitland or "Y Ty gwyn ar Daf" (The White House on the Taf) in Dyfed is pure conjecture, resting on no ancient authority;[129] the foundations associated with the name of Paulinus are Llangors church in Breconshire[130] and the chapel of Ystradffin, anciently known as "Capel Peulin," on the borders of Cardiganshire and Carmarthenshire.[131] If regard be now had to the early inscriptions bearing the name, they will be found to be three. One on a stone now in Margam church is the epitaph of "Cantusus," set up (so the legend is construed) by his father "Paulinus";[132] another at Llandysilio in Dyfed marks the resting-place of "Clotorigi" (Clodri) son of "Paulini";[133] the third, found at Maes Llanwrthwl and now kept at Dolau Cothi, Carmarthenshire, is more elaborate and may be thus rendered—"Keeper of the faith and constant lover of his country, Paulinus lies here: he was a most devoted follower of the right".[134] It is possible that this last inscription, with its

13th June (see Mostyn MS. 88) and who was connected with St. Winifred (Penn. ii. 179), with S. Senan of Scattery Island, Clare, who was commemorated on 8th March.

[128] *Cambro-Br. SS.* 122. See also p. 137; *Lib. Land.* 99.

[129] Whitland is a township in the parish of Llangan and, until the foundation of the Cistercian abbey, had no ecclesiastical associations.

[130] See *Arch. Camb.* IV. xiv. (1883), 44-5, 144, 146, 153, 154, for twelfth-century references to Llangors as the church of St. Paulinus.

[131] It is "Capel Pylyn" in Speed's map of Carmarthenshire, and is reasonably identified by Rees (*Welsh SS.* 187) with the chapel of St. Paulinus mentioned as subject to the abbey church in a Strata Florida document of 1339 (*Str. Flor.* App. li.).

[132] *Inscr. Chr.* No. 77; *Lap. W.* 38-9; *Arch. Camb.* V. xvi. (1899), 145-6. The stone was formerly at Port Talbot and was a Roman milestone before it was converted into a gravestone.

[133] *Inscr. Chr.* No. 97; *Lap. W.* 111-2; *W. Phil.* (2), 397-8. In *Celtic Folklore*, p. 535, Rhys seeks to connect the "marinilatio" of this stone with the church of Paulinus at Llangors.

[134] Gibson, 624; *Inscr. Chr.* No. 82; *Lap. W.* 79-81; *W. Phil.* (2), 392. When first described by Llwyd, the stone was a footbridge at "Pant y Polion," which is, I am informed still the name of a field on Bron Deilo farm, opposite Maes' Llanwrthwl.

CHAP. V.

emphatic terms of praise, may record the virtues of the Paulinus of tradition, but, in view of the fact that the name was in common use at this period, even this must not be regarded as certain, and, in general, it may be said that the history of this "saint" cannot be eked out by means of the "Paulinus" inscriptions.

In the case of the more famous of the Welsh "saints," further evidence is available in the shape of regular lives, recording for the edification of the faithful the great deeds and marvellous experiences of men who appear in a variety of trying situations as the constant favourites of Heaven. Lives of this kind no doubt contain in most cases a substantial nucleus of truth and may be used, if due caution be exercised, for historical purposes. But, as they are in their very nature panegyrics of particular saints, in which everything is subordinated to the enhancement of the hero's glory, the element of exaggeration (not to speak of the avowedly miraculous) is from the beginning not absent and it grows more and more pronounced as the story is told and retold in successive ages. Hence it is much against the lives of the great monastic founders of Wales—Dewi, Padarn, Teilo, Cadog, Illtud and Cybi—that not one of them can in its present form be assigned to an earlier date than the era of the Norman Conquest, that is to say, five hundred years after the period with which these documents are concerned.[135] It would be folly for this reason to question the existence of Dewi and his companion saints, or to deny that they founded many of the churches which bear their name, but it must be held that we know little of their real history. Great as is the fame of Dewi Sant, who has for ages been recognised as the patron saint of Wales, for the historian he is but a lay figure compared to Gildas.

The life of Dewi,[136] better known as St. David, is, it should

[135] Most of these lives were edited, with English translations, by W. J. Rees for the Welsh MSS. Society in *Lives of the Cambro-British Saints* (Lland very, 1853). It is to be regretted that the text of this volume, in the words of Rhys (*W. Phil.* (2), 425), "teems with inaccuracies"; for a long list of important corrections see *Cymr.* xiii. 76-96. The principal MS. source used for this edition was Cottonian MS. Vespasian A. xiv. (ff. 13-94), written about 1200; the lives of St. David, St. Cadog, St. Gwynllyw, and St. Illtud appear, however, to have been composed about a century earlier (*Cymr.* xi. 127-9).

[136] Dewi represents the popular and Dafydd the learned form assumed by David in Welsh (Loth, *Mots Latins*, 160).

be said, in all likelihood the oldest and most trustworthy of the group. It was written about 1090 by Rhygyfarch, son of Bishop Sulien of St. David's, who belonged to a family of scholars and had access to such records as the cathedral could supply.[137] It certainly seems, in its account of the early monastic discipline of St. David's, to embody ancient materials and to describe institutions which had long fallen into abeyance. Thus, in spite of its late date and general legendary air, this life perhaps merits closer attention than most compositions of the class to which it belongs. St. David, according to this narrative, was the son of Sanctus, a king of Ceredigion, and Nonnita, a nun of Dyfed; he was born in the latter region, at the spot on the north shore of St. Bride's Bay now marked by St. Nonn's Chapel,[138] when King Tryffin and his sons ruled over Dyfed. The date thus indicated, *viz.*, about 520,[139] is probably not far wrong; as to the parentage, all that can be said is that the reverence shown towards the memory of Nonnita, or, to use the better-known form, Non, not alone in Wales, but also in Cornwall, Devon and Brittany, seems to give her an assured historical position, though the idea that she was a nun at the time of St. David's birth may fairly be set down as due to a misunderstanding of her name.[140] In later life she probably became, like Samson's relatives, a convert to the monastic life, and hence the churches dedicated to her at Llannon[141] and Llanerchaeron in Cardiganshire, Llannon in Carmarthenshire, Alternon in Cornwall, Bradstone in Devon and Dirinon in Brittany.[142] Sanctus or Sant is a much

[137] *Cambro-Br. SS.* 117-43. For Rhygyfarch ("michi autem qui Ricemarchus nominor") and his connections, see chap. xii. extra note. On this life depend that composed by Giraldus Cambrensis (iii. 377-404) and the Welsh "buchedd," for the earliest text of which see *Llyfr yr Ancr*, 105-18.

[138] Fenton (2), 63; Jones and Freem. 227, 243; *Arch. Camb.* V. xv. (1898), 345-8.

[139] The pedigree of the royal house of Dyfed makes "Triphun" the grandfather of "Guortepir," the "Vortipori" of Gildas (*Cymr.* ix. 171).

[140] Several instances of the personal name "Nonnita" occur (*W. Phil.* (2), 404), one in a Cornish inscription of about this period (*Inscr. Chr.* No. 10; *Arch. Camb.* V. xii. (1895), 54). Giraldus had the "sanctam monialem" of Rhygyfarch before him, but thought it desirable to suppress it. No importance need be attached to statements providing Non with local connections (*Myv. Arch.* II. 23 (415), 37-8 (423); *Iolo MSS.* 82-3, 101, 110, 124).

[141] A chapel (now ruined) under Llansantffraid (*Arch. Camb.* V. xiv. (1897), 165-6).

[142] "Buhez Santes Nonn," a Breton miracle play, was found in a MS. of about 1400 at Dirinon and printed at Paris in 1837; the text was re-edited by

CHAP. V.

more shadowy personage, and better evidence than we have at present is needed to prove that St. David was of royal blood and grandson of Ceredig ap Cunedda Wledig.[143]

The saint, it is further said, was baptised by St. Ailbe of Emly[144] (who died about 530) and spent his earliest years at Henfynyw,[145] Cardiganshire, in a school apparently taught by one "Guistilianus," a bishop and his cousin on the father's side.[146] After taking priest's orders, it is added, he went to the school of Paulinus, already mentioned, and was there for very many years. It would seem as if in these passages two different accounts of St. David's education had been combined, more especially as the ninth-century life of Paul Aurelian offers a third, mentioning "Sanctum Devium" among the famous pupils of Illtud.[147] Rhygyfarch's next excursion is into the region of pure legend, when he tells how his hero founded, before he made his home in Mynyw, twelve famous monasteries, among them being the well-known English foundations, Repton, Croyland, Leominster and Bath! He is on surer ground when he brings the saint back to Mynyw, in its Latin form, Menevia, and recounts the struggles he had with the chieftain of the district, one "Baia Scottus," whose fort is still shown at "Clegyr Foia" (Boia's Rocks),[148] ere he was allowed to settle peaceably in "Glyn Rhosin," the little valley ever since inseparably associ-

E. Ernault in *Rev. Celt.* viii. pp. 230-301, 405-91. The story is taken entirely from Rhygyfarch's life, save for some additions from Geoffrey of Monmouth.

143 Sanctus is "Sant" in the older Welsh authorities (*Myv. Arch.* II. 23 (415); *Llyfr yr Ancr*, 106), the form "Sandde" being an eccentricity of the Iolo MSS. (82, 101, 110, 124). He does not appear in the pedigree of the royal house of Ceredigion, which is carried to Ceredig through a son "Iusay" (*Cymr.* ix. 181). In the "Buhez," Ceredig is named as the saint's father.

144 "Helue Menevensium (read, Muminensium) episcopo." He probably owes his place in the legend to the existence near St. David's of a Llaneilfyw or St. Elvie's.

145 I follow the explanation of Giraldus (iii. 384), that the "Vetus Rubus" of Rhygyfarch is a translation of Henfynyw by some one who thought, as Giraldus did himself, that Mynyw was from the Irish muine, a bramble.

146 Possibly the "Justinianus" whose astonishing legend is given in Capgrave's *Nova Legenda Angliæ* (ed. Horstman, 1901, ii. pp. 93-5) and who was commemorated at Llanstinan and at Capel Stinan, near St. David's (Fenton (2), 64; Jones and Freem. 224).

147 *Rev. Celt.* v. p. 421.

148 Excavations conducted by Mr. Baring-Gould in 1902 showed that the spot had been occupied by a people in the Early Iron stage of civilisation (*Arch. Camb.* VI. iii. (1903), 1-11). It need not be supposed that Boia and his clan were much above this level.

ated with his name. That he found a Goidel in possession in this remote corner of Dyfed is most likely[149] and opposition to a monastic settlement may well have come from a self-willed landowner who did not at all repudiate the name of Christian.

After the settlement in St. David's, the life suggests that, save for one important exception, the saint's wanderings came to an end and that henceforth his energies were devoted to the work of organising and controlling the monastic community he had got together in this remote angle of Britain. The exception is the journey to Jerusalem which, according to the legend, he made in company with Padarn and Teilo and which had as its issue his consecration as "archiepiscopus" by the Patriarch, but this passage in the life is without doubt purely mythical, the intention being to show that St. David was not beholden for his episcopal authority to any ecclesiastic in the West. Though he was reverenced in later ages in Devonshire,[150] in Cornwall,[151] and in Brittany,[152] and was in close intercourse with the monastic founders of Ireland, with men like St. Maedhog of Ferns[153] and St. Senan of Clare,[154] there is nothing to show that he travelled in those regions; the influence he wielded was as abbot of the monastery of Mynyw or Tyddewi and the founder of daughter monasteries in other parts of South Wales.

The type of monasticism which prevailed at St. David's was of the most rigorous kind. The abbot himself was known as "Dewi Ddyfrwr,"[155] David the Waterdrinker, and for ages his successors were under a solemn obligation to abstain from meat.[156] In the picture drawn by Rhygyfarch of the ancient but vanished order of the fraternity, monks are seen yoked to the plough in place of oxen, others dig and hoe the ground

[149] P. 121.

[150] At Thelbridge and at Ashprington.

[151] At Davidstow.

[152] At S. Divy, near Landerneau.

[153] The "Aidus" of the life in *Cambro-Br. SS.* 232-50. In Rhygyfarch's text he appears as "Aidanus" (130) and "Maidoc" (133), the latter being an affectionate derivative from the former name (*Arch. Camb.* V. xii. (1895), 36-7). Ferns, the seat of his monastery, is "Guernin" in the one passage and "aquilento," *i.e.*, marsh (absurdly rendered "north" on p. 4361), in the other.

[154] *Acta Sanctorum*, March, vol. i. (8th day), 772*a* (Venice, 1735).

[155] Life of Paul Aurelian (*Rev. Celt.* v. p. 421), Rhygyfarch (118), Giraldus Cambrensis (iii. 379), *LL.* ii. 318, *Iolo MSS.* 300, 301. *Lib. Land.* 128 suggests a somewhat different interpretation, and Mr. Phillimore regards the original meaning of the epithet as an open question (Owen, *Pemb.* 206-7).

[156] Gir. Camb. vi. 104 (*Itin.* ii. 2).

CHAP. V.

in religious silence, others carry saws for the felling of timber. No one may claim anything as his own, not even the sorry skins he wears; the careless use of such a phrase as "*my* book" is an offence to be expiated by severe penance. It would appear certain, therefore, that St. David's was a monastery of that stricter pattern which caused Gildas, if the extracts cited under his name on this subject are really his,[157] so much anxiety in his later years. Monks, he complains, are forsaking their old allegiance in many monasteries of the ancient and less exacting type in order to join communities having a more rigorous ideal, in which the eating of meat, the drinking of all beverages save water, the use of horses and carriages are abjured. Bread is eaten by measure; oxen are discarded so that the zeal of the brethren may show itself in the drawing of ploughs, and meanwhile, such is the burden of his lament, there is a notable falling off in Christian charity and a dangerous uprising of the pharisaic spirit. If Gildas and David did, as is dimly suggested by these extracts, champion opposing schools of ascetic thought, it is certain that the school of David left the deeper impress upon the Welsh mind; as Christianity had in the first instance made good its foothold in Wales through the powerful appeal of monasticism, so now Celtic enthusiasm cast its suffrage in favour of the more uncompromising exponents of the monastic creed.

That St. David was a bishop[158] may be without hesitation believed, and no doubt every abbot who succeeded him in the headship of the monastic community of Mynyw held the same office. He may even, by contrast with men of inferior fame and influence, have been known as "archiepiscopus" or "chief bishop".[159] But there is no warrant for supposing that he sought to wield any authority as metropolitan, or archbishop in its later sense, over the British Church, either from St. David's or any other centre. Geoffrey of Monmouth, having made Dubricius Archbishop of Caerleon, is naturally led to indicate David as his successor in that dignity;[160] Rhygyfarch is less

[157] Printed by H. and St. (i. 108-13), Mommsen (pp. 86-8) and Williams (pp. 256-70), who are all disposed to regard them as genuine.

[158] He is styled "Dauid episcopus moni iudeorum" in Harl. MS. 3859 (*Cymr.* ix. 156).

[159] For this use of the title see *Cymr. Trans.* 1893-4, 131.

[160] *Hist. Reg.* ix. 15; xi. 3.

concerned about ecclesiastical order, and, while claiming for his hero the position of metropolitan, represents the office as conferred upon him by general acclamation after his wonderful preaching to the multitudes assembled at the Synod of Brefi. But in the days of St. David the system of dioceses, under which each bishop has assigned to him for his exclusive rule a definite extent of territory, was clearly not known in Wales, and still less could there be an archbishop recognised as supreme from end to end of that country.

Nothing could well be more legendary than the account of the Synod of Brefi as it has come down to us. The Pelagian heresy has revived (though Gildas, it should be noted, has not a word to say about a relapse which, had it really occurred, must have deeply moved him), and 118 bishops meet at Brefi in Ceredigion to proclaim the true faith to the immense throng there gathered together. But not one of them can make himself heard, and matters are at a standstill until it is suggested that Daniel and Dubricius shall fetch the Saint of Mynyw. David is with difficulty persuaded to return with them to the synod and leaves them on the way to raise from the dead the only son of a widow. But, when at last he reaches Brefi, he is master of the situation; the ground beneath his feet rises into a little hill (on which now stands the church of Llanddewi), and his voice, resonant as the sound of a trumpet, reaches the farthest limits of the assembly. Fantastic as is this story, the Synod of Brefi may not itself be mythical; it is known from Bede[161] and from the life of St. Samson[162] that the bishops of the Britons were accustomed to meet in such gatherings, and, if there was no occasion to discuss Pelagianism, there were other burning questions, notably those connected with the monastic life, which made counsel and joint action very necessary.

St. David died, as is well known, on the 1st of March; the year of his death cannot, unhappily, be fixed with the same precision. Probably that intended by the Irish *Chronicon Scotorum*, *viz.*, 588, is not far from the mark,[163] and he would

[161] *H.E.* ii. 2. [162] P. 583*b*.

[163] The entry is simply "Dauld Cille Muine". So Tighernach (*Rev. Celt.* xvii. p. 158) has "Dabid Cille Muni"; Harl. MS. 3859 also leaves out the "obiit". Thus all three notices clearly come from a common, probably

CHAP. V.

thus be a contemporary of Gildas, but somewhat younger. The fame he acquired in later ages, culminating in his adoption by Welshmen generally as the patron saint of their country, is to be explained by the very large number of churches (Rees reckons fifty-three[164]) in all parts of South Wales which were regarded as under his protection. In many cases the dedication is probably not one which dates from St. David's own day, but, when all deductions have been made, it still remains true that, within the limits of South Wales, he had an exceptional position in respect of the many important churches, like Llangyfelach in Gower, Llanarthneu on the Towy,[165] Glascwm in Elfael, and Dewchurch Magna in Herefordshire, which owned allegiance to his memory. The only saint who seems to have been regarded as in any way his rival was Cadfael, familiarly known as Cadog and Catwg, the founder of Llancarfan in Morgannwg, and a saint of great reputation in that quarter of Wales.[166] In the life of Cadog, written about 1075 by one Lifric, who was son to Bishop Herwald of Llandaff and "magister" of Llancarfan,[167] it is said that David summoned the Synod of Brefi while Cadog was away on pilgrimage and that his reluctance to take precedence of so distinguished a saint was only overcome by the strict injunctions of an angel. When Cadog returned, no one for a while ventured to tell him what had occurred, and, when at last the news was broken to him, he gave vent to most unsaintly anger, which was only appeased by another angelic interposition. It is noteworthy in this connection that none of the ancient churches of the king-

an Irish, source, and the later date implied in the Welsh chronicle, *viz.*, A.D. 601, is perhaps due to an attempt to connect the saint with the "Sinodus urbis legion" ascribed to that year (*Cymr.* xi. 156). If the statement of Rhygyfarch, that he died on a Tuesday, were to be accepted, the year might be given with some confidence as 589.

[164] *Welsh SS.* 45.

[165] Llanarthneu appears in a poem by Gwynfardd Brycheiniog, a contemporary of the Lord Rhys ap Gruffydd, as "llan adneu" (*Myv. Arch.* I. 271 (194); *Lit. Kym.* (2), 155). It is, therefore, no doubt, the "Depositi Monasterium" of *Cambro-Br. SS.* 117, "adneu" being the Welsh legal term for a deposit (*LL.* i. 244, 258, 484; Wotton, *Glossary*, *s.v.*). At the same time, this current derivation was probably wrong, Arthneu being really a proper name; *cf.* the "lan hardneu" of *Lib. Land.* 279.

[166] His life, from Vesp. A. xiv., is printed in *Cambro-Br. SS.* 22-96. For the name Cadfael (in old Welsh, Catmail), see pp. 25, 28.

[167] *Cambro-Br. SS.* 80; *Lib. Land.* 271, 273, 274.

dom of Glywysing, lying between the Tawe and the Usk, are dedicated to St. David; this was the special domain of Cadog, who was sprung from the princely house of the district, his father Gwynllyw (commemorated at St. Woollo's, Newport) being the ruler who gave his name to the ancient cantref of Gwynllwg.[168] Thus there would appear to be some ground for the belief that Dewi and Cadog were not close fellow-workers, while both tradition and the evidence of dedications go to show that Dewi worked harmoniously with the other two monastic pioneers of the South, with Padarn or Paternus of Llanbadarn Fawr in Ceredigion and with Eliud, familiarly known as Teilo, the patron of many a Llandeilo in South Wales.[169] But, if there was jealousy in Glamorgan of the fame of the Demetian saint, the rivalry of Cadog never became elsewhere serious, for his renown always remained a strictly local affair.

NOTE TO CHAPTER V. § i.—*Harleian MS.* 3859.

This MS., which at one time belonged to the abbey of Montauban in the South of France, includes, among other writings unconnected with Wales, a copy of the *Historia Brittonum* attributed to Nennius (ff. 174*b*-189*b*), followed by a set of Latin annals, a number of genealogies of Welsh and Cumbrian princes, a list of British cities, and the tract *De Mirabilibus Britanniæ* (ff. 189*b*-198). Various estimates have been given of the age of this little collection; Petrie assigns it to the tenth century (*Mon. Hist. Br.* 68), Hardy to the eleventh (*Catalogue of Materials for British History*, i., No. 778), Maunde Thompson to the beginning of the twelfth (*Cymr.* ix. 145-6). The point is not, however, of the first importance, since it has been clearly shown that the Harleian MS. is not an original in respect of these documents, but is derived from an older MS. written in the Hiberno-Saxon hand. The parent MS. may be confidently assigned to the end of the tenth century, in view of the fact that the principal pedigree given is that of Owain ap Hywel Dda, who died in 988, and that the annals come to an end in his reign. This conclusion is also supported by the spelling of the Welsh names, which are uniformly in the Old-Welsh form.

The MS., therefore, represents a tenth-century contribution to the history of Wales, and the information given in the annals and the genealogies is of high value. Both have been printed, with scrupulous care, by Phillimore in the ninth volume of the *Cymmrodor* (152-83), where also will be found a full introduction (141-51). Less satisfactory is the edition of the annals in the volume entitled *Annales Cambriæ*, which appeared in the Rolls series in 1860 under the editorship of John Williams Ab Ithel. Harl. MS. 3859 is MS. A. of this edition, in which it is awkwardly combined with MSS. B. and C. of the thirteenth century.

[168] *Cymr.* vii. 118-9; xi. 40-1. The oldest known form of the name is given in Harl. MS. 3859, *viz.*, Guinnliguiauc (*Cymr.* ix. 167), for Gwynllywiog.

[169] For the lives of Padarn and Teilo see *Cambro-Br. SS.* 188-97 and *Lib. Land.* 97-117 respectively. Both contain friendly references to St. David.

CHAP. V.

The annals begin with a year which appears to be A.D. 444 and run on, so far as the marking of the years is concerned, to 977, though the last event recorded is under 954. The year of our Lord is nowhere given, the only addition to the successive entries of "an(nus)" being the figure set against every tenth year which gives the number of that year, counted from the first (see the facsimile in the Rolls edition). As a record of events set down from year to year, these annals obviously belong to St. David's; after 809 no bishops are mentioned save those of that see, while of them there is a fairly complete account. It is known from the story of Asser that learning was not without its devotees at St. David's during this age. But, while the later entries are undoubtedly of contemporary authority, the earlier ones have no claim to be put on the same footing. It has often been pointed out that the basis of the chronicle was furnished by some Irish source, also used by Tighernach and the Irish annalists who followed him (*Mon. Hist. Br.* 92-3; *Ann.* C. xv. xvi.; *Cymr.* xi. 139). Nor is it unlikely that, as suggested by Skene (*Chronicles of the Picts and Scots*, 1867, xxviii.), it was this Irish document which provided the starting-point of A.D. 444, otherwise not easily explained, for the Annals of Ulster assign to this year the foundation of Armagh and the beginning, therefore, of organised Christianity in Northern Ireland. But, besides this foreign source, the earlier annals depend to a great extent on the *Historia Brittonum*, and probably upon other similar traditional accounts of the doings of the Britons. In the eighth century the notices are predominantly northern, and are, for the most part, such as would naturally occur in a Strathclyde chronicle. It is not until the age of Offa is reached that the entries begin to wear the aspect of a contemporary record kept in South Wales, and it is from this point only that the chronicle takes the position of a historical authority of the first class.

NOTE TO CHAPTER V. § ii.—*MSS. and Editions of Gildas.*

Gildas's work was not popular in the Middle Ages ("raro invenitur," says William of Newburgh, who had lighted upon a copy) and few MSS. are available for the determination of the text. Of those extant the most important is Cottonian MS. Vitellius A. vi., which belonged to the abbey of St. Augustine, Canterbury, and was written in the eleventh century. It was used by the early editors of Gildas, but suffered severely in the Cottonian fire of 1731 and was thus neglected in the nineteenth century, until Mommsen showed in 1894 that much of it was still legible and of great value for purposes of textual criticism. In the same edition another important MS. was used, *viz.*, that now kept in the public library of Avranches (No. 162), which came originally from the neighbouring abbey of Mont St. Michel. The readings of this MS. had not been given in any previous edition; it is of the end of the twelfth century, and, though corrupt and interpolated, supplies a useful check upon the Cottonian MS. There are two MSS. of Gildas in the Cambridge Public Library; Dd. i. 17 came from Glastonbury and belongs to about 1400; it is clearly a copy of the Cottonian MS. and is valuable chiefly as evidence of what that MS. once contained. Ff. i. 27 was the property of the Cistercian abbey of Sawley in Yorkshire and is a thirteenth-century MS. It is a copy of a MS. written by one Cormac, in which great liberties were taken with the original.

The first editor of Gildas was the Italian Polydore Vergil, who used the Cottonian MS. and one akin to that of Avranches. This edition appeared in 1525. In 1568 John Josselin, Latin secretary to Archbishop Parker, published a second, based upon the Cottonian MS. and its Cambridge derivative, Dd. i. 17. Thomas Gale next included Gildas in his Scriptores XV. (Oxford, 1691), and for the first time made use of the older Cambridge MS., Ff. i. 27, by no means to the advantage of the text. Nearly a century and a half went by ere another attempt was made to give to the world a text of Gildas, and the edition of Joseph Stevenson, published by the English Historical Society in 1838, was in some respects the least satisfactory of all. Stevenson relied on the Cambridge MSS. and the early editions, and appears to have taken it for granted that no better authorities were to be found; the Cottonian MS. he does not even mention. Gildas finds a place in the huge volume entitled *Monumenta Historica Britannica* (1848) and also, with the omission of the historical portion, in the first volume of *Councils and Ecclesiastical Documents* (London, 1869), but both Mr. Petrie and Mr. Haddan, while aware of the importance of the Cottonian MS., believed it to be lost and brought no fresh material to the study of the text. In 1894,[170] however, appeared the *Monumenta Germaniæ Historica* edition, under the superintendence of Mommsen; for this full use was made both of the Cottonian and the Avranches MSS. and textual problems were for the first time adequately discussed in a detailed introduction. In the edition issued by Hugh Williams for the Cymmrodorion Society (1899-1901), the text of Mommsen is reprinted with an English translation and notes.

Gale was the first to divide the work into "Historia" (cc. 1-26) and "Epistola" (cc. 27-110), the source of this error (in which he was followed by Stevenson) being the fact that the MS. to which he pinned his faith, *viz.*, Ff. i. 27, ends with c. 26. In no other MS. is there any break at this point, and the monk of Rhuis, in his life of Gildas (p. 97), joins the end of c. 26 to his citation of c. 27 in the most natural manner possible. What the original title of the work was it is difficult to determine; in the Cottonian MS. it was apparently described as *De Excidio Britanniæ.*

The authenticity of the *De Excidio* as a real production of the early sixth century is no longer seriously questioned. The MSS. are all of late date, but the extensive use of the work by Bede, who mentions "Gildus" by name (*H.E.* i. 22), makes it impossible to suppose it of later date than A.D. 700, and the efforts of Thomas Wright (*Biographia Britannica*, i. 115-35) and A. Anscombe (*Academy*, 1895) to find a place for it, either as a whole or in part, in the seventh century have been quite unsuccessful.

The Rhuis life was first printed from a defective Fleury MS. in Dubois' *Floriacensis Bibliotheca* (1605), 429-63, whence it was taken by Bolland for the *Acta Sanctorum* (Jan. (29), II. 958-67). Mabillon in *Acta Sanctorum Ordinis S. Benedicti* (i. 138-52) used a Rhuis MS. to supply some of the defects of the Fleury MS., but was not able to add the missing close. Mommsen edits (pp. 91-106) from the printed sources. In c. 34 reference is made to an event stated to have happened in 1008, but it is not unlikely that, as Williams suggests (*Gildas*, p. 318), these later chapters are an addition to the original life, furnishing no clue as to its date. The Glastonbury life was first printed by Stevenson in his edition of Gildas, from Burney MS. 310 (British Museum), written in the priory of Finchale, near Durham, in 1381, and a MS. copied from this in the sixteenth century (Royal MS. 13 B. vii.). Phillimore pointed out in 1890 (*Cymr.* xi. 79) how the most valuable MS. of all, C.C.C.C. MS. 139 (which is of the twelfth century), had been neglected, and cited some of its readings. Mommsen's text (pp. 107-10) is based on this and the Burney MS.

[170] This is the date of the separate issue of the "Gildas and Nennius" fasciculus—the whole volume (tom. xiii.) is dated 1898.

CHAPTER VI.

STRUGGLE OF THE CYMRY AND THE ENGLISH.

(For this period I have made much use of Mr. Plummer's editions of Bede's *Ecclesiastical History* and of the Anglo-Saxon Chronicle. *Celtic Britain* is still indispensable. Mr. Skene devoted much labour to the elucidation of the history of this period and embodied the fruit of his researches in *The Four Ancient Books of Wales* and *Celtic Scotland*. But his analysis of the material he used was not sufficiently searching, and many of his conclusions rest in consequence on a very insecure basis.)

I. THE MEN OF THE NORTH.

CHAP. VI.

THE first event on record in the history of the struggle between the English and the Britons who were under the sway of the northern gwledig is the foundation by Ida of the kingdom of Bernicia. Bede gives the year as 547,[1] a date which he no doubt inferred from the particulars given in the old list, kept from an early period, of Northumbrian kings and the years of their rule.[2] Whether Ida founded an entirely new settlement or was raised to the dignity of king by a body of Anglian warriors already established on the Northumbrian coast is a point as to which information is wanting, but it is likely that any colony previously settled in this region was insignificant, and that it was from the middle of the sixth century that the Britons who

[1] *H.E.* v. 24.

[2] The references to the treatment of the "infaustus annus," 633-4, in *H.E.* iii. 1, 9, afford absolute proof that there was such a list in existence in Bede's time and that he regarded it as a trustworthy record. In point of fact, the Moore MS. of *H.E.* has appended to it (see *Mon. Hist. Br.* 290) a table of this kind which appears to have been entered in the MS. in 737, two years only after the historian's death. It gives the length of Ida's reign, with Bede, as twelve years, and the data it furnishes, assuming that Æthelfrith died in 616, would fix the accession of Ida at 547. The same list appears, with the accidental omission of the one-year King Glappa, in the *Saxon Genealogies* (*Hist. Britt.* c. 63); Simeon of Durham has it also (*Hist. Reg.* § 12), but with a number of errors of transcription. The list in Fl. Wig. i. 6 differs in important respects; it appears to me to have been altered so as to bring it into conformity with the Anglo-Saxon Chronicle, *s.a.* 588.

dwelt on the banks of the Forth, the Tweed and the Tyne had reason to be genuinely alarmed at the progress of the Teutonic invader. The centre of Ida's power is indicated by the fact that tradition ascribes to him the foundation of Bamborough,[3] a coast castle between Berwick and Alnwick, which long remained an important royal stronghold. The people over whom he bore rule called themselves Baernice,[4] a name which was possibly derived from that of the Brigantes who anciently occupied this region[5] and was transferred into Welsh in the forms Byrneich and Bryneich.[6]

During the second half of the sixth century war must have been all but incessant between the Bernician interlopers and the older inhabitants of these northern lands. No details of the conflict have, however, been handed down, save the brief notices contained in the little tract which a Briton of the district put together at the end of the seventh century and which now appears, in four MSS., at the end of the *Historia Brittonum.* In this document (commonly known as the *Saxon Genealogies*)[7] the names are mentioned of five kings of Bernicia who succeeded Ida and preceded Æthelfrith, and of two of them it is said that British chieftains waged war against them. These were Theoderic, a son of Ida, who reigned from 572 to 579—"against him Urien and his sons valiantly did battle"—and Hussa, who was king from 585 to 592—"against him the four kings, Urien, Rhydderch the Aged, Gwallog and Morgan, fought".[8] In 592 a grandson of Ida, Æthelfrith son of Æthelric, obtained the crown, a man whom Bede terms a very Saul for plundering his enemies; no English leader, he says, made himself master of more British land, either by driving out the Britons or reducing them to servitude.[9] Thus

[3] A.S. Chr. MS. E. *s.a.* 547. *Cf.* also the difficult passage in the *Saxon Genealogies* (*Hist. Britt.* c. 61, end), which I read: "(i)unxit (as in the "Nennian" recension) Dinguayr(u)i guurth Berneich," *i.e.*, he joined Dinguarwy, or whatever the form should be, to Bernicia. So Zimmer, *Nenn. V.* 307; on p. 80 he has another suggestion.

[4] A.S. Chr. MS. E. *s.a.* 634.

[5] *Celt. Br.* (2), pp. 113-4.

[6] Byrneich is the older form; see Mommsen's edition of the *Hist. Britt.* pp. 201 (Berneich, Bernech), 204 (Birneich), 205 (Berneich, Birnech); *Bruts*, 101 (Byrneirch), 102 (Byrneich), 103 (Byrneich).

[7] See note on p. 116.

[8] *Hist. Britt.* c. 63. The dates are calculated from the list of kings referred to above.

[9] *H.E.* i. 34.

CHAP. VI.

at the end of the century Bernicia had become, out of small beginnings, a most formidable power.

It seems most probable that it was this struggle, continued by the Britons with varying but on the whole decidedly adverse fortune until the middle of the seventh century, which created the national name of Cymry.[10] Hitherto, the general designation of the race holding power between the Severn and the Forth had been "Britons," in modern Welsh "Brython"; this distinguished them alike from the Goidels, Scotti, or Irish on the one hand and from the English on the other. But in the extremity which now beset them, in face of the resistless advance of the English, not in Bernicia alone, but in the kingdom of Deira also, to the south of the Tees, and throughout Mid Britain, Brython and Goidel would seem, along the whole of this line, to have agreed to cast aside race distinctions and to recognise only the common name of "Combroges" or "fellow-countrymen," fighting for freedom under the authority of one gwledig. Only thus does it seem possible to explain the late appearance of the name in history, its extension to the North, where it is still preserved in Cumberland, the "land of the Cymry," and its failure to reach the Britons of Devon, Cornwall and Brittany, between whom and the more northerly Britons there was kinship, but, so far as can be seen, no martial alliance.

The leaders of the Cymry in this long and obstinate conflict were the men known to tradition as "Gwŷr y Gogledd," the Men of the North.[11] No single figure towers above the rest, as in the age of Arthur or of Maelgwn Gwynedd, though it may be presumed that the office of gwledig was still in existence; the Britons were clearly much divided and fought under the leadership of local chieftains. Four of these are mentioned in the *Saxon Genealogies* as opponents of Hussa, *viz.*, Urien ap Cynfarch, Gwallog ap Llyenog, Morgan (ap Coleddog?) and Rhydderch ap Tudwal. Others whose names

[10] The view here adopted is that of Rhys (*Celt. Br.* (2), pp. 115-6, 139; *W. People*, p. 26). For the derivation and application of the name, see the note appended to this chapter.

[11] Peniarth MS. 45 (formerly Hengwrt MS. 536) gives "Bonedd Gwyr y Gogledd" (Pedigrees of the Men of the North), as printed in *IV. Anc. Bks.* ii. p. 454. But these pedigrees are to be found in a much more trustworthy form in Harl. MS. 3859, as printed by Phillimore in *Cymr.* ix. 169-82.

have been handed down are Llywarch ab Elidyr (surnamed the Aged), Clydno Eiddin, Gwrgi and Peredur his brother, Gwenddoleu ap Ceidio. Of most of these little can be said save that they seem to be real historical personages, but of one or two a few facts are authentically recorded. The author of the *Saxon Genealogies* had for some reason or other a special interest in Urien,[12] whom he describes as the most brilliant war-leader on the British side; he besieged the English for three days and three nights in the island of Lindisfarne,[13] but, in spite of his services to the cause of British freedom, fell a victim to the jealousy of Morgan, who contrived his death in the course of the expedition. Urien continued to be for many centuries, under the name of Urien of Rheged, a figure of importance in Welsh legend, but his exploits against the Irish of South Wales, the fame of his son Owain, lord of three hundred ravens, and of his daughter Morfudd, beloved of Cynon ap Clydno Eiddin, and his death at the hands of Llofan Llawddifro, all belong to the realm of fable rather than of history.[14] Rhydderch ap Tudwal, known to the older writers as Rhydderch the Aged,[15] but in later times as Rhydderch the Open-handed (Hael),[16] is another British leader who may be said to be something more than a name for the historian. In Adamnan's life of St. Columba,[17] written at the end of the seventh century, he is spoken of as a friend of that saint, who ruled at the Rock of Clyde, the Allt Glud of the Britons, now known as Dumbarton.[18] He had many enemies, of whom he stood in daily fear, and in his

[12] In addition to the account of Urien himself, there are references to a son Rhun (c. 63) and a great grand-daughter Rhiein(melth) (c. 57).

[13] "Insula Metcaud". *Cf.* "Inis Metgoit" of Tighernach (*Rev. Celt.* xvii. p. 182).

[14] See *Arth. Legend*, cap. xi., where perhaps overmuch emphasis is placed on the mythological element.

[15] "Riderch hen" in the pedigree (*Cymr.* ix. 173) as in the narrative (c. 63).

[16] He appears, with Nudd and Mordaf, as one of "Tri hael Ynys Prydain" (Triad i. 8 = ii. 32 = iii. 30).

[17] I. 15.

[18] The old-Welsh form, Alt Clut, in which "Alt" = hill, height, is found in the Namur MS. of Bede (*H.E.* i. 1) and in Harl. MS. 3859 (*Cymr.* ix. 166); it seems to be preserved also in the name of the Arthurian warrior "tarawc allt clwyt" (*Mab.* 138). More common, however, is the Irish Ail (= rock, the "Petra" of Adamnan and *H.E.* i. 12) Cluaithe, whence the ordinary Alclud. Dumbarton is Dunbretan, the fort of the Britons.

CHAP. VI.

anxiety sent a private message to the prophet of Iona to know whether he was destined to fall by their hands. Columba's answer was that he would escape all their wiles and die in his own house, reposing on his couch of feathers, a prophecy which, according to Adamnan, was literally fulfilled. Rhydderch and Columba being on these terms, it is easy to credit what Jocelin of Furness, writing at the end of the twelfth century, says of the relations between the ruler of Dumbarton and another saint of the period, *viz.*, Kentigern or Cyndeyrn, the founder of Glasgow.[19] The hostility of "Morken," who may be the "Morcant" or Morgan of the *Saxon Genealogies*, had driven Kentigern from the banks of the Clyde to North Wales, where he founded the monastery of Llanelwy or St. Asaph. But when Rhydderch obtained supreme power in the North, there was a change of attitude towards Christianity, or rather, it may be supposed, towards monasticism; the new ruler was in full sympathy with the aims of Kentigern and invited him to return to his old field of operations. There was a memorable meeting at Hoddam (in Dumfriesshire), where the saint for a time took up his abode; in the course of a few years the monastic centre of Glasgow was founded, not far from Rhydderch's stronghold of Dumbarton. It has been suggested that Rhydderch attained his commanding position as the result of the battle of Arderydd, fought at Arthuret, near Carlisle, about 575, and that he then defeated a semi-pagan host and achieved a Christian victory;[20] but in the course of ages, so thick a legendary haze has gathered round the history of this famous encounter[21] that one may not venture to say more of it than

[19] Life as edited by A. P. Forbes in *The Historians of Scotland* (vol. v. Edinburgh, 1874), cc. 23, 24, 29-33.

[20] *IV. Anc. Bks.* i. pp. 66, 175. Harl. MS. 3859 assigns "bellum armterid" to the year 573 (*Cymr.* ix. 155), but its dates ought not hereabouts to be accepted without question. All the known forms of the name, including "Armterid" and the "Arywderit" of *Blk. Bk.* 2*b*, 31*b*, imply the spelling Ar*d*ery*dd*, and Skene had no ground for using the form Ar*dd*ery*d*, save the wish to support his view that the site of this battle was in the neighbourhood of Arthuret, a little north of Carlisle. Arthuret was, however, Ar*t*uret in the thirteenth century (*Tax. Nich.* 319) and the identification, which rests on a passage in the fifteenth-century edition of the chronicle of Fordun (ed. Goodall, Edinburgh, 1759, i. 135-6), mentioning a battle "cunctis in hac patria constitutis satis noto, quod erat in campo inter Lidel et Carwanolow situato," needs no such illicit garnishing.

[21] For the legends about Rhydderch and Arderydd and various interpretations of them, see the mediæval Latin poem entitled "Vita Merlini" (Die Sagen von

that it was a triumph won by Rhydderch over Gwenddoleu ap Ceidio.[22] Possibly it was the real turning-point of his career; his power, at any rate, was by some means or other firmly established, for the family of Rhydderch, in a collateral branch, furnished kings of Cumbria or Strathclyde for many generations.[23]

How the Cymry fared in their struggle with the Anglian kings of Deira and with the chieftains who won Mid Britain for the Teutonic race it is beyond the power of the historian to say, for we have no trustworthy information on the subject until Bede raises the curtain upon the doings of Æthelfrith at the beginning of the seventh century.[24] The most prominent of the princes of the Southern Cymry in this age was Rhun, son of Maelgwn Gwynedd, who succeeded to his father's authority in North Wales about 550, but tradition has nothing to say of any fighting between him and the English. Yet it leaves in the mind a fairly definite impression of the man as one of the notable figures of the second half of this century.[25] In the mediæval romance known as *The Dream of Rhonabwy*, Arthur and his knights are represented as receiving from their enemy, Osla of the Broad Knife, a request for a six weeks' truce. The king gathers his counsellors together to consider the proposal and thereupon the whole group makes its way to the spot where a great, tall man, with red-brown, curly hair, sits apart. Rhonabwy in his vision asks the reason of this extraordinary

Merlin, San-marte, Halle, 1853); the Welsh poems printed in *IV. Anc. Bks.* ii. pp. 3-5, 18-28, from the Black Book of Carmarthen; Davies's *Mythology and Rites of the British Druids* (London, 1809), pp. 469-74; *Lit. Kym.* (2), 198-267; *Dict. Nat. Biog. s.v.* Rhydderch Hael.

[22] The name of Gwenddoleu is perpetuated in Carwhinelow, near Arthuret, anciently Caerwyndlo (*Bye-Gones*, 1st Oct. 1890, p. 483) and Carwanolow (note 20 above).

[23] See Harl. MS. 3859, Pedigrees V. and VI. (*Cymr.* ix. 172-3).

[24] The elaborate speculations of Dr. Guest, as contained in *Origines Celticæ* (London, 1883), have been accepted to a surprising extent by Stubbs, Freeman, Green and other writers of sound judgment. But they rest on the flimsiest foundations, and in particular take no account of the established rules of Celtic or Teutonic philology. See W. H. Stevenson in *Engl. Hist. Rev.* xvii. (1902), pp. 625-42.

[25] For Rhun see Harl. MS. 3859, Pedigree I. (*Cymr.* ix. 170); Jesus Coll. MS. 20 (*Cymr.* viii. 87); *Mab.* 159, 160; *LL.* i. 104; Triad i. 9 = ii. 8 = iii. 25 and i. 22 = ii. 43 = iii. 28; *Dict. Nat. Biog. s.v.* Rowlands (*Mon. Ant.* p. 148) makes him give his name to Caerhun on the Conway, which is perhaps rightly so explained.

CHAP. VI.

proceeding, and is told that this is Rhun ap Maelgwn Gwynedd, whose privilege it is that all shall come and take counsel of him, not he of others. Rhun and Arthur did not, of course, live in the same age; yet the privileged position assigned to Rhun in the story may well be an echo of a real predominance held by him as gwledig in succession to his father. The reference to his stature seems, also, a historical touch: for the poets call him "Rhun *Hir*"[26] (it will not be forgotten that Maelgwn o'ertopped his fellow-princes) and there is a triad, the Three Golden-shackled Men of Britain, which makes him out to have been of so gigantic a frame that special arrangements were necessary for getting him seated on a horse's back.

One incident only in Rhun's career is recorded, and this brings him into relation with the Men of the North. According to the story preserved in the oldest copy of the Venedotian version of the Welsh Laws,[27] Elidyr the Bounteous was slain, while on a visit to North Wales, by the men of Arfon at Aber Meweddus, not far from Clynnog.[28] This brought down upon the district a punitive expedition from the North, led by Rhydderch Hael, Clydno Eiddin and other chieftains of the Cumbrian region, who gave Arfon to fire and sword. How Rhun comported himself during the progress of this avenging onslaught is not stated, but, when it was over, he organised a great counter expedition, which carried the arms of Gwynedd as far as the Forth. It was to supply historical grounds for the claim of Arfon to lead the van in the Venedotian host that this narrative was first put on record, and the tale is duly told how the battle stood still on the banks of the northern river until a message from Gwynedd ended all strife by an authoritative decision in favour of the men of Arfon. Nevertheless, in spite of some legendary features, the tradition probably rests on a basis of fact, and shows, what one is very ready to be-

[26] *Myv. Arch.* I. 189 (140).

[27] Peniarth MS. 29 (Black Book of Chirk), referred to as A. in Owen's edition of the Laws. It is of the early part of the thirteenth century. The section "Breiniau Arfon" is also found in E., which is a transcript of A. See *LL.* i. 104-6.

[28] Eben Fardd drew attention in *Cyff Beuno* (Tremadog, 1863) to the fact that a brook which runs into the Desach from Bron yr Erw is called "yr afon Wefus" (p. 66). A link between this and the "Mewedus" of MS. E. of the Laws (*Camb. Reg.* ii. 308) is supplied by "Moweddus," included in a list of the possessions of Clynnog church in *Rec. Carn.* 257.

lieve, that the struggle with the English was not too absorbing to allow room for internal conflict.

There is excellent evidence that these encounters, whether with the foreign foe or among the Cymry themselves, were the theme of poets who sang their glories, while they were still recent, in the Brythonic tongue. It has been already shown that the Welsh tribes retained, in spite of the Roman occupation, their native system of poetry and music, owing its origin, most likely, to the Druidic discipline.[29] Thus there is no difficulty in accepting the statement of the *Saxon Genealogies* that in the age of Ida, *i.e.*, about 550, Talhaearn the "Father of Fantasy" was famous in poesy, and that Aneirin, Taliesin, Blwchfardd, and Cian, known as the Wheat Singer, were all at the same time renowned composers of British verse.[30] It is true that of the five names thus signalised only the first two were known to Welshmen of the Middle Ages, and even the fame of Aneirin was not as widely diffused as might have been expected,[31] but this tells in favour of the notice as really ancient and not the product of the Middle Ages, when Welshmen had different ideas as to the great singers of the sixth century. At that period the "Cynfeirdd" or "Primitive Poets" of the Welsh people were understood to be Aneirin, Taliesin, Merlin (in Welsh Myrddin) and Llywarch the Aged; Talhaearn, Cian and Blwchfardd had been forgotten,[32] and two

[29] See p. 86.

[30] *Hist. Britt.* c. 62: "Tunc Talhaern Tataguen in poemate claruit, et Neirin et Taliessin et Bluchbard et Cian, qui vocatur Gueinth (read Guenith) Guaut, simul uno tempore in poemate Britannico claruerunt". For explanations of this passage see *Nenn. V.* 103, and *Cymr.* xi. 135. Three MSS. read "Tata*n*guen," whence the ridiculous "Talhaiarn *Tad Tangwn*" of Iolo MSS. 77; *cf.* 79 and 128.

[31] This is suggested not only by the "*et* Neirin," for an original *a*neirin, of Harl. MS. 3859, but also by the gross blunder made in "Llyfr Gwyn Rhydderch" and afterwards in the Red Book of Hergest in copying Aneurin's title of "mechdeyrn beirdd," *i.e.*, prince of bards, which is taken to be "merch Teyrnbeirdd," daughter of Teyrnbeirdd! See *Cymr.* vii. 98-9. The mediæval form is always Ane*i*rin.

[32] Talhaearn and Cian are both mentioned in the poem called "Angar Cyfyndawt" (*Myv. Arch.* I. 34-5 (35); *IV. Anc. Bks.* ii. p. 130, 131), but it may be conjectured that the poet was drawing upon Nennius. Llanfair Talhaearn in Denbighshire is an ancient chapel of the cathedral of St. Asaph, dedicated to the Virgin, and owes its name to its position in the township of Talhaearn (Thomas, *St. Asaph.* 386). In the Black Book of Carmarthen the title "Tad awen" is given to one "tedei" (fo. 32*a*), from whom is derived the "Tydain Tad awen" of the Third Series of Triads (Nos. 57, 92, 93) and Davies's *Celtic Researches* (159, 160) and *Mythology* (193, 526).

CHAP. VI.

other names had taken their place in the roll of great bards of the sixth century, of which it may be said that Myrddin has a suspiciously mythical air and that Llywarch Hên was a chieftain of whose devotion to bardism there is no satisfactory evidence.

To what extent the poems ascribed in mediæval MSS. to Taliesin and Aneirin may be regarded as the work of those poets is a question which has occupied critics for a century and has not yet received a final solution.[33] It is indeed certain that not one of these poems has come down in a sixth-century dress, and certain, also, that many of them were written in the Middle Ages with an eye to political conflicts then raging and were merely assigned to an ancient bard, as were the Myrddin poems, for stage effect. But it still remains doubtful whether some of these warlike strains, in which the setting is Cumbrian rather than Welsh, primitive rather than mediæval, may not embody fragments of the older music, fitted to the diction of a later age. This is a possibility which has to be seriously considered in the case of the principal work attributed to Aneirin, the "Gododin".[34] Though it no doubt contains many late additions, its principal theme, the ill fortune of the Brython on the field of Catraeth, seems to belong to early Cymric history and to have nothing to do with the Wales of the Middle Ages. Catraeth has not been satisfactorily identified,[35] but Gododin or Gododdin has been generally taken to be the country of the Otadeni or Votadini, placed by Ptolemy between the Tyne and the Forth.[36] The difficulty of interpreting the poem also deepens the impression of antiquity it conveys; it wears the aspect of a genuine relic of a long-forgotten strife, a massive boulder left high on its rocky perch by an icy stream which has long since melted away.

> The men went to Catraeth ; merry was the host.
> The grey mead was their drink and their poison too.

[33] The chief works dealing with the question have been Sharon Turner's *Vindication of the Genuineness of the Ancient* British *Poems* (London, 1803), Stephens' *Literature of the Kymry* (Llandovery, 1849), Nash's *Taliesin* (London, 1858), and Skene's *Four Ancient* Books *of Wales* (Edinburgh, 1868).

[34] For the Gododin see *Myv. Arch.* I. 1-16 (1-20); *IV. Anc. Bks.* i. pp. 374-409; ii. pp. 62-92, and the editions by John Williams Ab Ithel (Llandovery, 1852) and Thomas Stephens (published in parts by the Cymrodorion Society, 1888).

[35] For the philological objections to Catterick see *Arth. Legend*, 240-1.

[36] *W. People*, p. 98.

Such was the melancholy story—a tale of valour and high daring brought to the biting of the dust by lack of self-governance, a tale the pitiful recollection of which, though it told of humiliation and defeat, the Cymry diligently kept alive through the ages.

II. The Celtic Churches and Rome.

"He who acts as guide to the barbarians, let him do penance for thirteen years, that is, if there does not ensue a slaughter of Christian folk and the shedding of blood and lamentable captivity. When these follow, let the man abandon his arms and spend the rest of his life in penance."[37] Such was the temper in which the Cymry waged their conflict with the English; the war against the heathen invader was to be a crusade, in which no relations were to be permitted with the enemy, and what in other wars was common desertion became treason to the Christian faith. Briton and Englishman were forbidden to have dealings with each other, and the mutual suspicion and hostility thus engendered brought it about that no effort was made by the older inhabitants of the island even to convert the new-comers to their own religion. In the *Life of Beuno*, a saint who belongs to the beginning of the seventh century, it is said that, after having been for some time settled at Berriew, near the Severn, Beuno one day heard an Englishman's voice on the further side of the river egging on his dogs to the chase of a hare. Whereupon he turned where he stood and without delay went back to his followers, bidding them make up their baggage and prepare for instant removal. "For," said he, "the kinsmen of yonder strange-tongued man whose voice I heard across the river setting on his dogs will obtain possession of this place, and it will be theirs, and they will hold it in ownership."[38] The life is late and the incident may be fictitious, but the spirit breathed in these words was most certainly that which possessed the British Church in St. Beuno's day.[39] Where the Englishman planted his foot, it was held that there was no place for missionary effort.

[37] This is one of the canons attributed to the synod of the "Grove of Victory" (H. and St. i. 118).

[38] *Llyfr yr Ancr*, 120-1; *Cambro-Br. SS.* 14-5. "Buchedd Beuno" is ascribed to the thirteenth century (*Cymr.* xi. 129).

[39] Bede complains of it (*H.E.* i. 22).

CHAP. VI.

This was the posture of affairs when in 597 a Roman mission despatched by Pope Gregory I., under the leadership of Augustine, head of the convent of St. Andrew's in the imperial city, landed in Kent and secured the adhesion to the Christian faith of its king, Ethelbert, and the Kentish people. Ethelbert was not only king of Kent, but had also made himself overlord of all the English kingdoms south of the Humber; hence, his change of religion at once affected a very wide area, quite apart from its importance as the first step in the process of winning England for Christianity. After the preliminary difficulties had been overcome and the work of the mission set on a firm basis, Augustine was certain to avail himself of the far-reaching authority of the Kentish king to get into touch with the Christians of the unconquered West, and the question of the relations which were to exist between him and the British Church would call for immediate settlement.

For 150 years there had been no intercourse between the Christians of the British Isles and those of the Continent, with the exception of that carried on through Brittany, the British colonists of which appear to have had almost as little to do with their Frankish neighbours as had the insular Britons with their English foes. The state of things which now arose was the fruit of this isolation; the Celtic Churches had not shared in the general movement of Western or Latin Christianity, but had travelled in a path of their own making. Conservative in some respects, they had innovated in others, and their successful breaking of new ground, their conversion of the heathen Picts, the fame of their seats of learning, had given them confidence in themselves and made them little disposed to give up at the bidding of an outside authority customs and institutions which had come down from the early ages of Christianity. Hence the situation was one which required careful handling, and it was unfortunate for the cause which Gregory had at heart that his representative had none of the gifts of a diplomatist, but relied on the authority bestowed upon him by the pope and thus assumed from the first that supremacy which he should have attained by policy and self-restraint. Gregory himself, it should be said, showed little appreciation of the true nature of the problem when he handed over to Augustine all the bishops of Britain, "so that thou mayst teach the unlearned, fortify the weak by thy exhortations, and by the exercise of thy authority reduce the perverse to obedience"[40] Ecclesiastics who had long been accustomed to the fullest independence were not likely to be won over by this rough and ready adaptation to their case of the methods of the schoolmaster. CHAP. VI.

There was no insurmountable barrier, it would seem, between Augustine and the British bishops.[41] No theological differences parted the Roman from the Celtic Church, for the notion that the latter was the home of a kind of primitive Protestantism, of apostolic purity and simplicity, is without any historical basis. Gildas shows clearly enough that the Church to which he belonged held the ideas current at Rome in his day as to the sacrifice of the eucharist and the privileged position of the priest.[42] The Roman missionaries knew of nothing against the Christians of Britain before they landed in the island, but on the contrary held them in high esteem for their reputed holiness of life,[43] nor is it to be supposed that Augustine would have asked them to join him in preaching the gospel to the English if he had not known them to be, from the Roman point of view, of unquestionable orthodoxy.[44] It was, no doubt, the case that they had not been used to acknowledge any special authority over other churches as vested in the Bishop of Rome; in the eye of Gildas,[45] every bishop sits in the chair of St. Peter and has entrusted to him the keys of the kingdom of heaven. Yet this was due to Celtic isolation and not to any anti-Roman feeling; the Irish missionary Columbanus, sturdy champion though he was of Celtic independence in matters ecclesiastical, nevertheless says of the pope—"By reason of Christ's twin apostles (Peter and Paul), you hold an all but celestial position, and Rome is the head of the world's Churches, if exception be made of the singular privilege enjoyed by the place of Our

[40] *H.E.* i. 27 (Plummer, p. 53).

[41] On the whole question see H. and St. i. 152-5; Warren, *Liturgy and Ritual of the Celtic Church*, pp. 63-82; Zimmer, *Celtic Church in Wales and Ireland*, pp. 60-1; *Cymr. Trans.* 1893-4, 99-101, 103-7.

[42] Williams, *Gildas*, p. 159.

[43] See the letter of Laurentius and his comrades in *H.E.* ii. 4.

[44] The views of F. V. Conybeare on this subject (*Cymr. Trans.* 1897-8, 84-117) have been shown to be baseless by H. Williams (*Zeit. Celt. Ph.* iv. 541-5).

[45] C. 66 (sedem Petri apostoli inmundis pedibus usurpantes). *Cf.* c. 109.

CHAP. VI.

Lord's resurrection (Jerusalem)".[46] When this much was conceded, it was but a short step to the acknowledgment of such claims as were put forward by Rome at this early stage in the history of the papal power.

The only extant account of the conferences which took place, probably in 602 or 603, between Augustine and the leading clergy of Southern Britain, is that contained in the *Ecclesiastical History* of the Venerable Bede.[47] As a witness, Bede labours under the disadvantage of being a warm partisan of the Roman against the Celtic party, the breach being still unhealed when he wrote in the early part of the following century. But, prejudiced as he was, he had the instincts of a historian, and his narrative allows us to see pretty plainly the point of view of the opposite party. If he tells the story of the blind man whom the Britons could not cure, but who forthwith received his sight from the Roman envoy, he has also preserved the much more interesting anecdote, which he got, no doubt, from a British source, of the hermit who, when consulted by his fellow-Britons as to the line of action they should follow, bade them take their cue from Augustine's own bearing and deportment—if he paid them the courteous attention of rising on their approach, let him be submissively heard as a true servant of Christ; if, on the other hand, he kept his seat, in arrogant assumption of superiority, let them have nothing to do with him. Augustine, according to the story, did not rise, and from that moment the spirit of discord and suspicion had the upper hand. Whatever measure of historical truth may lie in this story, it has undoubtedly symbolic value; it contains the British justification of the refusal to work with the new Archbishop of Canterbury, and in recording it Bede gives proof of his honesty and diligence as a chronicler of the past, his willingness to make use of any material that lay ready to his hand.

The first conference, arranged with the help of King Ethelbert, took place not far from the estuary of the Severn at a spot (probably the modern Aust) which long bore, in memory

[46] Letter to Boniface IV. in *Monumenta Germaniæ Historica* (new series), Epistolae, tom. iii. pp. 174-5. *Cf.* Warren, *Liturgy and Ritual of the Celtic Church*, pp. 38-9.

[47] *H.E.* ii. 2. For the date see H. and St. iii. 4, and Plummer's *Bede*, ii. p. 73.

of the event, the name of Augustine's Oak[48] Certain bishops and divines attended on behalf of the Britons, and, having listened to the demands of Augustine, asked that the matter should be adjourned for the consideration of a fuller and more representative assembly. This was duly arranged; to the second conference there came seven British bishops and many learned men, especially, says Bede, from the great monastery of Bangor, presided over at that time by abbot Dunod. The reference is undoubtedly to Bangor on the Dee, where a monastery had been established in the middle of the sixth century by Deiniol or Daniel, the founder of the original Bangor on the Menai Straits.[49] It seems likely that the conference was held not far off, and the "Sinodus urbis legion" assigned by Harleian MS. 3859 to the year 601[50] may well refer to some clerical assembly got together at Chester in connection with these negotiations. It would be of the utmost interest to know who were the leading figures on the British side, but the attempt even to fix the sees of the seven bishops who met Augustine is a hopeless one,[51] and all that is certainly known is that the conferences were a failure. According to Bede's account, Augustine expressed his readiness to overlook many peculiarities of the Celtic Churches which were contrary to universal Christian custom, if only they would in three respects make a fresh beginning; let them adopt the Roman calculations for fixing the Easter of each year, "complete" the ordinance of baptism as was done at Rome, and join him in preaching the gospel to the English, and all would be well. But to none of these things would the Britons consent, nor, adds the narrative, would they accept Augustine as archbishop.

Throughout the period of severance between the Celtic and the Roman Churches great stress was laid on the divergence with

[48] "Augustinaes Ác" is not found out of Bede and no identification can therefore be confidently put forward. But it is in favour of Aust, the Austreclive of Domesday (i. 164*b*, 2), that it was known in Welsh as Penrhyn Awstin (Triad i. 30 = ii. 56) and that it appears as "aet Austin" in the charter of 692 or 693 which bestowed it on the see of Worcester (*Cod. Dipl.* i. 35). Green's objection (*Mak. Eng.* p. 224) disappears if we take Bede to be speaking of the boundaries of his own day.

[49] See note appended to this chapter.

[50] *Cymr.* ix. 156. The ascription of the death of Gregory to the same year is possibly an inference from Bede's "interea" at the beginning of *H.E.* ii. 2.

[51] H. and St. i. 148 and iii. 41; Plummer's *Bede*, ii. p. 75.

CHAP. VI.

regard to Easter. Like the question of the proper form of clerical tonsure, which Augustine does not seem to have raised, though it was keenly debated between the two parties in later times,[52] it forced itself on men's notice as a visible sign of discord, since the sudden transition from the gloom of Holy Week to the rejoicings of the Day of Resurrection was an event in the Christian year to catch the attention of the most careless, and to see one Christian still keeping the Lenten fast while another by his side was in the midst of the Easter revels[53] brought out in the clearest fashion how far they were from dwelling as brethren in unity together. Nevertheless, the divergence was one which did not issue from any theological principle, but was due entirely, as has already been suggested, to the long separation between the Celtic Christians and those of the Continent. From an early period it had been agreed to celebrate our Lord's Resurrection, not, like His Nativity, on a fixed date, but at the season of the Jewish Passover, historically so closely connected with it. The Passover has always been observed on the day of full moon (known as the fourteenth) of the first month of the Jewish ecclesiastical year, that month being the one which coincides with the spring equinox. When it was further decided that the Easter festival should always be held on Sunday, itself a weekly celebration of the Resurrection, and not on the day which happened to be that of the paschal full moon, the elements of a complicated problem had been got together, and for many centuries no agreement as to a uniform system seemed possible.[54] The Celtic Churches accepted the principles stated above; their Easter was not a fixed date, nor did it ever fall on any other day than a Sunday. But the rules which they followed in determining which Sunday should be Easter Day in any particular year were those which had been current in Rome at the beginning of the fourth century, while in the meantime at Rome itself changes had been successively adopted which had produced an entirely new system. In this way it came about that, as the result of one rule, the Celtic

[52] Plummer's *Bede*, ii. pp. 353-4.

[53] This occurred in the royal household of Northumbria under Oswy (*H.E.* iii. 25).

[54] For a full and lucid account of the technical questions involved see A. Giry, *Manuel de Diplomatique* (Paris, 1894), pp. 141-54. The Celts, as Zimmer says (*Celtic Church*, pp. 110-1), followed the older "supputatio Romana".

Easter often anticipated the Roman by a week, while occasionally, through the operation of another, it would fall no less than four weeks later. Among the Celts 25th March was the earliest possible Easter Day, 21st April the latest, while at Rome the range of oscillation was from 22nd March to 25th April. As a result of these conflicting calculations, it was the exception for the two Easters to coincide.[55]

There is considerable doubt as to the meaning of Augustine's second demand, with reference to the "completion" of baptism. It is most often understood as implying the absence of the rite of confirmation[56] or some defect in the manner in which confirmation was carried out.[57] As, however, this particular element of discord is not elsewhere touched upon, it was clearly not one of the first magnitude. The same cannot be said of the British refusal to accept Augustine's third condition, namely, that Briton and Roman should join hands in the great undertaking of the evangelisation of the English kingdoms. It is, unfortunately, nowhere stated in express terms why this task was declined, so that the grounds of the refusal can only be conjectured. Race hatred, the fruit of a century and a half of race conflict, will no doubt supply a partial explanation, as it explains the fact that nothing had yet been done by the Britons themselves in this direction. But the conviction is forced upon one that this was not the sole reason, and it is a fair inference from the narrative of Bede that the claim of Augustine to exercise ecclesiastical supremacy over the whole island was the real stumbling-block. Where pride of race told was in indignation at the thought that the British Churches, the origin of which lay far back in a distant past, were to be disposed and ordered at the will of a mere missioner to the English, living among these Christians of yesterday and making their interests at all times his first consideration. The Britons may even have pictured to themselves the spectacle, which was actually witnessed in little more than fifty years, of an Englishman seated in the chair which it was sought to invest with such dignity and authority.

The breach having been once made, there is no doubt that the Britons did their best to keep it open. They made use

[55] See the tables of Giry, pp. 187-8, 212-3.

[56] Plummer's *Bede*, ii. pp. 75-6.

[57] *Trans. Cymr.* 1893-4, 103-6.

against those who conformed to the Roman system of that weapon of excommunication which had already been found by the Celts a far too handy resource in their domestic disputes about monasticism.[58] "It is to this day," writes Bede in 731, "the fashion among the Britons to reckon the faith and religion of Englishmen as naught and to hold no more converse with them than with the heathen."[59] This had begun as early as the time of Laurentius, the next successor of Augustine at Canterbury, who complains that one Dagan, an Irish bishop, had not only refused to eat at his table, but would not take his food anywhere under the roof which sheltered him.[60] In the days of Aldhelm, who died in 709, the Britons would make no use of pots and pans which had served for a Saxon meal until they had been thoroughly cleansed and scoured.[61] It was a losing battle which the Celtic Churches were fighting, since they could not hope to maintain their traditions, which were traditions merely and represented no great principle, against the growing influence of Rome, yet it was fought none the less bitterly for that reason.

III. Destruction of Cymric Unity by Northumbria.

At the beginning of the seventh century the English attack upon the Cymry became, in the hands of Æthelfrith, a most threatening movement. For the first twelve years of his reign, *viz.*, from 592 to 604, he was, if the author of the *Saxon Genealogies* is to be trusted,[62] king of Bernicia only, his southern border being the Tees, or possibly the Tyne;[63] in the latter year he annexed the neighbouring English kingdom of the Deiri (known in Welsh literature as Deifr),[64] expelling from

[58] See the fragments ascribed to Gildas (H. and St. i. 108-12).

[59] *H.E.* ii. 20. [60] *Ibid.* 4. [61] H. and St. iii. 271.

[62] "Eadfered Flesaurs (the epithet has not been explained) regnavit duodecim annis in Berneich et alios duodecim in Deur; viginti quatuor annis (so *H.E.* i. 34) inter duo regna regnavit" (*Hist. Britt.* c. 63). It is true that the acceptance of this chronology involves the abandonment of the usual view, based on entries in the Anglo-Saxon Chronicle, that Deira was annexed by Ethelric, Æthelfrith's father, on the death of Ælle as early as 588. But a much better authority than the Chronicle, *viz.*, Bede's short chronicle (*Mon. Hist. Br.* 96), speaks of the English north of the Humber as under the rule of Kings Ælle and Æthelfrith in the days when Kent was receiving the gospel, so that there is no difficulty in accepting the statement that the former lived until 604.

[63] For the limits of Bernicia southward see Plummer's *Bede*, ii. p. 120.

[64] Rhys (*Celt. Br.* (2), p. 291) connects Deifr with the Welsh "deifr,"

it the young Edwin, son of its former king, Ælle. He now held an exceedingly strong position, and, though the predominance of Ethelbert prevented him from exercising much influence south of the Humber, north of that river he was without a rival. In 603 he had been attacked by Aidan, king of the important Irish or "Scottish" colony which had established itself in Argyll, with a large army which probably included a contingent of Cymry from the region of the Clyde; but Aidan sustained a crushing defeat at Degsastán (The Stone of Degsa),[65] probably Dawston at the head of Liddesdale.[66] "From that day to this," says Bede, "no king of the Scots dwelling in Britain has dared to take the field against the English race." It was probably the distinction he achieved through this victory which emboldened Æthelfrith soon after to lay his hands upon Deira, and it resulted from this further acquisition that he was brought into touch with the southern Cymry, with the men of Gwynedd and of Powys and the dwellers along the Mersey and the Ribble.[67] Thereupon opened the second stage in the relations between the English and the Cymry—that which led in the space of about fifty years to the final separation of the northern from the southern section of the defeated nation and thus set Wales and Strathclyde travelling their several ways.

By what route Æthelfrith pushed forward to Chester there is nothing to show. But it was near this city that, about the year 615,[68] he won his most famous victory over the Britons. Bede gives in his *Ecclesiastical History*[69] some account of

waters, and assumes an original Debria or Dobria. It is strange, if this be so, that the labial is not represented in the early forms Deur (*Sax. Gen.*), Deiri and Deri (Bede).

[65] *H.E.* i. 34. [66] *IV. Anc. Bks.* i. 177.

[67] In *Iolo MSS.* 86, "Teyrnllwg" is said to be the ancient name of the region between the Dee and the Cumbrian Derwent. But this is probably a mere inference from the name Cadell Deyrnllwg, which in its oldest form, as given in *Hist. Britt.* c. 35 (ed. Mommsen, p. 176), is "Catell Durnluc" (the Blackhanded). See *Cymr.* vii. 119.

[68] Bede gives no date, but says incidentally that Augustine (*ob.* 604 or 605) had died "multo ante tempore". This rules out the conjectures of the Anglo-Saxon Chronicles (605, 607) and points to the period 610-6. Harl. MS. 3859 assigns "Gueith cair legion" to 613 (*Cymr.* ix. 156), which is also the year implied in *Ann. Ult. s.a.* 612. The notice in Tighernach is as follows: "K. ui (which, if correct, would be 611 or 616) . . Cath (the battle of) Caire Legion ubi sancti (*i.e.*, the monks) occissi sunt et cecidit Solon mac Conain rex Bretanorum et Cetula rex cecidit. Etalfraidh uictor erat, qui post statim obit" (*Rev. Celt.* xvii. pp. 170-1).

[69] *H.E.* ii. 2.

CHAP. VI. the battle; unhappily, he was only interested in what may be regarded as an accident of the struggle. It was his purpose to show that on this occasion a prophecy uttered many years before by Augustine was fulfilled, to the effect that, if the British clergy would not join him in preaching to the heathen English, they would assuredly be the victims of their barbaric rage. Accordingly he tells the familiar story of the appearance on the battle-field, after a three days' fast, of many hundreds of monks from the not far distant monastery of Bangor, who were stationed in what was supposed to be a place of safety under the protection of one Brochwel,[70] and from that post of vantage began to implore the blessing of God upon the arms of their fellow-countrymen. Æthelfrith asked the meaning of this strange spectacle, and, on being told, bade his troops forthwith carry by storm the citadel of prayer; "for," said he, "if they cry to their God against us, they fight against us as surely as do those who bear weapons". The command was obeyed; Brochwel and his men fled at the first onset, and no less than twelve hundred "saints" are said to have been put to the sword. Such was the massacre of the monks of Bangor—a piteous tragedy, yet one which beyond a doubt had often been paralleled in the relentless warfare between the pagan invader and his Christian foe. As to the main issues of the battle, Bede has nothing to say, except that Æthelfrith's decisive victory was not won without considerable loss on his own side.[71] This disposes of the view, which is also, it may be added, inconsistent with the later history of Cheshire,[72] that the battle of Chester was at once followed by a Northumbrian occupation of the plain around the city.[73] Genuine as the victory was, it was pretty certainly not one to have results of this kind: Æthelfrith withdrew from the district, and shortly after, in 616,

[70] "Brocmail" can hardly be Brochwel Ysgythrog, ruler of Powys, for his grandson, Selyf ap Cynan, was slain in this very battle. Nor is it likely he is the "Brocmail" of the year 662 in Harl. MS. 3859 (*Cymr.* ix. 158). The name was, in fact, a very common one; see *Cymr.* ix. 177, 178, 179, 181, 182, and, for the early form "Brohomagli," *Inscr. Chr.* No. 158, *Lap. W.* 202, *W. Phil.* (2), 372.

[71] "Non sine magno sui exercitus damno."

[72] *Cymr.* x. 23 (A. N. Palmer). The dialect of Cheshire is Mercian in its affinities, not Northumbrian; see Darlington, *Folkspeech of South Cheshire* (Eng. Dialect Soc., London, 1887).

[73] *Mak. Eng.* pp. 242-5 and map.

met his death on the banks of the Idle in battle against Rædwald of East Anglia.[74]

So far as can be seen, the leader of the Cymry in the battle of Chester was Selyf (or Solomon), son of Cynan of the White Car son of Brochwel of the Tusks, who, as representative of the ancient line of kings of Powys, was the natural defender of the valley of the Dee.[75] The Welsh and the Irish notices of the battle name him as the most notable among the slain, and one of the Triads reckons him among the British heroes who were avenged from their graves;[76] this may be a reference to the mythical British victory, which, according to Geoffrey of Monmouth, almost immediately wiped out the disgrace of the day of Chester,[77] or it may be merely an allusion to the fact that Æthelfrith lived but a short time to enjoy his triumph. There is no evidence that the forces of Gwynedd took any part in the battle, for, though the chronicle in Harl. MS. 3859 assigns to the same year the "falling asleep" of Iago (Jacob), son of Beli[78] and grandson of Rhun ap Maelgwn,[79] it does not connect the event with its notice of "Gwaith Caerlleon"; moreover, "dormitatio" is almost always used of the death of an ecclesiastic and suggests that Iago, if at any time king of Gwynedd, had by this time resigned that office and withdrawn to the quiet of a monastery.[80] Thus the ruler of Môn and Arfon and the inheritor of the claims of Maelgwn Gwynedd at the time was probably Cadfan, who appears in the pedigrees as the son of

[74] *H.E.* ii. 12. As to the date, the year 616 appears to be the one which is required by the figures of Bede; see *H.E.* i. 34; ii. 14; and especially ii. 20. It is also the year implied in the old list of Northumbrian kings (*Mon. Hist. Br.* 90). That MS. E. of the Anglo-Saxon Chronicle has 617 is of no importance, in the light of the evidence drawn from older and better authorities.

[75] For the pedigree of Selyf see *Cymr.* ix. 179 (Harl. MS. 3859); viii. 87 (Jesus Coll. MS. 20 (Evans, *Rep.* ii. p. 31)). "Garwyn" appears in the Old-Welsh form "Carguinn" in *Cambro-Br. SS.* 79, as corrected in *Cymr.* xiii. 80; *cf.* also the "garrvin" of *Blk. Bk.* fo. 14*b*. "Ysgythrog" is from "ysgythr," a tusk, for which see *LL.* i. 312, *Mab.* 122, 135.

[76] Triad i. 65 = ii. 30 = iii. 76.

[77] *Hist. Reg.* xi. 13. Palmer thinks the second battle may be historical and may underlie the "Gwaith Perllan Fangor" of Triad i. 66-7 = ii. 38 (*Cymr.* x. 22-3).

[78] *Cymr.* ix. 156. [79] *Ibid.* 170.

[80] Triad i. 39 = ii. 29 = iii. 48 says, indeed, that one of his own men cleft his skull with an axe, but this may be due to confusion with Iago ab Idwal, who was killed "a suis" in 1039. Iago ap Beli was reputed a benefactor of the cathedral church of Bangor (Browne Willis, *Survey*, 184).

CHAP. VI.

Iago ap Beli.[81] Nothing is known of this king from any ancient literary source,[82] but the caprice of time, which has overwhelmed so many other memorials of vastly greater interest, has spared us his tombstone.[83] After long serving as the lintel of the south door, it is now within the church of Llangadwaladr in Anglesey, and its inscription reads "Catamanus rex sapientisimus opinatisimus (most renowned) omnium regum," language which is reasonably interpreted to mean that he claimed, as hereditary "gwledig," a primacy among the chieftains of the Cymry.[84] As the foundation of the church is traditionally attributed to Cadfan's grandson, Cadwaladr,[85] the inscription may not actually date from the year of the king's burial, but the form of the name[86] and the characters employed point pretty clearly to the seventh century.

If Cadfan is to be reckoned among the obscurer personalities of Welsh history, his son and successor Cadwallon[87] holds a place in the forefront of those who have earned the grateful remembrance of the Welsh race by vigorous championship of the national cause. The memory of his great duel with Edwin of Northumbria, carried on with marked ill fortune for many years, but ending in the defeat and death of the English king, deeply impressed itself on the minds of his fellow-countrymen, so that Edwin became the typical English antagonist,[88] and every bold defender of the freedom of Wales was hailed as a new Cadwallon.[89] This was, indeed, the last great struggle between

[81] *Cymr.* ix. 170. Though this is fairly good authority, the number of names (five) in the pedigree between Maelgwn (*ob. circa* 550) and Cadwaladr (*ob.* 664) makes one a little sceptical.

[82] Geoffrey of Monmouth (*Hist. Reg.* xi. 13; xii. 1) is here, as elsewhere, a mere romancer.

[83] *Mon. Ant.* 156 (157); *Arch. Camb.* I. i. (1846), 165-7; *Inscr. Chr.* No. 149; *W. Phil.* (2), 160, 364; *Lap. W.* 190-1.

[84] *Celt. Br.* (2), pp. 127-8.

[85] *Myv. Arch.* II. 33 (421).

[86] Brythonic "Catamanus," for an earlier "Cat*u*manus," is on its way to become the old Welsh "Catman".

[87] For the pedigree see *Cymr.* ix. 170. Bede's form "Caedualla" is due to the influence of the name of Ceadwalla of Wessex.

[88] See *Myv. Arch.* I. 194 (143), where a twelfth-century militant bard says—

Gwalchmai y'm gelwir, gal Edwin ac Eingl.

("Gwalchmai am I called, a foe to Edwin and every Englishman.")

Cf. Blk. Bk. fo. 24*a* (*IV. Anc. Bks.* ii. 17)—a poem of about the same date.

[89] See the poem from the Red Book of Hergest in *Myv. Arch.* I. 121-2 (96-7); *IV. Anc. Bks.* ii. 277-9, which has no relation to the battles fought by the Cadwallon ap Cadfan of history and must commemorate the deeds of some mediæval prince.

Briton and Englishman for supremacy in the island, and the overthrow of Edwin for a brief space raised hopes that Britain might yet be snatched from the grasp of the Teutonic conqueror. The fall of Cadwallon a year later scattered these hopes to the winds, and, though the contest with Northumbria was not abandoned, it had henceforth little prospect of success, and on the death of Penda, who furnished it with Mercian support, it came suddenly to an end.

The death of Æthelfrith in 616 had brought about a dynastic revolution in Northumbria. Power was seized by Edwin, the representative of the royal line dislodged from Deira in 604, and thus, while the two kingdoms still remained under one head, it was the southern and not the northern realm which now wielded supremacy. Edwin had spent his youth—he was now thirty-one—in exile, fleeing from court to court to escape the ruthless enmity of Æthelfrith; during his wanderings he had lived in East Anglia, and also, if we may accept the evidence of the Triads, in Gwynedd, for his name is included in a trio of "Three Chief Oppressors of Môn, nurtured within the island".[90] He soon showed the energy and resolution to be expected from one who had been trained in the austere school of adversity. Attacking the British kingdom of Elmet, or Elfed, as it would now be written, which lay around our Leeds, he completely subdued it and drove King Ceredig from his throne.[91] By this conquest the chief barrier which parted Deira from the Irish Sea was removed, and very shortly afterwards Edwin must have effected that breach between the Cymry of the North and those of Wales which the battle of Chester foreshadowed, but did not actually bring about. His relations with the other English kingdoms, over all of which save Kent he established his ascendancy, his acceptance of Christianity at the instance of a Roman missionary from Canterbury, and his assumption of something like imperial state invest his short reign with great interest, but for the historian of Wales his most notable achievement was his conquest of what Bede calls the Mevanian islands, lying

[90] I. 81 = ii. 56 (end). Geoffrey of Monmouth's account (*Hist. Reg.* xii. 1) of the nurture of Edwin and Cadwallon together no doubt rests on this tradition.

[91] *Hist. Britt.* c. 63; *Mak. Eng.* pp. 253-7. For Ceredig see *H.E.* iv. 21 ("rege Brettonum Cerdice"); he may be the "Ceretic" of Harl. MS. 3859, *s.a.* 616 (*Cymr.* ix. 157), but in that case the year is most probably wrong.

CHAP. VI.

between Britain and Ireland,[92] in other words, of Anglesey and Man. Such a conquest implies the equipment of a fleet, which was probably fitted out at Chester; [93] not only was this necessary for any operations against the Isle of Man, but it was repeatedly shown under the Norman and early Plantagenet kings that nothing could be effected against Anglesey without naval assistance, so strong were the natural defences of the island on the landward side. With a fleet in possession of the Irish Sea, troops flushed with victory over the Britons of Elmet, and borders secured from attack by the greatness of his name, Edwin entered upon what was the first English invasion of Wales with notable advantages in his favour.

It may be judged from Cadwallon's later history that there was no lack of spirit in the defence. But tradition has nothing to say of his share in the campaign, and only commemorates the valour of one Belyn of Lleyn, who is described as fighting Edwin with his "teulu" or warband at "Bryn Edwin" in Rhos,[94] and also at Erethlyn, near Eglwysfach, in the same region.[95] Rhos, lying as it does between the Clwyd and the Conway, was just the region in which to oppose the progress of any expedition making its way to Anglesey, and the Hill of Edwin may be that known at present under the slightly altered form of Bryn yr Odyn, not far from Llanelian. The brave stand of Belyn and his doughty followers was, however, made in vain, for the struggle closed, after having been waged apparently for some years, with the retreat of Cadwallon to the little island of Priestholm or Ynys Lannog, off the coast of Anglesey, where

[92] *H.E.* ii. 5, 9. The description given of the two islands in c. 9 shows clearly that Anglesey is meant to be one, but Bede had no warrant for extending the name "Mevania" to this island, which is always Mona and Môn in the ancient writers. As for "Meuania," it is found in certain authors, *e.g.*, Orosius (*Adv. Pag.* I. ii. § 82), as a name of the Isle of Man, being probably a misreading of "Menauia," which again is the Celtic "Manavia" or Manaw (*Celt. Heath.* pp. 663-4).

[93] *Mak. Eng.* p. 257.

[94] Triad i. 49 = ii. 40 = iii. 27. That Belyn belongs to history and not merely to fable is shown by the "Belin moritur" of Harl. MS. 3859, *s.a.* 627 (*Cymr.* ix. 157).

[95] Triad ii. 19, in which "yn" must be read before Erethlyn (Erythlyn in the Red Book). The name appears in the old one-inch Ordnance map as "Hiraethlyn"; for the better form "Pennant Ereithlyn" see Thomas, *St. Asaph*, p. 538.

he was hemmed in by Edwin's fleet.[96] It was now, in all probability, that the flight to Ireland took place,[97] which is vouched for by tradition [98] and which must have made Edwin's triumph for the moment complete.[99]

But ere long the wheel of fortune took a sudden turn. Cadwallon, on his return to Wales, entered into an alliance with Penda, who had stepped forward as the leader of the Mercians, the English settlers in the basin of the upper Trent.[100] The motives of Penda are not difficult to discern; he was a pagan and remained until his death the chief upholder of heathenism among the English; he resented as a Mercian the ascendancy of Northumbria. There is more to wonder at in the attitude of Cadwallon, for never before, so far as can be seen, had Briton and Englishman made common cause in any quarrel that had arisen in the island. The British king had, however, realised, in the light of recent events, that his first concern must be to

[96] "Obsessio Catguollaun regis in insula glannauc"—Harl. MS. 3859, *s.a.* 629 (*Cymr.* ix. 157). As the fall of Edwin is assigned to 630, the year is probably 632.

[97] *Celt. Br.* (2), p. 131.

[98] Triad i. 34, which says, however, that he was an exile for seven years. Geoff. Mon., in deference to the tradition, takes Cadwallon to Ireland (*Hist. Reg.* xii. 4), but soon moves him on to Brittany ("Armoricam," whence the "Armonicam" of Reginald's life of St. Oswald—Sim. Dun. i. 345—*cf.* 350), so that he may be restored by Breton help. A poem in the *Book of Taliesin* (*IV. Anc. Bks.* ii. p. 206; *Myv. Arch.* I. 74 (62)) has a reference to the story—

Pan dyfu gatwallawn Dros eigyawn iwerdon.
("When Cadwallon returns o'er the Irish sea")—

but the poet is no doubt using the old tradition in the interests of some prince of his own day.

[99] Wm. Malm. was the first to suggest that Anglesey was so called in consequence of Edwin's reduction of it, the name being really "isle of Angles or English" (*Gesta Regum*, ed. Hardy, i. 69). There are many objections to this derivation. One fails to see why the very brief occupation under Edwin should have led the English ever afterwards to speak of this as by pre-eminence their island. Further, the name does not make its appearance until the eleventh century; Alfred's version of *H.E.* ii. 5, 9, has "Monige" for the Mevanian islands (Plummer's *Bede*, ii. p. 94) and MSS. C. and D. of the Anglo-Saxon Chronicle have *s.a.* 1000 the same form for Anglesey (*Mon. Hist. Br.* 407). "Angles ege" is first found in MS. E. *s.a.* 1098. Philological difficulties have also been pointed out (*Academy*, 2nd June, 1894, p. 458) and altogether, the derivation proposed by Dr. H. Bradley and supported by Mr. W. H. Stevenson (*Descr. Pemb.* i. 322-3) is much to be preferred. Starting from the form Ongulsey found in the Orkneyinga Saga (Rolls ed., p. 70), they connect the name with the Norse öngull, a fiord, and interpret as "the island of the strait".

[100] *H.E.* ii. 20. According to some Welsh pedigrees, Cadwallon married Penda's sister (*Bye-Gones*, 1st Oct. 1890, p. 480).

CHAP. VI.

break the power of Edwin, and that in the furtherance of this purpose he must not be over scrupulous as to the means he employed. He had no reason to dread the triumph of Mercia, a state as yet in its infancy, and Penda's religion was no stumbling-block to one who did not regard the English Christians, followers of the ways of Rome, as brethren in the faith. In 633 Cadwallon and Penda met Edwin in battle, defeated and slew him, and for a time had Northumbria at their feet. The scene of this memorable encounter cannot, unfortunately, be fixed with certainty. Bede gives the name of the place as Haethfelth and conveys the impression that it was in Deira, or not far distant from its borders; [101] accordingly, Hatfield, near Doncaster, has been a popular identification.[102] The *Saxon Genealogies*, on the other hand, speak of this battle as "bellum Meicen," [103] and later Welsh traditions connect it with the Meigen which is known to have lain somewhere near the Breiddin, on the borders of Montgomeryshire and Shropshire.[104] On the whole, it is most likely that the battle was fought in the north, at a spot known to the Cymry as Meigen, and that this was subsequently confused in Welsh literature with the more familiar Meigen on the confines of Powys.

During the year which followed the overthrow of Edwin, Northumbria was entirely at the mercy of the British king and his Mercian ally.[105] It was treated as a conquered country and pitilessly ravaged; no respect was paid by either of the two victors to the nascent Christianity of the district. Cadwallon was the dominant spirit, and it is clear that his policy was

[101] See the reference in *H.E.* ii. 14 (end) to ravages which followed the fight. The Berne MS. of *Hist. Reg.* xii. 8 has, it should be noted, "hedfeld" and not "Hevenfeld," as in Giles's edition. Geoffrey knows only the English names of the battle-fields of this period.

[102] Smith in *Mon. Hist. Br.* 171; *Mak. Eng.* pp. 269-71; Plummer's *Bede*, ii. pp. 115-6.

[103] *Hist. Britt.* c. 61, which is the source of the entry in the chronicle in Harl. MS. 3859, *s.a.* 630. For an explanation of the "Mei*cer*en" of the Rolls editor (*Annales Cambriæ*, ed. J. Williams Ab Ithel, 1860, p. 7), see *Cymr.* ix. 157; xi. 147.

[104] Triad i. 63 = ii. 15 suggests that Meigen was in Powys, and the poem styled "Marwnad Cadwallon" associates it with the Severn and Dygen (*IV. Anc. Bks.* ii. p. 277; *Myv. Arch.* I. 121 (97)), the latter being in full Dygen Freiddin (*Myv. Arch.* I. 193 (142)). According to *Iolo MSS.* 18, there was a place of the name ("Meigen Cil Ceincoed"), on the banks of the Rhymni.

[105] *H.E.* ii. 20; iii. 1.

purely destructive; his aim was not to subjugate Northumbria, but to ruin it. On the death of Edwin, Bernicia and Deira had again become separate kingdoms; a son of Æthelfrith's, Eanfrith, had seized the crown of the northern, a cousin of Edwin's, Osric, that of the southern state. Cadwallon set himself to make an end of both rulers. He defeated and slew Osric in the summer of 634, finding his opportunity when that prince endeavoured to shut him and his army within the circuit of a walled town;[106] in the autumn of the same year he lured Eanfrith to his camp and despatched him also. With a very large army, to which had flocked, no doubt, the Cymry alike of the north and of the south, in eager expectation of a final triumph over the Saxon foe, he planted himself in the heart of Northumbria, on the hills that slope northwards towards Hexham and the Tyne.

A second son of Æthelfrith's, named Oswald, had, however, at once stepped into the place of his brother Eanfrith, and, with a small body of troops on which he could thoroughly rely, marched south to contest with Cadwallon the supremacy of Bernicia. The two brothers had spent the reign of Edwin in exile among the Scots of Argyll and had there been imbued with the principles of the Christian faith, which they received, of course, in their Celtic form. Eanfrith's creed was, it would seem, but lightly held, for he abandoned it on his accession; Oswald, on the other hand, had embraced the new religion with all the earnestness of a singularly noble character, and the tale was long told how, on the day before the battle which he fought with Cadwallon, he had set up a rough wooden cross, the first ever seen among the English of those parts, and had knelt at its foot with his soldiery to pray for victory in the coming struggle. The spot bore the name of Heavenfield; it lay close to the Roman Wall, not far from the point where this is cut by the North Tyne, and the devotion of later ages, which held the place to be one of the most sacred in Northumbria, raised there the chapel of St. Oswald's, which marks it to this day.[107] The following night Oswald's army resumed

[106] Often supposed to be York, but Bede obviously did not know its name.

[107] *H.E.* iii. 2. There is nothing in the narrative of Bede to suggest that there was any fighting at "Hefenfelth" or St. Oswald's. On the contrary, he states explicitly that Cadwallon and his army were overwhelmed at "Denises-

CHAP. VI.

its march and at daybreak surprised the host of Cadwallon, as it lay encamped some 10 miles further south, on the banks of a stream now known as Rowley Water. In spite of the disparity of numbers, the rout of the British was complete and the death of Cadwallon made it irretrievable defeat.[108]

The year of Cadwallon's ascendancy in the North showed that, though the courage of the Cymry ran high, they did not possess the secret of rule. They failed to follow up their victory in the field by any measures which might incline the defeated Northumbrians to accept their overlordship, and accordingly the question whether they would reconquer the island or be driven into the highland regions of the West was really settled by the events of this year. Some time went by ere the contest with Northumbria was abandoned, but its issue was henceforth certain.

Oswald established himself as king of the whole of Northumbria, and, according to the testimony of Bede,[109] was not inferior in the extent of his power to Edwin himself But no such struggle with the Cymry as marked his predecessor's reign is coupled either by history or by tradition with his name, and nothing is known of his relations with the successor of Cadwallon, if indeed any Welsh prince was able at this time to assert his claim to the office of "gwledig". His chief enemy was Penda of Mercia, and it was Penda who, in 642, when he had ruled over the Northumbrians for some eight years, attacked and slew him in the battle of Maserfeld.[110] There is

burna," which has been shown to be several miles to the south (Plummer's *Bede*, ii. pp. 122-3). This harmonises well with the fact, to which Bede and an equally good authority, Adamnan (*Vita Sancti Columbæ*, i. 1), bear witness, that Oswald, with a much smaller army, won his victory over the thousands of Cadwallon by means of a night march, followed by an attack at dawn. It was, says Adamnan, "felix et *facilis* . . . victoria".

[108] In the *Saxon Genealogies* the battle is called "bellum Catscaul" (*Hist. Britt.* c. 64), whence the "ca*n*tscaul" of Harl. MS. 3859, *s.a.* 631 (*Cymr.* ix. 157). Skene's derivation of the name from "cad ys guaul," the battle at the Wall (*Celtic Scotland*, 1876, i. p. 245), is quite impossible, not to speak of the high probability that the battle was not fought at the Wall at all. The recent habit of dating it 635, instead of 634, is due to a misunderstanding of Bede (Plummer's *Bede*, ii. p. 121).

[109] *H.E.* ii. 5 ("sextus Oswald . . . hisdem finibus regnum tenuit").

[110] *Ibid.* ii. 9-13; for the date see v. 24. The *Sax. Gen.* calls this "bellum Cocboy" (*Hist. Britt.* c. 65), a name which cannot be used either for or against the Oswestry identification.

no evidence that the Cymry had any part or lot in this battle, though it would seem probable that it was fought not far from their borders. For, while no ancient authority furnishes any hint as to the situation of the battle-field, a local tradition,[111] which was in existence at the time of the Norman Conquest, fixed it at Oswestry, the Oswald's Tree (in Welsh "*Croes* Oswallt," *i.e.*, Oswald's Cross), from which the place derived its name, being taken to be the wooden post or stock on which was set by Penda's orders the head of the fallen king. When Oswald came to be regarded as an English saint and martyr, a church was raised on the spot to his memory; hard by may still be seen Oswald's Well, once highly esteemed for its healing virtues and at that time overshadowed by Oswald's Ash, of which remarkable legends were also told. On the whole, there is much in favour of this identification; it is implied in Bede's account of the miracles which signalised the spot that it lay in a wild region sometimes visited by British wayfarers,[112] and there can be no difficulty in imagining the Mercians as having pushed so far west,[113] for Penda's name is preserved in that of Llannerch Panna, near Ellesmere,[114] and perhaps in that of Pontesbury between Shrewsbury and Montgomery.[115]

The victory of Maserfeld made Penda for many years the chief power in Southern Britain. Northumbria became again a divided kingdom, and the Mercian leader was able not only to control affairs in Deira, but also to harass by constant plundering expeditions the furthest limits of Bernicia, ruled over by Oswald's brother, Oswy.[116] So far as can be judged, he had at all times the support of the Cymry, and about 645

[111] See the life of Oswald by Reginald of Durham, printed in part by T. Arnold in the Rolls edition of Simeon of Durham (vol. i. 1882), and especially pp. 350, 356-7. The earliest mention of Oswestry by that name is in Earl Hugh's charter to Shrewsbury abbey (*Mon. Angl.* iii. 520 "Oswaldestre"; in the foundation charter it is "ecclesiam sancti Oswaldi," *ibid.*).

[112] *H.E.* iii. 10 ("quidam de natione Brettonum . . . iter faciens iuxta ipsum locum").

[113] Green, who supposed that Shrewsbury did not become English until the time of Offa (*Mak. Eng.* pp. 419-20), was thereby led to set aside the view that Maserfeld was in North-west Shropshire.

[114] This name, which may be a translation of the English Penley (*Bye-Gones*, 1st Oct. 1890, p. 480), appears in Peniarth MS. 176 in the more regular form of Llanerch Banna (Evans, *Rep.* i. pt. 2. p. 979). For Panta, the Celtic spelling of Penda, see *Hist. Britt.* cc. 60, 64; *Rev. Celt.* xvii. pp. 181, 185, 194.

[115] Pantesberie in Domesd. i. 255*b*, 1.

[116] *H.E.* iii. 16, 17.

CHAP. VI.

a struggle, noticed only by the Irish annalists,[117] took place between Oswy and the Britons of Strathclyde or of Wales, in which it is highly probable that Penda played a secret, if not an open part. Gwynedd was ruled over at this time by Cadafael son of Cynfedw, who was not of the stock of Maelgwn, but is ranked by the Triads among the Three Peasant Kings of the Isle of Britain.[118] Cadwallon had, indeed, left a son Cadwaladr, but he was probably at the time of his father's death of tender years, and would seem to have had to wait for his crown for a considerable period. Other Welsh leaders of the period are not known to history, but there is little doubt that they acted with Penda, and that most of them were in the army which in 655 [119] marched upon Bernicia with the intention of overwhelming Oswy. It was the crisis of that king's career; he was shut up in the strong fortress of Iudeu, which lay somewhere near the Firth of Forth,[120] and was forced to deliver up to Penda the treasures of the royal hoard, the heirlooms he had received from his ancestors and the rich spoils of many a victory over the Britons. These the Mercian king distributed, with the pride of a conqueror, as largess to his followers, and the delight of the Cymry at recovering their ancient possessions made memorable for years to come the "Restoration of Iudeu".[121] The army then returned in triumph, and it was probably as the serried hosts were passing through Deira, in the careless mood of men who had achieved their purpose, that Oswy burst upon them and in the battle of Winwaed Field [122] routed the great confederacy, slew the

[117] Tighernach in *Rev. Celt.* xvii. p. 186 (Cath Ossu inter eum et Britones); *Ann. Ult. s.a.* 641.

[118] I. 76 = ii. 59 = iii. 26. III. 48 seeks to make him the murderer of Iago ap Beli; it is not a very likely story.

[119] Bede gives the date in *H.E.* v. 24.

[120] *Celt. Br.* (2), pp. 133, 151, 268; *W. People*, pp. 115-6. The difficulty in identifying the "urbem quae vocatur Iudeu" of the *Sax. Gen.* (*Hist. Britt.* c. 64, end) with the "urbem Giudi" of *H.E.* i. 12, which is almost certainly Inchkeith, might be met by supposing that Bede had confused an "urbs Giudi" and an "*insula* Giudi".

[121] I follow the *Sax. Gen.* here rather than Bede, because the phrase "Atbret Iudeu" must have had its origin in an actual restoration. "Atbret" is now "edfryd"; *cf. Gr. Celt.* (2), p. 900.

[122] Not yet identified, though, with Bede's words before one ("hoc autem bellum rex Osuiu in regione Loidis . . . confecit"), it is difficult to avoid placing it in the West Riding. The suggestion that here (*H.E.* iii. 24) "Loidis" means

implacable enemy of his house, and finally freed Northumbria from the domination of Penda and his British allies. Cadafael escaped destruction by making for Gwynedd with all his men the night before the encounter, which led the wits of the day to affix a new epithet to his name, *viz.*, Cadafael Cadomedd, "The Battle-seizer who battle declines".[123] But among the thirty noble leaders who fell around Penda there must have been no small number of Britons, the last of their race seriously to contest with the English the supremacy of the isle of Britain.

CHAP. VI.

Oswy's victory enabled him to reach a height of power and influence attained by no earlier English king. He was recognised alike by Saxon, Angle, Briton, Pict and Scot as the supreme ruler of Britain, and after his death in 671 a good part of his authority was retained by his son Egfrith. This final victory of Northumbria over the Cymry put an end to the existence of the latter as a united force and irrevocably divided the Cumbrians from the Welsh. Thus the year 655 forms an epoch of great importance in the history of the Welsh people; it closes the period of definition, during which they were gradually marked off from the other inhabitants of these islands and constituted a separate people; it brings upon the stage a nation, isolated and self-contained, dependent henceforth upon its own resources for its development.

NOTE TO CHAPTER VI. § i.—*The Name "Cymry".*

Zeuss first proposed in 1853 the "Combroges" derivation and cited the similar form "Allobroges," explained by an early commentator on Juvenal, *Satires*, viii. 234, as meaning "men of another land" (*Grammatica Celtica*, first ed., p. 226). It has now been generally adopted; see *Urk. Spr.* 221; *W. People*, p. 26. Among obsolete derivations mention may be made of the following. Geoffrey of Monmouth, in order to explain Cambria, the Latinised form of Cymru, invented a Kamber, son of Brutus (*Hist. Reg.* ii. 1), who does not appear in the original Brutus legend, as given in various forms in the *Historia Brittonum.* Theophilus Evans (*Drych y Prif Oesoedd*, ed. 1740 and reprint of 1902, p. 7) in 1715 derived Cymry from Gomer, son of Japheth, who had from the time of Josephus (*Ant. Jud.* I. vi. 1) been regarded as the ancestor of the Gauls (*Hist. Britt.* c. 18: "primus, Gomer, a quo Galli"). This derivation soon ac-

Lothian seems far-fetched; it would be unlike Bede not to warn his readers that the name is not the same as that which he mentions in ii. 14, where the reference is unmistakably to a region in Deira.

[123] *Hist. Britt.* c. 65. The *Sax. Gen.* call the battle "strages Gai campi" (probably translating some such form as "Maes Gai").

CHAP. VI.

quired great popularity among Welshmen, who have not yet given up the habit of speaking of themselves as "hil Gomer" and of their language as "yr Omeraeg". A more specious explanation was that which connected Cymry and Cimbri, the name of a tribe now definitely assigned to the Teutonic family, though long supposed to be Celtic (*Rev. Celt.* xix. p. 74). This was first put forward in the sixteenth century by Humphrey Llwyd (*Commentariolum*, ed. Moses Williams, London, 1731, pp. 65-6) and caught the fancy of many capable historians, including the penetrating critic, Thomas Stephens (*Lit. Kym.* first ed., 1849, Pref.). John Walters proposed in his *Dissertation on the Welsh Language* (1771) a native derivation, from "cyn" = first, original and "bro" = country, giving the word the sense of "aborigines" (so W. O. Pughe's *Dictionary, s.v.* Cymmro), but, as is pointed out by Zeuss (*Gr. Celt.* (2), p. 207), this combination yields, not "Cymro," but "Cynfro". For the distinction between the two prefixes "kom, kon" and "kentu," see *Urk. Spr.* 86 and 77. It ought, perhaps, to be added that the ever delightful George Borrow makes an original contribution of his own to the discussion of this question, which shall be given in his words: "The original home of the Cumro was Southern Hindustan, the extreme point of which, Cape Comorin, derived from him its name" (*Wild Wales*, appended note).

The main facts as to the early use of the name are given by Phillimore in *Cymr.* xi. 97-100. Its first appearances are in connection with the history of Cumbria, not of Wales, and it was only very slowly adopted by Welsh writers as a substitute for the ancient "Brython," "Brittones". Thus it is unknown, not only to Gildas, Bede and Nennius, but also to Asser, the *Liber Landavensis*, and the compilers of the older parts of the *Annales Cambriæ*. But there is one important exception; "Cymro," "Cymraes" and "Cymry" are of fairly common occurrence in the Welsh Laws, and, although the MSS. of these are of comparative late date, the terminology they employ is no doubt ancient. See *LL.* i. 96, 98, 152, 206, 208, 508, 530, 646, 694, 750; ii. 94, 100, 114. In these passages, however, the "Cymro" appears to be, not so much a member of a particular race, as one holding a definite legal status. He is usually distinguished from the "alltud" or landless man, and occasionally from the "caeth" or slave. He is, in fact, the "treftadog" or "priodor," whether bond or free, the man who has landed property or expectations. It is possible, therefore, that the term had a legal before it had a historical application and the use of "Cymry" in the sense of "co-proprietors" may have prepared the way for its adoption as a badge of national union.

NOTE TO CHAPTER VI. § ii.—*Bangor.*

The idea that "bangor" denotes in Welsh a primitive type of monastery is due to the Glamorgan school of antiquaries, one of whom expressly says (*Iolo MSS.* 114): "the bangors preceded the monasteries and afterwards disappeared, with the exception of those which became monasteries". The theory took its rise from the fact that some half-dozen Celtic ecclesiastical sites actually bear the name; to these the writers of the Iolo MSS. added another dozen, such as Bangor Illtud (Llanilltud Fawr) and Bangor Dathan (Caerwent), which were entirely of their own invention. It was a further help to this explanation that the name Bangor had long been explained as derived from "ban," high, conspicuous, lofty, and "cor," a choir (see Davies, *Dict. s.v.* ban). But it has lately been pointed out that, where "bangor" occurs as a common noun, it has a very different meaning, *viz.*, the binding part of a wattle fence (Evans, *Dict. s.v.*), and the suggestion has been put forward that the first monastic site so called took its name from the wattle enclosure surrounding it, while the other monasteries were called Bangor in honour of the first and most famous (A. N. Palmer in *Cymr.* x. 16-7; *cf. Cymr.* xi. 83-4). If this be so, there can be little doubt that the original Bangor was that on the Menai Straits, known to this day among Welshmen as "Bangor *Fawr* (the Great) yn Arfon," and to be identified with the "Bennchor moer in Britannia" the burning of which is mentioned by *Ann. Ult. s.a.* 631 (really 634). This monastery is commonly said to have been founded in the early part of the sixth century, so that the famous Bangor of Belfast Lough, established by Comgall about 558 (*Chron. Scot.* and *Ann. Ult. s.a.*) may well have been modelled upon it. Nor is there any difficulty in regarding Bangor Iscoed, which is Bede's "Bancor" and "Bancornaburg," as an offshoot also; the true tradition appears to make Deiniol, the founder of episcopal Bangor, its patron saint (see below). Of the other places bearing the name little need be said. Bangor on the Teifi is an ancient church dedicated to St. David (*Myv. Arch.* I. 271 (194)), but there is nothing to show that it was ever the seat of an important monastery. Capel Bangor near Aberystwyth was not an ecclesiastical site until 1839; it takes its name from the adjacent farm of Maes Bangor. CHAP. VI.

The "Bancornaburg" of *H.E.* is, of course, an English derivative, explained as meaning "the stronghold of the men of Bangor" (Plummer's *Bede*, ii. p. 75). The existence of the form and Bede's use of the present tense ("vocatur") are not favourable to the view which is sometimes expressed (*Cymr.* x. 15) that the monastery did not survive the famous massacre of Æthelfrith's day. It has not been observed that the name was still current, in the form "Bankeburw," at the end of the thirteenth century (*Tax. Nich.* 248).

"Dinoot," which represents the old Welsh Dunôt (with the narrow *u*), from the Latin Donatus (*Celt. Br.* (2), p. 304), is given by Bede as the name of the abbot of Bangor-on-Dee in Augustine's time. But a little consideration will show that this cannot be the father of Deiniol and the son of Pabo Post Prydain mentioned in the old genealogies (*Cymr.* ix. 174; *Myv. Arch.* II. 23 (415)) and in the Triads (i. 11 = ii. 31 = iii. 71). For this Dunod is everywhere represented, not as a "saint," but as a mighty warrior; he belongs, moreover, to the beginning and not to the end of the sixth century. There is, so far as I know, only one passage which can be cited in support of the ascription of this church to Dunod ap Pabo, *viz.*, *Iolo MSS.* 105, and elsewhere in these notices (113, 127, 129) the view is taken that it was Deiniol who had the chief share in the matter of its foundation. That this is the sounder tradition is shown by the fact that two of the ancient chapels of Bangor, *viz.*, Marchwiel and Worthenbury, are dedicated to Daniel, that there was in the parish a "Daniel's Well" (*Cymr.* x. 19) and that the parish wake or annual festival followed St. Deiniol's day, formerly 11th September (*Iolo MSS.* 152; Evans, *Rep.* i. p. 17), but now, as the result of the change of style, 22nd September (*Arch. Camb.* IV. vii. (1876), 297; Thomas, *St. Asaph*, p. 799). It is, of course, quite possible, and even likely, that Bede's "Dinoot" was of the family of Deiniol.

CHAPTER VII.

THE AGE OF ISOLATION.

I. The Determination of the Welsh Border.

CHAP. VII.

Though there is little contemporary evidence as to what took place in Wales during the two hundred years which followed the battle of Winwaed Field, the indirect evidence leaves no doubt as to the political condition of the country. From the royal genealogies preserved in Harleian MS. 3859 and from the Welsh laws, no less than from the scanty notices of the annalists, it may with confidence be inferred that the Welsh were during this period under the rule of minor chieftains, "kings" of districts which were often of less extent than a modern Welsh county, and that, if any one of these claimed, by right of ancestral dignity, pre-eminence among his fellows, the utmost to which he could attain was an honorary primacy, carrying with it no important practical consequences.[1] The ambitious hope of recovering Britain from English domination had for ever faded and with it had ended the mission of the gwledig; henceforth, the conflict with the English would be a border warfare, waged against the kings and ealdormen of Mercia, in countless skirmishes and border forays, under many local leaders, and centuries would go by ere the spectacle would again be beheld of a great national movement led by a prince whose authority was recognised by the whole of Wales.

In this and the following two chapters the history of this period of subdivision and local independence will be treated, not chronologically, for any attempt to weave the scattered strands into a thread of continuous narrative must prove a failure, but topically, each branch of the subject being taken separately. The establishment of a border between the English

[1] See p. 231 below.

and the Welsh peoples, the progress of the Welsh Church, the geographical and territorial divisions of Wales, the social life and the characteristic institutions of the Welsh will be in turn discussed, and the way will thus be prepared for the study of mediæval Wales, when a certain measure of stability has been reached in these matters and the main interest lies once more in the action of individual princes and of their opponents.

Little is known of the process by which the boundary between the English and the Welsh was evolved. No record has been preserved of the English conquest of Cheshire, Shropshire or Herefordshire, and one can but conjecture the course of events in this region during the seventh and the eighth centuries. On the whole, it appears likely that it was the earlier and not the later of these two centuries which witnessed the triumphs of Mercia along the border, and that the great age of territorial expansion was that of Penda (d. 655) and his energetic son, Wulfhere (d. 675). Chester and its neighbourhood, though not occupied by Æthelfrith as the result of his famous victory,[2] probably fell into Mercian hands not long afterwards; this may well have been one effect of the fall of Cadwallon. If it may be supposed that St. Werburh had a convent here before the translation of her relics to the place from Hanbury in 874, it was thoroughly English as early as 680, for she was a daughter of King Wulfhere.[3] To this it may be added that the fact that Bede gives the monastery of Bangor Iscoed an English name, *viz.*, Bancornaburg,[4] implies that, when he wrote in 731, the English border was not far from the Dee. In Shropshire the evidence is in the same direction. It has already been suggested that Penda's name is preserved in that of Llannerch Panna, near Ellesmere, and that the battle of Maserfeld was fought at Oswestry.[5] In the next generation, Wulfhere gave his name to a Wulfheresford in the hundred of Mersete,[6] which was known to the Welsh as

[2] See p. 180.

[3] Fl. Wig. i. 32, 265. The date of the translation is from Higden, who was a monk of St. Werburgh's (*Polychr.* vi. 126).

[4] *H.E.* ii. 2.

[5] P. 189.

[6] "In Merset hund. Rogerius comes tenet Wlferesforde. Rex Edwardus tenuit" (*Domesd. Shrops.* i. 259*b*, 2). No identification is suggested by Eyton (*Shrops.* xi. 43).

CHAP. VII.

"Rhyd Wilfre ar Efyrnwy,"[7] and must, therefore, have been close to Llanymynech or Melverley. Shrewsbury itself is not mentioned until a comparatively late date,[8] but the nunnery at Wenlock, not far to the south-east, was founded by St. Milburh, who was a cousin of St. Werburh,[9] so that this district must have been in English hands before the end of the seventh century and was not won for Mercia, as has been sometimes supposed,[10] by the victorious sword of Offa. That English Herefordshire was also conquered about the middle of the seventh century (if not earlier) does not admit of any doubt. This was the region of the Hecana or Magesaetas, who formed a separate kingdom under Merewald, a brother of Wulfhere,[11] and from about 680 a separate diocese, with Hereford as the seat of the bishop.[12] The *Liber Landavensis*, compiled from old records at Llandaff in the twelfth century, places as early as the age of Oudoceus, *i.e.*, the first half of the seventh century, the overthrow of the Britons in the triangle formed by the Dore, the Worm and the Wye,[13] and it is indeed evident that, in the interests of the security of Hereford, this tract of country must have been seized about the time of the foundation of the city. The general effect of the evidence, therefore, is to make

[7] *Mab.* 144.

[8] The earliest reference to Shrewsbury (if the document be genuine) is to be found in Ethelred's charter to Wenlock, done in 901 "in ciuitate scrobbensis" (*Cod. Dipl.* ii. 137). It next appears in the Anglo-Saxon Chronicle, MS. F. *s.a.* 1006.

[9] Fl. Wig. i. 33, 265; Wm. Malm. *G.R.* 78, 267 (i. 110, 369-70).

[10] Green (*Mak. Eng.* pp. 419-20; *cf.* also maps on pp. 395 and 429) adopted too readily the statement of Welsh writers that Offa conquered the country between the Wye and the Severn and thus brought about the transference of the capital of Powys from Pengwern (*i.e.*, Shrewsbury) to Mathrafal on the Vyrnwy. The first to put forward this view was David Powel in his *Historie of Cambria* (1584), and it does not appear that he had any warrant for doing so (see p. 17 of reprint of 1811). There was an ancient tradition that Shrewsbury, which has been long known to Welshmen as "Amwythig," had once borne the name of "Pengwern" and that on the site of St. Chad's Church had stood the palace of Brochwel Ysgythrog, prince of Powys (Gir. Camb. vi. 81 (*Itin.* i. 10), 169 (*Descr.* i. 4); Historia Monacellae in *Arch. Camb.* I. iii. (1848), 139). But nowhere in the older sources is it suggested that the ruin of Pengwern was brought about by Offa. Rhys thinks (*Celt. Br.* (2), 141) that "Scrobbesbyrig" is a translation of "Pengwern".

[11] Fl. Wig. i. 265.

[12] *Ibid.* 41, 238; *H.E.* v. 23 (Ualchstod), with Plummer's notes (ii. 341; *cf.* also 222).

[13] *Lib. Land.* 133-4.

it fairly certain that at the beginning of the eighth century, the age of the greatness of Mercia, that state had already reached, in the main, its westernmost limits, and that the work of Offa, important though it was, lay rather in the direction of definition than of conquest.

During the years 716 to 757 Mercia was ruled by Ethelbald, who was the principal English monarch of his day, holding Wessex for the greater part of his reign in subjection and towering above Northumbria and its feeble line of kings. There is, however, no record of any warfare carried on by him against the Welsh,[14] and all that is known of the border conflict which no doubt went on incessantly during this period is that in or about 722 the Welsh won two victories in South Wales, the one at a " Pencon " or " Pencoed," not yet identified, and the other at Garth Maelog, which was probably the place of that name near Llanbister in Radnorshire.[15] It is under Ethelbald's successor Offa, who was king of Mercia from 757 to 796, that the struggle between Welsh and English again emerges into the light of history, just at the stage when the final limit is being set to the westward progress of English colonisation.

Offa was one of the most powerful kings of the early English period, formidable in Kent, Wessex and East Anglia, and dealt with as an equal by his mighty neighbour, Charles the Great. Thus it is not at all surprising that he should have shown vigour and resourcefulness in his treatment of the Welsh, to whom his realm lay open from the Severn to the Dee. A battle of Hereford between Welsh and English is recorded under the year 760;[16] whether he was concerned in this it is

[14] By the " Wealas " of *A.S. Chr.* 743 I understand, as generally in this part of the Chronicle, the West Welsh, or men of Cornwall and Devon. Ethelbald came to the aid of Cuthred as his overlord.

[15] " Bellum hebil apud cornuenses. gueith gart mailauc. cat pencon. apud dexterales brittones. et brittones uictores fuerunt in istis tribus bellis " (Harl. MS. 3859 in *Cymr.* ix. 160). The present Caerfaelog, or Cyfaelog, close to the village of Llanbister, was formerly " Gardd (for Garth) Vaelog " (Dwnn i. 266). Another possible identification is with Garth Mailwg, near Llantrisant, Glamorganshire; there is, however, some evidence that this is properly Garth Milwg (*Lib. Land.* 384). I know no reason why Garth Maelog should be placed, as is done by Powel (p. 12), in North Wales.

[16] " Bellum inter brittones et saxones, id est gueith hirford " (Harl. MS. 3859 in *Cymr.* ix. 161). The Dyfnwal ab Tewdwr mentioned in the same annal was a prince of Strathclyde; see the pedigree on p. 172.

CHAP. VII.

not possible to say, but his name is expressly coupled by Harleian MS. 3859 with two raids which were made upon Welsh territory in 778 and 784.[17] These attacks seem to have been made on so large a scale as to attract the special notice of the chronicler, but they were probably not intended as part of any scheme for the conquest of Wales, for the enterprise particularly connected with the name of Offa is the boundary dyke which he caused to be raised along the Welsh border, and the rearing of which at enormous cost must be looked upon as a deliberate closing of the era of conquest.[18] Attempts have, indeed, been made to discredit the traditional account of the origin of this great earthwork and to show that it is much older than the age of Offa. But they have been signally unsuccessful. It is true that the older English and Welsh chronicles, for the most part, have nothing to say of the digging of the dyke, but the testimony of Asser,[19] a Welshman familiar with England who wrote less than a century after Offa's death, outweighs the silence of the other sources and makes it all but absolutely certain that the popular name of the dyke preserves the true account of its origin. It has been pointed out that the form and disposition of this entrenchment prove it to have been cast up by an Eastern folk for protection against dwellers in the West; the ditch or fosse is always on the western side, and wherever the line of a cliff or escarpment is followed, the face of this is always to the west. That the dyke is also post-Roman is clear from the discovery in it at the Ffrith, near Hope, of relics of a Roman settlement which were disturbed when it was erected, and when the theory that it was prehistoric has thus been disposed of, there seems no

[17] *Cymr.* ix. 162. The entry in *Ann.* C. MS. C. *s.a.* 795, "Vastatio Rienuch ab Offa" no doubt refers to an expedition into Dyfed (Rheinwg), which anticipated that of Cenwulf in 818.

[18] A. N. Palmer has admirably discussed the leading problems connected with the dyke in *Cymr.* xii. 65-86. See also *Arch. Camb.* II. i. (1850), 72-3; III. ii. (1856), 1-23; III. vi. (1860), 37; IV. vi. (1875), 275-81, and Stevenson's *Asser*, pp. 204-5.

[19] "Rex nomine Offa qui vallum magnum inter Britanniam (his usual name for Wales) atque Merciam de mari usque ad mare facere imperavit" (c. 14). The passage was copied by Sim. Dun. ii. 66, and a little later by the author of the twelfth-century life of St. Oswald (Sim. Dun. i. 353). There is no allusion to the dyke in Harl. MS.3859, *Ann. C.*, or the older *Bruts;* what is said on the subject by the Gwentian Brut (*Myv. Arch.* II. 473-4 (686)) should be entirely disregarded.

reason for depriving Offa of the credit of the undertaking, which has been ascribed to him by English and Welsh tradition alike for the past ten centuries. CHAP. VII.

According to Asser, the dyke ran from sea to sea, and in order to be a complete boundary, it was no doubt requisite that it should do so. Both the northern and the southern end are, however, difficult to trace. No vestiges of the dyke have been found to the south of Bridge Sollers on the Wye,[20] about 6 miles above Hereford, unless the entrenchments which line the east bank of that river between Monmouth and Chepstow are to be regarded as part of the great work. From the fourteenth century to the time of Pennant it was supposed that the northern end lay at Basingwerk, near Holywell,[21] but the earthworks here, though locally known as "Clawdd Offa," were shown in the first edition of the Tour of 1773[22] to be part of Wat's Dyke, which, lying a few miles to the east of Offa's Dyke, runs parallel to it as far as the borders of Montgomeryshire.[23] The western dyke probably touched the sea not far from Prestatyn,[24] but its course, except for a short length near Newmarket, is quite uncertain through the greater part of Flintshire. Near Treuddyn Church its traceable course begins;[25] the line of the "vallum" may thence be followed without serious interruption through Adwy'r Clawdd (The Gap in the Dyke), Ruabon, Chirk Castle Park, Selatyn, Llanymynech and Llandysilio to the Severn. Here intervenes a break of about 5 miles and it is reasonable to suppose that the river itself was treated for this distance as the boundary. At Buttington the dyke re-appears and thence runs southward through Forden, Lymore near Montgomery, Mainstone, Knighton (the Welsh

[20] *Archæological Survey of Herefordshire* (1896), p. 7.

[21] Higden (*Polychr.* ii. 34) was the first to place the end of the dyke between Basingwerk and Coleshill (collem carbonum). He was followed by Gutyn Owain in the Book of Basingwerk (*B.T.* MS. E. p. 8), Humphrey Llwyd (*Comment.* (2), 64), and Edward Llwyd (Gibson, 587).

[22] Penn. i. 31.

[23] For Watt's Dyke, or "Clawdd Wad," see Penn. i. 349-50. Palmer thinks it may also have been thrown up by Offa (*Cymr.* xii. 75). The notion that the space between the two dykes was neutral ground cannot be traced further back than Churchyard's *Worthiness of Wales* (1587).

[24] *Arch. Camb.* III. iv. (1858), 335-42 (Guest); *Cymr.* xii. 79-80.

[25] For the course of the dyke see the old maps (one inch to the mile) of the Ordnance Survey, Sheets 79, 74, 60, 56; Penn. i. 350-2; *Radnorsh.* (2), pp. 123-4 *Archæological Survey of Herefordshire*, p. 7.

CHAP. VII.

name of which is "Tref y Clawdd," the Town on the Dyke), and Discoed to Knill, near Kington in Herefordshire. Henceforward its course is broken; a portion has been traced near Lynhales and another on the north side of the Wye near Bridge Sollers, but beyond the latter point, as has been already stated, no sign of it can be perceived; for reasons which can only be conjectured, Offa did not think it necessary to place any barrier between himself and the men of Ewias and Erging.[26] It is obvious that a power which possessed no standing army could have made no other use of this dyke than as a boundary, the violation of which it visited with penalties, and such, it must be supposed, was the purpose of Offa in erecting it. In the twelfth century it was believed that by an ordinance of the builder of the dyke every Welshman found with a weapon on the eastern side of it had his right hand forthwith cut off.[27] Whether such a decree was ever issued by Offa or not, it may safely be said that the main intention of the dyke was to mark definitely the frontier between the two races and so to signify to the Welsh on the one hand, how far they might come, and on the other, that no further aggression at their expense was intended. What was English was to remain so, but no more Welsh "trefs" were to be turned into English "hams" and "tons". It is probable that for many years the border had not sensibly advanced; while the plains had been won with comparative ease, the tide of invasion had washed in vain against the immovable ramparts of the Welsh mountains, and on the lower slopes of these the line was now drawn which was to separate English and Welsh for centuries and indeed separates them at many points to this day.

A study of the older place names along the dyke brings out clearly the fact that it was a real national border line. To the east of it the village names are of English origin, Suttons, Astons, Actons, Middletons, Newtons of the ordinary type;[28] to the west, the names are, save for some exceptions to be

[26] The ordinary view, that the Wye served as the boundary from Bridge Sollers to Monmouth, seems to me to leave the Welsh much too near Hereford for that city's safety.

[27] John of Salisbury (*Polycraticus*, vi. 6) ascribes the law to Harold, Walter Map (*De Nugis*, ii. 17, p. 86) to Offa, but with the substitution of "foot" for "right hand".

[28] This was noticed by Humphrey Llwyd (*Comment.* (2), 64-5).

presently noted, Welsh in formation, from Rhuddlan and Diserth in the north to Bleddfa and Llangynllo in the south. In Flintshire, it is true that the facts have been somewhat obscured by the process of reconquest carried on by the Welsh in later years; yet the help of Domesday is hardly needed to enable one to see Preston in Prestatyn, Westbury in Gwespyr, Merton in Mertyn, Bishopstree in Bistre,[29] and thus to bring to life again the English settlement which once occupied the region of Englefield or Tegeingl almost as far as the Clwyd. In the neighbourhood of Wrexham, Chirk and Oswestry, the dyke still forms the dividing line between the two peoples, as it does in the Welshman's popular phrase, when he speaks of England as "y tu draw i Glawdd Offa" (the other side of Offa's Dyke). In Montgomeryshire and Radnorshire the English village names extend at certain points a mile or two to the west of the dyke; cases in point are Leighton, Forden, Hopton, Waterdine, Pilleth, Cascob and Radnor.[30] These are ancient English settlements, for they are mentioned in Domesday, and it must be understood that hereabouts, even after the making of the dyke, the process of English colonisation for a little time went on without check. The portion of the dyke just north of the Wye seems to have become obsolete as a frontier not long after its erection, as the result of the settlement of Eardisley and the surrounding villages, which threw the Welsh back upon the outlying ridges of Radnor Forest.

By the action of Offa the border between Welsh and English was thus to a large extent fixed. The border warfare was, however, not brought to an end, nor yet the forays into the heart of Wales by means of which Mercia at this time demonstrated her strength and kept the Welsh in awe. In 796, the year of the death of Offa, a battle was fought at Rhuddlan, in which, it may be conjectured, the English sought to defend their new frontier in Tegeingl.[31] Under Offa's successor, Cen-

[29] The Domesd. forms are Prestetone (269*a*, 2), Wesb(er)ie (*ibid.*), Meretone (269*a*, 1) and Biscopestreu (269*a*, 2).

[30] *Trans. Cymr.* 1899-1900, 123-4.

[31] "Bellum rud glann" (Harl. MS. 3859 in *Cymr.* ix. 163). The entry "Caratauc rex guenedote apud saxones iugulatur" comes two years later (798) in all the old authorities, and it was not until the time of Powel (p. 17) that the two notices were merged and the foundation laid for the popular account of the defeat of Caradog in the battle of Rhuddlan Marsh (Morfa Rhuddlan).

CHAP. VII. wulf, the English in 816 harried Rhufoniog, which lay west of the Clwyd, and the region of Snowdon itself; in 818 they penetrated into Dyfed. Cenwulf died in 821 at Basingwerk,[32] perhaps in the course of a new campaign against the Welsh, nor did his death, though it marks the end of the period of Mercian greatness, lead to a cessation of the attacks upon the men of the west, for in 822 the Welsh fortress of Degannwy, once the secure stronghold of Maelgwn Gwynedd, was destroyed and the realm of Powys was overrun. Shortly afterwards, however, the supremacy of Britain passed from Mercia to Wessex, and, when Mercia further began to feel the weight of the Norseman's sword, the Welsh were able to breathe more freely.

II. The Early Welsh Church: its Organisation.

While the kings of Mercia were confining the Welsh people within limits which grew daily narrower, the Welsh Church was also being more and more cut off from the rest of the Christian world. Little by little the Celtic communities outside the borders of Wales adopted the Roman Easter and so abandoned the original Celtic position, that the insular traditions ought to be maintained against any innovation hailing from the Continent.[33] First, the Southern Irish yielded to Rome during the papacy of Honorius I. (625-38); next, the Northumbrian Church, an offshoot of Iona, declared for the See of Saint Peter at the famous Synod of Whitby in 664. Through the influence of Adamnan, abbot of Iona and biographer of St. Columba, the Northern Irish followed suit at the very end of the seventh century. Iona itself was for some years obdurate, but after seeing its Pictish branches forced to accept the Roman customs, gave up the struggle in 718. It was probably about this time that the Britons of Strathclyde gave way, and about 705 a large section, if not the whole, of the men of Devon and Cornwall were won over to the Roman cause by Abbot Aldhelm of Malmesbury. In the middle of the eighth century it is most likely that the people of Wales were

[32] "Transit el liu de Basewerce," says Geoffrey Gaimar (v. 2240), a late authority, but here quoting, no doubt, some lost record.

[33] Zimmer, *Celtic Church* (1902), pp. 77-86; H. and St. ii. 6; i. 673.

the only considerable community of Christians in these islands who maintained the old attitude of isolation from Rome. CHAP. VII.

This position of solitary protest could not be long retained, and accordingly it is not surprising to find the Welsh in their turn forced to give way in the early part of the reign of Offa. The submission to Rome was all the more thorough inasmuch as it was not, apparently, brought about by foreign arms but by a peaceful revolution within the country itself. In the year 768, says the sole authentic record of the event, "Easter was altered among the Britons, the reform being the work of that man of God, Elbodugus".[34] According to the untrustworthy Gwentian Brut,[35] South Wales did not yield without a conflict, but it is obvious that the particulars which it gives have been invented in order to bring out the independence of that part of the country and its unwillingness to follow the North in basely truckling to Rome. History knows nothing of any struggle of the kind, and the character of the prime mover in the matter suggests that the change was really due to the feeling of the abler and more spiritual leaders of the Welsh Church that they were, by a meaningless conservatism, cutting themselves off from the religious life of Christendom. Elfodd (for such would be the modern Welsh form of the name of Elbodug)[36] is a somewhat shadowy figure, but it may be inferred from the epithet "homine Dei" that he was a monk;[37] tradition makes him a member of the monastic community of Caer Gybi or Holyhead.[38] He must have embarked upon his movement of reform at a comparatively early age, for he lived more than forty years after its successful completion, to die in 809 with the title of "chief bishop in the land of Gwynedd".[39] This greatness, however, he attained in later

[34] "Pasca commutatur apud brittones emendante elbodugo homine dei" (Harl. MS. 3859 in *Cymr.* ix. 162).

[35] *S.a.* 755, 777, 809.

[36] The "Elbodugo," "Elbodg" of Harl. MS. 3859 and the "Elvodugi," "Elbobdus" of the MSS. of Nennius (ed. Mommsen, pp. 143, 207) represent the old Welsh Elbodug and Elbodu, to be compared with Arthbodu (*Lib. Land.* 80) and Gurbodu (*ibid.* 230). *Cf. Gr. Celt.* (2), p. 22; *W. Phil.* (2), 386.

[37] *Trans. Cymr.* 1893-4, 129. *Cf.* the Welsh "meudwy," a hermit, which is for "meu duiu," servus dei (*Urk. Spr.* 198).

[38] *Myv. Arch.* II. 42 (425). Other evidence seems to point to a connection with Abergele (Thomas, *St. Asaph*, p. 351).

[39] "Elbod(u)g archi episcopus (in) guenedote regione migrauit ad dominum" (Harl. MS. 3859 in *Cymr.* ix. 163).

CHAP. VII.

life; his victory, there is reason to think, was not the victory of the prelate or man of affairs, but of the scholar and student. Nennius in the next generation introduces himself as author with the proud title of "disciple of Elfodd,"[40] whom he elsewhere styles "most saintly of bishops";[41] incidentally, he allows us to see that his master was a student of the works of Bede.[42] Slight as are these indications, they seem to show that it was the learning and devotion of Elfodd which won this battle for him, and no authority which he wielded as metropolitan or as bishop of Bangor, titles, be it observed, one is not warranted in attaching to his name.[43]

Thus the schism between the Christians of Wales and those of the rest of Western Europe came to an end, for the submission in respect of the observance of Easter undoubtedly carried with it submission in regard to other points of difference so far as these were considered to be a breach of Catholic unity. Welshmen came, in common with other dwellers in the Western world, to regard Rome as the centre of the religious world, and Welsh princes and prelates adopted the fashionable habit of pilgrimage to the holy city which held the bones of St. Peter and St. Paul.[44] Nevertheless, the Welsh Church still retained in many respects the marks of its Celtic and monastic origin; acknowledgment of the supremacy of Rome by no means implied at this period the acceptance of a uniform system of worship and church organisation, so that there was still room left in Wales for the growth of distinctive features of church life. It will now be convenient to take a brief survey of that life as it manifested itself in the centuries preceding the Norman Conquest.

40 "Ego Nennius Elvodugi discipulus" (ed. Mommsen, p. 143).

41 "Elbobdus episcoporum sanctissimus" (ed. Mommsen, p. 207).

42 It was Elfodd and another bishop, one "Renchidus," who pointed out to him that Edwin of Northumbria was really baptised by Paulinus of York, and not, as the old British record alleged, by Rhun ab Urien. Nennius cut the knot by treating the two men as one and the same.

43 "Archi episcopus" was at this time a title of honour merely and did not necessarily imply metropolitan authority (*Trans. Cymr.* 1893-4, 131). Elfodd is styled bishop of Bangor by late writers only (*Gwentian Brut s.a.* 755; *Iolo MSS.* 117, 127), who could not imagine an Archbishop of Gwynedd seated at any other place.

44 Recorded instances are those of Cyngen of Powys in 854, Hywel (of what line is uncertain) in 886, Hywel Dda in 928, and Bishop Joseph of Llandaff in 1045.

The salient fact in the history of the Welsh Church at this time is that the principal churches, those having ancient traditions and a position of honour and prestige, were in the hands of communities of clergy which in origin, whatever they may have in time become, were monasteries.[45] Primitive Welsh law divides churches into two classes, *viz.*, "mother churches" and those of less consideration.[46] The former are treated as always having an abbot (abad), who should be a cleric and lettered (dwyfol lythyrwr), with a community or "clas" of canons (cynonwyr), including at least one priest (offeiriad). In the smaller churches there are no abbots or canons, but merely parsons and priests. The "clas" was an important and responsible body; it received the half of all payments made to the church,[47] succeeded to the movable property of the abbot when he died,[48] and decided finally all disputes arising among its members.[49] Though the "claswyr" are not styled monks, but canons, the title of their chief officer, the abbot, and the manner in which they consumed in common the revenues of the Church, afford strong evidence that the "clas" was at first a monastery, smaller, no doubt, than the great monastic establishments of the sixth and seventh centuries, but of the same general type and in many cases, for instance at Llantwit and St. David's, carrying on the traditions of the age of the saints.[50]

This view of the organisation of the Welsh Church in the early Middle Ages does not rest for support solely upon the statements of the Welsh Laws; it is confirmed by many inci-

[45] The otherwise admirable discussion of this subject in A. N. Palmer's essay on "The Portionary Churches of Medieval North Wales" (*Arch. Camb.* V. iii. (1886), 175-209) would have gained greatly in point if the evidence for the *monastic* origin of mother churches had been fully appreciated.

[46] *LL.* i. 78-80 (Ven.); 432-4 (Dim.); ii. 842 (Lat. B.)

[47] *LL.* i. 434 (§ 3); ii. 842 (§ 6). [48] *Ibid.* ii. 10 (§ 27). [49] *Ibid.* (§ 28).

[50] For other references to the "clas," see *LL.* i. 106 (clas Bancor a rey Beuno); ii. 63 (yclaswyr ar personeit; kanys vynt yssyd berchenogyon ar yr eglvys); Buchedd Gr. ap Cynan in *Arch. Camb.* III. xii. (1866) 42 (ar escop ae athraon a holl clas er arglwyd dewi). "Monastica classis" is found in Rhygyfarch's life of St. David (*Cambro-Br. SS.* 127), a phrase which suggests a derivation from "classis" = "corpus, collegium" (Ducange *s.v.*). The word occurs in place names; Higher and Lower Clas are two hamlets of the parish of Llangyfelach, an ancient Dewi church; Clas Garmon is a township of the parish of St. Harmon's; Treclas contains the parish church of Llanarthne, for which see note 165 to chap. v. The head of the body of clergy at Caergybi (Holyhead) was styled "penclas" (Penn. iii. 73).

CHAP. VII.

dental references to the churches themselves to be found in the literature of the period. The *Liber Landavensis*, for instance, bears witness to the existence of many monastic churches in South Wales; the head of the church of Llancarfan (anciently Nant Carfan) is described as "abbas Sancti Catoci"[51] and "abbas Carbani vallis";[52] at Llantwit Major there is "abbas Sancti Ilduti,"[53] at Llandough, near Cardiff, "abbas Docguinni".[54] Abbots also appear at Caerwent, Moccas, Garway, Welsh Bicknor, Llandogo and Dewchurch, and, if, as is most likely, "princeps" was but an alternative title, Bishopston in Gower and Penally may be added to the list.[55] In 1188 the church of Llanbadarn Fawr, near Aberystwyth, had an abbot, though in this case, as in others in Wales at this period, the title was held by a layman, who, having first got himself recognised as the advocate or guardian of the shrine, had afterwards appropriated its landed endowment.[56] Nor was the case different in North Wales. In 1147 there was an abbot of Towyn in Meirionydd,[57] while in 856 the death is recorded of a "princeps" of Abergele.[58] Llandinam had its abbot in the middle of the twelfth century,[59] and as late as the fifteenth the memory survived of the abbot and "claswyr" of Llanynys.[60] The churches

[51] *Lib. Land.* 140, 143, 144 (Catmaili, the older form, occurs on p. 131).

[52] *Ibid. passim.* For the form Nant Carfan, see also the colophon to Caradog's *Life of Gildas* (ed. Mommsen, p. 110), and the life of Gwynllyw in *Cambro-British Saints* (p. 149). Geoffrey of Monmouth seems to be responsible for *Llan* Carfan (*Hist. Reg.* xii. 20).

[53] *Lib. Land. passim.* "Abbas lannildut" occurs once (145).

[54] *Ibid. passim.* For the identification see *Margam Abb.* 3.

[55] *Ibid.* 222 (guentonie urbis), 164 (mochros), 166 (lann guruoe), 164 (lann garthbenni), 223 (lann enniaun, id est lann oudocui), 164 (lann deui), 145 (lann cynuur; *cf.* 239, in monasterio sancti cinuuri, id est lann berugall), 149 (aluni capitis).

[56] Gir. Camb. vi. 120-1 (*Itin.* ii. 4).

[57] "Moruran abat y ty gwyn" (*Bruts*, 315; *B.T.* 174) has been generally taken for an abbot of Whitland, but the part played by him is altogether unsuited to a Cistercian monk and the difficulty vanishes when it is remembered that Cynfael, the scene of the incident, is close to Towyn Meirionydd.

[58] "Ionathan princeps opergelei moritur" (Harl. MS. 3859 in *Cymr.* xi. 165). For the ancient importance of Abergele church see Thomas, *St. Asaph*, pp. 350-2.

[59] "Dolfin abbas Llandina*n*" (the correct form of the name) is among the witnesses to a Trefeglwys charter granted by Madog ap Maredudd, who died in 1160 (*Arch. Camb.* III. vi. (1860) 331).

[60] According to a petition of Griffin Young to Pope Boniface IX. (*Papal Letters*, iv. 349), the revenues of Llanynys (in Dyffryn Clwyd) were anciently divided into twenty-four portions called "claswriaiethe," instituted for the main-

mentioned in this list are among the oldest and most important in the country, so that it is plainly not with monasteries in the ordinary sense of the term that we have to do, but with the general framework of church organisation.[61] CHAP. VII.

In the case of the four cathedral churches, the title of abbot was from the first merged in that of bishop, always regarded in Wales as the more honourable, notwithstanding that in Ireland and Scotland matters were usually reversed. Yet evidence is not wanting that they, too, were served by communities of the same pattern. When Bishop Bernard of St. David's (1115-1148) came into possession of his see, he found there a body of "claswyr," who regarded the cathedral revenue as a common stock for their support and had not divided it, as was usual elsewhere, into canonries or prebends for the maintenance of a fixed number of clergy.[62] They were continuing the traditions of the "monasterium" of Asser's day. Llandaff is also termed a "monasterium";[63] it rejoiced, indeed, in the name of archmonastery, which was probably meant to emphasise its supremacy as the mother house over the other convents founded in honour of St. Teilo.[64] Were there any ancient accounts of Bangor and St. Asaph, they would probably tell the same tale. It is, indeed, likely that chance alone determined which of the many monasteries founded in the sixth century should permanently become episcopal sees. At the beginning of the tenth century seven important churches in the kingdom of Dyfed were traditionally known as "esgoptai" or episcopal houses.[65] Mynyw headed the list and still retained its bishop.

tenance of twenty-four perpetual portionaries called "abbatathelaswyr" (*i.e.*, abad a chlaswyr). To one of these, the portion of David the priest, was assigned the cure of souls. I am indebted to Mr. J. R. Gabriel for calling my attention to this document.

[61] The fact that "llan," meaning at first a monastery, came to be applied to all churches alike is further proof of the monastic origin of the older Welsh Churches. See note 122, chap. v.

[62] Gir. Camb. iii. 153 (*Men. Eccl.* ii). The form "glaswir" for "claswyr" is, of course, inaccurate, but the substitution of *g* for *c* in this word seems to have been not uncommon. Thus Jocelin of Furness explains Glasgu as "cara familia" (*Life of St. Kentigern*, ed. Forbes, p. 182) and "Y Klas ar Wy" (Pen. MS. 147), which was Clastbirig in the twelfth century (Fl. Wig. *s.a.* 1056 in *Mon. Hist. Br.* 608), has since become Glasbury.

[63] *Lib. Land.* 144, 214. [64] *Ibid.* 74, 75, 129; *Cymr.* xi. 131-2.

[65] *LL.* i. 556-8 (Dim.); ii. 790-1 (Lat. A.), 869 (Lat. B.). The section on "saith esgopty Dyfed" is clearly primitive and in all probability formed part of the original "law of Hywel".

CHAP. VII.

But the other six houses, *viz.*, "Llan Ysmael" (St. Ishmael's on Milford Haven), "Llan Degeman" (Rhoscrowther), "Llan Usyllt" (St. Issell's near Tenby), "Llan Deulyddog" (Carmarthen), and a "Llan Deilo" and a "Llan Geneu" which cannot be identified, were presided over by simple abbots, and only in the higher status and privilege of these dignitaries was there any substantial recognition of the former standing of these churches as episcopal sees.[66] Llanbadarn Fawr in Ceredigion is another ancient church which early mediæval tradition alleged to have been at one time the seat of a bishop,[67] and it can hardly be doubted that other Welsh monastic centres were also ruled by bishop-abbots until the time came when the ideas of Christendom as to the necessity of parcelling countries into dioceses, with one bishop for each of these divisions, were accepted by the Welsh and the four principal houses of St. David's, Llandaff, Bangor and St. Asaph were recognised as supreme in their own quarter of Wales.[68]

Scarcely any direct evidence is to be got as to the life of the Welsh monastic communities in the days of their early zeal and activity. But the indications are that it did not differ greatly from the manner of life led by the monks of Ireland and Scotland during the same period, so that what is known from the life of St. Samson[69] and the early British peniten-

[66] For the situation of the seven churches see Aneurin Owen's notes (*LL.* i. 559); Fenton (2), 218-9; *Descr. Pemb.* i. 296, 304, 307, 308, 310. There is nothing to indicate which Llandeilo was meant, and several churches with this dedication, *e.g.*, Llanddowror and Llandeilo Abercywyn, lie between St. Issell's and Carmarthen. No Llangeneu is now to be traced in Dyfed. Lat. A. clumsily introduces "Egluyss Hwadeyn," *i.e.*, Llawhaden, into the list, thus betraying, as in § 13 (p. 791), the hand of a St. David's editor.

[67] Gir. Camb. (vi. 121-2 (*Itin.* ii. 4)) expressly states, what is implied in the "metropolis alta" and "antestes . . . Paternus" of the poem of Ieuan ap Sulien (H. and St. i. 665), that Llanbadarn was once "cathedralis". It was no doubt on the strength of this tradition that Geoffrey of Monmouth made Cynog "Lampaternensis ecclesiae antistes" (*Hist. Reg.* xi. 3). While the tradition itself is of historical value, no importance should be attached to the notice in *Gw. Brut, s.a.* 720, implying there was a bishopric of Llanbadarn at that date, and it is very unlikely, too, that the "Idnert" stone found at Llanddewi Brefi commemorates, as Edward Llwyd suggested, the murdered bishop of Gerald's account (Gibson, 644; *Lap. W.* 140; *Inscr. Chr.* No. 120).

[68] Some evidence of the monastic origin of Bangor and St. Asaph is afforded by the statement of Gir. Camb. (vi. 170 (*Descr.* i. 4)) that the former was under the patronage "Daniells *abbatis*" and by the reference to St. Kentigern's foundation of a monastery in "Llyfr Coch Asaph" (Thomas, *St. Asaph*, p. 179).

[69] Cited from the Bollandist text; see note 96 to chap. v.

tials[70] may be pieced out with the aid of Bede and of Adamnan, the biographer of St. Columba. It is certain, in the first place, that the monks did not inhabit a single building, but lived in separate huts or cells, which were surrounded by a wall or rampart, after the pattern of that which girt the various buildings of a royal court or "llys".[71] This was the "llan," or enclosure; within it were also the church, the abbot's cell, the "hospice" for the entertainment of visitors, and such necessary outhouses as the kiln in which corn was dried to fit it for the mill. None of these buildings were of stone, any more than those set up within the precincts of a "llys," which are known to have been of timber and wattle. The very church was of wood, for, according to Bede, stone churches were almost unknown among the Britons.[72] It is not surprising, under these conditions, that not a vestige remains of the buildings of any early Welsh monastery and that no part of any Welsh church now standing is anterior in date to the coming of the Normans.[73]

Entrance into the community was through the monastic vow, which was taken in the church on bended knee[74] and was known as the vow of perfection.[75] The man thus became one of the "brethren," a body of comrades among whom there was complete equality, but who owed unquestioning obedience in all things to their spiritual father, the abbot.[76] There were often other officers who relieved the abbot of some of his

[70] Cited from H. and St. i. 113-20. The MS. (Paris 3182) comes from Fécamp Abbey and ultimately from Brittany. It is of the eleventh century (Bradshaw, *Collected Papers*, 1889, pp. 473-4).

[71] See, especially, *V.S. Columb.*, with its references to the "ecclesia" or "oratorium" (i. 8, 32; iii. 23), the "hospitium" (i. 31, 32; ii. 39), the abbot's cell (i. 35; iii. 21, 22), and the "canaba" (i. 45). In i. 3 mention is made of the "vallum monasterii" at Durrow. There was a hospice in the monastery of Piro (*Acta SS.* July, vi. 579*b*).

[72] "Ecclesiam de lapide, insolito Brettonibus more" (*H.E.* iii. 4). In *Lib. Land.* 277, the erection of a wooden church about 1060 at Llangarran in Archenfield is mentioned, and it would seem likely that churches generally in that district were of light construction, in view of the large number which Bishop Herwald is said to have consecrated during the fifty years of his episcopate.

[73] So, substantially, Allen in *Monumental History of the British Church* (1889), p. 43.

[74] *V.S. Columb.* i. 32.

[75] H. and St. i. 118 (§ 9).

[76] "Offensus quis ab aliquo debet hoc indicere abati, non tamen accusantis sed medentis affectu, *et abas decernat*" (H. and St. i. 115 § 18).

CHAP. VII.

duties, a priest who offered the eucharistic sacrifice,[77] a cook or steward who saw to the food supply,[78] occasionally a teacher [79] and a scribe.[80] But none of these trenched in any way upon the authority of the abbot. Election by the monks appears to have been the regular mode of appointing an abbot in the larger monasteries, but considerable influence was exercised by the bishops of the district,[81] and another important factor made itself felt at an early period, namely, the force of blood relationship. Although the inmate of a monastery was regarded as having divorced himself from all family ties, it was nevertheless the fact that abbots sought to secure for their own relatives the succession to their offices. One instance of the kind has already been given; it will be remembered that Illtud had a nephew who confidently expected to succeed to the position held by his uncle and who was filled with jealousy when he saw that the dazzling virtues of Samson might bring about the ruin of his hopes.[82] This incident reveals clearly the exact situation; there was no rule of hereditary succession, but merely a presumption in favour of relatives, which would not stand against the claims of a really brilliant outside candidate. Nevertheless, it is worthy of note that, of the eight abbots who ruled over Iona and its daughter houses in the seventh century, all save one are known to have been relatives, near or distant, of St. Columba.[83] In the dependent monasteries, the heads of

[77] See *Lib. Land.* for "presbiter Catoci" at Llancarfan (268, 272, 273), "sacerdos" and "presbiter S. Ilduti" at Llantwit (257, 272), "sacerdos" and "presbiter Docunni" at Llandough (249, 258, 268, 272), "presbiteri tathiu" at Caerwent (270). In the Book of St. Chad (*Lib. Land.* pref. xlvi) is "sacerdos teiliav".

[78] When Samson is made "pistor" of Piro's monastery, he is thus addressed by Dubricius: "omnia bona quae in hac cella, Deo donante, abundant ad dispensandum tibi praecipio" (581*b*). Elsewhere in the life the "pistor" and the "oeconomus" are distinguished (577-8).

[79] *Lib. Land.* has "doctor Catoci" (273), "magister sancti catoci" (271, 274). *Cf. Cambro-Br. SS.* 82-3, for the constitution of the "clas" at Llantwit Major.

[80] "Dissaith scriptor" (*Lib. Land.* 224) recalls the "scribe" of Irish monasticism, for whom see Warren, *Liturgy and Ritual of the Celtic Church*, p. 18.

[81] Samson was elected abbot in place of Piro by the suffrages of the monks ("consilio facto . . . omnes voluerunt"), but Dubricius was the moving spirit (582*a*).

[82] 577*b*. Compare the story told in the same life of the desire of Dubricius to hand on his office to an unworthy favourite (probably a relative called Morinus (589*a*)).

[83] See the genealogical table in Fowler's edition of *V.S. Columb.*

which were appointed by the abbot of the parent community, there was still further scope for the exercise of family partiality; the appointment by St. Columba of a maternal uncle as head of "Hinba insula"[84] and by St. Samson of a paternal uncle as head of the monastery ceded to him in Ireland[85] are instances of what was no doubt a common practice. The inherent right of noble blood to rule was in this age not questioned, either in Church or State, and when a family of good birth had once given an abbot to a particular monastery, their interest in it and influence over it tended to become permanent.

The monks were at first entirely supported out of the lands immediately attached to the monastery, which they tilled with their own hands. Other endowments were regarded with suspicion, as likely to lower the high spirit of monastic self-denial,[86] and though they inevitably came, as the monastery grew in reputation, until each important "llan" had scores of rent-yielding estates in different parts of the country, this was a departure from primitive ways and ideas. All the early authorities agree in representing the monks as engaged in agriculture and the care of cattle. "He who breaks his hoe," runs one of the provisions of the monastic code ascribed to Gildas, "where it had no fracture before, let him pay for the damage by extra work or keep a special fast."[87] They went out to their various tasks, assigned to them by the abbot or his representative, in the morning and spent a long day in the fields, to return at nightfall for the one set meal of the day.[88] The fare was of the plainest, its main constituents being bread, butter, cheese, eggs, milk and vegetables, but meat and beer were not altogether excluded, save in the monasteries bound

[84] *V.S. Columb.* i. 45.

[85] 582*b*. "Avunculus" is used for "patruus".

[86] Bede says of the Irish monks who settled in Northumbria under Oswald and Oswy that none of them accepted "territoria ac possessiones ad construenda monasteria, nisi a potestatibus saeculi coactus" (*H.E.* iii. 26).

[87] H. and St. i. 115, § 26.

[88] The "discipuli" of Piro went out in the morning "ad opus exercendum" (579*b*). *Cf. V.S. Columb.* i. 37 (fratres, post messionis opera, vespere ad monasterium redeuntes); iii. 12 (dum fratres, se calceantes, mane ad diversa monasterii opera ire praepararent); iii. 23 (ad visitandos operarios fratres . . . in occidua insulae Iouae laborantes parte). The monks of Bangor Iscoed lived "de labore manuum suarum" (Bede, *H.E.* ii. 2). H. and St. i. 114, § 15, shows that the "cena" covered a good deal more than half the daily ration of food.

CHAP. VII.

by rules of special severity.[89] Drunkenness, though esteemed a serious offence, was not altogether unknown.[90]

Manual labour was, of course, not the sole occupation of the monks. Much time was given to the study of the scriptures,[91] and writing absorbed the energies of those brethren who had special qualifications for this work.[92] There was each day and night a regular succession of services in the church, when portions of the Psalter were chanted in Latin, the universal language of the Western Church.[93] On Sundays and saints' days there was also a celebration of holy communion, while the holiday character of the day was further marked by a general cessation of labour and a more generous diet.[94] Wednesdays and Fridays, on the other hand, were days of fasting[95] and the season of Lent was always observed with great rigour.[96] The saints' days observed included not only the festivals recognised by Christendom at large, but also the anniversaries of the great figures of the Celtic Church, whose death-days were treated as heavenly birthdays and made an occasion for feasting and rejoicing.[97]

Hard work and assiduous devotion were not the only means of moral discipline provided by this ancient monastic system. There were also severe penalties for all lapses from the monastic standard of purity and simplicity. The monastic virtues were humility, readiness to obey, almsgiving, and above all, chastity, and any breach of these obligations was punished in proportion to the gravity of the offence. In the more serious cases a period of "penitence" was prescribed, during which the offender was excluded from communion, placed upon fasting diet, and required constantly to ask pardon for his sin. Penitents were sometimes grouped together in particular monasteries, where they were sent to work out their discipline; often, however, they

[89] H. and St. i. 113, § 1; 115, § 22; 119, § 11.

[90] For legislation dealing with it see H. and St. i. 114, § 10; 118, § 2; 119, §§ 3, 4; for the actual case of Piro see the life of St. Samson, 582*a*.

[91] *V.S. Columb.* i. 24.

[92] Columba was a notable scribe (ii. 8, 9, 16; iii. 15).

[93] H. and St. i. 115, § 19; Williams, *Gildas*, p. 282.

[94] *V.S. Columb.* ii. 1, 44; iii. 12, 17.

[95] *Ibid.* i. 26; Bede, *H.E.* iii. 5.

[96] Dubricius spent every Lent in the monastery of Piro (581*b*).

[97] *V.S. Columb.* ii. 45; iii. 11; *Life of St. Samson.*

were banished to distant countries, the enforced pilgrimage being added as a further item to the sum of penance.[98]

In their relations with the outside world the early Celtic monks resembled the friar rather than the cloistered monk of mediæval times. Custom did not limit them to the precincts of their monastery, but, subject to the authority of their abbot,[99] allowed them to wander hither and thither on errands appropriate to their calling. In the early period, when heathenism had not completely relaxed its hold upon the country, they went about preaching,[100] and thus the monastery came to be regarded, not merely as a home for pious recluses, but also as the natural ecclesiastical centre of the district in which it stood. Monks were often charged with special commissions which took them far from their place of settlement, or were suffered as "peregrini" to undertake long journeys on which they had set their hearts.[101] A monk might even be sent forth, with a number of companions, as bees from an old hive, to found a new community, and, in the days when ascetic fervour was at its height, it was always the ambition of such a band to discover some desert island or dell in the heart of the forest in which they might live the life of self-denial.[102] Thus it was that the isles of the Atlantic coast in Ireland and Scotland came to be "isles of the saints," that the islands of Priestholm, Bardsey, St. Tudwal, Ramsey, Caldy and Barry on the Welsh seaboard also offered asylum to men weary of the turmoil of the world, and that on the mainland many a monastic "Diserth" or "desert" arose in what was once a forest solitude.[103]

It must, of course, be understood that the picture of Welsh monastic life which has just been drawn will only hold good

[98] For the penitential system see H. and St. i. 113-20; Williams, *Gildas*, pp. 272-5.

[99] *V.S. Columb.* i. 6.

[100] Bede, *H.E.* iii. 5, 26; *Life of St. Samson.*

[101] The "peregrinus" appears in Bede (*H.E.* iii. 19), the *Life of St. Samson* (582*b*, 584*a*), and *V.S. Columb.* ii. 39; iii. 7. The British bishop Marcus in the ninth century spent the end of a long and busy life in voluntary exile at the abbey of St. Médard, near Soissons (Mommsen's *Nennius*, pp. 120, 172).

[102] *V.S. Columb.* i. 6, 20; ii. 42.

[103] For this use of "desertum" and its Welsh and Irish equivalents see *Cymr. Trans.* 1893-4, 113; *Descr. Pemb.* i. 260. Three churches in Wales bore the name, *viz.*, "Y Ddiserth yn Nhegeingl" (*Bruts*, 369), "Y Ddiserth yn Elfael" (Pen. MS. 147) and "Y Ddiserth yn Rhos" (Evans, *Rep.* i. p. 971), now Llansantffraid Glan Conway.

CHAP. VII.

for the early monks, those who founded the Welsh Church in the sixth, seventh and, one may perhaps add, eighth centuries. As the primitive ideals lost their fascination, as the monasteries gathered wealth and the monk's life became one of ease, maintained at the expense of the labour of others, degeneration set in, and the havoc caused by the Danish attacks of the ninth century added another element of disorder. How rapidly a monastic system might absorb, like some subtle poison in the veins, the secular spirit is shown by Bede's letter to Archbishop Egbert of York, in which he complains that within thirty years the monasteries of Northumbria, once famous for their unworldly purity, had to a large exent become secular institutions, in which no monastic rule was observed. The two most important changes which affected the Welsh communities were the growth of territorial endowment and the abandonment of the celibate life. The first process must have begun early; it was the natural way in which a prince or wealthy landowner paid honour to the memory of the local saint or atoned for some injury done to the Church. On the margins of the Book of St. Chad, a MS. of the Gospels which was at Llandaff during the ninth century and part of the tenth, are several entries of that period typical of the method by which the greater churches grew rich.[104] "This writing sheweth," runs one, "that Rhys and the tribe of Grethi have given to God and St. Eliud (*i.e.*, Teilo) Trefwyddog . . . its render is forty loaves and a ram in the summer, in the winter forty loaves, a sow and forty sheaves (of oats). . . . He that shall keep this compact shall be blessed, he that shall break it shall be cursed, of God."[105] Such were the gifts which in the course of three or four centuries made St. David's, Bangor, Llandaff, St. Asaph, Clynnog, Llancarfan, and other churches the centres of groups of manors or hamlets of rent-paying serfs. The abbot was no longer an apostle, a worker of miracles, a terror to evil-doers, but simply a mighty landowner. The vow

[104] The marginalia of the Book of St. Chad are given in facsimile, with a full discussion of their meaning, in *Lib. Land.* pref. xlii-xlviii and the accompanying plates. See also Bradshaw, *Collected Papers*, 1889, pp. 458-61.

[105] "Mannuclenn" is not otherwise known, but, judging from the ordinary "dawn bwyd" of a South-Welsh servile "tref" as given in the Laws (*LL.* i. 532-4, 770), I regard "sheaf" or "handful" (from "manucla" = manua, a bundle) as a far more likely explanation than the "sucking pig" of *Lib. Land.* xlv.

of poverty, though still so far observed that the monk had no property of his own, had lost most of its meaning through the great accession of riches to the community. As for the vow of celibacy, that probably went more gradually, as the result of the position held by the monks in so many cases as clergy in the chief or mother church of the locality. Although the monk took a vow which put marriage out of the question, no such solemn obligation was entered into by the cleric, and the objection to a married clergy, though very general in the Middle Ages and enforced by reformer after reformer, did not rest upon any fundamental law of the Church; it was partly a matter of sentiment, arising out of the belief that the monastic ideal was the higher one, and partly a matter of policy, based on well-founded dread of the rise of a system of hereditary succession. Whether in any particular age and country the clergy were actually married men and founded families depended upon the local public opinion, and in Wales it seems clear that in and after the ninth century clerical marriage and family property in church offices were pretty firmly established. Among the clergy who witness the grant of freedom to Bleiddud son of Sulien and his heirs entered in the Book of St. Chad is "Cuhelyn son of the bishop," *i.e.*, of the Bishop Nobis who then presided over Llandaff,[106] and in the same century another Bishop Nobis, seated at St. David's, was followed in the see by a relative named Asser, who became famous as the biographer of King Alfred.[107] At the era of the Norman Conquest the system had reached its height. The sons and grandsons of Sulien, who was Bishop of St. David's from 1073 to 1078 and again from 1080 to 1085, were the leading clergy of the diocese for the best part of a century, and when Giraldus Cambrensis says that in Wales sons regularly succeed their fathers in church livings,[108] his statement is confirmed by the evidence of the *Liber Landavensis* that this was quite the rule in the district of Archenfield, then altogether Welsh, at the end of the eleventh century.[109] While there are no documents which make it possible to trace the gradual dis-

[106] *Lib. Land.* xlvi.

[107] "Expulsione illorum antistitum qui in eo (*i.e.*, St. David's) praeessent, sicut et Nobis archiepiscopum (for this title see note 43), propinquum meum, et me expulit" (c. 79).

[108] *Works*, iii. 130; *cf.* vi. 214 (*Descr.* ii. 6).

[109] *Lib. Land.* 275-7.

CHAP. VII.

appearance of the celibate ideal, it is indubitable that a change of this kind was brought about, were there no evidence other than that afforded by St. David's, where in the sixth century Dewi preached and practised a pitiless austerity and in the thirteenth century the canons lived with their wives, as Giraldus complains, under the very shadow of the cathedral.[110]

Yet there were, let it not be forgotten, certain communities which kept the primitive discipline as late as the time of Giraldus, favoured by their isolation from the world. One such occupied Priestholm,[111] off the easternmost point of Anglesey, a body of hermits who still followed the custom of maintaining themselves by the labour of their own hands and whose rigorous asceticism was such that no woman was ever allowed to enter the island. The soil was hallowed by the bones of departed anchorites without number, and the very animals of the place, it was believed, were in league with the powers above, for any quarrels which ruffled the surface of this peaceful and sheltered community were forthwith avenged by inroads made on its supplies by the little field-mice of the island. Bardsey, the "Ynys Enlli" of the Welsh, was held by a group of hermits of the same pattern,[112] and had, in consequence, a high reputation throughout Wales for sanctity. The dearest wish of the Welsh warrior or poet, as he approached the end of his stormy career, was to be buried in "the beauteous isle of Mary," where the heaving ocean made a girdle round the churchyard and where he might share the sleep of twenty

110 *Works*, iii. 128-9. In South Wales the law recognised as legitimate the sons of clerics who had not taken priest's orders, but the son of a priest was "begotten against law" (*LL.* i. 444 (Dim.); 760 (Gw.); ii. 857 (Lat. B.)).

111 Gir. Camb. vi. 131 (*Itin.* ii. 7). The name Priestholm (Priests' isle) is of Scandinavian origin. In Welsh the island was known originally as Ynys Lannog ("insula glannauc" in Harl. MS. 3859—*Cymr.* ix. 157), from the mythical Glannog, father of Helig Foel and grandfather of certain local saints (Bonedd y Saint in *Myv. Arch.* II. 24, 30, 45 (416, 419, 426)). This is the name which Gir. Camb. gives as "Enislannach" and, in an unfortunate excursion into the fields of Welsh etymology, explains, by reference to "llan," as "insula ecclesiastica". Ynys being a feminine noun, the disappearance of the *g*, which led him into this pitfall, is quite regular for Welsh of this period. "Ynys Seiriol," due to the close connection of the island with Seiriol's church of Penmon, appears to be much later, while "Puffin Island" is a modern tourists' designation.

112 Gir. Camb. vi. 124 (*Itin.* ii. 6). Rhys derives the Welsh name from an original Ynys Fenlli and connects it with Benlli Gawr (*Arth. Legend*, 354).

CHAP. VII.

thousand saints, "the pure-souled dwellers of Enlli"[113] Nor were these stricter communities confined to the islands of the coast; there was one at Beddgelert, in the rocky heart of Snowdon, a body of clergy who led a celibate life and were given to self-denial and the practice, as became their situation on the confines of Eifionydd, Ardudwy, Arfon and Arllechwedd, of hospitality.[114]

These groups of celibates or "meudwyaid"[115] appear to have been the only monasteries in the strict sense which survived among the Welsh at the era of the Norman Conquest. There were no Benedictine houses until the Norman conquerors of South Wales brought into the country this type of monastic foundation, and upon the native Welsh, it will be seen in a later chapter, no impression was made by any movement of this kind until the middle of the twelfth century, the great age of Cistercian expansion. Thus the men under vows (diofrydogion) mentioned in the Welsh Laws, who have abjured women, the eating of flesh, and riding on horses, men of peculiar sanctity whose concurrence gives special virtue to a judicial oath, are probably the members of these celibate communities,[116] together with another class which was to be found at all times in Wales from the introduction of Christianity to the age of the Protestant Reformation, namely, solitary hermits, dwellers in isolated cells. This type remained unchanged, however much communities might alter, throughout the ages; the holy man consulted by the British clergy before they went to their second conference with Augustine[117] is represented six centuries later by Wechelen, the hermit of Llowes in Elfael, who was regarded by the whole countryside as a prophet and a

[113] See the "Deathbed of Meilyr the Poet" (Marw Ysgafyn Veilyr Brydyt—"ysgafyn" is explained in *Mots Latins*, 215) in *Myv. Arch.* I. 192-3 (142). The translation in *Lit. Kym.* (2), 13-5, gives the general sense, but is not to be trusted in details. For an important early account of Enlli see *Lib. Land.* 1-5 (story of Elgar).

[114] Gir. Camb. iv. 167. The place is not named, but is clearly Beddgelert.

[115] For "meudwy" see note 37 above.

[116] *LL.* i. 408, 594 (Dim.), 688, 750 (Gw.); ii. 769, 794, 803 (Lat. A.), 836, 850 (Lat. B.)—all South-Welsh texts; the inclusion of "gwyr diofrydog" in a "rhaith" was not apparently usual in Gwnyedd. Some of the texts have "llien" for "cic".

[117] Bede, *H.E.* ii. 2.

CHAP. VII.

healer of the sick and whose guidance and ghostly counsel were sought, poor and illiterate though he was, by so considerable a person as Giraldus Cambrensis.[118] The "gwr ystafellog" (chambered man) appears in the Laws, in virtue of the payment due on his death to the lord of the district in which he lived,[119] and from the same source it is known that there were women anchorites, singular among all Welshwomen in that they also paid this "ebediw" or heriot, which was otherwise only exacted from men.[120] This was because other women paid an "amobyr" or marriage-fee, which would never become due in the case of a woman vowed to life-long seclusion.

The "mother churches" of monastic origin were well distributed over the whole of Wales, and their position in the earlier ages of Welsh Christianity is accurately defined in the name which has been given them of "missionary churches"[121] Every important "clas" had its "out-stations," to use the language of modern missions, for each of which one or more of the members was responsible and which became in time a chapel of the mother church. Thus the "clas" of Cybi at Holyhead had chapels at Bodedern, Llandrygarn and Bodwrog, while in Powys traces of the supremacy of Meifod as the old ecclesiastical metropolis of the district in which it stood are found as far afield as Llanfair Caereinion and Alberbury. In this way may be explained the rise of a very large number of the churches which ultimately, through the assignment to them of the tithes of certain definite areas around them, became the parish churches of to-day. They were at first the mission stations of the mother churches. But a number of churches remain which cannot be accounted for in this way, and these, it is reasonable to suppose, were erected by the efforts of laymen, who wished to make provision for their own spiritual needs. Churches built in this way seem to have been far fewer in Wales

[118] *Works*, i. 89-93 (De Rebus, iii. 2); i. 175 (Invect. vi. 20).

[119] *LL.* i. 492, § 24 (Dim.), 686, § 11 (Gw.); ii. 12 (from a Venedotian source), 797 (Lat. A.), 885 (Lat. B.) all fix his "ebediw" at 24d.

[120] *LL.* i. 96, § 52 (Ven.), 492, § 25 (Dim.), 686, § 12 (Gw.); ii. 12, 797 (Lat. A.), 885, which give the payment variously as 12d. and 16d. Aneurin Owen, following Moses Williams (Wotton, 585), translates "ystafellog" as "cottar" (i. 687), but the "sanctimonialis" of Lat. A. and B. is conclusive as to the meaning.

[121] Palmer in *Arch. Camb.* V. iii. (1886).

than in England, possibly because building in wood was so much simpler and less costly that there was here no occasion to invoke the aid of wealth when a new sanctuary was to be raised. But the "king's chapels," the churches built for the use of the lord of territory and his train at the principal courts of his kingdom, were certainly of this type. According to what seems to be the old law, the chapel of the court, in which the men of the court worshipped,[122] was one of the buildings which the king's villeins were to put up and keep in repair;[123] it had a permanent chaplain, who lived in the "maerdref," the hamlet attached to the court,[124] but its chief officer was the "offeiriad teulu," the king's priest, who followed the king as he travelled from court to court, acted as his chaplain and secretary, and received the bulk of the religious offerings of the king and his courtiers.[125] He was the real parson of the royal chapels and his office was naturally in the gift of the king.[126]

III. The Early Welsh Church: Art and Literature.

(The chief authority upon Celtic art in Christian times is the late J. Romilly Allen, whose book on the subject, dealing also with the earlier art of the pagan epoch, appeared in 1904. Use has also been made in this and other chapters of the handbook written by Mr. Allen for the Society for Promoting Christian Knowledge, entitled *The Monumental History of the Early British Church* (London, 1889). The stones are fully described in *Lap. W.*—discoveries made after 1879 are dealt with in *Arch. Camb.* See also articles by Mr. Allen in *Arch. Camb.* V. x. (1893), 17-24; xvi. (1899), 1-69.)

What has been said of the ruling tendencies in the Welsh Church during the centuries which followed the age of Gildas and Dewi suggests that, though much quiet and enduring

[122] *LL.* ii. 68, § 69.

[123] The "cappel" appears in Dim. (*LL.* i. 486) and Gw. (i. 772), and was found, there is reason to think, in the copies of the laws used in the compilation of Lat. A. and B.—see ii. 785, 828. In Ven. (i. 78) the list of nine buildings is otherwise made up, but this may well be due to the fact that in the thirteenth century royal chapels were no longer built in the old haphazard fashion.

[124] The "offeiriad teulu," like other members of the court, had no house there; he lodged with "caplan y dref" (*LL.* i. 358, 634), "sui capellani" (ii. 755), or "cappellani sub eo servientis" (ii. 819, 897). In Ven. (i. 16, 52) this officer is styled "clochydd," *i.e.*, bellringer or sexton.

[125] Ven. i. 16-18; Dim. i. 364; Gw. i. 638.

[126] "Ni ddyly esgob bersoni neb ar sapelau y brenin heb ei ganiad" (A bishop ought not to appoint any one to the king's chapels without his consent)—Ven. i. 18, MSS. A., E. MSS. B., D. read differently, but assert the same principle.

CHAP. VII.

work was done, there was a loss of originality and a declension from early spiritual ideals. This impression is not removed if one looks at the intellectual output of the period, the permanent records of its activity in the spheres of literature and art. It was not a great epoch or an epoch of great men; though in touch with Ireland,[127] the home at this time of a valuable culture of native growth, Wales was but feebly moved by this life across the sea and rather shared the backwardness of the rest of Britain and of Western Europe.

Of the architectural work of the period it is impossible to judge, for it has been already stated that nothing remains of any church built in Wales before the Norman Conquest.[128] Even if it be true that all churches of the time were not of wood, and occasionally one was built of stone, it seems clear that the conditions were such that architecture had as an art no scope for development.[129] The only memorials in stone which have survived as evidences of the artistic culture of the period —and these are fairly abundant—are the carved stone crosses and inscribed stones which stood in the graveyards and on other consecrated spots connected with the early churches. In respect of these a direct succession may be observed from the standing stones bearing inscriptions in Latin capitals or ogam characters, or both, which were discussed in Chapter IV. of this work. At first the stones are without ornament, save an occasional incised cross, and the later date is inferred merely from the form of the letters, which are no longer capitals but of the type known as minuscule. There is a stone of this description in the churchyard of Llanwnnws, Cardiganshire, which is believed to be of the early part of the ninth century and bears a Latin legend that may be thus rendered: "Whosoever may decipher this name, let him utter a benediction on the spirit of Hiroidil son of Carotinn".[130] Still older is the inscription on the stone at Caldy Island; to the old ogam epitaph was

[127] The British bishop Marcus, to whom the copyist of the Vatican MS. erroneously ascribes the *Historia Brittonum*, was educated in Ireland in the early part of the ninth century (Mommsen's *Nennius*, pp. 120, 172).

[128] P. 209.

[129] Allen, *Celtic Art*, p. 179.

[130] "*Quicunque* explica*uer*it h*oc* no*men* det benedixionem pro anima hiroidil filius carotinn" (*Arch. Camb.* V. xiv. (1897), 156-8). See also *Inscr. Chr.* No. 122; *Lap. W.* 144; *Arch. Camb.* IV. v. (1874), 245-6, and V. xiii. (1896), 135. The "nomen" is the *χps* which is placed at the head of the cross.

added about A.D. 750 the following: "And I have marked it with the sign of the cross. I beseech all that pass hereby to pray for the soul of Cadwgan."[131] Meanwhile the art of illuminating manuscripts had reached a high pitch of perfection in Ireland, and a special Irish style of decoration had been evolved, in which the curves and spirals of the earlier Celtic world were grafted upon the interlacing ribbon and key-pattern work of Christian art and results achieved of wonderful complexity and artistic merit. Nothing more beautiful of its kind can be imagined than the illuminated border and initial work in the Book of Kells, a copy of the gospels prepared in the first half of the eighth century for the use of one of the most famous of the monasteries of St. Columba. In the course of time the principles of design followed in the decoration of books were applied to the ornamentation of stone monuments, and the sculptor's art produced the graceful stone crosses, covered with intricate ornament, of which many examples are to be found in Scotland and Ireland. The ninth century is believed to have been the age in which the highest degree of skill was attained by the Celts in craftmanship of this kind.[132] In Wales the same causes were at work, evolving a native art of sculpture out of primitive and Christian decorative elements, but with less felicitous results. A good deal of carving in the Celtic style was at this period executed in the country; nearly a hundred stones—if fragments be taken into the reckoning—with Celtic ornament upon them have come to light in such ancient centres of church life as Penmon, Corwen, Meifod, St. David's, Margam, Llantwit Major, Penally, Nevern and Llanbadarn Fawr. But it is agreed that the Welsh crosses are inferior in design and workmanship to the Irish ones; spirals are almost wholly absent, there is little figure sculpture, and there is less grace of form. The new style of decorating tombstones was adopted in Wales, but the artists and gravers had not the Irish cunning.

CHAP. VII.

Among the more notable of the Welsh crosses may be mentioned the two at Nevern and Carew, the former 12 and

[131] "Et singno crucis in illam fingsi: rogo omnibus ammulantibus ibi exorent pro anima catuoconi" (*Arch. Cam.* V. xiii. (1896), 98-103). See also *Inscr. Chr.* No. 94; *Lap. W.* 106-8; Fenton (2), 251.

[132] *Celtic Art*, pp. 286-8.

CHAP. VII.

the latter 14 feet high. The Carew cross bears, as was often the case with these elaborately sculptured monuments, the name of the artist, who appears to have been one Maredudd of Rheged.[133] An important group of these carved tombstones belongs to Glamorgan, where over thirty stones showing Celtic ornament have at various times been discovered. The Glamorganshire crosses, of which twelve belong to Margam and Llantwit Major, are often of remarkable form, having a short, broad shaft and a round head, and bear singular inscriptions, such as this on a stone at Llantwit Major: "In the name of the Supreme God begins the cross of the Saviour which Abbot Samson prepared for his soul and for the soul of King Ithel and Arthfael and Tecan".[134] It is noteworthy that the inscriptions on these crosses, when they extend beyond the mention of a name, are (with one exception)[135] written in Latin and not, as in Ireland, in the vernacular speech, which may be regarded as showing that such culture as was maintained in the Welsh Church ran on the traditional Roman lines, and was not, like the Irish, a native growth, drawing its inspiration from popular sources. The custom of setting up tombstones with minuscule inscriptions and Celtic ornament lasted as late as the end of the eleventh century and the advent of the Normans, for in 1891 there was discovered in St. David's Cathedral a memorial of this kind to Hedd and Isaac, sons of Bishop Abraham, who presided over the see from 1078 to 1080.[136]

Beyond the carved and inscribed stones little remains to tell of the degree of progress attained by the Welsh in artistic performance at this time. There is no evidence that they had the Irish skill in illuminating, for, though the Book of St. Chad was for a considerable time at Llandaff and was then known

[133] *Inscr. Chr.* No. 96; *Lap. W.* 119; *Arch. Camb.* V. xii. (1895), 186-190.

[134] "In nomine di summi incipit crux salvatoris quae preparauit Samsoni apati pro anima sua et pro anima iuthahelo rex et artmali et teca(n)" (*Inscr. Chr.* No. 62; *Lap. W.* 12; *Arch. Camb.* V. xvi. (1899), 147-150).

[135] This is the well-known stone preserved in Towyn Church, the inscription on which has never been satisfactorily explained and is possibly not genuine. See *Inscr. Chr.* No. 126; *Lap. W.* 158; *Arch. Camb.* V. xiv. (1897), 142-6 (Rhys).

[136] *Arch. Camb.* V. ix. (1892) 78; x. (1893), 281.

as "Efengyl Teilo,"[137] it came there by purchase[138] and may well have been produced by Irish art. Ancient bells, of the quadrangular Celtic form, have been found in two or three places in Wales, but only in one case was there any ornament.[139]

Learning did not wholly die in the monasteries of Wales. It is known, from the existence of MSS. of Ovid, of the poet Juvencus, and of Martianus Capella, in which many of the words are interpreted in old Welsh of the ninth century, that the studies of the monks were not confined to the text of the Scriptures, but ranged over a fairly wide field.[140] Nevertheless, the bad Latin of the inscriptions shows that composition in that language was at a low ebb, and there are in fact but two works written by Welshmen between 600 and 1050 which have survived, neither of them of much literary merit, though they are full of interest for the historian. They are the *Historia Brittonum* usually connected with the name of Nennius, and Asser's *De Rebus Gestis Ælfredi.* Many problems, into which it is not possible here to enter, cluster round the former of these two works; the date at which it was first put together, its original author, the relations to each other of the various MSS., are still under discussion.[141] But some facts stand out with sufficient clearness and enable an estimate to be formed of the significance of the work as an index to Welsh culture. About the year 800 a little collection of tracts on the history

[137] "Sit maledictus a deo et a teiliav, in cuius euangelio scriptum est" (*Lib. Land.* xlvi.).

[138] "Emit gelhi filius arihtiud hoc euangelium de cingal . . . et dedit pro anima sua istum euangelium deo et sancti teliaui super altare" (*Lib. Land.* xliii.). It is probably of the eighth century (*Celtic Art*, p. 175).

[139] *Arch. Camb.* IV. ii. 271-5; *Celtic Art*, pp. 196-201. The famous bell of St. David, called "Bangu" and kept at Glasgwm, was probably of this type (Gir. Camb. vi. 18 (*Itin.* i. 1)).

[140] For the old Welsh glosses see Bradshaw, *Collected Papers*, pp. 281-5, 453-88; *IV. Anc. Bks.* ii. pp. 1, 2, 311-4; *Gr. Celt.* (2), 1054-1063; *Arch. Camb.* IV. iv. (1873), 1-21.

[141] Earlier editions of the *Historia Brittonum* (Gale, *Scriptores XV.* 93-139, 1691; Gunn, 1819; Stevenson, 1838; Petrie, *Mon. Hist. Br.* pp. 47-82) have been superseded by that of Mommsen (*Monumenta Germaniae Historica: Chronica Minora saec.* iv. v. vi. vii.—Berlin, 1894), in which there is a complete critical apparatus, and use is made of an important MS. not known to the earlier editors, *viz.*, the Chartres MS. of about A.D. 900. In *Nennius Vindicatus* (Berlin, 1893) Zimmer had for the first time shown the true relation of Nennius to the work so commonly cited under his name, and in Mommsen's edition the "Nennian" passages are printed separately.

CHAP. VII.

and geography of Britain was known in Wales in a number of copies; it included the *Saxon Genealogies*, which has been treated in the earlier chapters of this book as a valuable authority for the sixth and seventh centuries,[142] and the rest of the collection may possibly be quite as old.[143] One copy, from which is derived nearly all the extant MSS., was transcribed by a man who had a special interest in the ruling family of Buellt and Gwerthrynion, districts bordering on the upper waters of the Wye;[144] a somewhat later copyist wrote in the fourth year of Merfyn Frych, ruler of Gwynedd, *i.e.*, about 829.[145] Another copy, compiled about 800, was the work of one "Nennius," or, to use the Welsh form, Nyniaw, who calls himself a disciple of Bishop Elfodd and freely edits the original "volume of Britain," as he terms it, which he has in his hands.[146] It is beyond dispute that the original author of the *Historia Brittonum* and its editor Nennius were very unskilful writers of Latin and had a very limited knowledge of the general course of history. The gulf between them and Gildas as Latinists is immense; fault may no doubt be found with the over-elaborate style of the older writer, but it was at any rate the fruit of profound study. The matter, too, of the *Historia* reveals to us a community in which folk-lore takes the place of learning. Use is made of some of the historians whose works

142 See note 84 to chap. iv.

143 This is Mommsen's view (Introd. 113, 117), as against Zimmer, who holds that the *Historia* was written about 800 (*Nenn. V.* § 10).

144 All MSS. save the Chartres MS., which is an imperfect copy, have the passage (c. 49), "Fernmail ipse est qui regit modo in regionibus duabus Buelt et Guorthigirniaun," and the descent of Ffernfael from Vortigern. According to Jesus Coll. MS. 20, Ffernfael's cousin Brawstudd was married to Arthfael of Morgannwg (see Pedigrees IX. and XIV. in *Cymr.* viii. 85, 86), which would indicate that this king flourished about 800—a conclusion also to be drawn from the number of generations between him and Vortigern.

145 The reference to the "annum quartum Mermini regis" (c. 16) is not found in the Chartres MS. or in the Irish version, and does not belong, therefore, to the original text of the *Historia*, or, apparently, to the Nennian edition. The year is no doubt the same as that given in many MSS. as A.D. 831 (Mommsen, p. 146), for it is not likely that Merfyn Prych obtained the throne of Gwynedd until the death, recorded by Harl. MS. 3859 under the year 825 (*Cymr.* ix. 164), of Hywel ap Rhodri, the last male representative of the line of Cunedda. 831 may easily, in fact, be an error for 829 (observe that the year of the *passion* is given as 796), the precise year required if Merfyn succeeded in 825.

146 As a disciple of Elfodd, Nennius must have lived about 800, and the same conclusion is suggested by the fact that the *Historia* was known under his name to the Irish scholar Cormac (836-908).

were current in ecclesiastical circles, of Jerome, of Prosper and of Isidore,[147] but inferences are drawn from the writings of these reverend fathers which would have greatly surprised them. Because the chronicle of Jerome used for the earlier part of the Roman period is without the computation of the year by means of its consuls, while the continuation of Prosper has them, it is gravely said that in the time of the Emperor Maximus "there began to be consuls at Rome and never afterwards were they called Cæsars"![148] An old list of seven emperors who visited Britain is taken, and it is assumed that save for the visits of these seven the Britons were independent of Rome; then the writer adds that, while he has only found the names of seven "in the ancient traditions of our elders," the Romans speak of two more; these, however, are Septimius Severus and Constantius, whom he has already, without realising the fact, included in his list.[149]

Nennius, it has already been said, styles himself a disciple of Elfodd, from which it may be inferred that he flourished about the year 800 and belonged to the party which desired a closer connection between the Welsh Church and the rest of Christendom.[150] No copy of the *Historia* exactly representing his edition of the work seems to have been preserved, but it has been reconstructed in its main features by the skill of Zimmer and Mommsen. In his preface Nennius represents himself, as was the manner of his kind, as an original compiler rather than a mere editor; "I have," he says, "gathered together all I could find not only in the Roman annals, but also in the chronicles of the holy fathers Hieronymus, Eusebius, Isidorus and Prosper, and in the annals of the Irish and the English and in our own ancient traditions".[151] Elsewhere he lays aside the pretence of originality and speaks with the voice of the mere copyist: "But since my master, priest Beulan, thinks the Saxon and other genealogies useless, I have refrained from copying them, but I have written out the 'Cities' and the 'Marvels of Britain,' as other scribes have done before

147 Mommsen, Introd. 114-5.
148 C. 26 (Mommsen, p. 166).
149 For the original list see the Chartres MS. (Mommsen, p. 163, note 4).
150 See section ii. of this chapter.
151 From the shorter preface. The longer is only found in one late MS. and is spurious (Mommsen, Introd. 126).

CHAP. VII.

me".[152] His purpose was to produce a new and enlarged edition of the *Historia*, but he found himself sadly destitute of material. The doctors of Britain, he complains, have kept no records of the history of the race; incessant war and pestilence have dulled the senses of the Britons, so that they have ceased to care about the memorials of their past[153] It must be confessed that Nennius did little to improve the text of the *Historia.* He had learnt from readers of Bede that to Paulinus, and not Rhun ab Urien, was due the credit of the conversion of Edwin of Northumbria,[154] and he knew that Septimius Severus died at York.[155] But it is an unhappy guess which identifies the mythical Ceredig, Hengist's British interpreter, with the historical king of that name who ruled the northern Elfed in the days of Edwin,[156] nor is it of any great advantage to have the lineage of Brutus, the progenitor of all Britons, traced to the accursed Ham instead of the more reputable Japheth.[157] Genuine as was the patriotism of the disciple of Elfodd, he had undertaken a task which was beyond the compass of his narrow powers.

A hundred years later another Welsh scholar appears in the person of Bishop Asser of St. David's.[158] A relative of Bishop Nobis, brought up in the famous monastery of Dewi and gradually promoted from the grade of scholar, through that of priest, to the highest dignity the place could offer him,[159] Asser

[152] Mommsen, p. 207.

[153] Preface. It is remarkable, as Zimmer points out (*Nenn. V.* 133), that the expression "hebitudo gentis Britanniae" is echoed in the early ninth century MS. (so Bradshaw) which speaks of the alphabet invented by "Nemniuus" in answer to the taunts of an English scholar, who said the Welsh had no native alphabet; this the Welshman did "ut uituperationem et *hebitudinem* deieceret *gentis suae*" (*Gr. Celt.* (2), 1059).

[154] See note 42 above.

[155] Mommsen, p. 165.

[156] *Ibid.* p. 178.

[157] *Ibid.* p. 151.

[158] I have, of course, used the recent edition of the life of Alfred by W. H. Stevenson (Oxford, 1904), in which the many difficult questions raised by the text of this work are for the first time fully and scientifically treated.

[159] "Illa tam sancta loca, in quibus nutritus et doctus ac coronatus (*i.e.*, tonsured) fueram atque ad ultimum ordinatus" (Stev. p. 64). I understand the last phrase to refer to his elevation to the episcopate; for, despite Stubbs (*Reg. Sacr.* (2), 217), it would seem clear that only a bishop of St. David's could speak of "omnia quae in sinistrali et occidentali Sabrinae parte habebam" and couple himself with Nobis as one of the "antistites" of the "parochia Sancti Degui".

was in every respect a child of the Welsh monastic system. Other influences, Irish and Breton, had in all probability contributed to the ripening of his scholarship,[160] but it is undoubtedly to the credit of St. David's that, when King Alfred was endeavouring to revive learning in Wessex by gathering foreign teachers at his court, it was able to furnish at least one man who could assist him in his design. Asser himself has told the tale, how the king summoned him from the further limits of the West to a conference which took place between them at Dean[161] in Sussex, how Alfred appealed to him to leave Wales and join the circle of scholars at the court, how he hesitated to abandon the interests entrusted to him in his native country, and how he finally agreed to a division of his time between the old and the new responsibilities. A long illness which kept him a prisoner for many weary months at Caerwent[162] postponed the fulfilment of the bargain, but it was ultimately approved, from motives of policy, by the monks of St. David's, and from this time forth Asser's connection with Alfred and with England was intimate, until he died bishop of Sherborne about 910.[163] Such a career leads one to look with interest into the work produced by Asser as an author. But the biography of Alfred is in many ways an unsatisfactory piece of writing. Its tone and spirit are admirable; throughout there is genuine enthusiasm for the patient, earnest hero who grappled with so many difficulties and ever set the loftiest ideals before him. But the arrangement is confused and shows no unity of purpose; the style is of the inflated and rhetorical type which was affected by many Western writers at this period; and nothing could be more abrupt than the conclusion. Asser stands on a distinctly higher level as an author than Nennius, but he is manifestly

[160] Stev. (xciii.) thinks the Frankish element in Asser's work may have come through Breton channels.

[161] Near Eastbourne (Stev. 312).

[162] So Stev. (313-4) understands the "Wintonia civitate" of the text, at once disposing of the serious difficulties raised by the ordinary rendering "Winchester". Caerwent (which is "guentonia urbs" in *Lib. Land.* 220, 222) was an ancient ecclesiastical centre, owing its foundation to one Tathiu or Tatheus (*Cambro-Br. SS.* 255-64; *Lib. Land.* 222, 243; *ibid.* 270, mentions five "presbiteri tathiu"). It also lay on the old Roman road which would take Asser from Wessex to St. David's.

[163] *A.S. Chr.* MS. A. *s.a.* Harl. MS. 3859 gives the year as 908 (*Cymr.* ix. 167).

inferior as a literary artist to Gildas, and, while posterity will ever be grateful to him for the picture of the good king he served, his work cannot be said to remove the impression that the life of the Welsh Church at this time ran a somewhat sluggish and pedestrian course.

CHAPTER VIII.

THE TRIBAL DIVISIONS OF WALES.

(For the materials of this chapter I have had to depend mainly upon my own studies, save that invaluable help has been derived from the notes of Mr. Egerton Phillimore in the various Cymmrodorion volumes and elsewhere.)

I. The Cantrefs of Gwynedd.

CHAP. VIII.

It will now be convenient to undertake a general survey of the political condition of Wales during the period 650 to 850, and this will of necessity be at the same time a topographical account of the country as it then was, since the story will not admit of being treated with reference to one central point, but must be separately told for each one of the many tribal areas into which Wales was at this time divided.

Anglesey,[1] the Mona of primitive times and the Môn of mediæval and modern Welsh, has been throughout the historic period a political unit. It is true that it is divided into three cantrefs, but these bear upon them, in their names of Cemais, Aberffraw and Rhosyr,[2] the marks of their origin as areas mapped out by the government with reference to the three principal courts of the chieftains of the island. The six commotes into which the three cantrefs are subdivided wear a more ancient aspect, but even they do not appear, with the possible exception of Tindaethwy,[3] to represent old tribal distinctions or anything but administrative convenience. Save for the great fen known as Malltraeth Marsh, which separates the commote of Menai from that of Malltraeth, the island has no important physical barriers; it lies low and, in marked contrast to the opposite mainland, has no mountain ranges or

[1] For the derivation of the name see chap. vi. note 99.

[2] The documents which record the names of the cantrefs and commotes of Wales are discussed in the note appended to this chapter.

[3] See p. 41.

CHAP. VIII.

high table-lands.[4] Hence it acquired importance in very early times as the great corn-growing district of North Wales; its proud sons dubbed it "Môn, the mother of Wales," since the abundant crops it yielded were sufficient, they said, to maintain the whole of Wales for one year.[5] In Bede's time it was known for its fertility,[6] and the number of parish churches it contains is an incidental proof of its ability in the Middle Ages to support a large population. It thus became, as soon as the Goidelic elements in it had been thoroughly subdued to the Brythonic, the chief seat of political power in Gwynedd and the residence, in particular, of the line of kings which claimed to represent Cunedda Wledig and Maelgwn Gwynedd. Physical and political causes combined to prevent in Anglesey that division into minor chieftaincies which was so common a spectacle in other parts of Wales.

After the fall of the great Cadwallon, the house of Cunedda was represented by his son Cadwaladr, who was king among the Britons in the days of Oswy of Northumbria.[7] None of his deeds have been recorded, yet he must have been a figure of some distinction, for the bards of later ages regarded his name as one to conjure with, and in days of national depression foretold his return, as was fabled of Arthur also, to lead the Cymry to victory.[8] He died in the great plague of 664[9] and

[4] According to *App. Land Com.* 259, only 188 acres of the surface of the county lie at a higher elevation than 500 feet above sea-level.

[5] Gir. Camb. vi. 127 (*Itin.* ii. 7), 177 (*Descr.* i. 6). Prydydd y Moch was familiar with the title; see *Myv. Arch.* I. 299 (211).

[6] *H.E.* ii. 9 (frugum prouentu atque ubertate).

[7] "Dum ipse (Osguid) regnabat, venit mortalitas hominum, Catgualart regnante apud Brittones post patrem suum, et in ea periit" (*i.e.*, Cadwaladr) (*Sax. Genealogies* in *Hist. Britt.* c. 64).

[8] *Cf.* the lines in the "Hoianau" (*Blk. Bk.* fo. 30*b*; *IV. Anc. Bks.* ii. p. 26),

A phan del Kadualadir y orescin mon
dileaur Saeson o tirion prydein.

("And when Cadwaladr comes to seize Anglesey, the English will be driven from the pleasant isle of Britain.")

[9] The plague in the reign of Oswy which, according to the *Saxon Genealogies*, carried off Cadwaladr, can hardly be any other than the famous pestilence of 664, for which *cf.* Bede, *H.E.* iii. 27. The chronicle in Harl. MS. 3859 gives the year of the king's death as 682, but it is of inferior authority to the *Sax. Gen.* Geoff. Mon. introduced another element of confusion by identifying Cadwaladr with Caedualla of Wessex and making him die, accordingly, at Rome on 20th April, 689 (*Hist. Reg.* xii. 14, where the Berne MS. reads "Cheduallam iuvenem," and 18, where "mayarum' is to be read for the "majurum" of Giles).

it is likely, notwithstanding his martial reputation, that he spent the close of his life as a monk, for the church of Eglwys Ael or Llangadwaladr in Anglesey claims him as its patron saint and founder, and churches were dedicated to him in other parts of Wales.[10] The situation of Llangadwaladr, some two miles from Aberffraw, suggests that this had already become the chief dwelling-place of the family, not to speak of the fact that Cadfan's tombstone is in the same church, carrying back the connection with the district a couple of generations earlier.[11] Henceforth Aberffraw, a cluster of dwellings on the little lift which rises above the sand-flat at the mouth of the Ffraw, was the "principal seat" of Gwynedd,[12] and its possession was held to confer a dignity and precedence which no other title could supply. CHAP. VIII.

The successors of Cadwaladr were men of no note, whose sway did not extend, it would seem, beyond the limits of Anglesey. The death of Khodri Molwynog, son of Idwal, son of Cadwaladr, is recorded under the year 754,[13] and the family then passes out of sight until in the early part of the ninth century two sons of Khodri, Hywel and Cynan, are found battling against each other for the lordship of Môn. In 816 the death of Cynan, whose chief stronghold was in the commote of Tindaethwy, left the field clear for Hywel, who no doubt ruled over Anglesey until his death in 825. When Hwyel died, the male line of Maelgwn Gwynedd was at an end and its claims were transferred to another house by Ethyllt, the daughter of his brother Cynan.[14]

It may be mentioned that there were other royal courts in Anglesey than that of Aberffraw. In Talybolion, Cemais[15] commanded the little harbour of Porth Wygyr, widely known

[10] *Welsh SS.* 299-301. In 1352 the vill of "Eglussell" was held "de sancto Cadewaladre rege" (*Rec. Carn.* 46).

[11] See p. 182.

[12] "Eisteddfa arbennig" is the phrase of the Dimetian Code (*LL.* i. 346).

[13] "Rotri rex brittonum moritur" (Harl. MS. 3859 in *Cymr.* ix. 161). Other sources add nothing of value save Rhodri's pedigree and distinguishing epithet, the latter not yet satisfactorily explained (*Cymr.* ix. 169-70; *Bruts*, 257; *Cymr.* viii. 87).

[14] The chief authority is Harl. MS. 3859 (chronicle and pedigrees). *Ann. Ult.* also record *s.a.* 815 (= 816) the death of "Conan mac Ruadhrach rex Britonum". It has been very generally assumed that Merfyn Frych succeeded immediately on the death of Cynan Tindaethwy; on this point see chap. vii. note 145.

[15] *Rec. Carn.* 63-5.

CHAP. VIII.

in the Middle Ages as the northernmost point of Wales,[16] while Twrcelyn had its royal manor at Penrhos Lligwy.[17] Llanfaes, not far from Beaumaris (which is a creation of Edward I.), was the court of Tindaethwy[18] and before Newborough commenced its career as an English-made borough, it had been, under the name of Rhosyr, the centre of the commote of Menai.[19] This was in accordance with the rule that each commote should have its own "llys" or royal vill, at which the lord of the country received the renders of the men of that commote, whether freemen or serfs. In addition, there were in the island two important ecclesiastical centres, the "clas" founded by Cybi at Caer Gybi,[20] under the shadow of the mountain—the highest in Anglesey—known to English sailors as the Holy Head,[21] and the similar foundation of Seiriol at Penmon, with its offshoot on the adjacent isle of Priestholm or Ynys Lannog.[22] Penmon and Caergybi flank the island on its eastern and western sides respectively, and readers of Matthew Arnold will hardly need to be reminded of the tale told of the two founders, that they journeyed once a week to meet each other at the wells of Clorach, "in the bare midst of Anglesey," until the Western saint, ever facing the warm beams of the sun, became Cybi the Swarthy (Cybi Felyn), while his companion from the East, with the sunlight always falling upon his back, remained Seiriol the Fair (Seiriol Wyn).[23]

Facing Anglesey, in one long serrated line, are the heights

[16] *Cymr.* xi. 43. It is the "portus Yoiger" of Gir. Camb. vi. 165 (*Descr.* i. 1); for other early references see *Myv. Arch.* I. 74 (62), 194 (143), 270 (193); Triad i. 5 = iii. 65.

[17] *Rec. Carn.* 70-2.

[18] There is an interesting survey of Llanfaes, as it was in 1294, the year before that in which the building of Beaumaris was commenced, in *Trib. System*, App. pp. 3, 4.

[19] *Rec. Carn.* 83-5.

[20] See pp. 130, 218.

[21] The fourteenth-century English romance of "Gawain and the Green Knight" brings Gawain past "alle the iles of Anglesay" and "the Holy Hede" (vv. 698-700, ed. Morris).

[22] See p. 216. That Penmon was a monastic church of the ancient type is made certain by the grant in 1237 to the prior and canons of Ynys Lannog of "totam abbadaeth (*i.e.*, abbacy) de Penmon" (*Mon. Angl.* iv. 582).

[23] The story first appears in the notes to Richard Lloyd's *Beaumaris Bay* (1800), p. 2, though it was known to Lewis Morris (*Celt. Remains*, p. 351). It should be explained that in his well-known sonnet ("East and West") Matthew Arnold misses the precise point of the two epithets and so tells the legend not quite convincingly.

of the "stronghold of Gwynedd,"[24] the region known to the Welsh as Eryri, "the haunt of the eagles,"[25] and to the English by the no less romantic name of Snowdon, "the hill of snows".[26] This was the mountainous rampart which, stretching from the mouth of the Conway to the Rivals, at all times protected Anglesey and the intervening district of Arfon from serious attack on the landward side, and few sights are more impressive than the distant prospect of this mountain wall, rising in peak after peak along the horizon, as it may be seen from Aberffraw and many another point of vantage in Southern Anglesey. Nor was Eryri merely a barrier of crag and moorland, a rocky, marshy wilderness. Hidden within its folds were mountain glens, such as Nant Peris in Arfon and Nant Ffrancon in Arllechwedd, where the herbage was of the finest and the woods sheltered deer and nurtured swine. Just as it was reckoned that Anglesey could feed with corn the entire population of Wales, so it was held that the pastures of Eryri could furnish grazing for all the sheep and cattle in the country.[27] It was not only a citadel, but a citadel which, in the summer season, at any rate, could not easily be starved into submission.

The region which lay opposite to Anglesey, from the summit of the Rivals to the river Cegin between Bangor and Llandegai, was appropriately known as Ar-fon, *i.e.*, the land over against Môn.[28] The cantref thus named extended not only between the limits just specified, but also far into the heart of Eryri; the vale of Nantlle and the pass of Llanberis

[24] "Kedernit gwyned" (*Mab.* 62, 63). *Cf.* *Bruts*, 292: "mudaw hyt ymynyded eryri. Kanys kadarnaf lle adiogelaf y gael amdiffyn yndaw rac y llu oed hwnnw".

[25] The *Hist. Britt.* (c. 40) contains a reference to "montibus Hereri" (according to some MSS. "Heriri"), where was situated the "arx" of Ambrosius, *i.e.*, Dinas Emrys, near Beddgelert. It is not so long since eagles ceased to haunt these mountains—see Williams, *Observations on the Snowdon Mountains* (1802), pp. 2, 3.

[26] An early instance of the use of the name is to be found in *A.S. Chr. s.a.* 1095, MS. E. (Snawdune). It is properly the equivalent of Eryri (Gir. Camb. vi. 135 (*Itin.* ii. 9)) or Snowdonia, and was not used in the Middle Ages, as now, to denote merely the summit. The Welsh name of this, known to every Welshman to-day as "Y Wyddfa," was anciently "Y Wyddfa Fawr," or the Great Burial-place, since the bones of Rhita the Giant were supposed to be entombed in the cairn which crowned it (*Celt. Folklore*, pp. 474-9).

[27] Gir. Camb. vi. 135 (*Itin.* ii. 9), 170 (*Descr.* i. 5).

[28] Gir. Camb. vi. 124 (*Itin.* ii. 6).

CHAP. VIII.

were within its borders. It is aptly described by the author of *Breuddwyd Macsen Wledig* as a land of which the seaboard ran side by side with the champaign, the woodlands with the mountain.[29] The cantref was conceived as divided into four strips or belts, the maritime, the agricultural, the forest and the highland belt, rising in terrace fashion above each other until the central mass of Snowdonia was reached. It was a rich and diversified country and nourished a race of great independence of spirit. The men of Arfon claimed it as their right to lead the van in the hostings of Gwynedd and therewith demanded many other privileges, such as the liberty to fish in the three chief rivers of the district (probably the Saint, the Gwyrfai and the Llyfni), the right to declare, against their neighbours of other cantrefs, the boundaries of Arfon, and the privilege of sleeping, when they visited the king's court, in the "neuadd" or common hall with the royal heir and the squires of the court.[30] Arfon was a true tribal district, in which tribal consciousness was keen and alert. At some period or other in its history, the ancient cantref was, like many another, divided into two commotes. The river Gwyrfai, flowing from Llyn Cawellyn under the foot of Snowdon to the western end of the Menai Straits, furnished the dividing line, and from that day to this has separated the commote or hundred of Uch Gwyrfai (Above Gwyrfai) from that of Is Gwyrfai (Below Gwyrfai). The cantref contained several notable civil and ecclesiastical sites. Oldest of all was Carnarvon,[31] the Segontium of the Romans, known to the Welsh as Caer Saint yn Arfon and often more briefly as "Y Gaer yn Arfon," which is the source of the modern name. Legend had much to say of the past glories of this place. It was the burial-place of Constantine the Great and the home of Elen of the Hosts, the British wife of the Emperor Maximus. Here Brân the Blessed was found by the bird which brought under its wing the tale of the woes endured by his sister Branwen in Ireland, and here Beuno the saint up-

[29] "Gwlat a oed kyhyt y maestir ae mor. kyhyt y mynyd ae choet" (*Mab.* 83).

[30] "Breiniau Arfon" (The Privileges of Arfon), a tract found in two MSS. of the Ven. Code (*LL.* i. 104-6).

[31] For references to Carnarvon see *Hist. Britt.* c. 25; *Mab.* 34, 88; *Cambro-Br. SS.* 18. A charter in favour of Penmon priory was issued by Llywelyn ab Iorwerth at "Kaerinarvon" on 15th October, 1221 (*Mon. Angl.* iv. 582).

braided King Cadwallon for offering to him land which had been unlawfully wrested from its infant proprietor. The fort on the hill of Llanbeblig—for it was the building of the Edwardian castle which drew Carnarvon down to the margin of the strait—was clearly the ancient centre of the cantref, the original home of its chieftains, though in later times it was eclipsed in importance by Dolbadarn.[32] The two chief sanctuaries of Arfon were Bangor and Clynnog. Of the former, Bangor Fawr yn Arfon, the seat of the bishops of Gwynedd, some account has already been given;[33] it is enough to say here that the whole of the north-eastern corner of the cantref, from the Cegin to the modern village of Portdinorwic, formed part of the possessions of the see, and that a solid barrier of Church land thus intervened between the men of Arfon and those of Arllechwedd.[34] The "clas" of Celynnog Fawr was little inferior in importance to that of Bangor; it had lands in Lleyn and Anglesey as well as in the neighbourhood of the church, and St. Beuno, its founder and protector, was reckoned among the mightiest of saints. Not many years have elapsed since the whole countryside brought their children to Beuno's Well to be healed of their ailments, and paid an annual tribute to Beuno's Chest (Cyff Beuno) to ensure the prosperity of their flocks and their herds.[35]

To the east of Arfon lay Arllechwedd, for the most part a rugged, stony region, a land of declivities, as its name implies, and hence playing no important part in the early history of Wales. Its two strips of fertile, low-lying territory, the one bordering on the sea and the other on the river Conway, which was the eastern limit of the cantref, were known re-

[32] *Rec. Carn.* (17-22) shows the tenants of Is Gwyrfai as joining in the maintenance of the manor of Dolbadarn.

[33] See note appended to chap. vi.

[34] *Rec. Carn.* 93-5, 231.

[35] The "clas" of "Beuno," with that of Bangor, was to protect the special rights of the men of Arfon (*LL.* i. 106). Clynnog is Celynnog, the hamlet of holly trees; see B. *Saes. s.a.* 977 and 1151 (*B.T.* is wrong in both passages); *Llyfr yr Ancr*, 124; *Buch. Gr. ap C.*, 36. Clynnog Fechan was close to Llangeinwen, Anglesey, and belonged to Clynnog Fawr (*Arch. Camb.* I. i. (1846), 310-11; *Rec. Carn.* 257). There is a list of the possessions of the house in *Rec. Carn.* 257 (*cf. Arch. Camb.* I. iii. (1848), 253-5). For the antiquities and traditions of the place see B. Willis, *Bangor*, pp. 299-305; Penn. ii. 396-400; *Arch. Camb.* I. iii. (1848), 247-57; "Cyff Beuno," a Welsh account of the parish by Eben Fardd, schoolmaster and poet (Tremadoc, 1863).

CHAP. VIII.

spectively as Arllechwedd Uchaf (Upper) and Arllechwedd Isaf (Lower) and with these two commotes was associated that of Nant Conwy,[36] which lay west of the Conway from Dolgarrog to its source. The royal court of Arllechwedd was at Aber of the White Shells (Gwyn Gregin),[37] a favourite residence of the later rulers of Gwynedd; Trefriw, perched on the hillside just above the highest reach of the tidal portion of the Conway, was the manor of Nant Conway when the district came into the hands of the English, but Dolwyddelan must have been at one time the chief stronghold of the lord of the commote. The Church had no great foothold in Arllechwedd until the foundation of the Cistercian abbey of Aberconwy in 1186; there was no important "clas" within its bounds, and probably none of its churches stood higher in popular repute than that of St. Tudclud at Pennant Machno (now condensed into Penmachno),[38] which is shown by its ancient Christian tombstones to be a foundation of the fifth or sixth century.[39]

The great tongue of land thrown out by Eryri to the west has long been known by the name of Lleyn, which is said to signify the land of spearmen.[40] It is a remote, sea-locked region, lying off the track of the main currents of Welsh life, but its green straths and swelling knolls, only here and there broken into by mountain masses, are fertile and luxuriant, and the district has always maintained a considerable population. Three commotes went to make up the cantref of Lleyn. Dinllaen, so called from the "dinas" or cliff castle on the little peninsula of Porthdinlleyn, was the northernmost, stretching from the Rivals to Carn Fadryn; its royal manor was at Nevin.[41] From Carn Fadryn to Aberdaron a second com-

[36] So Pen. MS. 163 (Evans, *Rep.* i. p. 952), which is right on this point against the other old lists. The five churches of the commote are assigned to the deanery of Arllechwedd in the Norwich Taxation (*Arch. Camb.* V. xi. (1894), 30) and the silence of the Statute of Rhuddlan as to Nant Conwy is only to be explained by the assumption that it was included in "candreda de Arthlegaph".

[37] The full name is given in Pen. MS. 147 (Evans, *Rep.* i. p. 913) and *Myv. Arch.* II. 30 (419).

[38] Penanmagno in *Rec. Carn.* 9, Pennam'achno in the Norwich Taxation (*Arch. Camb.* V. xi. (1894), 30). Llyfr John Brooke (Evans, *Rep.* i. p. 913) and B. Willis, *Bangor*, p. 274, give the name of the saint correctly; in Ecton's *Thesaurus* (third edition, p. 495) it is printed as Tyddud, which misled Rees (*Welsh SS.* 332).

[39] *Inscr. Chr.* Nos. 135-7; *Lap. W.* 175-7.

[40] *Celt. Folklore*, i. p. 226.

[41] *Rec. Carn.* 35.

mote extended, which apparently took its name of "Cymydmaen" from a famous "Maen Melyn" or "Yellow Rock" forming part of the promontory which faces Bardsey.[42] The court of this commote was at Neigwl.[43] The third commote, which skirted the shores of Cardigan Bay from St. Tudwal's Isles to the river Erch, originally bore the name of Cunedda's son Afloeg, but Afloegion was in time corrupted into Gaflogion and Cafflogion.[44] Pwllheli was the ancient centre of this commote.[45] The church lands of Lleyn were extensive, for, in addition to the numerous vills which were the property of the see of Bangor and those which belonged to Clynnog Fawr, the cantref itself contained the important "clas" of Aberdaron, whose abbot was lord of a very considerable part of Cymydmaen.[46] Pilgrims were constantly passing through to Bardsey, and the necessary provision for them helped to give the church a special title to the wide domains which it held in the peninsula.

There is scarcely anything to show who ruled in Arfon, Lleyn and Arllechwedd in the eighth century. But the mention in Harl. MS. 3859 of a King Caradog of Gwynedd who was slain by the English in 798[47] leads one to surmise that the pedigree of Hywel ap Caradog to be found in the same authority[48] is that of the royal line of his district. It goes back to Cynlas (no doubt the Cuneglasus of Gildas), cousin of Maelgwn Gwynedd and great-grandson of Cunedda.[49] As it is not carried beyond Hywel, who belonged to the early part of the ninth century, it may be conjectured that the three cantrefs were,

[42] "Maen Melyn Lleyn" is close to Braich y Pwll. It was famous in the fourteenth century; see Dafydd Nanmor's reference in his "cywydd" to the golden hair of Llio of Gogerddan—

Mae'r un lliw a'r maen yn Llŷn.
('Tis of the same hue as the stone in Lleyn.)

[43] *Rec. Carn.* 38. A farm near Llandegwining still bears the name of Maerdref.

[44] See p. 117. [45] Under the name of Porthely (*Rec. Carn.* 25, 29, 31, 32).

[46] There are early references to the church and clergy of Aberdaron in *Buch. Gr. ap C.* (116; *Myv. Arch.* II. 596 (729)) and *B.T.* p. 122 (*Bruts*, 295; *B. Saes. s.a.* 1112 (= 1115)). For the "abadaeth" as a territorial area see *Rec. Carn.* 252 (composition of the year 1252 between the abbot of Bardsey and the secular canons of Aberdaron), and *cf.* the "abadaeth" of Penmon (*Mon. Angl.* iv. 582).

[47] "Carataue rex guenedote apud saxones iugulatur" (*Cymr.* ix. 163).

[48] *Cymr.* ix. 172. [49] See p. 133.

CHAP. VIII.

under Merfyn Frych, combined in one kingdom with the ancient realm of Anglesey. Henceforth Môn and Arfon are rarely divorced from each other.

The rugged heights which surround the north-eastern corner of Cardigan Bay were, according to tradition, the portion of Cunedda's son Dunod (Donatus), and here, therefore, was the cantref of Dunoding.[50] It was, says the primitive narrator of the story of King Math, the best of all cantrefs for a young man to rule over,[51] which may be taken to mean that as a rough and craggy region, it tried and disciplined the powers of the budding chieftain, not suffering him to fall into ignoble sloth and self-indulgence. It was cut in twain by the broad tidal estuary known as "Y Traeth Mawr" (The Great Sands), which was previous to its reclamation from the sea in 1811 a most formidable barrier, and it thus fell at an early date into the commotes of Eifionydd and Ardudwy, names which soon eclipsed and drove out of current use the ancient one of Dunoding. Eifionydd, named after Dunod's son, Eifion,[52] was the northern commote; it lay between the Erch and the Traeth, and, in historical times, the home of its lords was on the rock now crowned by the ruins of Criccieth Castle, though there is reason to think that the mound at Dolbenmaen marks the site of an earlier royal residence.[53] Ardudwy was a large but thinly populated area; from the Festiniog valley in the north to the Mawddach estuary in the south it was chiefly moor and mountain, but a fertile strip along the coast was known as Dyffryn Ardudwy (The Plain of Ardudwy). Among the famous sites within it were Harlech, where Brân from the height of the Castle rock watched the coming of the ships which brought the king of Ireland and his train to beg the hand of his sister Branwen,[54] and Mur y Castell, where Llew held his court amid

[50] For the name see, in addition to the ordinary lists, Jesus Coll. MS. 20 (*Cymr.* viii. 85), *Iolo MSS.* 122, *Mab.* 73. On the analogy of Glywysing and Dogfeiling, the ending should be -ing and not -ig. Ffynnon Dunawd, near Eisteddfa in Eifionydd, probably commemorates a saint and not the son of Cunedda (Y Gestiana, gan Alltud Eifion: Tremadoc, 1892, p. 9).

[51] *Mab.* 73.

[52] "Ebiau(n) map Dunaut map Cunedda" (*Cymr.* ix. 178). For the form *cf.* Meirionydd, Elenydd and Maelienydd.

[53] *Bye-Gones*, viii. (1903-4), p. 180.

[54] *Mab.* 26 (hardlech yn ardudwy ynllys idaw).

the broken walls of the dismantled Roman encampment.[65] It was a land which bred hardy wielders of the lance,[66] a nurturer of warriors rather than of churchmen, for neither here nor in Eifionydd were there in early times any churches of the first rank and the ancient church holdings were not considerable. The local dynasty, tracing its origin to Dunod ap Cunedda, appears to have held its own until well on in the tenth century.[67]

The districts so far dealt with belonged to the ancient Gwynedd, sometimes called by way of distinction Gwynedd above Conway.[58] East of the river Conway came Gwynedd below Conway, which does not seem to have been entitled to the name originally, for the natural explanation of the name "Y Berfeddwlad" (The Middle Country) which it also bore is that it was the land which lay between Gwynedd and Powys.[59] The four cantrefs of the Middle Country were Rhos, Rhufoniog, Dyffryn Clwyd and Tegeingl,[60] belonging for the most part to the great upland plateau of eastern North Wales, but cleft by the rich expanse of the Vale of Clwyd, a fertile, corn-growing tract of which each cantref had its share. Rhos was bounded by the Clwyd, the Elwy, the Conway and the sea; along the east bank of the Conway it sent a long arm southwards as far as Capel Garmon. The Llandudno peninsula was included in it and formed the commote of Creuddyn, which is now in a different county from the main body of the cantref, but was anciently reckoned one of its members. One may, indeed, surmise from the name Eglwys Rhos that this was the original Rhos from which the cantref took its title and that the derivation is to be sought in the Goidelic word for "promontory" rather than in the Brythonic for "moor" [61] The two other

[65] *Mab.* 74 (lys idaw yn y lle a elwir mur y castell). The fort is described on p. 68.

[66] "Sunt . . . his in partibus lanceae longissimae" (Gir. Camb. vi. 123 (*Itin.* ii. 5)).

[67] None of the persons named in the Dunoding pedigree in *Cymr.* ix. 177-8, appear elsewhere, so that dating is difficult, but the usual method of calculation (three generations to a century) will bring Cuhelyn, with whom the pedigree ends, to about 930.

[58] "Gwyned ewch Conwy" (B. *Saes. s.a.* 1175).

[59] *Cymr.* xi. 174.

[60] In a document in Rymer (4), i. 267, dated 30th April, 1247, the four "cantredos" of "Pernechelad" are given as "Ros, Rowennok, Defrencluc et Anglefeld".

[61] Both are derived from the same Celtic original (*Urk. Spr.* 312).

commotes were Uwch Dulas and Is Dulas, to the west and east respectively of the little river Dulas. Of the sites of the cantref, none ranked higher than Degannwy, the royal manor of Creuddyn, associated by tradition with the glories of the rule of Maelgwn,[62] known to have been a stronghold in the ninth century,[63] and only eclipsed as the principal fortress of the district when Edward I. built Conway on the opposite side of the river. Possession of the rock of Degannwy, which, like that pictured in "The Bard,"

> Frowns o'er old Conway's foaming flood,

was hotly contested in the long border strife between Welsh and English, and its vicissitudes furnish no bad index of the alternate rise and fall of the fortunes of the men of Gwynedd. The cantref also contained some important churches, such as Abergele, once the mother church of a wide district, but afterwards reduced to a state of dependence upon St. Asaph,[64] and Llandrillo or Dinerth, a church of similar standing.[65]

Rhufoniog was an inland cantref; the broad moorlands of Hiraethog were for the most part within its limits, which to the north and east were defined by the Elwy, the Clwyd and the Clywedog. The river Aled furnished the dividing line of the two commotes of Uwch Aled and Is Aled; there was a third commote, called Ystrad or Cymeirch, which lay between the Lliwen and the Clywedog. Rhufoniog plays no important part in the early history of Wales; though there must have been a fortress on the limestone rock of Denbigh, the Welsh Dinbych, long before the time of Edward I., it is only then that the place enters into the light of history, and no list has been preserved of the princes of this region or of the neighbouring cantref of Rhos during the period which preceded the absorption of the district in the realm of Gwynedd.[66] Much of it, in fact, was in episcopal hands; the bishop of Bangor had Llanrhaeadr,[67] and

[62] P. 129. [63] P. 202.

[64] Thomas, *St. Asaph*, pp. 350-1. For the "princeps opergelei" who was head of the "clas" in 856 see *Cymr.* xi. 165.

[65] Thomas, *St. Asaph*, p. 548. It was an important church in 1137 (*Buch. Gr. ap* C. 128 (734)).

[66] *Ann.* C. MS. B. *s.a.* 816 mentions a "regnum Roweynauc" in a notice clearly derived from an ancient source.

[67] *Rec. Carn.* 112.

no small proportion of the revenues of the bishop of St. Asaph was drawn from the manors of the see in Henllan, Llansannan, Llannefydd and Llangerniew.[68] CHAP. VIII.

Dyffryn Clwyd was a much richer cantref, though it did not cover the whole of the famous vale, but only the southern portion, from Bodffari to Derwen. The most important of the three commotes into which it was divided bore the name of Dogfeiling [69] and it is a reasonable assumption that this was once the designation of the whole cantref, marking it out as the realm of Dogfael, son of Cunedda Wledig.[70] Like Rhufoniog, it has no recorded early history, though there is in this cantref as in the other a site pretty clearly indicated by its name and its natural advantages as that of an early stronghold. Ruthin, which is by interpretation Khudd-ddin, the red fort, occupying a ridge of red sandstone in the centre of the Vale, was the centre of the commote of Dogfeiling and became the seat of the lord's castle when at the end of the thirteenth century Dyffryn Clwyd was transformed into a marcher lordship. Ecclesiastically, the cantref, with the adjacent commote of Cymeirch, was associated with Gwynedd above Conway, for, when evidence is forthcoming as to the boundaries of the Welsh dioceses, it is found to be part of the diocese of Bangor, though surrounded by that of St. Asaph.[71] The fact has also to be noted—and here may lie the explanation of the anomaly—that the bishop of Bangor was a principal owner of land in the cantref, being lord of almost the whole of the commote of Llannerch, which consisted of the modern parishes of Llanfair and Llanelidan [72]

The fourth cantref included in the Middle Country was known to the Welsh as Tegeingl.[73] Under the later princes of Gwynedd, Tegeingl was a region which took in the whole of our Flintshire as far south as Connah's Quay and Cilcen, and

[68] Thomas, *St. Asaph*, p. 180.

[69] Evans (*Rep.* i. p. 914, footnote 9) gives, from Cardiff MS. 14, the constituent parishes of the three commotes of Dyffryn Clwyd.

[70] *Descr. Pemb.* 201 (note by E. P.).

[71] This was the case at the time of the Norwich Taxation of 1254 (*Arch. Camb.* V. xi. (1894), 31). In 1859 Bangor gave up the deanery of Dyffryn Clwyd in exchange for that of Cyfeiliog.

[72] *Rec. Carn.* 113-5.

[73] The accent falls on the first syllable. For the suggested derivation from the tribal name "Deceangli," see *Celt. Br.* (2), pp. 81, 290; *Arch. Camb.* V. ix. (1892), 165; *W. People*, p. 94.

CHAP. VIII.

was divided into the three commotes of Rhuddlan, Coleshill and Prestatyn. But it has already been shown that this district was seized by the English of Mercia not later than the end of the eighth century,[74] and all the evidence goes to show that the bulk of it remained in English hands until it was reconquered by Owain Gwynedd in the twelfth. Even the names of the commotes show how late was the organisation of this country as a Welsh cantref, for they bear the names of the castles built by the Normans to secure their hold upon the district. At the period which is now under consideration, Tegeingl was a part of Mercia, save perhaps the portion around Llanelwy or St. Asaph, where the bishops of this quarter of Wales maintained a precarious and uneasy footing on the storm-swept frontier between the two races. It is true that nothing is known with any certainty of the history of the see before the twelfth century, but the place was then regarded as a bishop's seat of old standing and some ancient title no doubt underlay the extensive claims of the successors of St. Kentigern to territorial lordship in the northern part of the Vale of Clwyd.

II. The Cantrefs of Powys.

Central Wales may be regarded as a broad table-land, through which rivers great and small furrow their way in winding courses to the sea, but which has few clearly marked mountain ranges or stretches of fertile plain. The ancient kingdom of Powys[75] took in most of this region, extending in its widest limits from the neighbourhood of Mold to the river Wye, near Glasbury and Hay.[76] It included some productive districts, such as the lower valley of the Dee and the well-watered meadows of the upper Severn, so that its children were not altogether without warrant in hailing it as "Powys, the Eden of Wales"[77] But most of it

[74] Pp. 201-2.

[75] The view of Zeuss (*Gr. Celt.* (2), pp. 1053-4), that the name is to be connected with the "poues = quies" of the Oxford glosses and to be interpreted as meaning "settlement," still holds the field (*Celt. Br.* (2), p. 218).

[76] In the "Dream of Rhonabwy" (*Mab.* 144) the limits of Powys are given as "oporford (*i.e.*, Pulford, near Chester) hyt yg gwauan yg gwarthaf arwystli" (some point near Llangurig in South Montgomeryshire). But this was in the twelfth century, after the separation from the province of "Rhwng Gwy a Hafren".

[77] "Powys paradwys Cymry" (*Myv. Arch.* I. 114 (92); *IV. Anc. Bks.* ii. p. 259).

was pastoral upland, a country well fitted to be the nurse of a race of hardy, independent warriors, lovers of tribal freedom, haters of the sluggish and toilsome life of the lowland tiller of the soil, and tenacious holders of ancient privileges.[78] Such were the men of Powys, inheritors of the old Brythonic traditions, in whom incessant warfare with the Mercian English kept alive the ancient tribal characteristics.

Tribal independence does not seem, however, in this case to have brought about the division of the country into separate chieftaincies, for, so far as the scanty records show, there was but one kingdom of Powys and this maintained its unity until it was absorbed in the kingdom of Gwynedd in the ninth century. The founder of the dynasty was one Cadell Ddyrnllug (the Blackfisted?), a contemporary of St. Germanus.[79] He was, so the story ran, the swineherd of the tyrant King Benlli, and, when the gates of the royal stronghold were churlishly shut against the saint and his companions, offered the shelter of his cottage to the men of God and killed and dressed for their supper the calf of his solitary cow. The inevitable sequel follows; fire from heaven struck the citadel of Benlli (which was probably perched on Moel Fenlli[80] in the Clwydian range), so that it was instantly consumed and never again rebuilt, while Cadell and his nine sons became kings of Powys. Their progeny still ruled the country when the *Historia Brittonum*, which is our authority for the legend, was composed.[81] Whatever may be the historical basis of the story, it is certain that the family which governed Powys during the period 600-850 traced their origin to Cadell. The Selyf ap Cynan who fell in the battle of Chester was his descendant in the seventh generation,[82]

[78] See Cynddelw's poem entitled "Breiniau Gwŷr Powys" in *Myv. Arch.* I. 257 (186).

[79] *Hist. Britt.* cc. 32-5; pedigrees in Harl. MS. 3859, as given in *Cymr.* ix. 179, 181, 182, with Phillimore's notes. The old Welsh "Durnluc," for which see *Cymr.* vii. 119, was altered at an early date (see, for example, Jesus Coll. MS. 20 in *Cymr.* viii. 87) to "Deyrnllwg," and thus was evolved the mythical region of Teyrnllwg, placed by *Iolo MSS.* 86, between the Dee and (apparently) the Cumbrian Derwent.

[80] The hill-fort on Moel Fenlli was occupied in the Roman period (p. 89 above) and there is a Llanarmon, under the patronage of St. Germanus, not far off.

[81] "Et a semine illorum omnis regio Povisorum regitur usque in hodiernum diem" (*Hist. Britt.* c. 35). The passage is found in all the MSS. of the *Historia.*

[82] P. 181.

CHAP. VIII.

and the Elise to whose memory was erected the monument popularly known as "Eliseg's Pillar" stood as his representative in the tenth.[83] Elise was the son of Gwylog and Sanan, daughter of Noe ab Arthur of Dyfed;[84] he flourished in the middle of the eighth century, and, so far as can be ascertained from old readings of the now obliterated inscription on his monument, waged successful war against the English. His grandson Cadell died king of Powys in 808[85] and was succeeded by his son Cyngen. Under Cyngen the realm of Powys was reduced to sore straits, for in 822 it was overrun by the English, but this was but a temporary check, since Cyngen, who set up the stone cross to his great-grandfather's memory, was clearly in possession of Ial, and speaks, indeed, of the whole realm of Powys as though it were under his sway. After a long reign he closed his career with a pilgrimage to Rome, where he died in or about 854, the last king of Powys of the line of Cadell.[86]

During the period which is now being dealt with much of what was reckoned Powys in later ages was in the hands of the English. The line of Offa's Dyke not only ran through Tegeingl, but also intersected the districts known in the Middle Ages as the commotes of Ystrad Alun and Yr Hob and of Maelor, the English Bromfield; it left little to the Welsh save moor and mountain. It would appear that the ancient home of the kings of Powys in this part of their dominions was the commote of Ial, a long strip of upland which took in the western part of the valley of the Alun and abutted upon the Dee where it works its devious way through the gorges of Llangollen. Here was the hill-fort, named after Brân, a famous figure of Celtic story,[87] which guarded the upper waters of the

[83] The inscription on "Eliseg's Pillar" is only known from a transcript by Edward Llwyd. See Penn. ii. 7-10; *Arch. Camb.* I. i. (1846), 17, 32; VI. ix. (1909), 43-8. At present hardly a word can be read (*Lap. W.* 200). Romilly Allen points out that in form the monument belongs to a well-known Mercian type (*Arch. Camb.* V. xvi. [1899], 19). According to Phillimore, Llwyd's Elise*g* is probably a misreading of Elise*t*, which represents Elise*dd*, the old form of Elise and Elis (*Cymr.* ix. 181).

[84] *Cymr.* ix. 175. [85] Harl. MS. 3859 *s.a.* [86] *Ibid.*

[87] A doublet of the name Dinas Brân appears to be preserved in Dinbren or Dinbran, the name of the township in which the castle stands. See *Goss. Guide*, pp. 130-1. The township is now, with the rest of the parish of Llangollen, in the Nanheudwy division of the hundred of Chirk, but appears to have been originally in Ial.

" wizard stream " ; here was the pillar which told of the valour of King Elise, and here was the ancient church, Llanarmon yn Ial, which commemorated the services of St. Germanus to the founder of the fortunes of the house of Powys.[88] Ial was the heart of Northern Powys and remained in the possession of the Welsh as long as they retained their independence. Higher up the Dee was the small commote of Glyndyfrdwy, not yet rendered famous by the exploits of its great chieftain, Owen Glyndwr, and still more to the west the valley broadened out into the plain of Edeyrnion, a commote which took its name from Edern, or Eternus, ap Cunedda. No record is preserved of any dynasty deriving its origin from Edern and it is probable that the district, with the two subsidiary commotes of Dinmael and Glyndyfrdwy, was at an early date brought under the sway of the rulers of Powys. It included one important church, that of Corwen or Corfaen,[89] where there is an ancient cross of the same type as Elise's Pillar.[90]

Westward of Edeyrnion lay the border cantref[91] of Penllyn, of which the centre was Llyn Tegid or Pimblemere,[92] now Bala Lake. Ardudwy and Meirionydd hemmed it in on the west and it was thus exposed to the attacks of the men of Gwynedd, to whom it ultimately fell in the days of Llywelyn ab Iorwerth. Encircled by lofty mountains, which enclose as in a girdle the broad waters of the lake and their fringe of meadows, the land is one of legend rather than of history, playing but a small part in the conflicts of mediæval Wales, but rich in romantic memories. It was the realm of Gronw the Radiant, who stole the love of the magic bride of Llew Llaw

[88] It was probably the Llanarmon to which Gruffydd ap Cynan made a death-bed gift of ten shillings (*Buch. Gr. ap C.* 128 (734)). There was a special cult of Germanus in Powys, for the five principal churches dedicated to him are within the old bounds of the province (Rees, *Welsh SS.* 131; add to the four mentioned Castle Caereinion). In this connection it is interesting to note that the saint was mentioned in the inscription on Elise's pillar.

[89] For the old form see *Bruts*, 324; B. *Saes. s.a.* 1164; *Tax. Nich.* 286; *Arch. Camb.* I. ii. (1847), 241.

[90] *Arch. Camb.* V. xvi. (1899), 19.

[91] So treated in all the lists, though styled a cymwd in the Statute of Rhuddlan (*LL.* ii. 908) and the Record of Carnarvon (261).

[92] The name first appears in Gir. Camb. vi. 176 (*Descr.* i. 5), where the form is " Pemmelesmere ". Rejecting the impossible derivation from " pum plwyf," the five parishes of Penllyn, one may suggest that Penllyn itself furnishes the first element of the compound.

CHAP. VIII.

Gyffes and perished miserably by the hand of the injured husband;[93] Llywarch the Aged, warrior and poet, is said to have lived there in the sixth century and to have held his court on the mound near Llanfor Church which bears his name;[94] even the great Arthur took his place among the legendary heroes of the lakeside, for was not Caer Gai the home of his foster-father Cynyr and the young Cai ap Cynyr the companion of his boyish sports?[95] Caer Gai may have been the royal residence at the head of the lake from which the district took its name of Penllyn (Lakehead), although in later times Y Bala, which signifies "The Outlet,"[96] was the seat of the chief stronghold of the region.

The mountain ridge which divides the valley of the Dee from that of the Ceiriog formed the backbone of the commote of Nanheudwy,[97] which included an important church, once the mother church of a wide area,[98] but apart from Llangollen was undistinguished. Another commote of the second rank was Cynllaith, watered by the stream from which it took its name and having as its centre the church of Llansilin. Sycharth, which was perhaps the ancient "llys" of the commote, had not yet become famous as the home of Owen Glyndwr. Further south came the rich commote[99] of Mochnant, the "fair wooded country" of a mediæval Welsh poet,[100] where the valley of the Tanat broadens out into a fertile plain beneath the very shadow of the Berwyn range. In the twelfth century political conflicts brought about a division of this region into the two commotes of Uch Rhaeadr and Is Rhaeadr (Above and Below Rhaeadr), and from that day to this the rushing stream

[93] *Mab.* 74-81. The mound at Pont Mwnwgl y Llyn anciently bore, it is said, the name of Gronw Befr (Penn. ii. 215).

[94] "Pabell Llywarch Hên," a stone enclosure, and "Castell Llywarch," a mound, have long been known at Llanfor (*Camb. Reg.* i. 192; Evans, *Rep.* ii. p. 453; Penn. ii. 209; Lewis, *Top. Dict. s.v.* Llanvawr).

[95] See *Goss. Guide*, p. 153; *Celtic Folklore*, p. 693; note 62 to chap. iii. above.

[96] Gibson, 662; Evans, *Dict. s.v.*

[97] This form may represent "Nannau Dwy," "the glens of Dee". *Cf.* the "Nanneudui" of *Ann.* C. MS. B. *s.a.* 1132.

[98] Thomas, *St. Asaph*, p. 505-6.

[99] The original Mochnant was a commote (*Mab.* 62, kymwt ym powys a elwir . . . mochnant).

[100] Llywarch ap Llywelyn calls it "uochnant kein amgant coedawc" (*Myv Arch.* I. 305 (215)).

which takes its name from the well-known waterfall in the Berwyns has been a boundary line, first separating Powys Fadog from Powys Wenwynwyn and then the county of Denbigh from that of Montgomery. But the region is naturally one; it found its ecclesiastical centre in Llanrhaeadr Mochnant, the church of St. Doewan, which was still served by a college or community of clergy as late as the days of Edward I.[101] Pennant, the church of the female saint Melangell, was also an ancient sanctuary, remarkable to this day for the girth of its venerable yews, but it lay hid in a fold of the mountains, remote from the centre of the commote, and can never have held the dominant position of Llanrhaeadr.

The river Cain gave its name to the cantref of Mechain,[102] which took in the whole of the valley of this stream and was bounded on the south by the river Efyrnwy, now known as the Vyrnwy. A great forest in its centre divided it into the commotes of Mechain Uwch Coed and Mechain Is Coed (Above and Below the Wood).[103] It was one of the most desirable parts of Powys, with abundance of land suited for tillage and no lack, at the same time, of fish and game. "Llys Fechain," the court of the cantref, stood on the banks of the Cain to the east of Llanfyllin, and its site is probably indicated by the mound known as Tomen Gastell.[104] "Llan Fechain," the prince's chapel, dedicated to that special patron of Powys, St. Garmon, was not far off. But Llanfechain was far outshone in importance as a holy place by the church of Meifod, on the southern border of the cantref.[105] Founded by a scion of the royal house of Powys, Tysilio son of Brochwel of the Tusks (Ysgythrog), ruled by a "clas" which could offer bards and other wayfarers a regal hospitality, and wielding authority over the daughter churches of Pool, Guilsfield, Alberbury and

[101] *Tax. Nich.* 286*a* (ecclesia de Rauraeader); Thomas, *St. Asaph*, p. 520.

[102] For the first part of the name (= field, plain) see *Urk. Spr.* 198, *s.v.* magos. It is seen also in Machynlleth, Mathafarn, Mathrafal and Mallwyd (*Goss. Guide*, cxix.).

[103] The townships of the two commotes of Mechain, save for the parish of Llanfyllin, are given in *App. Land Com.* 451.

[104] Llys Fechain is a township in the parish of Llanfechain (Thomas, *St. Asaph*, p. 755).

[105] For the church of Meifod see Thomas, *St. Asaph*, pp. 774-81; for Tysilio, *Welsh SS.* 277-79. Cynddelw's poem is printed in *Myv. Arch.* I. 243-7 (177-9).

CHAP. VIII.

Llanfair Caereinion, Meifod was the premier church of Powys, and, until the foundation of the Cistercian abbeys of Ystrad Marchell and Valle Crucis, was the chosen burial-place of its kings.[106] Its praises were sung by Cynddelw—

> Stately is the holy place by candle shine,
> Gracious its men with their long drinking-horns of flashing blue.[107]

It was "a privileged monastery," a "sepulchre of kings," lifting its proud head above the flooded meadows of Efyrnwy.[108]

A number of smaller commotes lined the Severn from Melverley to Berriew. Deuddwr, the land of the "two waters," occupied the peninsula formed by the confluence of the Vyrnwy and the Severn; Ystrad Marchell lay around the church of Guilsfield, of which the Welsh name is Cegidfa (Hemlock Field); Llannerch Hudol was a small tract to the south and west of Welshpool. The dwellers in these lands fronted the Mercian villages on the western slopes of the Long Mountain, Buttington, Leighton, Forden, and the rest, and, keepers as they were of the fords of the Severn, were chiefly intent upon the border warfare. Romance might tell of the halcyon days when Arthur and his attendant knights had spread their camp for a full mile along the river in the plain of Argyngroeg,[109] but such ease and security were not known in the age of Offa. It is possible that Pool itself, called Welsh Pool to distinguish it from Poole in Dorset, may owe its origin to an English settlement,[110] thrown across for the defence of a ford, though there was on the hillside hard by a Welsh ecclesiastical foundation, known to the natives as Trallwng Llywelyn, or Llywelyn's Bog.[111] A little further south was the strong post

[106] Madog ap Maredud (d. 1160) and Gruffydd Maelor (d. 1191) were buried at Meifod.

[107] "Berth y lloc wrth lleu babir,
Berth y chlas ae chyrn glas gloyuhir."

"Pabir" is a variant of "pabwyr," the two being derived from different forms of "papyrus" (*Mots Latins*, p. 192). "Clas" and "lloc" both suggest the monastic origin of the church; the latter, from the Lat. "locus" (*Mots Latins*, p. 182; *Gildas*, ed. Williams, p. 262), is retained in the compound form "mynachlog".

[108] "Breiniauc loc," "guydva brenhined," and "balch y lloc rac y llifeiryeint" are the phrases referred to.

[109] *Mab.* 148.

[110] It would otherwise have hardly had an English name.

[111] *Bruts*, 290, 339. The name is explained by Edward Llwyd (Gibson, 653); *cf.* also *Cymr.* xi. 39, where a number of similar forms are given.

of Castell Coch, which became in later times, under the name of Powis Castle, the principal fortress of Southern Powys. The ancient capital of this region was, however, in a remoter and safer quarter. Mathrafal, regarded in Welsh mediæval literature as the "principal seat" of Powys and one of the three royal residences of Wales,[112] stood on the banks of a tributary of the Vyrnwy, a little above Meifod. In front was a fertile plain, yielding the necessary produce for the royal kitchen and stable; behind stretched in wave after wave the rolling hills of the great commote of Caereinion. This was the heart of Southern Powys, where its princes might hope to find in their direst extremity a refuge from English or Norman attack.

In the cantref of Cydewain, which lay between the Rhiw and the Severn, was the church of Aberriw (now Berriew), where St. Beuno fled from before the face of the invading English,[113] and the fortified steep of Dolforwyn, fabled by some to have witnessed the drowning of the hapless Sabrina in those dim days of which Geoffrey of Monmouth has told the story with such surprising particularity.[114] A cantref which filled a far larger space in Welsh history was Arwystli, the land of the head waters of the Severn. It was originally, no doubt, a part of Powys, but an early connection sprang up between its chieftains and the realm of Gwynedd, so that it was frequently treated as belonging rather to Aberffraw than to Mathrafal, and, in particular, it became permanently attached to the bishopric of Bangor.[115] As in the case of Mechain, its two commotes were known as Uwch Coed and Is Coed, from a stretch of forest in the midst of the cantref; the respective manors or royal courts appear to have been at Talgarth, near Trefeglwys, and Caersws. There were also in the cantref two notable churches. Llandinam was the mother church of

Trallwng is now pronounced Trallw*m*; *cf.* "carlwm" for the older "carlwng" (Evans, *Dict. s.v.*).

[112] *LL.* ii. 50, 380, 584. It should be added that the position of Mathrafal is not as well attested as that of Aberffraw and Dinefwr, and the story of the transference of the capital thither from Shrewsbury in the eighth century is of modern growth (note 10 to chap. vii.).

[113] Chap. vi. note 38.

[114] *Hist. Reg.* ii. 5. Local tradition, and not Geoffrey, is responsible for fixing the site of the tragedy here (Penn. iii. 186).

[115] *Trans. Cymr.* 1899-1900, 157.

CHAP. VIII.

Llanidloes and Llanwnnog; it had an abbot as late as the twelfth century and was still held by a group of clergy at the time of the Edwardian conquest.[116] Llangurig was not so wealthy, but could also boast of a "clas," as well as of a patron saint, St. Curig, who was in high esteem as a worker of miracles in the surrounding district.[117] The bishop of Bangor had a manor at Llanwnnog, to which he no doubt resorted when his duties brought him to Arwystli.[118] Beyond Arwystli was Cyfeiliog, the westernmost of the commotes of Powys proper, which just touched the sea at the head of the tidal estuary of the Dovey. Its position on the confines of Gwynedd, Powys and Deheubarth made it the scene of many a conflict, and often did war rage around the stronghold of the chief at Tafolwern. The sister commote of Mawddwy was sheltered, on the other hand, by the beetling crags of Aran Fawddwy, and its history was uneventful; in its inmost retreat was "y Llan ym Mawddwy," the spot hallowed by the bones of St. Tydecho, who had withstood the great Maelgwn Gwynedd himself, and, it was reverently believed, still kept watch and ward over the fair fields of the commote.[119]

The cantref of Meirionydd may be reckoned as in some measure a part of Powys, for its ancient name was Cantref Orddwy, or the cantref of the Ordovices.[120] But, from the time of the Meirion or Marianus (grandson, as was alleged, of Cunedda) who gave it its more familiar name, it appears to have been for many generations under the rule of its own dynasty, represented about 870 by a certain Cynan ap Brochwel.[121] One or two interesting names occur in the pedigree of this line. Gwrin Farfdrwch (of the Ragged Beard),

[116] *Arch. Camb.* V. xi. (1894), 29 (Arustly); III. vi. (1860), 331 (Dolfin abbas Llandinan); *Tax. Nich.* 291*b*. Llandina*n* is the old spelling; see *Cymr.* xi. 46-7.

[117] The township of Llangurig (divided into Llan i fyny and Llan i waered) formed the manor of "Clas Arwystli" (*App. Land Com.* 451). See Gir. Camb. vi. 17-8 (*Itin.* i. 1) for the virtues of St. Curig's crosier.

[118] *Rec. Carn.* 115.

[119] *Camb. Reg.* ii. 375-8. The poem there printed calls Tydecho

"Crefyddwr cryf o Fawddwy
Ceidwad ar eu holl wlad hwy."

("A great man of religion from Mawddwy and guardian of all their land.")

[120] *Celt. Br.* (2), pp. 302-3.

[121] Pedigree XVIII. in Harl. MS. 3859 (*Cymr.* ix. 178).

who perhaps gave his name to the neighbouring church of Llanwrin, furnished Geoffrey of Monmouth[122] with one of the figures of his ever-shifting panorama, that of the just and clement king who found the ancestors of the Irish cruising aimlessly about in the seas to the north of Britain and gave them the island in which they afterwards became so mighty a people. Another of the line bore the name of Idris, still commemorated in that of the loftiest of the many heights of Meirionydd; for Cader Idris was the chair of no Druid or astronomer, but takes its name from a brave descendant of Meirion, who fell in battle on the banks of the Severn about 630.[123] The realm which obeyed this forgotten dynasty extended from the estuary of the Dovey to that of the Mawddaçh and further included the valley of the Wnion. It was a land of rocky confusion, where crag rose above crag; "shaggy and fearsome," says Giraldus, beyond any other region of Wales.[124] Shepherds perched on two opposing peaks might exchange abuse in the morning, but the day, he avers, would be far advanced ere they could meet in the valley bottom to settle their differences. Yet Meirionydd had its stretches of fertile soil. In the heart of the cantref, where the Disynni spreads itself out ere it is lost in Cardigan Bay, was "Tywyn Meirionydd," the Sandy Plain of Merioneth, where St. Cadfan founded in the sixth century a notable church.[125] Towyn was not inferior in importance to any save the two cathedral churches of North Wales; it was the mother church of the whole of the commote of Ystum Anner,[126] it had an abbot in the twelfth century,[127] and, again recalling Llandinam, was held by a number of clergy in the days of Edward I.[128] Like

[122] *Hist. Reg.* iii. 11, 12.

[123] "Strages sabrine et iugulatio iudris" (Harl. MS. 3859, *s.a.* 632—*Cymr.* ix. 158). *Cf.* the notices of Tighernach—"cath Iudruis rig Bretan (the battle of Idris, king of the Britons) qui in eo cecidit" (*Rev. Celt.* xvii. (1896), p. 182)—and of the Annals of Ulster, *s.a.* 632 (=633)—"bellum Iudris regis britonum". The date is in harmony with the position of Idris in the pedigree. *Cf. Goss. Guide*, 79; it should, however, be added that in the Celtic annals "jugulatio" often refers, as probably here, to ordinary killing in battle, and does not of necessity imply throat-cutting.

[124] Gir. Camb. vi. 122-3 (*Itin.* ii. 5).

[125] There is a full account of Cadfan in *Welsh SS.* 213-5. For the so-called Cadfan stone see note 135 to chap. vii.

[126] B. Willis, *Bangor*, p. 276.

[127] Note 57 to chap. vii.

[128] *Tax. Nich.* 291*b*.

CHAP. VIII.

Meifod, the place had its poet, one Llywelyn Fardd,[129] who sang in the twelfth century of the

> Lofty fane of Cadfan by the margin of the blue sea,

and prayed for its welfare—

> Prosper may its turf and its corn and its seed,

nor forgot its abbot, the liberal rewarder of poetic merit, for at Towyn there was

> Peace and mead borne in vessels
> And easy converse exchanged with a bard.

Less is known of the civil sites of the cantref It was divided by the Disynni into the two commotes of Talybont and Ystum Anner, two names which may indicate two ancient seats of the lords of Meirionydd, for there is a mound at Talybont (near Llanegryn), and Ystum Anner can be located at Llanfihangel y Pennant, where stands the fortified rock of Castell y Bere. But history speaks of castles also at Cynfael, near Towyn, and Cymer, near Dolgelly, and it is not easy to say which stronghold was the temporal, as Towyn was the spiritual, centre of the district in the days of its independence.

The southern portion of the ancient Powys was known in the Middle Ages as "Rhwng Gwy a Hafren," the land betwixt Wye and Severn.[130] It was a district which formed no part of the patrimony of the rulers of Powys descended from Bleddyn ap Cynfyn (d. 1075), but many circumstances point to its having once been included in the province. Tradition alleged that the southern limit of Powys was Rhyd Helyg on the Wye, near Hay; [131] in 1176 Bishop Adam of St. Asaph sought to establish a claim to the whole of Rhwng Gwy a Hafren, no doubt on the plea that his diocese covered the whole of Powys,[132]

[129] *Myv. Arch.* I. 360-2 (248-50). If one sets aside as the work of a later hand the poem to Owain ap Gruffydd ap Gwenwynwyn, the rest of the poems attributed in the *Myvyrian Archaiology* to Llywelyn Fardd fall naturally into the latter half of the twelfth century. The common date, 1230-1280, is a clumsy attempt to reconcile hopeless anachronisms.

[130] The form occurs, not only in the lists of cantrefs and commotes, but also (in Latin) in Gir. Camb. i. 30, 35 (*De Rebus*, i. 5, 6); vi. 19 (*Itin.* i. 1).

[131] *Iolo MSS.* 31; *Camb. Qu. Mag.* iii. 403.

[132] The claim to Kerry was avowedly only a first step or trial of strength. See Gir. Camb. i. 32-3 (totam . . . terram usque Vagam (Wye) . . . occupare proposuit).

while the early history of our Radnorshire, so far as it can be unravelled, seems to make it an Ordovician country.[133]

Setting aside the two small commotes of Keri [134] and Cymwd Deuddwr,[135] of which the former is now in Montgomeryshire,[136] Rhwng Gwy a Hafren comprised the commote of Gwerthrynion and the cantrefs of Buellt, Elfael and Maelienydd. Buellt, being so much of our Brecknockshire as lies north of the Epynt range, was not entitled geographically to be reckoned among the lands between the Wye and the Severn, but the *Historia Brittonum* shows that about 800 it was joined with Gwerthrynion under the rule of Ffernfael,[137] and thus it was no doubt included in the term as the definition of a political area. The mountains of the north of Buellt are separated from those of the south by the broad valley of the Irfon, and here, or close by, were the chief sites of the cantref, the courts of the four commotes of Treflys, Penbuellt, Dinan and Is Irfon,[138] the ancient church of Llanafan Fawr, where the tomb of Afan Buellt was shown, chief of the saints of this region,[139] and St. David's church of Maes Mynis, which dominated Is Irfon and was the mother church of Llanfair ym Muellt (St. Mary's in Buellt), the modern Builth.[140] Gwerthrynion was on the opposite side of the Wye, occupying the region between that river and the Ieithon. The name is obviously formed from

[133] On the whole question see the discussion in Owen, *Pemb.* i. 203 (Phillimore).

[134] "Keri" is mentioned in *Mab.* 62. The modern village bearing the name is properly Llanfihangel yng Ngheri (Pen. MS. 147 in Evans, *Rep.* i. p. 915).

[135] Omitted from the lists. It is represented by the parish of Llansantffraid "Cwm Toyddwr"—see Pen. MS. 147 (Evans, *Rep.* i. p. 915, *K. dayddwr*); *Reg. Conway*, p. 9 (Comottewthur); Owen's *Pemb.* i. 203. The "two waters" are the Wye and the Elan; from the latter is probably derived another name of the commote, *viz.*, Elenydd or Elenid (*Mab.* 62; Gir. Camb. i. 117; vi. 119, 138, 171, 173; *W. People*, p. 45; Owen's *Pemb.* i. 203).

[136] In all the lists of cantrefs and commotes Ceri is associated with Gwerthrynion or Maelienydd, not with Cydewain or Arwystli; this is also implied in its position in the diocese of St. David's and was common ground between the disputants in 1176 (Gir. Camb. i. 35 (*De Rebus*, i. 6)).

[137] *Hist. Britt*, cc. 48, 49; note 144 to chap. vii. above.

[138] Treflys is close to Llangammarch, Llys Dinan, near Newbridge on Wye. The court of Is Irfon was probably at Llanfair, where Builth Castle was afterwards raised; Penbuellt would seem to have been in the southern part of Llangammarch parish (Carlisle).

[139] *Welsh SS.* 208-9.

[140] *Ibid.* 53.

CHAP. VIII.

Gwrtheyrn, better known in its older guise of Vortigern, and the legend of the country was that the notorious bearer of that name had fled hither to escape the fulminations of St. Germanus, and that after his death his descendants had been settled in the commote as its rulers.[141] Some alleged that the tyrant had actually come to his shameful end in "the castle of Gwerthrynion on the river Wye," by which is probably meant Rhayader, but there were several other claimants for this distinction.[142] It is certain, however, that the early chieftains of Gwerthrynion traced their origin to Gwrtheyrn Gwrthenau, and it should further be noted that here, as in other quarters of Powys, there was a church under the patronage of Germanus. St. Harmon's, where there is known to have been a "clas,"[143] was probably pointed out by tradition as the spot where the saint, with all the clergy of Britain, prayed on the bare rock for forty days and forty nights for the conversion of the reprobate king.[144]

South Radnorshire was occupied by the cantref of Elfael, separated from Buellt and Brycheiniog by the swift-running stream of the Wye. Save along the banks of this river the cantref was a region of grassy highlands and did not rank as one of the coveted tracts of Wales. The broad-backed chain of hills to the south of Aberedw served to divide it into the commotes of Uwch Mynydd and Is Mynydd (Above and Below the Mountain), which had in Norman times their respective castles of Colwyn and Painscastle; what strongholds had in earlier days been held by the native chieftains in these two commotes there is little evidence to show. Of the ancient churches of Elfael the most notable was undoubtedly Glascwm. It was one of the greater Dewi churches, founded, as was believed, by the saint himself,[145] and here was kept a most precious legacy of his, the portable bell called "Bangu" which was endowed with miraculous powers.[146] In the White Bard

[141] *Hist. Britt.* cc. 47-9.

[142] Triad i. 91 = ii. 6. For the other stories see *Dict. Nat. Biog. s.v.* Vortigern.

[143] "Clas Garmon" is the name of one of the two townships of St. Harmon's (Carlisle).

[144] *Hist. Britt.* c. 47.

[145] Life by Rhygyfarch in *Cambro-Br. SS.* 123.

[146] Gir. Camb. vi. 18 (*Descr.* i. 1). *Cf. Cambro-Br. SS.* 136 (nola).

of Brycheiniog's catalogue of the churches raised in honour of St. David it is the CHAP. VIII.

> Church by the green hillside,
> Towering among the thickets, a sanctuary that faileth not.[147]

Its "clas" was a daughter community of the great house of Mynyw, and Glascwm thus came to be regarded as a manor of the bishop of St. David's, whose rights in the place have not yet become wholly extinguished.[148]

In its physical features the cantref of Maelienydd,[149] extending from the Teme to Radnor Forest and the neighbourhood of Llandrindod, was not dissimilar. The Ieithon was its principal river, winding its way south through miles of gorse-clad moor and upland pasture. From an early period the cantref was divided into three commotes,[150] which took their names from the principal royal residences within them. Rhiwlallt lay along the Lug, where stood, near Llangynllo, the spot, known to the English as Weston, which originally bore the name.[151] The "swydd" or "shire" of Buddugre was the northern portion of the cantref, the particular Buddugre or "Hill of Victory" which formed the centre of this commote being on the banks of the Ieithon.[152] The "swydd" of Dinieithon was the southern limb of Maelienydd, and no doubt the "din," or fortress, on the Ieithon from which it took its name was that of Cefn Llys, where the river winds around and almost isolates a steep hill which must have been in primitive as in Norman days a natural stronghold of great importance. Of the saints of Maelienydd none could compare in importance

147 " A glascwm ae eglwys gyr glas uynyt
Gwyteluod aruchel nawd ny achwyt" (*Myv. Arch.* I. 271 (194)).
The Red Book text has "*e*chwyd," with the same meaning.

148 *Black Book of St. David's*, 291, 331; Carlisle, *Top. Dict.*; *App. Land Com.* 445.

149 No doubt derived from a proper name which would in old Welsh be Mailgen. There is no ancient authority for the form "Moelynaidd" favoured by Jonathan Williams (*Hist. Radn. passim*). The deanery of Maelienydd included Keri and Gwerthrynion, and some of the lists appear to make the cantref no less extensive; in the oldest, however, that in Dom. viii., it has three commotes only.

150 For a list (not very carefully put together) of the parishes and townships of these commotes see *Radnorsh.* (2), 142 (Nos. 3, 4, 8).

151 L. G. Cothi, 239, 243, 245, 246, 330.

152 It is the "Bedd Ugre" of the maps. For the true form see *Bruts*, 409, *Cymr.* ix. 328; for the meaning and other instances, Evans, *Dict. s.v.*

CHAP. VIII.

with Cynllo, the sphere of whose influence, in this and the neighbouring district of Gwerthrynion, included no less than thirteen modern parishes.[153] His principal church was at Llanbister, to which accrued the largest income of any church in the archdeaconry of Brecon.[154]

III. The Cantrefs of Deheubarth.

The original "dextralis pars Britanniae" or "Deheubarth Kymry" embraced the whole of South Wales, in which sense the term is used by Asser[155] and by those who drafted the charters in the *Liber Landavensis*.[156] But in later parlance[157] the name Deheubarth came to be restricted to the realm, which included most of the South Welsh area, formed by the accretion of Ceredigion, Ystrad Tywi and Brycheiniog around the ancient kingdom of Dyfed, and in this sense it was exclusive of Gwent and Morgannwg. In the present section an attempt will be made to trace the earlier history of the constituent elements of this later Deheubarth.

Ceredigion, the territory which Ceredig ap Cunedda is said to have carved for himself out of the country of the Demetæ, appears to have had throughout its history the same borders as the modern county of Cardigan,[158] which thus hands on the tradition of the territorial unity of this district. Its bounds are given by a man of Ceredigion in the eleventh century[159] as follows—to the east, lofty mountains; to the west, the ocean; north and south, broad rivers (*i.e.*, the Dovey and the Teifi)—and this is still a good general description. The eastern boundary, from Glandovey to Lampeter, crosses and recrosses the watershed of Plynlimmon in somewhat devious fashion, but it is still true to say that Ceredigion is a land between the mountains and the sea, with all its rivers, including the two

[153] I refer to Llanbister, Llangynllo, Nantmel and their chapels as given by Rees (*Welsh SS.* 351).

[154] *Tax. Nich.* 274*b* (Lanbyst, £30 : 13 : 4).

[155] C. 80. *Cf.* note in Stev. 233-4. Asser more than once has "Britannia" in the sense of Wales (cc. 7, 79 (*bis*)).

[156] *Lib. Land.* 161, 162, 163, 169, 192, 212, 223, 230, 237.

[157] In *B.T.*, for instance.

[158] There is some evidence of an extension of Ceredigion at one period so as to include the cantref of Cemais (Owen, *Pemb.* i. 222-3), but this can only have been a temporary success of its chieftains.

[159] Ieuan ap Sulien of Llanbadarn about 1090 (H. and St. i. 664-5).

which make its northern and its southern border, running westward. Its eastern barrier of lonely moorland, though lacking the beauty of outline of the Snowdonian range, served a similar defensive purpose, and the stranger who set greedy eyes on Ceredigion, whether Brython or Norman or Englishman, usually made his attack from the north or from the south.

For some 400 years, if the evidence of the royal pedigree[160] is to be trusted, this country was ruled by the descendants of Ceredig. Some of the names recorded are undoubtedly historical. Seisyll, who was king about 730, embarked on a career of conquest and added to Ceredigion the three cantrefs of Ystrad Tywi, the whole dominion being henceforth known from the name of its founder as Seisyllwg.[161] The death of his son Arthen is chronicled under the year 807.[162] The last of the line was Gwgon ap Meurig, a great grandson of Arthen, who is recorded to have been drowned in or about 871;[163] his sister Angharad was married to Rhodri the Great, king of North Wales,[164] and it was thus, no doubt, that Seisyllwg became incorporated with Gwynedd and Powys in one realm, which was shortly afterwards divided among the sons of Khodri.

Ceredigion is always spoken of as a land of four cantrefs.[165] But the names of the cantrefs were, with the exception of that of the northernmost, not generally current; the well-known divisions of the country were the ten commotes into which the four cantrefs were divided. Penweddig,[166] or, as it was sometimes called, "Y Cantref Gwarthaf,"[167] "the uppermost" cantref, formed an exception; the Ystwyth, stretching across the whole of Ceredigion, supplied it with a well-marked southern border, and it was thus a clearly defined and well-known area. It contained three commotes, of which Geneu'r Glyn lay north of the Clarach, Perfedd (so called as the midmost of the three)

[160] *Cymr.* ix. 180, No. xxvi.

[161] This is inferred from *Mab.* 25, where "Seisyllwch" is explained to be Ceredigion and Ystrad Tywi combined. *Cf.* Basil Jones, *Vestiges of the Gael in Gwynedd* (Lond. and Tenby, 1851), pp. 61-2; *Cymr.* xi. 56. Seisyllwg is also mentioned in *LL.* ii. 50 and Triad iii. 14.

[162] "Arthgen rex cereticiaun moritur" (Harl. MS. 3859 in *Cymr.* ix. 163).

[163] "Guoccaun mersus est rex cetericiaun" (*ibid.* 166).

[164] See p. 325.

[165] *Mab.* 25, 59; *Str. Flor.* Appendix, xxi.

[166] The *dd* is implied in the "penwe*t*ic" of *Blk. Bk.* fo. 33*a* and the "Penwe*th*ig" of Gir. Camb. vi. 175 (*Descr.* i. 5).

[167] *Bruts*, 410. *Cf.* "hyt yggwarthaf keredigyawn" (*Mab.* 62).

CHAP. VIII.

between the Clarach and the Rheidol, and Creuddyn between the Rheidol and the Ystwyth.[168] Forts and castles of all ages were dotted over this border land between North and South Wales, among the most notable being the hill-fortress of Pendinas, anciently known as Dinas Maelor.[169] The neighbouring harbour of Aberystwyth had not yet been formed, and Ystwyth and Rheidol fell into the sea a mile or so apart. Penweddig had ecclesiastical no less than military importance, for there was in it a "clas" of the first rank, that of Llanbadarn Fawr, founded by Padarn or Paternus of Brittany, which was once the seat of a bishop and still retained its abbot in the twelfth century.[170] Llanbadarn was the mother church of the whole of Penweddig,[171] and the community held as church land that part of the commote of Perfedd which lay next the sea.[172] A slender Celtic cross over 8 feet high still stands in the churchyard[173] as a memorial of the pre-Norman glories of the place, which are also faintly suggested by the chronicler who tells us that it was pillaged by the Danes at the end of the tenth century.[174]

Of the remaining commotes of Ceredigion, the northernmost was Mefenydd, which lay along the southern bank of the Ystwyth, from the sea to Cymwd Deuddwr. To the south-west came the little commote of Anhuniog, so called, no doubt, from an Annun or Antonius,[175] long forgotten, who ruled over it; it reached as far as the Aeron. The south-eastern angle of Ceredigion belonged to the commote of Pennardd, an extensive region which took in Tregaron, Llanddewi Brefi and

[168] Lewis Morris gives the bounds of the crown manor of Creuddyn in a document printed in Meyrick, *Card.* (1), 555-67. The (old) borough of Aberystwyth lay outside this manor, but it was probably taken out of the commote of Creuddyn, the northern and southern boundaries representing the old channels of the Rheidol and Ystwyth respectively. See the plan in the Report of the Boundary Commissioners of 1831. Morris also gives (*ibid.* 568) the bounds of the crown manor of Perfedd; the commote of the name included in addition Llanbadarn and its manor of Vainor.

[169] *Brython* (1860), iii. 331; Evans, *Rep.* i. p. 724. It was also known in Welsh legend as Rhiw Faelor (Triad ii. 11).

[170] See pp. 159, 208.

[171] It is the only church in the cantref mentioned in *Tax. Nich.*

[172] The church claimed all the land between the Clarach and the Rheidol by donation of Maelgwn Gwynedd (*Cambro-Br. SS.* 192).

[173] *Arch. Camb.* V. xiv. (1897), 152-3.

[174] *Ann. C. s.a.* 988.

[175] Haminiog and Harminiog are modern corruptions. For Annun = Antonius see *Cymr.* x. 86; *Mots Latins*, pp. 132-3.

the site of the future abbey of Strata Florida. In these three commotes, sometimes grouped with Penweddig under the name of Uch Aeron (Above Aeron), the most famous of the early sites was Llanddewi Brefi, known through the length and breadth of Wales as the scene of the miracle wrought by St. David when the hill of Brefi rose beneath his feet and formed a pulpit from which he addressed the synod and the attendant crowds there gathered together.[176] The "clas" which was subsequently formed there was naturally a daughter-house of St. David's, and Llanddewi, with the moorlands which rise above it to the east, became an episcopal manor and forest,[177]

From Caron
To the banks of the Towy, that fair and beauteous stream ;
From the Black Pool, where once was wrathful encounter,
To the Twrch, divider of lands and rocks.[178]

Is Aeron, or Ceredigion below Aeron, consisted of four commotes. Of these Caerwedros was a coast region, extending to Llangrannog; its castle stood, at any rate after the Norman Conquest, a short distance from Llwyn Dafydd.[179] Mabwnion spread its length from the neighbourhood of Aberaeron to that of Lampeter; part of the rich vale of Aeron, praised by the White Bard for its meadows of clover and the wealth of acorns in its woods,[180] fell within the compass of this commote. The two remaining commotes lay along the northern bank of the Teifi, one of the greater streams of Wales, in which the beaver still built in the days of Giraldus Cambrensis, though no longer to be found in any other river of Southern Britain.[181] It was a river of salmon, also, in which the coracle men took, as they do to this day, great catches of fish in the swirling eddies below

[176] See p. 157.

[177] *Blk. Bk. of St. David's*, 197-203; *App. Land Com.* 444; Meyrick, *Card.* (2), 250. The act of 1536 added "Landway Ureny," until then a marcher lordship, to Cardiganshire.

[178] "O garawn gan yawn gan ehoec
Hyd ar dywi auon uirein a thec
Or llyndu lled vu llid gyhydrec
Hyd ar twrch teruyn tir a charrec."
—Gwynfardd Brycheiniog in *Myv. Arch.* I. 272 (195).

[179] Meyrick, *Card.* (2), 233.

[180] "A henuyniw dec o du glennyt aeron
Hyfaes y meillyon hyfes goedyt."
—*Myv. Arch.* I. 271 (194).

[181] Gir. Camb. vi. 114 (*Itin.* ii. 3), 173 (*Descr.* i. 5).

CHAP. VIII.

the rocks of Cilgerran.[182] Iscoed and Gwinionydd, with their southward-sloping valleys and their meadows fringing the Teifi, were the two most desirable commotes of the land of Ceredig, and here was Rhuddlan Teifi, the Red Bank on the Teifi, where Pryderi, the legendary king of South Wales, entertained to his loss and dire misfortune the cunning Northern wizard, Gwydion ap Don, and his companions.[183] In later times the royal residence of Gwinionydd was at Pen Coed y Foel, near Llandysil,[184] and the bishop of St. David's had also an important manor in this region of which the ancient church of Dewi at Bangor was the centre.[185] Iscoed, too, had its sites of legendary and historical interest, though Cardigan town and castle had as yet no existence. At Crug Mawr was the conical hill, still a conspicuous object in the landscape around Cardigan, which legend associated with the cure of melancholy; he who bowed thrice before it would never again suffer weariness of soul, "though he might wander solitary in the uttermost parts of the earth"[186] Penbryn, on the sea coast, was another important early centre; here was the standing stone of Corbalengi,[187] and the discovery in the same neighbourhood of Late Celtic bronze objects resembling spoons[188] shows that it was a scene of active life in the shadowy period following the Roman Conquest.

Crossing the Teifi from this part of Ceredigion, the traveller of olden time found himself in the kingdom of Dyfed, which occupied the south-western peninsula of Wales. This was one of the last regions to feel the force of the Brythonic conquest, and more than one indication is afforded of the continuity here between the older life and the new. The country kept the name of its pre-Roman settlers; it was ruled by the same dynasty from the fifth century to the tenth, and further by a house which had no connection with Cunedda Wledig. No conquests by the kings of Dyfed are recorded; they represented the ancient and declining race; theirs was a waning star, and it was their part gradually to yield to the encroachments of the Brythons

[182] Gir. Camb. *ibid.* For the coracles see pp. 201-2 (*Descr.* i. 17).
[183] *Mab.* 61. Pentre Rhuddlan, near High Mead, indicates the site.
[184] Meyrick, *Card.* (2), 192.
[185] *Blk. Bk. of St. David's*, 211-35.
[186] This is the last of the "mirabilia Britanniae" (*Hist. Britt.* c. 74).
[187] See p. 119.
[188] *Arch. Camb.* IV. i. (1870), 205-7.

until their whole realm fell at last into the lap of a scion of the house of Gwynedd. CHAP. VIII.

At one time the Demetian country had formed a considerable part of the area of South Wales, and men spoke loosely of the whole land to the north of the Bristol Channel as Demetia.[189] But first had come the loss of Ceredigion; then, in the early part of the eighth century, the broad lands between the Teifi and the Tawe had been reft from Dyfed by the prowess of Seisyll;[190] until at the time of the Danish invasions the name had come to be restricted to the narrower region which is the Dyfed of mediæval literature. It was now bounded by the sea, the Teifi, the Tywi, and a line connecting these two rivers which may be taken as running due north from Carmarthen. The modern county of Pembroke was thus entirely included in Dyfed, but to it has to be added a substantial part of Carmarthenshire if an idea, however rough, is to be formed of the extent of the ancient kingdom. Its seven cantrefs[191] were of very diverse physical aspect, from the barren, rocky moors of Pebidiog to the sandy shores of Penfro, warmed by the southern sun, and the rich alluvial meadows of Cantref Gwarthaf. But, taken as a whole, it was a goodly realm, as may without difficulty be gathered from the circumstance that in the eleventh century it fell not only speedily, but irredeemably, into Norman hands.[192]

The kings of Dyfed drew their origin, according to one account, from a national hero of the name of Dimet,[193] according to another, from a branch of the royal line of the Deisi in Ireland,[194] but in either case from no Brythonic source. At the beginning of the sixth century the dynasty was repre-

[189] The various applications of the name Dyfed are fully discussed by Mr. Phillimore in *Cymr.* xi. 56-7; Owen, *Pemb.* i. 45-6, 199, 224, 257-8.

[190] *Hist. Britt.* c. 47 mentions an "arcem Guorthigirni quae est in regione Demetorum iuxta flumen Teibi". The reference is, no doubt, to the fortified "Craig Gwrtheyrn" which stands near Llandysul, but on the south side of the river and therefore in the later Cantref Mawr.

[191] *Mab.* 1, 25, 44, 57, 59; Gir. Camb. vi. 93 (*Itin.* i. 12); 166 (*Descr.* i. 2).

[192] The Welshman and the Norman united in its praise; "nyt oes seith cantref well noc wy," says Pryderi in the story of Manawyddan (*Mab.* 44): "terrarum omnium Kambriae totius . . . tam pulcherrima est quam potissima," are the words of Giraldus (vi. 93).

[193] See the pedigree (No. ii.) of the house in Harl. MS. 3859 (*Cymr.* ix. 171).

[194] *Cymr.* xiv. 112.

CHAP. VIII.

sented by Aircol or Agricola of the Long Hand,[195] whose name indicates that he inherited some Roman traditions, and who is further alleged to have been a good friend of the monastic movement of his day. St. Teilo was a subject of his, born at or near Pen Alun (now Penally) in the cantref of Penfro, and some of the lands in this neighbourhood, claimed in a later age by the see of Llandaff as heir to the saint, are maintained to have been given by the liberal hand of Aircol. His son and successor was the Vortiporius of Gildas, who bore the Roman title of protector and was buried at Castell Dwyran Church in the centre of his kingdom.[196] He, it need scarcely be said, was no patron of the monks, though it is equally certain that he professed the Christian religion. The crown of Dyfed passed on to men of lesser note; early in the eighth century it was worn by Rhain ap Cadwgan, in whose reign, no doubt, befell the loss of Ystrad Tywi, for the diminished realm thus left to the Western dynasty is occasionally called Rheinwg, by contrast with the Seisyllwg of the conqueror.[197] Rhain's grandson Maredudd died in 796,[198] on the eve of the Danish invasions, and it may be conjectured that the disorder which followed, nowhere more signally than in Dyfed, pushed the ancient dynasty into the background, for, after the death of Maredudd's grandson Tryffin in 814,[199] all trace of it is lost, until in the age of Asser one Hyfaidd ap Bledri is found ruling over the district, with a hereditary claim based on the descent of his mother from Maredudd.

The northernmost cantref of Dyfed was Cemais, which stretched along the coast from the Teifi to the Gwaun and southward across the Preselly range as far as the moors which fringe its southern slopes. It thus included the only mountain-

[195] *Lib. Land.* 118, 125-7, 129, 130. His court of "Lis castell" is traditionally located at Lydstep, near Tenby (*Arch. Camb.* III. xiii. (1867), 366; *Lit. Eng.* pp. 81, 188). In the Blk. Bk. his grave is vaguely said to be in Dyfed (fo. 35*a*; *IV. Anc. Bks.* ii. p. 35). *Cf.* Owen, *Pemb.* i. 223, for a reference to Aircol in the *Book of Taliesin*, quite misunderstood in *IV. Anc. Bks.* i. p. 448, and Evans, *Dict. s.v.* Aercol. For the Latin origin of the name see *Celt. Br.* (2), p. 256, and *Mots Latins*, p. 131.

[196] Pp. 115, 132. He was "boni regis nequam fili(us)," says Gildas (c. 31).

[197] See note on Rheinwg, Esyllwg and Fferyllwg appended to this chapter.

[198] "Morgetiud rex demetorum (moritur)," Harl. MS. 3859 (*Cymr.* ix. 162-3).

[199] "Trifun filius regin moritur" (*ibid.*). His uncle Owain, through whose daughter the crown descended to Hyfaidd, died in 811 (*ibid.*).

ous tract to be found in Dyfed, a region dotted over with cromlechs, cairns and barrows, fraught with ancient memories, the scene of many a romantic story. It was at Preselly the barons of the legendary King Pwyll met to expostulate with him upon the absence of an heir to the crown; it was there that the giant boar called "Y Twrch Trwyth" killed no less than eight of Arthur's knights.[200] The saint of the district was Brynach Wyddel (the Irishman), whose principal church was at Nanhyfer (now Nevern),[201] lying half-concealed in a fold of the leafy valley of the Nyfer. This was for centuries the most important ecclesiastical site in Cemais; ogam inscriptions mark it out as a Christian burying-place of the early period;[202] an elaborately carved Celtic cross over 12 feet high bears testimony to its standing in the age of the Danish incursions;[203] the massive church is a witness to its mediæval importance. Cemais was divided by the river Nyfer into the two commotes of Uch Nyfer and Is Nyfer, but there is no evidence to enable one to fix the ancient royal seats of these divisions. To the west of the Gwaun came the cantref of Pebidiog, which opposed a rocky front to the sea at St. David's Head; it resembled Anglesey, Giraldus observes,[204] in its bare and wind-swept aspect, but had not the kindly soil which made amends for the uncomely mien of the northern island. Poor as the country was, it was the home of a notable community, for here, in the little valley of Hodnant, within a few miles of the westernmost cape of Dyfed, was the church of Mynyw or Menevia, the mother-monastery of all the churches of Dewi. It is unnecessary to repeat here what has been said in earlier chapters of the fame of "Ty Ddewi" (David's House), of its origin in the sixth century, of the austerity of its "clas," and of the tradition of learning there maintained[205] Towards the end of the eighth

[200] *Mab.* 18, 138.

[201] Nanhyfer is for Nant Nyfer, "the valley of the Nyfer," and appears in Harl. MS. 3859 (if a little slip of the scribe, who wrote "*in*/mer," be corrected) as "nant nimer" (*Cymr.* ix. 165).

[202] The "Vitaliani" stone came originally from Nevern, and, after serving as a gatepost on Cwm Gloyn farm, is now there once more (Gibson, 638; *Arch. Camb.* V. xiii. (1896), 291). Another ogam inscription was discovered in the church in 1904.

[203] Gibson, 638-9; *Inscr. Chr.* No. 103; *Lap. W.* 100; *Arch. Camb.* V. xvi. (1899), 26.

[204] *Wks.* vi. 127 (*Itin.* ii. 7).

[205] See pp. 154-6, 227.

CHAP. VIII.

century the chronicle now most nearly represented by Harl. MS. 3859 began to be regularly kept at St. David's, and from this time forth there is a tolerably complete record of bishops of the see, beginning with Sadyrnfyw the Liberal, who died in 831.[206] No stone remains of the pre-Norman church and buildings, save a few fragments of tombstones bearing Celtic ornament, and no account has survived of the revenues of the "clas" at this period, though it may be assumed that they included, not only rents from distant manors, but also a very considerable annual render from estates in Pebidiog itself. It is, indeed, possible that the cantref as a whole had no other lord in early times save the successor of St. David.[207]

In the three southern cantrefs of Dyfed the traces of the ancient Welsh life have been almost entirely obliterated by the Norman Conquest and the Flemish and English settlements. The old place-names have disappeared, save in a few isolated cases; the old legends have been forgotten—only the carved and inscribed stones, monuments like the great Celtic cross at Carew, remain to tell, and this in the barest outline, the story of a civilisation which has been swept away as thoroughly as that which the invading English found in South-eastern Britain. Especially has this been the case in Rhos, the cantref which, lying between the West Cleddau, Milford Haven, and St. Bride's Bay, perhaps took its name, as did its namesake in the Berfeddwlad, from the promontory which it pushed out into the sea. Of the pre-Norman history of Rhos all that can be said is that it had a notable saint in Ismail or Ysfael, nephew of St. Teilo, whose church at St. Ishmael's or "Llanisan yn Rhos" was one of the seven bishop-houses of Dyfed.[208] Deugleddyf, a small cantref which lay, as its name indicates, between the eastern and the western Cleddau, furnishes little more to record; the church of Llanhuadein (now Lawhaden) was its chief ecclesiastical site and this had from an early period been a dependent church of St. David's, so that the place became an important

[206] "Saturbiu hail miniu moritur" (*Cymr.* ix. 164). The name appears as "Sadurnueu" in the catalogue transcribed by Giraldus (not, it would seem, without some confusion of the chronological order) from the records of the see (*Wks.* vi. 102-3 (*Itin.* ii. 1)).

[207] *LL.* i. 558 says Mynyw was to render nothing to the lord of Dyfed.

[208] *LL.* i. 558; ii. 790, 869; *Welsh SS.* 252; Owen, *Pemb.* i. 307.

episcopal manor.[209] Penfro, the "land's end" of Dyfed,[210] a long, low peninsula skirting the southern edge of Milford Haven, is in better case; the early history of this cantref has not been so completely forgotten. It had in Rhoscrowther, formerly Llandegeman, one of the bishop-houses of Dyfed;[211] even better known were Penalun (now Penally), one of the leading churches which honoured St. Teilo, and the ancient monastery of Ynys Byr, or Caldy Island, with its ogam inscription linking the settlement with the beginnings of monastic enthusiasm. Other famous sites, of which the associations were secular, were Arberth (our Narberth) in the north, the chief seat of Pwyll and his son Pryderi and the scene of most of their surprising adventures, Llonion, now absorbed in the bustling activities of Pembroke Dock, which was famous throughout Wales for its crops of barley,[212] and Dinbych y Pysgod (of the Fish), which was thus distinguished from its namesake in Rhufoniog, and was a stronghold of the lords of Dyfed ages before the English learned to call it Tenby.[213] Though Penfro was among the first of the seven cantrefs to fall under foreign rule and to lose its Welsh features and traditions, its past had been too brilliant to be altogether forgotten or to be obliterated by English "ton" and Norman "castle".

Eastern Dyfed was almost entirely included in the great Cantref Gwarthaf (the Uppermost Cantref), which extended from Narberth to Carmarthen and was made up of no less than eight commotes. Efelffre lay east of Narberth, Peuliniog —the land of Peulin or Paulinus—to the north, between the Taf and the eastern Cleddau;[214] Laugharne and Henllan Amgoed

[209] *Blk. Bk. of St. David's*, 137-67.

[210] Pembroke, like Builth, Brecknock, Cardigan and Kidwelly, is properly the name of a district, usurped in course of time by its principal castle. The cantref of Penfro is probably represented by the deanery of Pembroke or Castlemartin, for which see Owen, *Pemb.* i. 304-9.

[211] *LL.* i. 558; Fenton (2), 218-9.

[212] "Amhynny y diharhebir o heid llonyon" (Pen. MS. 12 = Heng. MS. 202, in *Cymr.* vii. 132). The Red Bk. has "llouyon" (*Mab.* 307), and in the first series of triads (No. 30) the name has become "llonwen". There is a reference to "llys Llonion" in "Cywrysedd Gwynedd a Deheubarth" (*Myv. Arch.* I. 73 (62)) and to its maer in *LL.* ii. 879, line 4 (amitei and llonion should be separated); *cf.* also *Lib. Land.* 124, 255; *LL.* ii. 306; *Lit. Eng.* p. 91.

[213] The maer of "Dyubyt" (read "Dynbyc") appears in *LL.* ii. 879 (*cf.* 306). Gir. Camb. (*Wks.* iii. 353) speaks of the abundance of fish in the harbour.

[214] Owen, *Pemb.* i. 388-9.

CHAP. VIII.

indicate the position of Talacharn and Amgoed; Ystlwyf or Ysterlwyf centred in Llanddowror;[215] Penrhyn, as its name shows, occupied the peninsula between the Taf and the Tywi;[216] Derllys came north of this,[217] and, last of all, Elfed, stretching along the western bank of the Gwili, was the border commote on the side of Ystrad Tywi. In this wide region there were many places which had importance in early times, but it suffices to mention Llan Deulyddog, one of the seven bishop-houses, built within the shelter of the ruined walls of the Roman Maridunum,[218] Meidrum, one of the greater Dewi churches, the "high-roofed fane, within the churchyard walls of which a host might meet," of the White Bard of Brycheiniog,[219] and Y Ty Gwyn ar Daf (The White House on the Taf), a royal residence of the princes of Dyfed which was afterwards made for ever famous by Hywel Dda. The seventh cantref of Dyfed was Emlyn, lying opposite to Ceredigion on the south bank of the Teifi. It was divided by the river Cuch into the commotes of Uwch Cuch and Is Cuch, which have ultimately fallen into different counties, so that the Cuch forms the boundary here between Pembrokeshire and Carmarthenshire. The most notable ecclesiastical site of Emlyn was Cenarth on the Teifi, the church of St. Llawddog, where there was a remarkable salmon-leap, said to be the work of the holy man himself.[220] Whether any earlier fortress preceded the Norman castle of Cilgerran there is no evidence to show.

The three cantrefs annexed by Seisyll to the realm of Ceredigion were known collectively as Ystrad Tywi, or Strath Towy, which was a convenient geographical description, but brings out unmistakably the fact that the district had no ancient or traditional bond of union. A number of commotes to the north and west of the Tywi were grouped together under the name of Y Cantref Mawr (The Great Cantref); others

[215] Owen, *Pemb.* i. pp. 206, 213. [216] *Ibid.* p. 206.

[217] The place now known as Derllys is, curiously, not within the modern hundred of Derllys at all, but in the parish of Merthyr and, therefore, in the hundred of Elfed.

[218] "Lann toulidauc ig cair mirdin" (*Lib. Land.* 62; *cf.* 124, 254).

[219] "A dewi bieu bangeibyr yssyt
Meidrym le ae mynwent y luossyt" (*Myv. Arch.* I. 271 (194)).
For the episcopal manor there see *Blk. Bk. of St. David's*, 234-41.

[220] Gir. Camb. vi. 114 (*Itin.* ii. 3).

between the Tywi and Brycheiniog formed Y Cantref Bychan (The Little Cantref), while the third cantref (Cantref Eginog) was made up of the three commotes which lay between the Tywi and the Tawe. The arrangement was artificial, being the result of a reconstruction which followed upon the ruin of the older and wider Dyfed. The Great Cantref was a broad upland region, bounded by the Tywi, the Teifi and the Gwili; there was good land along the margin of these rivers, but most of the soil was covered with a dense scrub, which afforded excellent cover for fugitives or for irregular troops, and thus made Y Cantref Mawr a stronghold of Welsh independence in the troublous times which were experienced by South Wales after the coming of the Normans.[221] In area the cantref rivalled Y Cantref Gwarthaf in Dyfed, containing no less than seven commotes, of which the situation may be roughly indicated as follows. Mabelfyw and Mabudryd, names which explain themselves as of dynastic origin, were the commotes which lay along the Teifi, the former including Pencarreg, the later Pencader. Widigada, extending from the Gwili to the Cothi, marched with Dyfed and was near neighbour to Carmarthen. Catheiniog, the land of St. Cathen ap Cawrdaf,[222] came next in order in the eastward direction; the church of Llangathen was within its limits. Maenor Deilo, or the Manor of St. Teilo, occupied the rich tract along the banks of the Tywi from Dinefwr to Llanwrda:[223] north of this was Mallaen, which ended in the moorlands of southern Ceredigion. The seventh commote was Caeo, which took in the upper valley of the Cothi and thus formed the heart of the cantref, the inmost retreat in a land where nature ever gave the sons of the soil her kindly, overshadowing protection.

In the Cantref Mawr was situated, in the commote of Maenor Deilo, the "principal seat" of the realm of Deheubarth,

[221] "Kantaredum magnum, . . . copiosa silvarum condensitate australis Kambriae civibus tutissimum in necessitate refugium" (Gir. Camb. vi. 80 (*Itin.* i. 10)).

[222] *Welsh SS.* 280.

[223] Part of this district, in the parishes of Llandeilo and Llansadwrn, lies in the modern hundred of Perfedd, which represents the two northern commotes of the Cantref Bychan. But the arrangement seems to be too complicated to be really ancient, not to speak of the express statement of Gir. Camb. (*Wks.* vi. 172 (*Descr.* i. 5)) that the Tywi was the dividing line between the Great and the Little Cantref.

CHAP. VIII.

the royal residence, the possession of which carried with it the primacy among the rulers of South Wales. This was Dinefwr,[224] an ancient stronghold which stood on the summit of a little hill overhanging the north bank of the Tywi. Its early history, like that of Aberffraw and Mathrafal, is unrecorded, but there was, no doubt, good reason for the position of honour it held in mediæval tradition. Not far off was the important church of Llandeilo Fawr, a principal "clas" of that saint, which contested with Llandaff and Penally the distinction of being the resting-place of his body.[225] As a Teilo church it was claimed in the twelfth century by the see of Llandaff,[226] but the hold of the bishop of St. David's over the place, however acquired, was substantial and the name Tir Esgob (Bishop's land) still preserves the memory of the episcopal manor of Llandeilo.[227] St. David's had other possessions in the cantref, notably at Abergwili, which after the Reformation became the principal residence of the bishop.

The Cantref Bychan only deserved its name by comparison with the Cantref Mawr, for it lined the southern bank of the Tywi for a distance of thirty miles, from Ystrad Ffin (The Border Strath) to a point not much above Carmarthen. It was, on the other hand, of no great breadth, forming a long strip of territory which was divided at two points so as to make three commotes. Of these Hirfryn was the northernmost, lying between the Tywi and Cantref Buellt; Y Cymwd Perfedd, or the Middle Commote, came next, extending to the Black Mountains; Is Cennen, so called because it was, for the most part, on the seaward side of the river Cennen, was the western limb, including within its bounds the upper waters of the Llwchwr. In the Cantref Bychan were Llanarthneu, a "clas" of St. David which, according to the saint's legend, had the custody of the mystic gifts bestowed before his birth upon his father,[228] Myddfai, a royal manor, where in later times there

[224] First mentioned in *Lib. Land.* 78 ("gueithtineuur," the "work" of Tinevwr). *Cf.* Gir. Camb. vi. 80-1 (*Itin.* i. 10), 172 (*Descr.* i. 5); *LL.* i. 346, ii. 831; *Letters, Hen. III.* i. 176; *Cymr.* xi. 45.

[225] A peaceful solution was provided, we are assured, by the miraculous appearance of *three* bodies (*Lib. Land.* 116-7).

[226] *Lib. Land.* 56, 62, 77-8, 133, 254.

[227] *Blk. Bk. of St. David's*, 262-75.

[228] *Cambro-Br. SS.* 117. For the grounds of the identification see chap. v. note 165.

dwelt a remarkable race of hereditary physicians,[229] and that eagle's nest of the lords of Is Cennen, perched on the top of a tall limestone bluff, the castle of Carreg Cennen [230]

According to the lists, the third cantref of Ystrad Tywi was known as Cantref Eginog. But this was a name which gained no popular currency; men knew the district only by the names of its three commotes, Cydweli, Carnwyllion and Gwyr. The occurrence of the form "Gwyr and Cydweli" [231] suggests that originally there were but two, and that Carnwyllion was carved out of Cydweli, which continued to be the name of the western half of this land between the Tywi and the Llwchwr. Thus the "land of Cadwal" [232] bordered on the former of these two rivers, dipping in gentle curves to its broad and sandy estuary, while the "land of Carnwyll" [233] lay along the other, rising in mountainous masses which confronted the eastern sun. The third commote of this cantref, which retains its ancient name in the slightly altered form of Gower, was the largest in all Wales; it included not only the cliff-bound peninsula which stretches westward from Swansea, but also the wilder country to the north, between the Llwchwr and the Tawe, as far as the foot of the Black Mountains. Within it were the ancient fanes of Llangyfelach, one of the most important of the Dewi churches, which is still an episcopal manor,[234] Ystum Llwynarth, now known as Oystermouth, where Illtud lived in holy seclusion and the credulous in later ages pointed out an altar which hung in mid air, with no visible support,[235] and Llandeilo Ferwallt, which as a "clas" of Teilo was claimed by the bishops of

[229] For "Meddygon Myddfai" see the work published under that name by the Welsh MSS. Society in 1861 (Llandovery).

[230] The castle is first mentioned in 1248 (*B.T. s.a.*), but it would seem to be an ancient stronghold from the fact that from it is derived the name of the township of Trecastell in which it stands.

[231] "Guir (et) Cetgueli" (*Hist. Britt.* c. 14). Gwyr and Cydweli are frequently mentioned in *Lib. Land.*, but there is only one reference to Carnwyllion (p. 247), and this in a thirteenth-century addition to the original MS.

[232] Owen, *Pemb.* i. 200.

[233] According to *Cambro-Br. SS.* 22, corrected as to the spelling in *Cymr.* xiii. 77, "Cornouguill" gave his name to "Cornoguatlaun".

[234] *Cambro-Br. SS.* 123, 136; *Blk. Bk. of St. David's*, 284-9; *App. Land Com.* 445. The place is styled a "monasterium" in both the passages from Rhygyfarch's life.

[235] *Hist. Britt.* c. 71, where the form is "Loyngarth"; *Cambro-Br. SS.* 177; *Arch. Camb.* IV. xi. (1880), 155.

CHAP. VIII.

Llandaff and thus acquired its modern name of Bishopston.[236] The homes of the ancient lords of Gower are not so easy to indicate; at Castell Llwchwr (or Loughor) some stronghold may have formed a link between the Roman fort and the Norman castle, but there is no good evidence of the fact. Swansea was in all probability but a stretch of sand, the haunt of sea-gull and plover.

Between the broad-backed Epynt range, the towering mass of the Black Mountains of Talgarth and the graceful peaks of the Brecknock Beacons lie the fertile valleys of the Usk and the Llynfi, here contracting in narrow woodland passes and there broadening out in luxuriant meadows. This was the land of Brycheiniog, which extended from Buellt and Elfael on the north to Gwent and Morgannwg on the south, and thus included the whole of our Brecknockshire save the first named of these four districts. From the earliest time of which Welsh tradition speaks, Brycheiniog was an independent realm; its foundation was attributed, not to any scion of Cunedda or representative of the Brythonic race, but to one Brychan, who was, on the father's side, at least, of Irish, *i.e.*, Goidelic, origin and from whom the country acquired the name it has ever since borne.[237] Brychan is one of the most shadowy figures of Welsh legend; twelve sons and twenty-four daughters, most of whom are said to have adopted the religious life, are assigned to him in the ancient lists, and the story tellers of Brecknock had much to tell of him and his deeds of prowess, of the hot temper which threw bold critics into jail and flung whatever was nearest to hand at the bearer of evil tidings, of his marvellous ride to meet the hosts of Deheubarth[238] with the fetter

[236] *Lib. Land.* Index, *s.v.* L. Merguallt.

[237] The earliest references to Brychan are in Gir. Camb. vi. 31-2 (*Itin.* i. 2) and *De Nugis*, 77-9, both especially valuable because of the familiarity of Giraldus and Walter with Brecknock and its people. The tract "De Situ Brychen-iauc" in Cottonian MS. Vespasian A. xiv. (ff. 10*b*-11*b*), written about 1200 and printed in *Cymr.* xix. 24-7, contains the earliest account of Brychan's origin and descendants, and was probably copied from a still older source (*Cymr.* vii. 105-6; Owen, *Catalogue*, p. 22). For other accounts see *Cymr.* viii. 83-4 (Jesus Coll. MS. 20), *Breconsh.* (2), Appendix No. vi. (Cognacio Brychan, from Cott. MS. Dom. i.), *Myv. Arch.* II. 29 (418-9), *Iolo MSS.* 111, 118-21, 140, *Welsh SS.* 136-60. I follow the figures of Jesus Coll. MS. 20, supported, as far as the daughters are concerned, by Giraldus.

[238] The MS. of Map (Bodl. 851) has "regem . . . de Heulard" (*De Nugis*, 77), which I take to be a copyist's error for "regem Deheubard".

hanging to his horse's foot, and of the crushing defeat he inflicted on the invaders, whose mutilated bodies furnished material for three great cairns heaped up on the field of slaughter. It was to Brychan, through his son Khain Dremrudd (the Red-eyed), that the later kings of Brycheiniog traced their descent, and, notwithstanding the large element of fable in the usual accounts of him, he may perhaps be regarded as the real founder of the dynasty. The pedigree has, however, come down in a corrupt form,[239] and it is not possible to fix with any certainty the place in it of the two or three historical kings of the country. All that can be said is that in the seventh century one Awst (Augustus) seems to have been the ruling prince of Brycheiniog,[240] that somewhat later Tewdwr ap Rhain and Elwystl ab Awst divided the sovereignty between them, until Elwystl was treacherously murdered by Tewdwr,[241] and that in the age of Alfred the realm was possessed by Elise ap Tewdwr.[242] Brycheiniog retained its independence until the tenth century was well advanced.

The region was divided into three cantrefs,[243] and the names of two of these, *viz.*, Cantref Selyf (the cantref of Solomon) and Cantref Tewdos (the cantref of Theodosius), suggest that this took place in connection with the division of the territory at some period in its history between three coinheritors.[244] But the early conquest of Brycheiniog by the Normans had, as in Rhos and Penfro, the effect of obscuring, though it did not quite obliterate, the ancient local divisions, so that little can be said with confidence of the cantrefs of this district or of the commotes into which they were divided.[245] Previous to the

[239] It was for some reason or other not included in the collection in Harl. MS. 3859. In Jesus Coll. MS. 20, No. viii. (*Cymr.* viii. 85), there appears to be some confusion with the line of Dyfed.

[240] *Lib. Land.* 146, 154.

[241] *Ibid.* 167. There are no data to enable one to fix the age of Gwrfan.

[242] Asser, c. 80.

[243] "Tribus cantaredis distincta conseritur" (Gir. Camb. vi. 28 (*Itin.* i. 2)).

[244] An annotator of the list of cantrefs and commotes in Cott. MS. Domitian i. fo. 124*b*, says that this happened on the division of Brycheiniog between the three sons, Selyf, Tewdos and Einon by name, of Einon ap Gruffydd ab Elise. Einon had the cantref of Talgarth.

[245] A comparison of the lists will show that Dom. viii. and the Red Book give radically different accounts of the composition of the three cantrefs; the former is followed by Pen. MS. 163 and (substantially) by Pen. MS. 50, but the account in the Red Book is to be preferred for several reasons—in particular, it

CHAP. VIII.

Norman invasion, the chief royal residence of the country was Talgarth, where Brychan himself is said to have held kingly state;[246] commanding the vale of Llynfi, it guarded the approach which was most likely to be chosen by an invading English host. One of the commotes of Brycheiniog bore the name of Llywel, so that it is not unreasonable to suppose that Trecastell, near Llywel Church, was another of the ancient strongholds of the kingdom. A third was Ystrad Yw, which stood in the little valley of the Rhiangoll and gave its name to a district which formed the south-eastern corner of Brycheiniog.[247] Of notable churches there was no lack in this quarter of Wales. The principal saint of the region was Cynog, son of Brychan, who suffered martyrdom; Merthyr Cynog (the "martirium" of Cynog) was the place of his burial and held a position of corresponding importance.[248] Another member of the same family, Cynidr, a grandson of Brychan, was also of high repute as a patron in Brycheiniog; to him belonged Y Clas ar Wy (the "clas" on the Wye), which the English termed Glasbury.[249] Llangors, one of the few churches which preserved the memory of Paulinus, was another ancient ecclesiastical centre; it is expressly termed a monastery, *i.e.*, a "clas," and was held by the bishops of Llandaff, who paid occasional visits to the reedy banks of Llyn Syfaddon.[250] Nor was the sister see of St. David's unrepresented, for as the White Bard, himself a native of Brycheiniog, reminds us—

is not tainted with the error which divides Ystrad Yw into three cymwds, *viz.*, Ystrad Yw, Crug Hywel and Eglwys Iail. The latter two represent in reality Ystrad Yw Isaf and Ystrad Yw Uchaf, Eglwys Iail being an old name of Llangynidr.

[246] *Cambro-Br. SS.* 23. Talgarth is, perhaps, the Garth Matrun of p. 272.

[247] *Arch. Camb.* VI. iii. (1903), 82-4.

[248] *Welsh SS.* 138-9. The torque of St. Cynog was famous in the twelfth century (Gir. Camb. vi. 25 (*Itin.* i. 2), 112 (ii. 2)) and the church of Merthyr was a hundred years later the best endowed in the deanery of Brecon (*Tax. Nich.* 273).

[249] The connection of Cynidr (for whom see *Welsh SS.* 148-9) with Glasbury is clear, notwithstanding that his place as patron of the parish has long been taken by St. Peter. See *Cambro-Br. SS.* 274 (sancti Kenider de Glesbyri), *Cart. Glouc.* i. 314-6, iii. 5 (ecclesiam sancti Kenedri) and *Arch. Camb.* IV. xiv. (1883), 227 (Kenedereschirch). There is still a Ffynnon Gynid(r) in the parish. Other churches originally dedicated to the same saint are Kenderchurch in Archenfield, which is the "lann cinitir lann i cruc" of *Lib. Land.* 277, Llangynidr and Aberysgir.

[250] *Lib. Land.* 146, 238, 255.

Garth Bryngi is Dewi's honourable hill,
And Trallwng Cynfyn above the meadows;
Llanfaes the lofty—no breath of war shall touch it,
No host shall disturb the churchmen of Llywel.[251]

It may not be amiss to recall the fact that these possessions of St. David's brought here in the twelfth century, to reside at Llandduw as Archdeacon of Brecon, a scholar of Penfro who did much to preserve for future ages the traditions of his adopted country. Giraldus will not admit the claim of any region in Wales to rival his beloved Dyfed, but he is nevertheless hearty in his commendation of the sheltered vales, the teeming rivers and the well-stocked pastures of Brycheiniog.[252]

IV. The Cantrefs of Morgannwg.

The well-sunned plains which, from the mouth of the Tawe to that of the Wye, skirt the northern shore of the Bristol Channel enjoy a mild and genial climate and have from the earliest times been the seat of important settlements. Roman civilisation gained a firm foothold in the district, as may be seen from its remains at Cardiff, Caerleon and Caerwent. Monastic centres of the first rank were established here, at Llanilltud, Llancarfan and Llandaff, during the age of early Christian enthusiasm. Politically, too, the region stood apart from the rest of South Wales, in virtue, it may be, of the strength of the old Silurian traditions, and it maintained, through many vicissitudes, its independence under its own princes until the eve of the Norman Conquest. It had its own bishop, seated at Llandaff, and never acknowledged the supremacy of David, whose sway was so mighty in the rest of Deheubarth.

Until the middle of the seventh century the political history of the district is obscure.[253] Tradition spoke of a King Glywys, who ruled over the greater part of it, namely, that portion between the Tawe and the Usk afterwards known as Glywysing, and whose sons, including Gwynllyw, the father of St. Cadog, divided their father's realm between them.[254] But the dynasty

[251] *Myv. Arch.* I. 271 (194). [252] *Wks.* vi. 33, 36 (*Itin.* i. 2).

[253] Without accepting every document contained in the *Liber Landavensis* as authentic, one may use the evidence supplied by the compilation in drawing the broad outlines of the history of the period, and this I have endeavoured to do.

[254] *Cambro-Br. SS.* 22, 145. The antiquity of the form Glywysing is shown by its appearance in *Hist. Britt.* c. 41 (Gleguissing in the best texts), the chronicle

CHAP. VIII.

was short-lived; in a generation or two its place was taken by another, represented about 630 by one Meurig ap Tewdrig, who held not only Glywysing but also the region between the Usk and the Wye known from the ancient tribal centre of Venta or Caerwent as Gwent. The legend ran that Meurig's father Tewdrig had been mortally wounded in conflict with the English at the ford of Tintern on the Wye,[255] and it is most probable that this river now formed the boundary between the two races for a considerable distance from its mouth. In due course, Meurig was succeeded by his grandson, Morgan ab Athrwys,[256] known as Morgan Mwynfawr or the Benefactor; this prince was a contemporary of Rhain of Dyfed and Seisyll of Ceredigion (*circa* 730), so that it was pretty certainly from him the realm gained the name, in later ages so familiar, of Morgannwg.[257] Morgan was succeeded by his son Ithel; in the next generation a division of the realm seems to have taken place between the sons of Ithel. Ffernfael ab Ithel, who died in 775,[258] was king of Gwent, where also his descendants bore rule,[259] until the line ended with his grandson, Ithel ab Athrwys, in 848.[260] The other sons, Rhys, Rhodri and Meurig, seem to have been kings of Glywysing, but the course of events west of the Usk in the

in Harl. MS. 3859, *s.a.* 864 (*Cymr.* ix. 165), and Asser, c. 80 (Gleguising). It did not include Gwent, and, on the other hand, while it included Gwynllwg (*Cambro-Br. SS.* 95), it was not, as is alleged in *Iolo MSS.* 18, a mere *alias* of it. In *Lib. Land.* the term seems often to be used loosely as an equivalent of Morgannwg (see pp. 137, 156, where Gwent is included), but this may well be due to the ignorance of the compiler.

255 *Lib. Land.* 141-2.

256 Athrwys does not seem to have ruled himself, unless he was under king in Gwent (*Lib. Land.* 165-6).

257 This view differs from that of Mr. Phillimore (Owen, *Pemb.* i. 208), who ascribes the origin of the name to Morgan the Aged (d. 974). It certainly does not occur in any good authority of older date; on the other hand, the "seven cantrefs of Morgannwg" were not as a whole under the rule of the later Morgan, and it seems but natural to suppose the name came into existence at the same time as Rheinwg and Seisyllwg. Since the elder Morgan's grandson Ffernfael died in 775, I do not think he can well be the "Morcant" of Harl. MS. 3859 *s.a.* 665; he belongs rather, with Rhain and Seisyll, to the beginning of the eighth century.

258 Harl. MS. 3859 *s.a.* (*Cymr.* ix. 162).

259 This may be inferred from the grants ascribed to Ffernfael and his sons in *Lib. Land.*

260 "Iudhail rex guent a uiris broceniauc (Brycheiniog) occisus est" (Harl. MS. 3859, *s.a.* in *Cymr.* ix. 165). His pedigree is given in the same MS. (*Cymr.* ix. 181-2) as far back as Tewdrig and, stopping short with him, implies that he left no descendants.

middle of the ninth century is involved in much obscurity, for, when the political arrangements of the district of Morgannwg are once more clearly revealed, about 870, Gwent is under the sway of a great-grandson of Ithel, one Meurig ab Arthfael ap Rhys,[261] while Glywysing has as its ruler one Hywel ap Rhys, of quite uncertain pedigree.[262]

Like Dyfed, Morgannwg was reputed a land of seven cantrefs.[263] Six of these were generally known; they were Gorfynydd, Penychen, Y Cantref Breiniol ("The Privileged Cantref"), Gwynllwg, Gwent Iscoed and Gwent Uchcoed ("Below" and "Above the Wood"). As to the seventh there was less agreement; the likeliest view is that it lay in our Herefordshire, where the two regions of Erging (Archenfield) and Ewias remained thoroughly Welsh up to the time of the Norman Conquest. The first five of these cantrefs bordered on the sea; each had its tract of fertile land along the coast and behind this a wide extent of mountain or forest; the "bro" or champaign country was thickly peopled, while the "blaenau" or mountain glens, now among the busiest seats of industry in the Empire, were left to the browsing cattle and the hunter's quarry. From the mouth of the Tawe to that of the Thaw (anciently the Naddawan) stretched the cantref of Gorfynydd;[264] here were the ancient churches of Margam and Llanilltud Fawr, the former of unknown history,[265] the latter a wealthy foundation, main-

[261] For Meurig's pedigree see Harl. MS. 3859 in *Cymr.* ix. 182. His position is indicated in *Lib. Land.* 200, 226.

[262] The pedigree of Hywel ap Rhys is not to be found in Harl. MS. 3859, probably because Owain ap Hywel Dda was unwilling to recognise the rights of the family. In Jesus Coll. MS. 20 (*Cymr.* viii. 85, No. ix.) he is connected with Ithel ap Morgan, but the pedigree is a generation or two too long and its details are not attested by other authorities.

[263] *Mab.* 59. *Cf. Cambro-Br. SS.* 145: "septem pagos rexit Gulat morgantie," though this is a wrong use of Gwlad Forgan.

[264] So termed in the Red Book of Hergest (*Bruts*, 412) and therefore to be explained, it may be, as the land beyond the mountain (from the point of view of Gower). Other forms found are Gorenydd (so practically in *Cymr.* ix. 331), Gorwennydd (Triad iii. 14) and, most unsatisfactory of all, Gro Nedd. For the boundary between Gorfynydd and Penychen see *Cambro-Br. SS.* 53. The commotes of the two cantrefs, as usually given, appear to me to be subsequent in date to the Norman Conquest. They are the "members" of the lordship of Glamorgan, and do not include its main body, now known as the Vale or "Bro". *Cf.* Owen, *Pemb.* i. 427.

[265] Marga*n* (the *m* does not occur in any ancient authority) was originally the name of a district, probably a commote of Gorfynydd; see Geoff. Mon. ii. 15:

CHAP. VIII.

taining with dignity the traditions of the days of Illtud, and both remarkable for the many examples they had to show of elaborate carving in the Celtic fashion. The wheel crosses of Margam and Llanilltud, adorned with intricate plait-work, form a group of monuments of great interest and bear witness to the existence in Gorfynydd in the ninth and tenth centuries of a school of carvers in stone of considerable technical facility.[266] The inscriptions which many of them bear have not cast much light upon the history of the period; probably, however, one may recognise the Hywel ap Rhys of Asser and the Liber Landavensis in the person who speaks in the following epitaph from Llanilltud: "In the name of God the Father and the Holy Spirit Houelt set up this cross for the soul of his father Res".[267] Llanilltud may well have been a royal burying-place, for its abbot was one of the three great ecclesiastics of the diocese of Llandaff and the revenues of its "clas" were drawn from many a manor of Morgannwg.[268] Across the Thaw was the cantref of Penychen,[269] extending as far as the Taff; this also contained two ecclesiastical centres of the first rank, the one the seat of the bishop of Morgannwg, the other at Nant Carfan (corruptly, Llancarfan),[270] the principal "clas" of St. Cadog and a match in affluence and historic dignity to the not far distant Llanilltud Fawr. The abbot of Nant Carfan ruled over a community of thirty-six canons, who included a priest, a master or teacher, a sexton, and three custodians of sacred relics; broad lands around

"in pago Kambriae qui, post interfectionem Margani, eius nomine, videlicet Margan, hucusque a pagensibus appellatus est". Merthyr Mawr was within it (*Lib. Land.* 224).

[266] *Lap. W.* 8-15, 25-30; *Margam Abb.* chap. x.; *Arch. Camb.* V. xvi. (1899), 136-68; Allen, *Celtic Art*, p. 186.

[267] Rhys does not accept this identification (*Arch. Camb.* V. xvi. (1899), 155), but this is because he is concerned to show that the stone may be of as early a date as the seventh century. As against this date see Allen, *Celtic Art*, p. 179.

[268] See *Lib. Land. passim* for "abbas sancti Ilduti" ("abbas Lannildut," 145). The "abbas Carbani vallis" (or "Sancti Catoci") and the "abbas Docguinni" (of Llandough near Penarth—*Margam Abb.* 3) appear no less frequently. There is no direct evidence as to the possessions of Llanilltud, but the statement of *Cambro-Br. SS.* 168 (habentes . . . singuli suam villam) rests, no doubt, upon fact.

[269] The district appears (as Penn Ohen) in Wrmonoc's life of Paul Aurelian (*Rev. Celt.* v. p. 418), and was therefore a well-known area in the ninth century.

[270] See chap. vii. note 52.

the settlement provided the means of its support.[271] There was nothing essentially different in the organisation of the cathedral church of Llandaff. The place of the abbot was taken, indeed, by the bishop, but in other respects the analogy was close. A "priest of Teilo" represented the later dean; twenty-four canons (if not a greater number) formed the "clas" or "household" of the saint,[272] and if the territorial claims of Llandaff, as put forward by enterprising bishops, were more ambitious than those of Llancarfan, this was a circumstance due to the wider distribution of Teilo churches than of those which claimed the protection of Cadog.

The Taff and the Rhymni, flowing south from the mountains of Brycheiniog in parallel valleys but a few miles apart, were the western and eastern boundaries of Cantref Breiniol. Wherein the privilege of this cantref stood is not stated by tradition; it is possible, indeed, that the name is of later date than the Norman Conquest of Glamorgan, for there are some indications that the ancient title was Senghenydd, a term limited in later times to that part of the cantref which lay north of the ridge of Cefn On.[273] The district contained no important church or ecclesiastical manor and may, therefore, have always been, as it certainly was in later ages, the chief seat of civil power in Morgannwg. But there is no good evidence that the site of Cardiff Castle was occupied by any royal residence in the interval between the ruin of the Roman fort and the choice of

[271] *Cambro-Br. SS.* 82-96. Both the "presbiter" or "sacerdos" and the "magister" or "doctor" of St. Cadog find a place in *Lib. Land.* (258, 268, 272, 273, 274).

[272] The "sacerdos teiliav" and the "familia teliaui" are mentioned in the marginalia of the Book of St. Chad (*Lib. Land.* xliii. xlvi.); for the former see also *Lib. Land.* 247, 258, 264, 273. Bishop Urban gives the number of canons (*Lib. Land.* 88).

[273] The "Tref Eliau in Seghenid" of *Lib. Land.* 255-7 has been supposed to be Roath (*ibid.* 382) and was certainly on the coast. Thus the term at this date included Cibwyr or Kibor, as well as the Senghenydd of later times, for the limits of which see Owen, *Pemb.* i. 258, and *Arch. Camb.* IV. viii. (1877), 264-9. Before its division into the commotes of Uwch Caeach and Is Caeach, Senghenydd was itself a commote, which is what Giraldus means when he calls it the fourth part of a cantref (vi. 170 (*Descr.* i. 4); *cf.* 34 (*Itin.* i. 2)—"kemmoti, id est, quartae partis cantaredi"). It may be added that the way in which he seems in this passage to leave Cibwyr out of account in his analysis of the constitution of the diocese of Llandaff suggests that the authority he followed used Senghenydd in the older and wider sense. The "Sein Henyd" of B.T. (*Bruts*, 353, 355, 359, 360, 363) is a place in Gower.

the spot by Robert Fitz Hamon as the head of his newly won lordship.[274] The remaining cantref of the old realm of King Glywys lay between the Rhymni and the Usk; it took from his son Gwynllyw the name of Gwynllwg which, in the form Wentloog, has survived to the present day.[275] On a height near the mouth of the Usk, looking out over the marshy flats of the Severn estuary, was the church of Gwynllyw (now St. Woollo's), served by a "clas," ruled by an officer, who, though he once may have been an abbot, was in more recent times a dean, and consecrated in the affections of the cantref by many a tale of miraculous help rendered to the men of Gwynllwg in their days of sore need and tribulation.[276] Another church of high standing in the cantref was Bassaleg, a "basilica"[277] of which the ancient traditions were submerged by the devouring tide of the Norman Conquest, but which is known to have been the mother church of most of the land between the Rhymni and the Ebbw.[278]

The two cantrefs of the kingdom of Gwent occupied the region enclosed by the Usk, the Wye, the Monnow and the sea. A great forest, of which a large portion still remains under the name of Wentwood, divided the low-lying tract along the Bristol Channel from the northern uplands and thus parted the realm into Gwent Iscoed and Gwent Uchcoed.[279] Of these two divisions the seaboard one, though much the smaller, was the more important. It was famed for its fertility; the renown of the wheat and the bees of Maes Gwenith, on the banks of the Troggy, passed for a proverb throughout the whole of

[274] So Mr. J. S. Corbett in the *Transactions of the Cardiff Naturalists' Society*, vol. xxxiii. (1900-1), pp. 26-7. Mounds of the type of that on which the keep is erected are no longer regarded as pre-Norman.

[275] See chap. v. note 168.

[276] *Cambro-Br. SS.* 145-57 (Vita S. Gundleii). The "decanus ecclesie" is mentioned on p. 156.

[277] The derivation is suggested by Prof. Hugh Williams (*Gildas*, p. 29). Notwithstanding the occurrence in mediæval Welsh literature of the form Maesaleg, this cannot be the Campus Elleti of *Hist. Britt.* c. 41, which is rather to be looked for in the neighbourhood of the Palus Elleti of *Lib. Land.* 148, *i.e.*, near the river Thaw in S. Glamorgan.

[278] In addition to the chapels of Henllys and Risca assigned to it by Rees (*Welsh SS.* 342), Machen, Bedwas, Mynydd Islwyn, and Coed Cernyw were regarded as chapels of Bassaleg about 1100 (*Cartae Glam.* i. 2).

[279] "Coit guent" is mentioned in *Lib. Land.* 262 (bounds of "Hennriu in Lebinid").

Wales.[280] Here the princes of Gwent held court,[281] and here was Caerwent, from which the region took its name, once the Silurian capital—if we may dignify it with such a name—but since the days of St. Tathan the ecclesiastical and not the civil centre.[282] The saint was reputed to have been a famous teacher, the head of a "studium" or college of the same monastic type as that of Illtud; he founded a "clas" of the first rank, of which an abbot had the direction. All the men of Gwent revered him as the father of their land, its guardian and the avenger of its wrongs. In Upper Gwent there were no sites of like importance. It was a thriving land, dotted over with churches, but its traditions were matters of local interest, which had not caught the fancy of Wales at large. The bishop of Llandaff, it should be added, drew no small part of his income from the prosperous plains of Gwent; important manors at Llangadwaladr (now Bishton), Merthyr Tewdrig or Mathern, Llaneuddogwy or Llandogo, and in the valley of the Trothy sent their produce to maintain the state of the great monastery on the Taff.[283]

Two outlying members of the older Morgannwg remain to be noticed, namely, Ewias and Erging.[284] The former lay between Brycheiniog and the valley of the Dore—a land of long and narrow mountain glens, of which the streams run southward side by side to the Monnow. Most of it is now included in the county of Hereford, which has also absorbed the richer

[280] Triad i. 30 = ii. 56 = iii. 101. The place is a little north of Llanfair Discoed (Owen, *Pemb.* i. 236).

[281] The royal court of "Lisarcors" was somewhere in lower Gwent (*Cambro-Br. SS.* 156), and so too the "palacium" to which King Caradog ab Ynyr moved when he resigned Caerwent to St. Tathan, for it was between that city and the Severn, perhaps at Caldicot (*Cambro-Br. SS.* 259).

[282] The life of St. Tathan, a saint's day homily ("cuius hodiernam festivitatem celebramus," p. 263) composed by a Norman writer (observe the use of "indigene" on p. 264), is to be found in *Cambro-Br. SS.* 255-64. Caerwent Church is now dedicated to St. Stephen, but evidence is not lacking to show that Tathan was the original patron—see *Ann. Theokesb. s.a.* 1235 (p. 96); *Iolo MSS.* 114, 132, 151. Hence the "presbiteri tathiu" of *Lib. Land.* 270 are clergy of Caerwent; the "abbas guentonie urbis" appears on p. 222, and on pp. 243, 245 a "lector urbis guenti".

[283] *Lib. Land.* 180-3, 141-3, 156, etc.; *Tax. Nich.* 280; *App. Land Com.* 446.

[284] The translator of "Brut y Brenhinoedd" perversely renders the "Wissei" and "Gewissei" of Geoff. Mon. as "Ergig ac Euas," the latter, it may be remarked, a late Welsh form (*Bruts*, 109, 127, 252).

district of Erging, known to the English by the name of Archenfield. Erging was bounded by the Wye, the Worm and the Monnow; though so close to the gates of Hereford, it was a stronghold of Welsh customs and ideas as late as the end of the twelfth century. The Welsh saints were honoured throughout the district, and among them St. David had a great church at Much Dewchurch,[285] and Dyfrig, who was (if we may believe his legend) by birth and residence a man of Erging, a group of churches which commanded the allegiance of the dwellers along the winding banks of the Wye.[286]

AUTHORITIES FOR EARLY WELSH TOPOGRAPHY.

I. Lists of Cantrefs and Commotes.

Four lists of the cantrefs and commotes of Wales are to be found in MS., representing the work of four editors or compilers. The oldest is probably that contained in Cottonian MS. Domitian viii. ff. 119-20*b* (printed, not very accurately, in Leland's *Itinerary*, ed. 1769, v. 16-20), for, though the writing is said to be of the fifteenth century, the forms of the names imply an original of the twelfth or thirteenth (*Cymr.* xi. 168). Next comes the list in the Red Book of Hergest, cols. 377-80, written about 1400 and printed, first in the *Myvyrian Archaiology*, II. 606-12 (737-40), where it is printed on the lower half of the page, and more recently by Rhys and Evans in *Bruts*, 407-12. A third list occurs in Hengwrt MS. 34 = Peniarth MS. 50 (Y Cwta Cyfarwydd), pp. 133-8, written about 1450 and printed in *Cymr.* ix. 326-31. The fourth is in Hengwrt MS. 352 = Peniarth MS. 163, pp. 57-60, and was transcribed by Gruffydd Hiraethog in the year 1543; it will be found in full in Evans, *Rep.* i. p. 952-54. The upper list in the *Myvyrian Archaiology* (II. 606-13 (735-7)) is substantially that of Gruffydd Hiraethog.

Not one of these lists can be implicitly trusted, though they go far to correct each other's errors. The Cottonian list is defective in the section Ceredigion and throughout is atrociously spelt, but in other respects it is fairly accurate. Its order is—Y Berfeddwlad, Powys (including Arwystli), Gwynedd (including Penllyn), Rhwng Gwy a Hafren, Deheubarth, Morgannwg. The chief mistakes are the misplacement of Nant Conwy, the transposition of Uwch and Is Rhaeadr (this runs through all the lists save that of Gruffydd Hiraethog), the omission of Buellt and serious confusion in Gwynllwg and Gwent. The Red Book list follows the order—Y Berfeddwlad, Gwynedd (including Penllyn, Cyfeiliog, and other border districts), Powys (including Arwystli), Rhwng Gwy a Hafren, Deheubarth, Morgannwg. In the North Wales portion there are many errors, but the Dyfed and Ystrad Tywi sections are almost flawless. The older Peniarth list follows the same order as Dom. viii. but places Arwystli at the end of Gwynedd; its chief defect is wrong bracketing, which extends to nearly every section. Morgannwg, where it was written, naturally shows the fewest blunders. Gruffydd Hiraethog's order is his own, *viz.*, Gwynedd (including Arwystli and Penllyn), Powys, Rhwng Gwy a Hafren, Deheubarth, with Morgannwg and Gwent sandwiched between Brycheiniog and Dyfed. This list professes to be based on a

[285] Rees, *Welsh* SS. 53.

[286] Chap. v. note 114.

survey (y messvrwyd ac i rranwyd ac i rivwyd) of all Wales made by Llywelyn ap Gruffydd (*ob.* 1282), who, however, was never in a position, despite the extent of his rule between 1267 and 1277, to make any survey of the kind. It is full of inaccuracies, such as those which mark the treatment of Cantref Bychan and Cantref Mawr, and names many commotes, such as Penal, Hafren and Trefdraeth, which had no real existence. Its unsupported evidence is of the very slightest value.

II. Boundaries of Cantrefs and Commotes.

Really ancient evidence on this head is most difficult to obtain, but there was so much continuity in the matter of local divisions, notwithstanding political changes, that late authorities may often be used with advantage. In many parts of Wales the rural deaneries corresponded closely to the civil areas, and assistance may therefore be derived from *Tax. Nich.* 272-94. The survey printed in *Rec. Carn.* 1-89 is arranged under commotes, so that for the counties of Anglesey and Carnarvon our information is pretty full. Modern hundreds and manors often preserve the ancient boundaries; for a list of the former and their constituent elements, see *App. Land Com.* 362-76, and for particulars as to crown, episcopal and private manors, *ibid.* 437-75. Hengwrt MS. 99 = Peniarth MS. 147, written about 1566, contains (pp. 5-22) a list of parishes (printed in Evans, *Rep.* i. pp. 911-20), grouped to a large extent under the old territorial names, but the scheme is only partially carried out and not always quite correctly. Special sources of information for particular districts are indicated in the footnotes to this chapter.

III. Maps.

No ancient map of the cantrefs and commotes of Wales is known to me. That of William Owen (Pughe), published in 1788 in the third edition of Warrington's *History of Wales*, is very largely guess-work of a clumsy kind, and it is to be regretted that the authors of *The Welsh People* should have given it a place in their book.

Note to Chapter VIII.—*Rheinwg, Esyllwg and Fferyllwg.*

That names of districts might be formed in Welsh by the addition of -wg to personal names is clear from the well-established cases of Morgannwg, Gwynllwg (for Gwynllyw—wg) and Seisyllwg. An instance is to be found in *Hist. Britt.* c. 70, where mention is made of a region styled "Cinlipiuc," of unknown situation, but certainly named after some Cunalipi (*Arch. Camb.* IV. xiii. (1882), 163-4) or Cynllib. The cases of Rheinwg, Esyllwg and Fferyllwg, nevertheless, present in one way or another no small difficulty. The clearest indication of the position of Rheinwg is to be found in the life of St. Padarn in Vesp. A. xiv., in which a tripartite division of South Wales between Padarn, Teilo and Dewi is said to have been made; Padarn took Seisyllwg, Teilo Morgannwg—" regnum autem Rein hec predicta iura ab episcopatu Sancti David accepit" (*Cambro-Br. SS.* 196-7). St. David's domain can have been none other than Dyfed, and as the pedigrees show that Rhain (in Old Welsh, Regin) ap Cadwgan, Seisyll ap Clydog, and Morgan ab Athrwys ruled over Dyfed, Ceredigion and Glywysing respectively about the beginning of the eighth century, the three names appear to fit easily, on this explanation, into their places. They are also found in conjunction in Pen. MS. 32 (MS. D. of the *Welsh Laws*), where they appear to be intended to explain what was meant by Deheubarth (*LL.* ii. 50). Rheinwg is, therefore, taken to be Dyfed by Basil Jones (*Vestiges of the Gael*, pp. 61-2) and Phillimore (*Cymr.* xi. 141). Some other passages which might be cited do not so easily lend themselves to this conclusion; for instance, the

CHAP. VIII.

"Vastatio Rienuch ab Offa" of *Ann. Camb.* MS. C. *s.a.* 795 and the allusions in *Cambro-Br. SS.*77, 79, to attacks on Glamorgan by kings of "Reinuc". Aneurin Owen was probably led by these references to suppose a connection with Rhain Dremrudd, son of Brychan, and hence his gloss to Reinwg in *LL.* ii. 50, note *b*, "a district in Brecknockshire". For this view there is something to be said; the notion that "Ereinwg" was the Welsh name for Southern Herefordshire has, on the other hand, nothing to support it. It was first put forward by Humphrey Llwyd (*Comment.* (2), 94) and popularised by Camden (*Britannia*, 550); in all likelihood it owes its origin to the Offa passage quoted above.

Esyllwg, there can be little doubt, is an antiquaries' form, having no genuine root in history. Welshmen did not give to their territories the names of women; moreover, the only Esyllt who appears in Welsh records is the famous Iseult of romance. Those who used the name claimed, in fact, a different origin for it, which, in the light of modern philology, has only to be stated to be promptly dismissed; they regarded it as the Welsh equivalent of Siluria! Its real source, as can easily be shown, was a misunderstanding of Seisyllwg. This name having become obsolete and its application forgotten, the passage in the *Laws* (already mentioned) in which it occurs became corrupt (*cf. LL.* ii. 50, 584, *Comment.* (2), 169, and *Iolo MSS.* 74). Humphrey Llwyd found the form "Syllwc" in some MS. and forthwith leapt to the conclusion that the region meant was that of the Silures (*Comment.* (2), 102). The view gained acceptance and "Esyllwg" (the reading of some copies) found its way as a supposed ancient name for Morgannwg into the third series of Triads (Nos. 14, 16, 37) and the notices printed in the *Iolo MSS.* (86). *Camb. Reg.* ii. 8 contains a tremendous list of alleged variants of Esyllwg (land) and Esyllwyr (people); like other lists in the same article, it is the coinage of the ingenious and original contributor.

Fferyllwg is another form open to the gravest suspicion. Fferyll or Fferyllt is the Welsh mediæval name of the poet Vergil, and, owing to the bard's reputation in the Middle Ages as a necromancer, became a common noun, denoting an alchemist (whence the modern "fferylliaeth," chemistry) or worker in metal (*Mots Latins*, pp. 167-8; *W. Ph.* (2), 205). But no character in Welsh history bears the name, and there is no early instance of the use of Fferyllwg to denote "Rhwng Gwy a Hafren" (*Iolo MSS.* 86). I believe the origin of the form is to be found in the old name of Hereford which appears as Fernleg (Camden, *Britannia*, 553), Ferleg (*Comment.* (2), 94) and Fferleia (*Radnorsh.* (2), 108). This became Ferlex (*Camb. Reg.* i. 57; *Breconsh.* (2), p. 36); Fferregs (*Breconsh.* (2), p. 38), and, when written by Welshmen, Fferyllwg (*Gw. Brut. s.a.* 838).

CHAPTER IX.

EARLY WELSH INSTITUTIONS.

(As indicated in the text, this chapter is primarily based upon the evidence afforded by the *Welsh Laws*, though much valuable matter for purposes of illustration is to be gleaned elsewhere. For an account of the MSS., editions and history of the Law of Hywel see chap. x., appended note. The following are the chief modern works which deal with the subject of the chapter; *Das Alte Wales*, von F. Walter (Bonn, 1859); Hubert Lewis's *Ancient Laws of Wales* (1889); Seebohm's *Tribal System in Wales* (1895); Rhys and Brynmor Jones's *Welsh People* (chap. vi.); Vinogradoff's *Growth of the Manor*, book i. (1905); Wade-Evans's *Welsh Medieval Law* (1909). In the notes references to the laws are only given in support of statements not easily verified; the note appended to the chapter explains why no use has been made of the Triads of Dyfnwal Moelmud.)

I. THE CENEDL.

FOUR leading institutions supplied the framework of the civil organisation of Wales in the early mediæval period. They were the cenedl, the tref, the cantref and the brenin, or, to use terms of more general application, the kindred, the hamlet, the tribe and the chief. The first was the basis of society, for the Welsh were, and long continued to be, in that stage in which the tie of kinship is paramount, overshadowing all other relations. "They are above all things," wrote a keen observer in the twelfth century, "devoted to their clan, and will fiercely avenge any injury or dishonour suffered by those of their blood."[1] The second was the economic unit, the area of co-operation for the production of food, both by tillage of the soil and otherwise. The third was the political and judicial unit, the district within which men acted together for peace and war, for the trial of causes, both criminal and civil, and for the maintenance of the chieftain and his court. In the fourth appears the monarchical element, binding together the community under one authority—a costly burden from the economic

[1] Gir. Camb. vi. 200 (*Descr.* i. 17).

CHAP. IX.

point of view, but able to offer in return, not only guarantees for the preservation of order within the state, but also—what was no less prized—satisfaction to the spirit of tribal pride and security from the inroads of detested rivals.

Our knowledge of these institutions in their detailed working comes chiefly from the documents known as the *Welsh Laws*, which are to be found in various widely differing editions of the twelfth and succeeding centuries, but are ultimately to be traced to a code prepared, as tradition avers, under the direction of Hywel the Good in the early part of the tenth. What precisely was done by Hywel and his advisers will be discussed in a later chapter; here it is sufficient to say that, while the code is our chief source of information for these institutions, it did not bring them into existence. The cenedl, closely bound up as it is with the blood-feud, is incontestably of ancient origin, linking the Welsh of the Middle Ages with their prehistoric ancestors. The tref appears, under that name, in the ninth century records entered in the Book of St. Chad, and is already an organisation for the regular supply of food.[2] Gildas bears ample witness to the fact that in the sixth century his countrymen were ruled by kings, whose power rested on the possession of military force, and who tried, imprisoned and punished criminals as part of the daily business of kingship.[3] As to the cantref, it may be in name of more recent upspringing than the other three, but the tribe or "gwlad" it represented undoubtedly had its roots far back in the history of the Welsh people.

The cenedl was the kindred or clan, extending far beyond the household or family, but not to be confounded, on the other hand, with the larger community formed by the people or tribe. It corresponded to the Latin "gens," the Greek γένος, the Teutonic "sib," and the Irish "fine". It was the body of kinsmen descended from a common known ancestor who, recognising their relationship, acted in concert in all family matters, such as giving in marriage, acknowledging sons, and, above all, waging the family feuds and ending them

[2] "Treb guidauc . . . hic est census eius" (*Lib. Land.* xlv.).

[3] See especially c. 27 ("reges habet Britannia . . . iudices . . . belligerantes . . . fures insectantes . . . in sede arbitraturi sedentes . . . vinctos in carceribus habentes"). In c. 109 there is a reference to "catastam poenalem".

by the payment and receipt of compensation. The unity of this body was maintained by the agnatic principle; the kinship, that is to say, which bound it together was reckoned exclusively through males, so that a man could only belong to one cenedl, which did not include his wife, his mother, or any maternal relative. In this respect the Welsh appear to have followed a rule which was widely current among the Aryan races.[4] Unlike the "gens," but like the "fine," the cenedl was further limited by being confined to kindred within a certain degree of relationship. The fifth cousin (in Gwynedd the sixth) was, at least for matters of the first importance, the outside man; "beyond this degree," the lawyers alleged, "there can be no computation of kinship".[5] Within this limit, on the other hand, every man knew his pedigree accurately; to quote Giraldus once more, "the most ordinary folk among this people keep careful count of the family pedigree"[6]

The cenedl was so far organised as to have regular officers, with privileges substantial enough to make it worth while to pay the king a fee for admission to them.[7] Of these officers the chief was the pencenedl, the "caput" or "magister gentis," whose duty is described in general terms as "to act with his kinsman in every need that might beset him".[8] He was the guardian, the champion against oppression, the corrector, too, if there should be occasion,[9] of the men and women of his clan. The office was not hereditary, in the sense of descending directly from father to son,[10] and so differed from the kingship of the tribe; rather it was elective, the heads of households of the cenedl choosing one of their number, when a vacancy occurred, to hold it for life.[11] Among a people who had no

[4] Schrader, *Prehistoric Antiquities of the Aryan Peoples*, tr. F. B. Jevons (London, 1890), pp. 397-9.

[5] *LL.* i. 226 (Ven. MS. B.). The difference in practice between Gwynedd and the rest of Wales explains the discrepancies which caused perplexity to Hubert Lewis (*Ancient Laws*, pp. 83-4) and Seebohm (*Trib. System*, pp. 78-81).

[6] Gir. Camb. *ut supra.*

[7] Dim. II. xxiii. 54, 55 = Lat. A. II. xvii. 5, 3 = Lat. B. II. xxxix. 3, 1.

[8] Ven. II. xix. 3. For the expression "ymyrru ag un yn rhaid" see *Mab.* 133-4.

[9] Dim. II. viii. 20.

[10] Gw. II. xl. 10, where it is added: "oes uodawc yw pen kynedlaeth".

[11] Details are wanting as to the method of election, but several points are clear. The office was held for life (see previous note); it did not pass automatically (as suggested in *LL.* ii. 516—"hynav o wr cyvallwy yn y genedl"), for the

CHAP. IX.

nobility, as distinguished from the free tribesmen, the pencenedl naturally ranked high in the social scale, and, judged by the worth of his life and honour in the tribal tariff, was only inferior in dignity to the immediate kin of the crown.

It was one of the specific duties of the pencenedl to stand at the head of his clan when it was necessary for the body to take action in respect of the receiving or denying of a son. The institution of marriage was, as one might expect in a Christian land, recognised and in honour among the Welsh, and involved important legal rights and obligations. But it was not a rule of Welsh law, at any rate in Gwynedd, that only sons born in wedlock should be deemed legitimate, should be members of their father's family and inherit his possessions.[12] The evidence of the legal texts, both direct and indirect, leaves no doubt that foreign censors had in the main good grounds for asserting that in Wales no distinction was made between lawful and natural children.[13] Not only had the teaching of the Church been without effect in this particular, but, what was still more remarkable in a community so tenacious of ancient customs, there had been a departure, too, from the Aryan ideal, which required in the freeborn son pure blood on the mother's no less than on the father's side.[14] In Wales it is clear that, when once the fact of paternity had been established by the proper legal procedure—the oath of affiliation not rebutted by legal denial—the son passed at once into his father's cenedl and could not henceforth be shut out from any of its privileges. It was the father who ordinarily denied or received, but, as the law allowed affiliation many years after the birth of the child,

law finds it necessary to provide for a possible vacancy (Ven. II. xxxi. 19 = Dim. II. viii. 30 = Gw. II. xxxix. 41 = Lat. A. II. viii. 19 = Lat. B. II. xliv. 6); it was held by an "uchelwr" or head of household (Ven. II. xviii. 8).

[12] Ven. II. xvi. 2 is quite explicit as to the opposition on this point between "Cyfraith Hywel" and "Cyfraith Eglwys". Some of the other texts draw a distinction between lawful and unlawful sons (*e.g.*, Dim. II. viii. 27), but the rules as to affiliation everywhere observed leave it hardly doubtful what the real practice was.

[13] "Paternam hereditatem filii inter se, tam naturales quam legitimi, herili portione dividere contendunt" (Gir. Camb. vi. 225. (*Descr.* ii. 9)). *Cf.* H. and St. i. 514 (gravamen No. 18 of church of St. Asaph against Llywelyn ap Gruffydd) and the provision of the Statute of Rhuddlan (*LL.* ii. 925): "quod bastardi de cetero non habeant hereditates et eciam quod non habeant propartes cum legitimis nec sine legitimis".

[14] Schrader, *op. cit.* pp. 391-2.

some provision was necessary in the event of his being dead. Then it was that the pencenedl, with seven men of the clan, took the place of his deceased kinsman and either "swore the lad away from the cenedl"[15] or formally received him into it. In Gwynedd there was a ceremony of reception, no doubt of ancient origin. The pencenedl took the hands of the youth within his own and kissed him, "for a kiss is the token of kinship". He then placed the right hand of the youth in that of the eldest of the assembled kinsmen, who also kissed him in token of the new relationship. Thus the boy passed from hand to hand until the last of the group was reached.[16]

The admission of a son to a cenedl was not only a matter of importance for the near kin, whose rights of inheritance were affected; it touched every member of the clan as adding another name to the long list of those who might claim his help in the matter of the payment of galanas. The vendetta, or blood-feud, was still an institution of undoubted vigour and vitality in mediæval Wales. So keen was the clan feeling of solidarity, so strong the bonds which united the cenedl, that no man could injure or insult, still less pursue to the death, the humblest of its members without drawing down upon himself the unanimous hostility and vengeance of the whole kin. Time could not extinguish the mortal quarrel; "they are ready," says Giraldus, "to avenge, not only new and recent injuries, but also ancient and bygone ones, as though but lately received".[17] At an early stage, however, the idea of compensation emerged as the corrective of the evils of a perpetual state of private war; the feud, if there was no other way of ending it, might be bought off. To this problem, then, the law addressed itself; in a case of "galanas"[18] or "enmity" arising out of a violent death—and how the killing cameabout, whether by accident or

[15] "Gwadu mab o genedyl" (Ven. II. xxxi. 7; Dim. II. viii. 30). The oath, as Hubert Lewis says (*Ancient Laws*, pp. 15-16), had strict reference to the fact and was not a mere refusal to receive.

[16] Ven. II. xxxi. 25.

[17] Gir. Camb. vi. 200 (*Descr.* i. 17). There was a proverb which ran "Hir y bydd chwerw hên alanas" (Evans, *Proverbs*, p. 560).

[18] From gal, gelyn, a foe. Galanas came to mean not only the effect of the feud, the wergild, or blood money, but also its cause, the deed of slaughter. Incidental evidence of the antiquity of the term is furnished by its survival, in the form "galnes," "galnys" (=satisfaction for slaughter), among the Strathclyde Britons (Acts of the Parliament of Scotland, vol. i. (1845), pp. 299-300).

CHAP. IX.

in self-defence or in cold blood, did not in the least affect the situation[19]—under what conditions might the honour of the one clan be appeased and the safety of the other secured. In the first place, provision was made for a formal declaration ot war; the charge of manslaughter must be publicly made and an interval left for the legal reply. This might take the form of a denial, supported by the oaths of a body of compurgators, or, failing this, there was an undertaking to pay the "galanas," wergild, or murder fine, the amount of which was fixed, in a scale duly graduated according to rank, for every member of the community. It is unnecessary to enter here into the elaborate arrangements prescribed by the laws for the collection and division of the galanas fund; for the present purpose it is enough to say that every member of the cenedl of the "llofrudd" (red hand) had to contribute a share fixed in amount by the degree of his relationship, and every member of the cenedl of the slain man received a share calculated upon the same principle. The matter was further complicated by the inclusion for the purposes of galanas of kin on the female side, a practice which was not strictly consistent with the idea of the cenedl as a purely agnatic body, but which finds more than one parallel elsewhere.[20] At last, after many conferences and much spinning of legal subtleties, the last penny was paid and "everlasting concord" established between the two kins. Should a single penny, however, be wanting of the galanas money, all that had been done was of no avail; the law "set vengeance free," since "a part is not the whole," and, though all the rest of the money was retained, the "llofrudd" might, for want of this one penny, be slain with impunity.[21] So narrowly did the ancient spirit of tribal honour watch its rights, so grudgingly did it yield to the state—for it was the king who, for a substantial consideration, took the leading part in the exaction of galanas—the power of setting limits to its inborn liberty of self-defence.

[19] *LL.* ii. 42, 44 (§§ 11, 12). The rule Dim. II. i. 35 = Lat. A. II. ii. 33 = Lat. B. II. i. 14 shows that killing in battle might give rise to galanas; the West Saxon law under Ine (§ 34) was in almost identical terms.

[20] It was also the English custom. *Cf.* Vinogradoff, *Growth of the Manor*, pp. 9-11.

[21] Ven. III. i. 18 (MS. B.). The phrase, "cyfraith a ryddha ddial," occurs in Dim. II. viii. 14.

Considerable independence was enjoyed by the adult members of the cenedl, and there are few traces, in the case of men, of that absolute paternal power which gave Roman fathers entire control of the destinies of their sons. In the matter of holding land, the patriarchal principle, which conceded no rights to the son while the father was alive, still held good among the higher classes, but otherwise the attainment of majority brought with it emancipation. At the age of fourteen[22] the young tribesman was withdrawn from the control of his father, who might no longer correct him,[23] and he became in the eye of the law a fully responsible person. His independence was secured by the provision that he was now to come into possession of his rightful share of the family goods;[24] he might then choose his career, might enter the royal service in some capacity, might tempt fortune in some distant land, or, if of home-keeping disposition, might settle in a house of his own on some corner of the family land and join in the cultivation of the patrimony under his father's direction.[25] Such was the position of the "bonheddig cynwynol," the "gentleman born," the scion of a free stock; the son of an aillt or villein reached manhood and responsibility at the same age, but his freedom to rove was limited by the laws of villein tenure.

The independent householder was naturally also the married man, and the laws facilitated early marriage by providing that at the age of twelve a girl should come into possession of her goods, the share of the family property which she was entitled to carry with her to a husband.[26] She still remained, however, under the government of her father and other relatives until marriage was effected, for the essence of a regular marriage from the point of view of Welsh law was the formal bestowal of the bride by her kindred.[27] Whatever may have been usual in the way of invoking a blessing from the Church, a ceremony which, it is to be remembered, the canon law did not treat as

[22] Ven. II. xxviii.; Dim. III. ii. 8; Lat. B. II. xliv. 3, 4.

[23] Ven. II. xxviii. 8.

[24] "Medu y da" (*ibid.*). "Da," *i.e.*, goods, chattels, must always be carefully distinguished from land, the ownership of which passed under entirely different conditions.

[25] The rules for the division of land on an uchelwr's death show that his sons were already settled upon it in various detached homesteads.

[26] Ven. II. xxx. [27] See especially Ven. II. i. 75.

CHAP. IX.

indispensable, the Welsh conception of a lawful marriage was one which recognised the ancient rights of the cenedl over its daughters, in which the father uttered the fateful words, "Maiden, I have given thee to a husband," [28] and the pencenedl received his fee from the bridegroom in recognition of the rights of the kindred as a whole.[29] It is likely enough that in primitive times the whole clan was solemnly consulted; in the story of Cilhwch and Olwen, the giant Yspaddaden Pencawr refuses to give the hand of his daughter until the matter has been laid before her four great-grandfathers and her four great-grandmothers, all of whom are alive; [30] in later practice, no doubt, the business was arranged more simply. It appears to have been more usual to wed within the clan than without it; "marry in the kin and fight the feud with the stranger" [31] was an old tribal saying, and Giraldus testifies how widely diffused in Wales among all classes was the custom, notwithstanding that it was reprobated by the Church, of marrying near kindred.[32]

The wedded wife, though no special privileges were enjoyed by her children on the ground of their legitimacy, was herself protected in many ways by the law. Her husband had not, as in ancient Rome, the power of life and death over her; in everything which concerned galanas she was still a member of her native cenedl and liable to be avenged by her father and her brothers.[33] Nor might she be beaten, save for serious offences specified in the codes.[34] While she had a limited control over all the joint property of the household, including the portion she had herself brought to the common stock, she had also certain personal possessions which were exclusively hers and of which nothing could deprive her.[35] Most important of all, the

[28] Dim. II. viii. 73 = Gw. II. xxxix. 35 = Lat. A. II. xx. 41 = Lat. B. II. xxiii. 37.

[29] Ven. II. xix. 1. It was but 24d. (a usual figure in the case of official fees), and cannot, therefore, be treated as a relic of the bride-price. As no other payment was made by the bridegroom to the relatives of the bride, it must be supposed that all traces had disappeared of the fact that originally the husband bought his wife from her kindred.

[30] *Mab.* 119.

[31] "Dyweddi o wngc, galanas o bell" (Evans, *Proverbs*, p. 550). "Dyweddi" = marriage in old Welsh, the preliminary ceremony of betrothal being unknown.

[32] Gir. Camb. vi. 213 (*Descr.* ii. 6).

[33] Ven. III. i. 38 (MS. B.).

[34] Ven. II. i. 39; Dim. II. xviii. 6.

[35] These included the "cowyll" or "hood," which is the Morgengabe of the Germans, the gift of the bridegroom to the bride on the morning after the

law gave her considerable protection against arbitrary divorce. The Church had not succeeded in making the marriage tie indissoluble; the ancient rule that a man might put away his wife, if so minded, was still valid, and in certain cases, for instance, when a king's wife bore him no heir,[36] was deemed to be very salutary. But the law took care that it should not be frivolously put into operation by providing for a substantial payment, known as "agweddi," to the divorced woman, and allowed even this only during the first seven years of marriage;[37] after the lapse of this period, the husband who had grown weary of his spouse and desired a younger partner had to resign to the first wife the half of all his possessions, exactly as if the separation had been brought about by his death.[38]

The study of the cenedl reveals to us the oldest elements in Welsh society, those which had resisted the influence of Roman law and government, of Christian ethical teaching, and of royal authority as exercised by Welsh chiefs. It carries us back into the Celtic foreworld, and discloses a system not at all unlike, in spite of variations of detail, that which prevailed among the Irish. It was the continuance of this system far on into the Middle Ages, when feudalism and the canon law had elsewhere wrought such mighty changes, which gave Welsh life its piquant interest, its individual tone and colour.

II. The Tref.

The structure of Welsh society as an aggregation of kins having been examined, it next falls to consider its relation to the land which it occupied and from which it drew its sustenance. Largely pastoral in its activities, concerned in the rearing of horses, cattle, sheep and swine, it was also to some ex-

wedding, and anything which the wife might have subsequently received from her husband in atonement for his offences against her.

[36] In the story of King Pwyll of Dyfed, it is related how the men of the land began to clamour at the end of the third year against an alliance which had yielded no royal heir (*Mab.* 17-18).

[37] From the mention of "resipiscendi poena statuta" one may infer that it was this system which led Giraldus to talk of marriages on trial as usual among the Welsh (vi. 213-4 (*Descr.* ii. 6)).

[38] A wife irregularly married, without the concurrence of the kindred, was not entitled to the full "agweddi," though she might not be put away without some compensation. At the end of seven years she attained the status of a wedded wife.

CHAP. IX.

tent agricultural, tilling the soil for crops of oats, barley and, more rarely, of wheat. The woodlands nurtured bees, which furnished the mediæval substitute for sugar; firewood and building material were supplied from the same quarter. Hunting, hawking and fishing were open to the free tribesman as means of adding to the family larder. Clothing was made at home by the inmates of the household, and only articles of special value were imported. Thus each community was to a very great extent self-supporting and economically complete; the calling of the smith, which was in great honour because it furnished the warrior with his weapons, was the only industrial one which appears to have been definitely specialised.[39] At the same time there was within the community itself some degree of organisation and division of labour, the lower classes serving the higher, and this leads to the consideration of the various grades into which Welsh society was anciently divided.

As among other primitive peoples, there was at the bottom of the social ladder a slave class, supplying most of the manual labour needed and possessing hardly any rights. The "caeth," whether male or female, was the absolute property of his owner; he belonged to no cenedl, and, if he were killed, no galanas arose; the slayer had merely to recompense his master for the loss.[40] If a slave struck a free man, he was liable to the loss of his right hand;[41] if he sought to escape from his thraldom, he might be recaptured anywhere, and the captor received a reward.[42] The class was probably at one time largely recruited by war, but in a later age it was no doubt chiefly maintained by that active slave trade which was kept going by the Danes of Ireland, notably at the ports of Bristol and Chester.[43] It was by means of slaves that much of the field-work of a Welsh homestead was performed; cutting and clearing wood, digging, and the like were thus accomplished, and so, too, the menial housework, grinding corn in the family quern, baking

[39] Smithcraft ranked with bardism and holy orders as one of three free vocations which a villein might not follow (Ven. I. xliii. 11 = Dim. II. viii. 7 – Lat. A. II. viii. 10 = Lat. B. I. xix. 2).

[40] Dim. III. iii. 8; Gw. II. xl. 23.

[41] Ven. III. i. 34; Dim. II. xvii. 44; Gw. II. v. 32; Lat. A. II. xv. 18; Lat. B. II. xxii. 17.

[42] Dim. II. xvii. 49; Lat. A. II. xvi. 1, 2; Lat. B. II. xxii. 23, 24.

[43] *Conq. Eng.* (2), pp. 443-5.

and washing.[44] The lot of a slave was more or less irksome and unpalatable according as the owner was of lower or higher rank; the sewing-maid who served the queen was happily placed,[45] while life was not worth living, if a current proverb is to be believed, for the thrall who was fated to do service to a villein.[46]

A second class which stood outside the tribal system was that of "alltudion" or aliens. The alltud, or "other-country-man," [47] was naturally in very many cases the foreigner from England, Ireland or the Continent, living in Wales as an exile, a hostage, or an adventurer, but foreign speech and alien birth did not, in the sight of the law, form the essence of the alltud status. What really made the alltud was the want of attachment to the soil; he was the man who had no claim upon any land in the district, whether as villein or free tribesman, the fifth wheel in the coach, for whom there was no place in the system of the country.[48] Nevertheless, if he chose to settle in the district, he received full legal protection, and his descendants might in time be recognised as proprietors. He was required to place himself under the protection of some owner of land, who gave him the foothold on the soil which he required; during three generations the bargain was revocable and the alltud tenant might leave, on condition of halving his chattels with his lord; the fourth man—such, at least, was the custom of Gwynedd [49]—became a landowner, and at the same time a villein bound to perpetual service.

All who held land or were entitled in due course to succeed to it were reckoned proprietors, inheritors or Cymry.[50] Each was a member of some cenedl, with a definite "braint" or legal status; high and low, they were parts of one system. Nevertheless, a broad and well-defined barrier separated the villein

[44] Ven. III. i. 33; Dim. II. xvii. 38, 47; Gw. II. vii. 17. For lavatrix = ancilla, see Lat. A. II. xviii. 12; Lat. B. II. xlii. 12, lv. 1, lvi. 1.

[45] Dim. II. viii. 49 mentions "nottwyd gwenigyawl y vrenhines," which is to be translated "the needle of the queen's domestic".

[46] "Da angheu ar eidywc taeawc" (Evans, *Proverbs*, p. 546).

[47] From a primitive "allo-touto-s," perhaps seen in the "matribus ollototis sive transmarinis" of a Roman inscription from Binchester (*Urk. Spr.* 22).

[48] See especially Ven. II. xiv. 1, 2, and xv. 8.

[49] Ven. II. xvi. 20-6.

[50] It is important to observe that the term "Cymro" was not a badge of freedom, but included the aillt as well as the bonheddig. See note appended to chap. v.

CHAP. IX.

holder of land from the free-born member of the tribe. The aillt or taeog, for he was known indifferently by either name, as well as by the borrowed one of "bilain,"[51] was distinguished in many ways as belonging to an inferior social grade. He was subject to a lord, who might be the king, or one of the free landowners. He had no place in the free court of the district in which he lived. Hunting and hawking were for him forbidden amusements, and therefore he received no more compensation for any dog of his which might be killed than was paid for a farmyard cur, or for any bird he lost than the value of a hen.[52] He might not leave the tillage of the soil for any liberal occupation; smithcraft, the bardic order, the Church were all closed against him.[53] He might not, indeed, quit the community in which he was bred and born, the corner of the social system which the law provided for him, and if he took to flight and deserted his lawful station, he paid forfeit with all his possessions, which were immediately seized by his lord.[54] All the conditions of his life show that he was regarded as by pre-eminence the cultivator of the soil, the man whose industry as farmer and stockbreeder was necessary to the life of the community.

Little light is thrown by the laws upon the way in which the aillt of an uchelwr or free landholder served his master and was associated for work with his fellows.[55] The code of Hywel was put together, primarily, in the interests of the crown, and accordingly in the documents derived from it matters in which the king had no concern are only incidentally treated. As to the king's aillts, there is, on the other hand, some information, and this reveals the villeins who provided for the needs of the court as grouped together in communities known as trefs.

[51] Aillt is the usual term in Ven., taeog and bilain in the other codes. Aillt is connected by Whitley Stokes (*Urk. Spr.* 21, as modified by 327) with the Irish "alt, ailt" = house, and taeog is no doubt from "ty," but the meaning is "a slave *having* a house" and not, as the "verna" of Davies, *Dict.* suggests, "a slave born in the house". "Alltud" and "aillt" have been much confused by late writers, but in the authoritative legal texts they are always carefully distinguished.

[52] Ven. III. xiv. 17; Dim. II. xiv. 18; Gw. II. xxi. 12; Ven. III. xv. 10.

[53] See note 39 above.

[54] Dim. I. xxix. 6; II. xii. 5; Gw. I. xxxv. 11; xxxvi. 12.

[55] Ven. II. xvi. 20-6 deal with uchelwrs' alltuds and aillts, and suggest that they were under much the same rules as those of the king.

The tref was originally the "house" or "dwelling-place";[56] a secondary meaning which it acquired was "hamlet, village," and this is what seems to be denoted in the case of these villeins—the group of villein homesteads clustered together for the purpose of common cultivation of the surrounding land.[57] Each taeogdref or villein hamlet was responsible as a whole for what was due from it to the king, and, while each man had his own house, farm stock and farm buildings, it is clear that for the important business of ploughing there was co-operation. The heavy wooden plough was drawn by a team of eight oxen, and to furnish these the tref clubbed together; each taeog became a member of what was known as a "cyfar" or plough fellowship, and it was a rule that in no taeogdref might the annual ploughing begin until every man had found his cyfar.[58] Each day's ploughing produced an "erw" or "cyfair," a strip of ploughed land of which the dimensions varied in different districts, but which was usually about ten times as long as it was broad.[59] When twelve erws had been ploughed, they were assigned in accordance with a standing rule among the contributors to the ploughing, including not only the owners of the oxen and the plough, but also the ploughman and the ox-tender, the latter being not a "driver" but a "caller" (geilwad), for he walked backward in front of the team and relied even more upon the power of his voice than upon his ox-goad.[60] It is likely that each hamlet had its ploughman and its caller, who made ploughcraft their special business. Whether the land ploughed by a villein plough-team had been previously

[56] *Urk. Spr.* 137, 334. The word occurs in the sense of "house" in the ninth-century glosses of Martianus Capella (*Arch. Camb.* IV. iv. (1873) 4); this is also the meaning which explains "adref," "athref," and "gartref" and very many of the trefs of local nomenclature.

[57] "Trefgordd" is also used to denote the villein hamlet; Dim. II. ii. 12, compared with Gw. II. ii. 12, shows that it was used interchangeably with tref.

[58] Gw. II. xix. 2. Ploughing began on 9th February (Ven. III. vii. 4).

[59] "Cyfar" = co-tillage, and "cyfeir" (now "cyfer," an acre) = a day's tilth, are carefully distinguished in the texts (for "cyfeir" see Ven. III. vii. 4; xxii. 236, 237; xxiv. 13), though not in Aneurin Owen's translation. MSS. D. B. C. J. K. of the Ven. code clearly identify the "cyfeir" and the "erw" in III. xxiv. 3 ("erw y gwydd a honno a elwir cyfeir y casnad"). A. N. Palmer has made a special study of the various customary acres of Wales; see especially *Arch. Camb.* V. xiii. (1896), 1-19.

[60] "Stimulatore praeambulo sed retrogradu" (Gir. Camb. vi. 201 (*Descr.* i. 17)). "Geilwad" = driver is found in Job xxxix. 7.

CHAP. IX.

allotted as arable land to the villeins individually or was common for this purpose to the whole of the tref is not made clear by the laws,[61] but it is certain that the erws lay in open fields, unprotected by ditches or hedges, and that it was customary to plough virgin soil from time to time in order to get the benefit of unexhausted land.

The tref of villeins, which as a cluster of homesteads is often styled "trefgordd," acted together for other ends than that of tillage. The cattle of the tref grazed together in the wide pastures which surrounded it under the eye of the village herdsman or "bugail,"[62] whose dog walked out at the head of the herd in the morning and followed its rear at night, a valiant protector against the wolves of the forest, not a penny inferior in legal worth to the best ox in the herd.[63] There was also a village smithy, a village kiln for the drying of corn, and a bath-hut, in which water was heated for special ablutions.[64]

Perhaps the most remarkable fact about the "taeogdref" or villein hamlet is that its folk held their land, not by right of kinship, but as members of the community. Land of this description, the Venedotian code explains, is not to be divided (like family land) between brothers, but the king's officers are to apportion it equally between all the men of the tref, whence it is known as "tir cyfrif" (reckoned land).[65] It is further explained that no land of this kind can revert to the lord for want of heirs, since, as another passage puts the case, the son's share of his father's erw is, in such a tref, no greater than that

[61] Ven. II. xvi. 22, referring to men who have become aillts, says they have their homesteads and land attached to these and "eu tir namyn hynny yn dir swch a chwlltyr (*i.e.*, arable land) rhyngddynt". On the other hand, III. xxiv. 17 suggests that the partners in the "cyfar" had land of their own which they could require the team to plough when it was their turn to receive an "erw".

[62] "Bugail," which now means shepherd, is properly neat-herd or cattle-tender (*Urk. Spr.* 178). For "bugail trefgordd," tending the cattle of different owners, see Ven. II. iv. 8; Dim. II. viii. 81; Gw. II. xxviii. 24. Lat. A. calls him "pastor communis uille" (II. v. 8); so Lat. B. II. xvi. 8.

[63] Ven. III. xiv. 19; Dim. II. xiv. 18; Gw. II. xxi. 14; Lat. A. II. xxiv. 30; Lat. B. I. xiii. 26.

[64] Ven. III. iii. 20; Dim. II. viii. 36; Gw. II. xxxix. 16; Lat. A. II. iii. 14; Lat. B. II. vi. 11.

[65] Ven. II. xii. 6; xviii. 7. It may be said, with reference to Vinogradoff, *Growth of the Manor*, p. 93, that in the laws, as in the extents, "tir cyfrif" is clearly always villein land. Save in the Triads of Dyfnwal Moelmud (for which see note appended to this chapter), there is nothing to suggest that a system of co-tillage existed in mediæval Wales among the free tribesmen.

of the furthest man in the tref.[66] There was no general shifting of the homesteads, for the law provided that each man should remain in undisturbed possession of his "tyddyn," with the home croft of four erws,[67] and further laid down the rule that a taeog should be succeeded in this holding by his youngest son.[68] But as to the general arable land, on whatever principle it was tilled, whether as private or as communal property, it is clear that it was not subject to any rights of inheritance, but was regarded as a common fund for the maintenance of the whole tref. Every taeog's son in the village, if he had attained the age of fourteen and was not, as the youngest son, his father's destined successor, was entitled, on each distribution, to a man's share of the land which was being divided.

Thus the village community is to be found on Welsh soil, though only among the unfree cultivators. It is natural to regard this class, holding a servile position and having few privileges, as the descendants of a conquered race,[69] and the system of tenure under which they worked is obviously ancient, telling of the long settlement on the land of the cultivating community. In view of what has been said in the early chapters of this history, one may therefore without undue boldness recognise in these aillts and taeogs the remnant of the Iberian people, the oldest tillers of the soil in Wales, reduced to servitude by wave after wave of Celtic conquest, by the might of the ancestors of the free tribesmen, whose institutions are now to be examined.

Besides the true tref, or village community of servile tenants, there was another tref, termed the free tref, which seems to have acquired its name through being, like the other, a definite area within which there was joint responsibility for the render due to the king. Every commote was divided into trefs, some of which were bond and some free; the free trefs, no less than the bond, paid each its annual contribution towards the maintenance of the court.[70] But the free tref was not a

[66] Ven. II. xxi. 2; *LL.* ii. 56, 64.

[67] For the home croft of four or eight erws, which went with every homestead or "tyddyn," see Ven. II. xii. 1; Dim. II. xxiii. 1; Gw. II. xxxi. 1.

[68] *LL.* ii. 64.

[69] Lewis, *Ancient Laws of Wales*, p. 47; *W. People*, p. 215; Vinogradoff, *Growth of the Manor*, p. 25.

[70] The Venedotian code makes the "maenol," containing four trefs, the unit which paid the king the free render of £1 (i. 188). But all the particulars it gives

CHAP. IX.

hamlet or body of villagers; there is clear evidence that the households of the better class in Wales were not grouped together in villages, but were scattered here and there over the face of the country. Observers were struck by the difference in this respect between England and Wales; "they do not foregather in cities, villages or castles," says Giraldus,[71] "but inhabit the woods like anchorites," and Archbishop Peckham a century later noticed the same love of solitude.[72] It may be pointed out that the map of Wales bears witness to this day to the divergence between English and Welsh custom in the matter of the distribution of the rural population.[73] Most of the Welsh parish churches stand almost alone, the houses, instead of forming a group as in England, with the church as its centre, being pretty evenly dispersed over the whole parish. The free tref was constituted by marking off a number of these scattered holdings and associating them in responsibility for the payment of a fixed portion of the free render of the commote. Such a tref might very well be occupied by a body of kinsmen, since kinsfolk would naturally settle together; it would be separated from other trefs by well-marked barriers.[74] But it would not be, like the taeogdref, a society of joint tillers of the soil, with interests closely intertwined, but merely a group of private owners, each pursuing his own way and holding his land separately.

In the free tref the landowner was the man variously known as the uchelwr (high man), gwrda (goodman) and breyr.[75] For

under this head have an air of unreality; from the phrase "Y dref uchaf (*i.e.*, next to Arfon) o arllechwed" used in *Mab.* 63 of Creuwyrion (for which see *Rec. Carn.* 12-13), it would appear that in Gwynedd, as elsewhere, the term "tref" was used to denote the fiscal unit which became the "villa" and township of later times. Vinogradoff (148) points out how among the English artificial and composite "túns" were formed for administrative and judicial purposes on the analogy of the real village settlements.

[71] "Non urbe, non vico, non castris cohabitant; sed quasi solitarii silvis inhaerent" (Gir. Camb. vi. 200 (*Descr.* i. 17)).

[72] "Il ne habitent pas en semble, mes menit chescun loinz de autre" (H. and St. i. 570).

[73] The distinction is one between Celtic and Teutonic practice, as pointed out by Meitzen. See the contrasted maps in *Social England* (1901), i. pp. 164, 165.

[74] For the meer between two trefs see Ven. II. xxi. 1; xxv. 1; Gw. II. xxxii. 1, 5.

[75] Breyr is a purely South-Welsh term, while uchelwr occurs chiefly in Ven., often in the form "mab uchelwr," in which, as in "mab aillt," "mab sant," the prefix merely indicates the gender. Gwrda is commoner in general literature than in the laws.

the attainment of this position it was necessary not only to be of free birth, a member of a free cenedl, but also to have been fully emancipated, to have been freed by death from the control of father and paternal grandfather. This, it has been stated above, was not necessary for the holding of personal property or "da"; the "boneddig cynwynol" might be a householder and owner of cattle, but he had no rights over the family land while his father was alive.[76] Thus the uchelwrs were not only a wealthy, but also an experienced class, who naturally took a leading position in all the affairs of the country; they were the nearest approach to a nobility to be found in Welsh society[77] and are sometimes dignified by that title.[78] They had alltuds and aillts who did them service; they hunted the deer in their forests and took the fish which were caught in their weirs. Each lived in a "neuadd" or hall, which, although rudely built of timber and wattle, like all the buildings of the Welsh, was a much more substantial affair than the mere "ty" of the taeog.[79] It was the privilege of the uchelwr to possess a harp[80] and he was a recognised patron of travelling bards.[81] He was the man of leisure and dignified ease, the organ of the public opinion of his commote, the adviser, the critic and the defender of the crown.

Nevertheless, the uchelwr was not the absolute owner of the land under his control. He had but a life interest in it, and could not give, sell or bequeath any part of it, to the detriment of the family whose patrimony it was.[82] It passed on from generation to generation by fixed laws of inheritance, which might not be set aside. The first principle observed was equal division on the death of an uchelwr among all sons. Daughters were excluded, because it was not for them to carry on the family traditions, but by marriage to secure heirs for other

[76] Ven. II. xxviii. 9.

[77] The triad defining the three sorts of men as a king, a breyr, and a villein (*LL.* i. 350) excludes a nobility in the ordinary sense.

[78] See *LL.* ii. 1083 (index, *s.v.* nobilis) and Gir. Camb. vi. 166 (*Descr.* i. 2: "nobiles qui Kambrice Hucheilwer quasi superiores viri vocantur").

[79] Ven. III. xxi. 2, 3.

[80] Ven. I. xliii. 2 = Dim. II. viii. 10.

[81] Dim. I. xviii. 1; Gw. I. xix. 2; Lat. A. I. xxii. 2; Lat. B. I. xxi. 10. I take the reference to the taeog to be contemptuous and a reflection on the taste of the bard who could choose such a patron.

[82] Ven. II. xv. 8; *LL.* ii. 270.

CHAP. IX.

proprietors.[83] All sons, on the other hand, took equal shares, since the purpose of the law was to maintain the tribe, not to keep the estate intact. Such favour as was shown fell to the lot, not of the eldest, but of the youngest son, for it was he who, among uchelwrs and villeins alike, succeeded to his father's homestead,[84] the others being expected to remain in the homes they had made for themselves on the family land during their father's lifetime. But the law went further even than this in its benevolent determination to provide a fit maintenance for every uchelwr and ordained that, after the equal division between brothers, there might be on occasion a similar division between first cousins and even one between second cousins, so as to prevent the rise of marked inequalities between uchelwrs who were nearly akin to each other. Thus arose a subdivision of the cenedl—the group of men descended in the male line from a common great-grandfather; they could inherit from each other in default of issue and formed the body which it was necessary to consult before any part of the land could, for however good a reason, be disposed of to an outsider.[85]

III. The Cantref.

The survey of mediæval Wales which was undertaken in the eighth chapter showed us a country divided into regions called cantrefs, each of which was again divided into two, three or more commotes. Both the cantref and the commote are repeatedly mentioned in the laws, but upon examination it becomes evident that they are not two separate institutions, the one subordinate in its working to the other, like the English shire and hundred; though the geographical facts at first sight suggest this, they must not be so interpreted. The leading feature of the commote is its court, for the trial of disputes among the free tribesmen, and this is sometimes called the court of the commote or the cantref But nowhere is there

[83] Ven. II. xv. 1; Dim. II. xxiii. 7 is less rigid, recognising a daughter's claim in the absence of any male heir. This relaxation is said in the Statute of Rhuddlan (*LL*. ii. 925) to be "contra consuetudinem Wallensem antea usitatam," but it may be that the stricter rule was confined to Gwynedd.

[84] The obvious exception in the case of the successor of a chief is duly noted in *LL*. ii. 578, 686.

[85] *LL*. ii. 270.

any shadow of a suggestion that a case might be taken from the commote to the cantref, as from a lower to a higher court, or that there were two distinct sets of officers for the two areas. In the laws it is the commote which appears as the living and active body, the references to the cantref being for the most part perfunctory, with a smack of antiquity about them.[86] It is further to be noticed that the commote does not appear in the earliest Welsh records,[87] while the names of the Welsh commotes wear in the main a much more modern air than those of the cantrefs. The conclusion is, therefore, not to be resisted that the commote or "neighbourhood" is of comparatively recent origin; when the cantrefs had become, through the growth of population and the development of more settled habits, too large to be convenient areas of tribal co-operation, they were divided by agreement into smaller districts, each of which had henceforth its own independent organisation.[88] There is good reason to think that this step had not been taken in South Wales before the appearance of the Normans, and that the commote dates from the end of the eleventh century.[89]

The machinery of the commote, therefore, is in origin that of the cantref, and, during the period which is now under consideration, it is with the cantref only that one has to deal. A further question naturally arises, whether the cantref itself is a primitive institution and may not have been the fruit of an early attempt at constitutional reform. This is certainly suggested by the derivation of the name; the area formed by the

[86] Ven. knows only of the court of the cymwd, but Dim. II. viii. 110 and 116 have "brawdwr cymwd neu gantref" and "llys cymwd neu gantref" is a common phrase in *LL.* ii. The only passage in which an office is associated with the cantref is Gw. II. xl. 9, where the king's footholder or "troediog" is called "eisteddiad cantref," a phrase which is no doubt to be regarded as an archaism. The cantref continued, of course, to be of importance as a geographical area after losing its political importance; see Dim. II. viii. 14; xxiii. 47-9; Gw. II. xxxix. 5.

[87] The term is not to be found in *Lib. Land.* It occurs twice in *Mab.* (31, 62).

[88] *Gr. Celt* (2). pp. 192, 207; *Urk. Spr.* 87.

[89] The usual list of the commotes of Morgannwg, besides including such obviously late forms as Tir yr Iarll and Tir yr Hwndrwd ("Tirhundred" in the Cottonian list), does not appear to account for Bro Morgannwg at all. In Dyfed again, Penfro, which was originally the name of a cantref, could not have become the name of a commote also until "Castell Penfro" had come to be known by the shorter title.

CHAP. IX.

grouping of a "hundred houses" or "hamlets" (can tref) would seem to be of unmistakably artificial origin. In point of fact, there is good evidence that the cantref is the historical successor of the "gwlad" or "tud," *i.e.*, country or tribe, the body of free tribesmen who, either as ancient settlers or as Brythonic immigrants, held sway as an independent community within bounds which clearly marked them off from their neighbours.[90] At some period which cannot now be precisely ascertained, the larger gwlads, such as Môn, Ceredigion, Brycheiniog, Ystrad Tywi, were divided into cantrefs, the smaller, such as Meirionydd, Dyffryn Clwyd, Buellt, became cantrefs themselves,[91] and thus the cantref everywhere took the place of the tribe as the means of enforcing justice and as the link between people and crown.

The cantref court was an assembly of the uchelwrs of the cantref, who as heads of households represented all the freemen of the tribe. There was no fixed place of meeting; indeed, it was customary in cases of dispute as to land to meet on the land which was the subject of the lawsuit.[92] The king presided, or, in his absence, his official representative; it was his "llys" or "gorsedd," the "high seat" of his jurisdiction.[93] In South Wales, the assembly formed, nevertheless, a considerable check upon his power, for it might, by its "dedfryd gwlad," or "judgment of country," declare him to have acted oppressively and obtain the reversal of the deed which had incurred its censure.[94] Giraldus bears witness to the extent to which in

[90] "Gulat" is used for cantref (or cymwd) in the "Privilegium Teliaui" in *Lib. Land.* 120 (line 10), and the "gladoet" of Ven. II. ii. 4 must be cantrefs. Gwlad and cantref are treated as synonymous in Dim. II. viii. 14; Gw. II. xxxix. 5; the "henwryeyth gwelat" of Lat. A. II. ix. 15 are the "heneuydyon cantref" of Lat. B. II. xxiv. 45. "Tud," the Irish tuath (*Urk. Spr.* 131), is of rarer occurrence; *cf.* however, the "castell teirtut" of *Lib. Land.* 134, said to be the meeting-point of Cantref Bychan, Cantref Selyf and Buellt.

[91] It is quite possible that at the time of the later division some of the smaller centres became commotes, as not requiring to be divided, and were then grouped together in artificial cantrefs, which never had a separate existence. This appears to have been the case in Powys, where many of the cantref names have an unreal ring and are not known otherwise than from the lists.

[92] Ven. II. xi. 9 (a hynny ar y tir), 10 (dyfod ar y tir).

[93] For "gorsedd" = court see Ven. II. xi. 51; Dim. II. viii. 15; *LL.* ii. 8 (§ 24). In *Mab.* 8, 32, 166, and in place names, it has the meaning of "mound," "tumulus," possibly because it was a royal habit to hold session on elevations of the kind.

[94] Dim. III. i. 17; *cf.* II. viii. 139.

the south the royal dignity and supremacy were prejudiced by this aristocratic independence; the realm of Deheubarth, he says, though much larger than either Gwynedd or Powys, is not so desirable a heritage, by reason of the number and insubordinate temper of its uchelwrs.[95] It is hardly fanciful to find in this difference between the political atmosphere of the north and that of the south the chief explanation of the fact that the princes who worked most successfully for Welsh unity were in the main of northern origin. At the stage of political development which the Welsh people had now reached, aristocratic freedom meant tribal isolation and weakness, while royal power in capable hands made for national union and strength. And in South Wales, not only did the uchelwrs keep a tight hold of the reins in matters of government, they also retained to the full their ancient judicial powers. In Gwynedd and Powys, though the king's gwrdas still sat on his right and on his left as the assessors of his court, their functions were purely ornamental; in every commote there was an official or professional judge, who took the business of judgment out of their hands.[96] There was no such officer in the south; "in Deheubarth," says the Dimetian code, "there is in every court a great number of judges, as aforetime before the days of Hywel the Good, to wit, every owner of land by privilege of that land, though it be not land of office".[97]

The tribal court dealt, it would appear, with all such questions requiring judicial settlement as arose among the free tribesmen. Of these the most important was the determination of disputes as to who was the lawful owner of land, a matter settled, as has been said, on the land itself, in full court, after elaborate pleadings and counter-pleadings. Besides the judges and the parties, there were in attendance the clerk or recorder, the "rhingyll" or usher and summoner of the court, and, in many cases, two professional pleaders, whose duty it was to conduct the parties through the mazes and pitfalls spread for the unwary by primitive rules of legal procedure.[98]

[95] Gir. Camb. vi. 166 (*Descr.* i. 2).

[96] Ven. II. xi. 10; Dim. I. xxxi. 1; II. viii. 110.

[97] Dim. I. xxxi. 2.

[98] The employment of a "tafodiog" or pleader was optional in the south (Dim. II. ix. 5); in Ven. II. xi. 10, the presence of a "cynghaws" on each side is assumed. That the advocate was a professional lawyer appears from *LL.* ii. 98 (§ 7), 146 (§ 33). For the "gwallawgeir" or "faulty word" see Dim. II. viii. 78.

Silence was proclaimed in the field, and no one might help plaintiff or defendant by any suggestion save his "canllaw" or "hand-rest," the friend specially assigned for this purpose. Witnesses gave evidence as to recent facts; the important question of ancestry was settled by the testimony of neighbouring landowners, which might not be gainsaid. The decision rested with the judges, who in South Wales chose one of their number to preside and announce the verdict.[99] Such in a few words was the nature of the proceedings in an action of "kin and stock"; other suits are not so fully described, but it may be assumed that they followed in great measure the lines of this, the most important. There was a process for obtaining temporary possession of land which was being claimed in the court, a process open only to the son of a former occupant and known by the remarkable name of "dadanhudd" or "uncovering". It is explained, and no doubt rightly, as the assertion by the son of his right to uncover the fire on the family hearth in succession to his father.[100] In the Welsh house, it is known from other sources, the fire, burning on an open hearth in the centre of the floor, was at bedtime covered up with peats or logs, so as to keep it gently smouldering until the morning, when it was again uncovered and set blazing with the aid of fresh fuel.[101] If the son claimed the right to uncover his dead father's hearth, it can only have been as the priest of a long-forgotten ritual, as the lawful head of the house ministering to the ancestral hearth-spirits, and thus the action of "dadanhudd" preserves in its name the one known trace among the Welsh of that ancestor-worship which was so widely practised among Aryan peoples, and has been held to be of greater significance for their religious history than the nature-worship rendered so familiar to us by the classical writers.[102]

[99] Dim. II. viii. 114.

[100] *LL.* ii. 140-2 (§§ 26, 27); Wotton, 565; Evans, *Dict. s.v.* Moses Williams aptly cites a couplet:

> "Anhuddwyd aelwyd; Duw a welo
> Dodi un heddyw a'i dadanhuddo".

[101] Gir. Camb. vi. 184 (*Descr.* i. 10) says "igne sicut die, sic et nocte tota, ad pedes (concubantium) accenso". *Cf.* Ven. II. i. 31; Lat. A. II. xix. 11; Lat. B. II. xxiii. 33.

[102] The subject in general is discussed in Coulanges, *La Cité Antique* and W. E. Hearn, *The Aryan Household* (London, 1870), its bearing on "dadanhudd" in *Trib. System*, pp. 81-3. There is no authority for the form "dadenhudd" and little warrant for the translation "reuncovering".

Another matter which came under the notice of the court of the cantref was the determination of boundaries.[103] It is to be observed, however, that more was involved in this than the ascertaining of the facts. Facts were, in an early Welsh court, often quite subordinate to status, and the mere will of the landowner of "higher privilege" was enough to give effect to his desire to extend his boundaries at the expense of a less privileged neighbour. Thus the Church meered against the king, the king against his subjects, the uchelwr against the aillt, the aillt against the alltud. Fable reflects the spirit of the law when it tells how the young prince Geraint of Cornwall traversed the borders of his realm with a company of guides, the best men of the land, and "the furthest mark which was shown him, this he ever seized on as his own"[104] The law forbade the carrying of the custom to ridiculous and violent extremes, but the love of encroachment remained deeply rooted in the national disposition; "the digging up of boundary ditches, the removal of landmarks, the outstripping of bounds, the occupation and extension of lands by hook or by crook," says Giraldus Cambrensis, "are a passion with this people beyond any other race."[105]

There was much that was primitive in the criminal law administered in the cantref court, while at the same time modern conceptions of crime as an offence against the well-being of the whole community and of penalty as a matter for the state and not for the injured individual had made considerable headway. The law of galanas, discussed in the first section of this chapter, retained most of the ancient leaven, being little more than an attempt to regulate and keep within bounds the primitive right of revenge. Where, however, there was no question of loss of life, offences were for the most part dealt with, not on the basis of tribal custom, but on the assumption that they touched the honour and prestige of the king, for whose broken peace due atonement must be made. Fighting, violent seizure of another's goods, attacks on the honour of women, involved the payment of a "dirwy" or special fine of twelve cows; a "camlwrw" or fine of three cows was levied for a large number

[103] For the law of meering see *LL.* i. 196, 536, 542, 762, 764, 774; ii. 76, 90, 148-50.

[104] *Mab.* 268.

[105] Gir. Cam. vi. 211 (*Descr.* ii. 4).

CHAP. IX.

of minor offences, such as contempt of court, neglect of official duty, unauthorised meddling with another's property. Penalties were imposed not only upon principal offenders, in case of murder, theft or house-burning, but also upon those who in one way or another were sharers in their guilty enterprises; this inclusion within the scope of the law of the "affeithiau"[106] or "affections" of a crime was no doubt an innovation due to some early reformer, for that it was of recent origin is shown by the fact that no part of the fine exacted from an accomplice to murder went to the relatives of the murdered man.[107] Theft, as was usual in primitive communities, was punished with great severity; it was taken for granted that the thief caught with the stolen property in his possession would fall a just victim to his captor's rage,[108] and the law only interposed to secure a fair trial of the issue whether there had been theft or not; upon condemnation the flagrant thief was ignominiously hanged.[109] The suspected thief who did not succeed in legally establishing his innocence was not executed, but escaped on payment of a heavy fine. As was inevitable, the adamantine rigour of the law of theft led to very careful definition of the crime. It was distinguished from violent seizure, which was esteemed comparatively venial, from taking in ignorance, and even from taking without permission, provided that there was in this last case no attempt at concealment or denial.[110] Finally, a remarkable provision in some of the codes exempts from the doom of theft the starving man who, after begging for three days and receiving nothing, helps himself to the food which he needs to keep him alive.[111] That every man had the right to live was a principle of the law, and the sentiment of the country demanded that every person of substance should keep open house, not only for ordinary travellers, but also for the

[106] A loan-word from the Lat. affectus, which had in law the sense of "animus, consilium".

[107] So Ven. III. i. 11, where the question is argued on grounds of principle against the "rey" whose view is doubtless embodied in Dim. II. iii. 13.

[108] *Cf.* Maine, *Ancient Law*, tenth ed. (1885), pp. 378-9.

[109] The captured thief, apparently a mouse, but really a wizard in that shape, is destined for the gallows in the story of Manawyddan (*Mab.* 54-5).

[110] "Lledrad," "trais," "anoddeu" and "anghyfarch" are defined in Ven. III. ii. 52-5; Dim. III. vi. 23-6. There was no penalty for "anoddeu" and only a camlwrw for "anghyfarch".

[111] Dim. II. viii. 94 = Lat. B. II. x. 1.

destitute and the friendless. Giraldus did but state the position in round, set terms when he said: "Beggars are unknown among this people, for all houses are open to every one alike. Liberality, especially in the form of hospitable entertainment, is deemed by them to be the chief of virtues."[112]

It is scarcely necessary to say that criminal procedure exhibited little of that careful sifting of evidence which is characteristic of a modern law court. The business of the cantref authorities was to get the parties face to face and then to commit the issue to the arbitrament of the powers above, invoked on either side by solemn oaths. Every charge was made upon oath and, broadly speaking, had to be met in the same way, testimony as to the facts being usually not admitted. But the single oath of the accused was rarely sufficient to rebut the charge; the presumption was too strong against him, and he was required to clear himself by means of a "rhaith," or jury, who supported him in his protestation that he was innocent. In South Wales the "rhaith gwlad" or "jury of the country" upon which an accused person had to rely was apparently chosen from among the members of the court[113] and numbered no less than fifty men. What had originally been an appeal to heaven on the part of the man's kinsmen had become something very like an appeal to the public opinion of the cantref. The religious character of the proceedings was, however, never entirely forgotten; oaths were sworn upon relics of the saints, and, as special penalties were believed to be in reserve for the men who by perjury dishonoured these visible symbols of a power not yet defunct, there was great anxiety to secure and tender to the opposing party the relic which had the greatest fame in the district as the avenger of any false oath that might be sworn upon it.[114] Gospels were of less account in this respect than such precious objects as the torque of St. Cynog or the bell of St. David kept at Glascwm, for the saints of Wales, like those of Ireland, were held to be pitiless in vengeance when their ire was kindled by an indignity.[115]

The system of civil and criminal law which has been lightly

[112] Gir. Camb. vi. 182 (*Descr.* i. 10). [113] Dim. II. viii. 135, 136.

[114] For the seeking of relics see Ven. II. xxxi. 6; Dim. III. vi. 19; Gw. II. xxxvii. 1.

[115] Gir. Camb. vi. 26, 27 (*Itin.* i. 2), 130 (ii. 7).

CHAP. IX.

outlined in this section—and limits of space will not allow the treatment of the subject on a more extended scale—was not confined in its working to the cantref court. Its rules were observed in the supreme court, in which the "ynad llys" or royal judge decided the disputes of the circle surrounding the king, in the courts held by the "maer" and the "canghellor" for the villein hamlets of the cantref,[116] and in those, altogether exempt from royal jurisdiction, in which bishop and abbot dispensed justice to their tenants. Yet it may well be believed that the court of the cantref, representing the ancient tribal freedom, was its true source and that other courts borrowed from this, the oldest, their ideas as to law and legal procedure.

IV. The King.

From the earliest period at which it is possible to study the organisation of the Welsh tribes, they were under the rule of chiefs or kings, whose power was substantial and unquestioned, backed as it was by the possession of troops. Of Ireland it has been said that it is "doubtful whether the public force at the command of any ruler or rulers was ever systematically exerted through the mechanism of Courts of Justice".[117] The evidence for Wales is in quite the opposite direction; as has already been pointed out, the kings of Gildas were energetic in the administration of justice,[118] and in the codes the figure of the chief or "arglwydd" is everywhere the dominant one, securing the observance of the law and profiting heavily by its penalties. This much had been done for the Celts of Britain by the spectacle of the majesty of Roman justice; they never abandoned the conception of the magistrate as one who "beareth not the sword in vain". The law of Hywel was compiled at the instance of a chief; it began with and discussed on the amplest scale the rites and customs of the court; it protected the royal interests at every turn. No satisfactory view of the social and political institutions of the early Welsh is, therefore, to be obtained without taking into fullest account the position, the privileges and the power of the king.

116 The court of the "maerdref" appears clearly in Ven. I. xxxiv. 8; xxxvi. 10; II. xx. 3, and it may be inferred from II. xviii. 1 that there were similar courts, under the "maer" and the "canghellor," in the other unfree hamlets.

117 Maine, *Early History of Institutions*, third ed. 1880, p. 43.

118 P. 128.

The head of the tribe was no longer known by the old Celtic title of rêx or "rhi";[119] he was the "brenin," the "high" or "noble" one,[120] the "arglwydd," the "lord" or "master," and less commonly, the "tywysog," the "captain" or "leader".[121] He might be the lord of a single cantref, playing with all ceremony and dignity the part of a monarch on that narrow stage, or master of the fifteen cantrefs of Gwynedd, with a principal seat at Aberffraw. No distinction is made by the codes in respect of title or ordinary legal status between the great and the little chief; all are "brenhinoedd" and "arglwyddi" alike, and the supreme rulers of Deheubarth and of Gwynedd are only distinguished from their fellows by the larger amount due to them as compensation for dishonour[122] The number of minor chiefs is a standing characteristic of Welsh political history down to the age of the loss of national independence; while the successful ambition of the bolder princes, bent on conquest and aggrandisement, was a force which ever tended to reduce it, there was another which no less persistently worked in the direction of increase. This was the habit of regarding the kingdom as an ordinary estate, liable on the death of the owner to division among all his sons.

No rule is given in the codes on the important question of the succession to the crown. The one point which they make clear is that the matter was settled, not on the occurrence of a vacancy, but in anticipation, during the lifetime of the reigning chief. The "edling,"[123] or next successor, held a

[119] *Urk. Spr.* 230. "Rhi" appears in poetry only, and the feminine "rhiain" usually denotes "dame, lady" (*cf.* however, the "rieingylch" of Gw. II. xxxv. 2).

[120] *Urk. Spr.* 171; *Celt. Br.* (2), p. 282.

[121] *Urk. Spr.* 269. Though "tovisaci" appears in an early Welsh inscription (*Inscr. Chr.* No. 159; *W. Ph.* (2), p. 372; *Arch. Camb.* V. xv. (1898), 373-7), it is a title unknown to the laws, and appears to have come into ordinary use as a translation of the Lat. princeps. "Teyrn" (from "tegernos," *Urk. Spr.* 126) is occasionally found (*LL.* i. 342, 660, 678).

[122] For the use of "brenin" and "arglwydd" interchangeably see especially Ven. II. vi. 28; the "guastraut arglyides" of Lat. C. I. i. 24 is the "gwastrod y frenhines" (queen's groom or squire) of the other codes. Dim. I. ii. 5 is decisive as to the use of "brenin" for chiefs of the second rank.

[123] A loan-word from the English "ætheling" = one of noble or royal birth. The native term "gwrthrych" or "gwrthrychiad" is occasionally found; see Ven. I. v. 1 (MSS. B. D.); Dim. I. v. 1; Gw. I. xiii. 2; Lat. A. I. v. (heading); *Mab.* 105. "Gwrthrych" is literally "what is looked at, an object"; the edling probably got the name from his place in the royal hall, where he sat facing the king.

CHAP. IX.

prominent and honoured position in the court of every king; he had no land of his own, but was maintained by the royal bounty, being the chief personage in that motley company of officials, troopers, menials, youths and vagrants which made up the king's recognised following or "gosgordd". He was of the king's near kin, is described, indeed, as his son, his brother or his nephew, but it is nowhere said in the ancient authorities [124] that he was of necessity the eldest son, and might only be a brother, if sons were wanting. It is, therefore, possible that the edling, like the Irish tanist, at one time obtained his position by election and did not step into it by mere right of birth. On the other hand, it should be remembered that, owing to the existence of the office of "penteulu," or captain of the guard, one usually important reason for making the monarchy elective, *viz.*, the military needs of the tribe, did not here apply. And, if regard be had, not to the legal authorities, but to the historical facts, it will appear at once that what was customary was the succession of the eldest son to the principal part of the royal inheritance, with the assignment to younger sons of certain cantrefs of less importance. The completeness of the cantref in itself, as a political and economic area, made this a fatally easy policy, and the tendency to division was further encouraged, as Giraldus points out,[125] by the institution of fosterage. In accordance with ancient custom,[126] royal infants were not brought up at the court, but at a very tender age were placed under the care of foster-parents, to whom they became united by lifelong ties of affection. "Foster-father" and "foster-brother" were terms of respect and endearment, while kings' sons who were brethren by blood grew up strangers to each other, knowing each other as brothers only by repute. Moreover, as the foster-parents were uchelwrs of wealth and influence, each one a power in his own cantref, every claimant for a share in the division of the realm had behind him the weight of the support of some locality, desirous of honour for its favourite prince.

[124] *LL.* ii. 304 (xxxix. 2) is from Peniarth MS. 36*c*, which is not earlier than the end of the fifteenth century (Evans, *Rep.* i. p. 370).

[125] Gir. Camb. vi. 211-2 (*Descr.* ii. 4).

[126] The ancestors of St. Samson are described as "altrices regum"; see chap. v. note 107.

The privileges which fell to the lot of the successful candidate for the dignity of "brenin" were many and various. In the figurative language of the law, he had eight "pack-horses," or agencies which, without effort or trouble on his part, brought wealth and laid it at his feet.[127] One was the sea, for any wreckage which its waves might bring ashore was accounted royal spoil.[128] Another was the waste, the land claimed by no tref and subject to no kind of occupation; this he might grant to alltuds for settlement in return for a fee.[129] Another was the thief who, not having been caught with his theft in hand, was allowed to pay a price for his neck; that price was forfeit to the king. Another was the offender whose crime was expiated by the payment of a "dirwy," or the lesser offender who made his peace with a "camlwrw" of three kine; "dirwy" and "camlwrw" alike went to swell the wealth of the chieftain. Every man and every woman not subject to a lesser lordship paid to the crown a fee of specified amount, the woman on marriage, the man on succeeding to land or other property; the man's "ebediw" (often treated as a death duty) and the woman's "amobyr" were usually of the same amount, and it was a rule of law that neither was due from the same person more than once.[130] Most sweeping claim of all, the "brenin" was, in respect of movable property, treated as the universal heir in default of children. While the dead man's land might be claimed by any relative within the degree of second cousin, none but a son or a daughter could touch his cattle and household belongings, and if he had left no child, the "rhingyll" of the cantref forthwith made his appearance and seized the whole as the "marwdy" (house of death) of the lord. In South Wales, the influence of the Church had secured recognition of the right of a dying man to make bequests out of his property

127 Ven. I. xliii. 12 = Dim. II. xi. 2 = Lat. A. II. xii. = Lat. B. I. xx.

128 Ven. II. xvi. 6; Dim. II. xxiii. 37, 38.

129 The waste is always the king's (in Latin "desertum regis") and there is no trace of any authority exercised over it by the community or tribe. See Ven. II. xvi. 21; xviii. 7; Dim. II. xii. 9; Gw. I. xxxv. 1; Lat. A. I. xxvii. 2; Lat. B. II. xxiv. 19; xl. 21.

130 Ven. II. i. 55. The "ebediw" is the heriot of Anglo-Saxon law, as may be seen from the case of the "penteulu" (Ven. I. vii. 23) and from the fact that the portion of the ebediw of a king's villein anciently payable to the lord was sixty pence, *i.e.*, the value of an ox (Lat. A. II. xxii. 8). For the equality of "amobyr" and "ebediw" see Lat. B. II. xxxix. 5; *LL.* ii. 574.

CHAP. IX.

on his death-bed, and thus the lord only got a "marwdy" in case of sudden death. In Gwynedd it was not open to a man to bequeath anything he had, and even the goods of a bishop, save his books and official vestments, passed on his death into the royal hands.[131]

These manifold sources of income, being casual and uncertain in their nature, were not to be relied upon for the daily maintenance of the chief and his retinue. This was provided by a system of food renders, which were brought as tribute by free and bond subjects alike for consumption in the royal court of the cantref; the king had also, it should be added, his own demesne land, tilled for him by the aillts of the maerdref or hamlet of the court, and considerable use was made of the right of "cylch" or free quarters. There may have been a time when the king himself went on progress among his people, who received him in hospitable wise in their own homes;[132] in the laws, however, there is no mention of a royal "cylch" of this description, and only the members of the court appear as going on circuit. The queen, the captain of the guard with his men at arms, itinerant bards from another country, the royal horses, dogs, and hawks with their custodians, were at various seasons sent round the cantrefs, to quarter themselves chiefly upon the villeins. But the "gwest"[133] or entertainment of the king, if it ever took this form, had in historical times assumed a different aspect. The cantref was divided into a number of trefs, of which some were bond and some free; each tref was made jointly responsible for the render twice a year to the royal residence in the cantref of a specified quantity of food and provender. The tribute of the free tref was known by the honourable name of "gwestfa," or entertainment due; it was a "gwledd," or feast,[134] provided by a "cwynosog," or supperer,[135] who prob-

[131] The Venedotian rule appears clearly from Ven. II. i. 13; for its special application to bishops (but not abbots, whose goods passed to their convents), see *LL.* ii. 10 and the St. Asaph gravamina of 1276 (H. and St. i. 512). The South Welsh custom (of which there are traces in the north: *cf.* Ven. II. xxviii. 9, MS. D, and H. and St. i. 513, No. 7) is mentioned in Dim. II. viii. 62. "Cymynnu" is the Lat. commendo.

[132] This is suggested by the *Mab.* phrases "cylchu Dyfed" (46) and "cylchu ei wlad" (59) used of Pryderi and Math respectively.

[133] Used for "cylch" in Gw. I. xv. 13.

[134] Ven. I. ix. 25.

[135] Gw. II. xxxix. 45; xl. 8.

ably attended to represent his tref on the evening when it was consumed.[136] Its chief constituents were flour, beef, mead or other liquor of the kind, and oats for the horses;[137] in later times it might, instead of being paid in its original form, be commuted for the sum of one pound, and it is of interest to note that in 1352 the render of the free vill of Gloddaeth in Creuddyn to the Prince of Wales still stood at this amount.[138] The villein trefs, notwithstanding the extent to which they were burdened by the system of progresses, were not free from the liability to provide food; their contributions were known as "food gifts" and consisted chiefly of meat (mutton in summer, pork in winter), cheese, butter and loaves of bread.[139]

Thus the whole cantref worked together for the maintenance of the royal court which formed its centre. This was the "llys" or "castell," at one time also called the "manor" or "maenol".[140] Here were the king's summer pastures, ranged over by his great herds of cattle, the produce of fine and forfeit and border foray. Here was the "board land," tilled for the service of the court by the only Welsh villeins who, like those of mediæval England, gave their labour as the rent of their holdings. Here was the "maerdref," the hamlet in which they lived together at the castle gates, ruled by the "maer biswail," the "dung bailiff," whose epithet contemptuously distinguished him from the great "maer" or bailiff of the cantref And here was the group of buildings, enclosed within a strong wall, which constituted the royal palace of the Welsh

[136] *Cambro-Br. SS.* 156 mentions a dean of the "clas" of S. Woollo's, Newport, who "visitavit curiam Lisarcors apud inferiorem Guentoniam, convivio regali functus; sic consuetudo erat tunc temporis per patriam".

[137] The pork and bacon of Ven. II. xxvi. 1 do not find a place in the free renders of South Wales.

[138] *Rec. Carn.* 1.

[139] The Book of St. Chad furnishes two early instances of the renders of servile trefs; see *Lib. Land.* xlv. and chap. vii. note 105. The transference of the lordship from the tribal chief to the Church in these cases, typical of scores of others, did not, of course, affect the obligation of the tenants.

[140] "Maeno*r*" (in Gwynedd, "maeno*l*") is a word of undoubted native origin, occurring in the marginalia of the Book of St. Chad (*Lib. Land.* xlvii.). It has nothing to do with the English manor, but is connected with "maen" (stone); probably it was first applied to the stone-girt residence of the chief, so as to distinguish it from the ordinary tref. Thence were derived the later meanings—(i) group of villein trefs (Lat. A. II. xiii. 9); (ii) a division of the cymwd in Gwynedd, scarcely to be distinguished from the ordinary tref (Ven. II. xvii.). For fuller discussion see *Cymr.* xi. 32-4, 57-8; *W. People*, pp. 218-9.

CHAP. IX.

chief. The testimony of Giraldus is hardly needed to convince us that the Welsh of his day had no lofty stone-built towers or stately halls;[141] for the language of the codes and the poverty in remains of such sites as Aber and Aberffraw show indubitably that all the buildings of the "llys" were timber structures, more substantial, no doubt, than those of the ordinary free household, yet essentially temporary and of little value. Security was not neglected; the castle wall had a gate, narrowly watched by a porter, whose house was just behind it; the place was strong enough to be used for the custody of prisoners;[142] and all night long, from the evening horn-blast until the opening of the gate in the morning, the watchman, a freeman of the country who had no daylight responsibilities, kept a close vigil and guarded the castle from nocturnal attack. But the buildings so protected were of the simplest kind.[143] The chief was the "neuadd" or hall, an oblong structure resting on six wooden uprights, of which two were placed at the one end, with the door between them, and two at the other; the central couple, having between them the open hearth, divided the hall into an upper section, or "cyntedd," where the king and the greater officials sat at their meat, and a lower section, or "is cyntedd," assigned to the less distinguished members of the royal train. Next in importance was the chamber, or "ystafell"; this was the king's private apartment, where he passed the night,[144] and it was also the queen's ordinary day-room, since it was not in accordance with ancient custom for women to join in the festivities of the neuadd. The outhouses or subordinate structures included a kitchen and larder, a mead brewery, a kiln or drying-house, a stable, a barn and a dog-house. All these the villeins of the cantref were to put up and keep in repair, a further proof, if one were needed, that they were of light construction and called for no exercise of the builder's art.

The king was served by a number of officers, whose duties

[141] Gir. Camb. vi. 200-1 (*Descr.* i. 17).

[142] Ven. I. xxxvi. 6; Dim. I. xxii. 2; Gw. I. xxxix. 7; Lat. A. I. xviii. 7; Lat. B. I. xxi. 16.

[143] In *Mab.* 46 mention is made of "tei y llys" at Arberth and in particular of the "neuadd," "ystafell" (so *Wht. Bk.*), "bundy," "meddgell" and "cegin".

[144] "Ystafell y brenin yr hon y bo yn cysgu ynddi" (Ven. I. xi. 4).

and privileges were carefully defined by the laws. Each had his appointed seat in the neuadd when the court was gathered together for the evening's festivity, each his proper lodging for the night in or about the castell, each his horse from the royal stable and his clothing from the royal store. The most responsible was the judge of the court, who decided all the disputes of the court and was, moreover, the king's perpetual counsellor, always with him, and required to be always sober.[145] He was admitted to his office at a solemn ceremony held in the chapel of the court, when he swore to do justice; he then received the symbols of his dignity, a throw-board from the king and a gold ring from the queen.[146] The judge of the court was the official examiner of all candidates for minor judicial posts in Gwynedd;[147] the great gate of the castle was thrown open to receive him, and he slept at night either in the king's chamber or with his head on the cushion on which the king had sat in the neuadd on the previous day. Thus was concrete expression given to the idea, which redounds not a little to the credit of a warlike people, that "judgeship is the greatest of all temporal things".[148] Other officers of the first rank were the "offeiriad teulu" or court priest, who was the king's secretary and the incumbent of the royal chapel, the "distain" or steward,[149] who was in supreme control of the castle, its furniture and the store of food and drink within it, and the "gwas ystafell" or chamberlain, who looked after the ystafell, guarded the royal treasure, and was the king's special messenger. A chief falconer, a chief huntsman, and a chief groom, each with a troop of underlings, had custody of the hawks, the dogs, and the horses which ministered to the outdoor recreations of the court. For the minstrelsy of the neuadd the "bardd teulu," or court poet, was responsible, though the pencerdd, or chaired bard, the head of the bardic fraternity in his country, might occasionally be present and in that case would take the lead. There were also attached to the court a physician, a mead-brewer, a cook, a doorkeeper, a candle-bearer, a smith, a woodman (who replenished the hearth),

[145] Ven. I. xliii. 1; Dim. II. viii. 19, 110.
[146] Dim. I. xiv. 20, 21.
[147] Ven. III. preface.
[148] Gw. I. xiii. 29.
[149] The "distain" is the English "discthegn" (Cod. Dipl. No. 715—*cf.* Kemble, *Saxons in England*, ii. p. 109).

CHAP. IX.

and a cupbearer. The footholder held the king's feet in his lap during the evening's revelry and guarded him from mischance during the riotous hours of carousal; the silentiary, who through the day was the distain's agent and deputy, struck the pillar opposite the king, and from time to time demanded silence; the rhingyll, the usher of the commote court, had also duties in the neuadd, for it was his business to stand in front of the hearth and protect the timber-built hall from the destruction by fire in which the recklessness of the festive company might but too easily involve it.

But beyond a doubt the most important element in the constitution of the court was the "teulu". In modern Welsh this word signifies "family," and there has been in consequence a very general failure to understand the nature of the old institution so termed, efforts being made to interpret it in terms of kinship.[150] As a matter of fact, members of a royal "teulu" were completely divorced from family life, for the word has in this connection its original meaning of "house-host,"[151] and the "gŵr ar deulu" was a guardsman or trooper, belonging to the royal bodyguard or standing company of household troops.[152] The teulu was a body of horsemen, fed, clothed and mounted by the king and in constant attendance upon him.[153] It was commanded by the "penteulu," or captain of the guard, who was always a near relative of the reigning chief and in his absence took his place in the hall.[154] The company might number as many as one hundred and twenty,[155] and it is easy to see that the possession of this little force, constantly under arms, was a source of great strength to the lord of a cantref in his dealings with his subjects. All the more was this the case in that the loyalty of the teulu was no mere affair of contract;

[150] *Camb. Reg.* i. 205.

[151] *Gr. Celt.* (2), p. 1068; *Urk. Spr.* 321. "Gosgordd" had anciently the same sense; see *Gr. Celt.* (2), p. 1067 (Familia, *goscor pi teilu*).

[152] Ven. I. vii. 13 makes this definition certain.

[153] Ven. I. vii. 16, 22; *LL.* ii. 68 (§ 69).

[154] In *Mab.* 144 Madog ap Maredudd of Powys offers his brother Iorwerth the office of "penteulu". Their father Maredudd appears to have been "penteulu" to his nephew Owain ap Cadwgan in 1113 (*Bruts*, 291). None but very late authorities use the term to denote an ordinary pater familias.

[155] This was the number of each of the three faithful and of the three faithless warbands (*Mab.* 305); Gruffydd ap Llywelyn had a warband of 140 in 1047 (*Trans. Cymr.* 1899-1900, 132-3, 168-9).

the bond which united its members to their lord was one of sentiment and honour, and it was held to be their duty to cling to him in the hour of his sorest need, to die in his defence and, if need should be, even in his stead. "Three faithless warbands of the Isle of Britain," runs an ancient triad, "the warband of Gronw the Radiant of Penllyn, who refused to receive instead of their lord the poisoned shaft aimed by Llew Llaw Gyffes; the warband of Gwrgi and Peredur, who deserted their lords at Caer Greu, and they under bond to fight Eda of the Great Knee on the morrow, in which fight they were both slain; and the warband of Alan Fergant, who stealthily left their lord on the road to Camlan—the number of each of these warbands was one hundred and twenty men."[156] In the teulu, in short, is to be found the Welsh representative of the English warband or company of gesiths; one may go still further back and say it embodies the spirit of the "comitatus," as described by Tacitus in his account of the Teutonic foreworld. In Wales, as in the primeval forests of Germany, it was a lifelong disgrace for the warrior-client to return alive from the battle-field on which the master lay dead; to defend the life and honour of one's lord, to make all one's own achievements merely tributary to his renown, was the holiest of obligations.[157]

It is abundantly clear that the teulu was not merely used by the king to suppress domestic disorder and to repel external enemies. A plundering expedition into a "gorwlad" or neighbouring kingdom is treated by the laws as an ordinary incident in the routine of its duties, and minute directions are given for the division of the spoil, which, it is assumed, will be chiefly in the form of cattle.[158] Once a year, indeed, for a period of six weeks, the king might lead, not the teulu merely, but all the men of his realm upon a warlike incursion into some distant land; even the aillts sent from each villein tref a man with an axe and a pack-horse to make rough quarters for the host.[159] Yet life was not quite so hazardous and insecure as

[156] Triad i. 35 = ii. 42 (*Mab.* 305) = iii. 81. The story of Gronw will be found in *Mab.* 80; "Eda Glinfawr (or gawr)" is Eata, father of Archbishop Egbert (*Hist. Britt.* c. 61), whose association with Gwrgi and Peredur (*ob. circa* 580) is an anachronism.

[157] Tacitus, *Germania*, cap. xiv.

[158] Ven. I. vii. 14, 18; xi. 11; xiv. 7; Dim. I. xvii. 11; xviii. 2.

[159] Ven. I. xliii. 15; II. xix. 7, 11; Dim. II. xi. 5, 6; Gw. II. xxxv. 2, 7; Lat. A. I. xxvi. 1; Lat. B. I. xviii. 12, 17.

CHAP. IX.

these plans for systematic border warfare would suggest. The lands of the church enjoyed unbroken peace, and, as they were extensive and often lay along the borders of cantrefs, the points at which a conflict might take place were not so numerous as might at first be supposed. Moreover, it was not the fashion to fight at all seasons of the year, for instance, in the middle of winter, when the weather was cold and cattle were out of condition.[160] Such limitations as these explain the popular saying quoted by Giraldus, that the eagle knows the place where it may find its booty, but not the time, while the raven, that other grim satellite of war and carnage, can tell the time, but knows not the place.[161]

NOTE TO CHAPTER IX.—*The Triads of Dyfnwal Moelmud.*

In the royal pedigrees in Harleian MS. 3859 a "Dumngual moilmut" appears as a grandson of Coel Hên and grandfather of "Morcant bulc," who may be the "Morcant" of *Hist. Britt.* c. 63. This reference makes it likely that there was a historical person who bore the name, a Northern British prince flourishing about A.D. 500. The next mention of Dyfnwal Moelmud is in the *Historia Regum* of Geoffrey of Monmouth, who makes him the son of Cloten, king of Cornwall, and ruler over all Britain about 450 B.C. Dyfnwal is represented as the author of the "leges quae Molmutinae dicebantur . . . quae usque ad hoc tempus inter Anglos celebrantur"; they dealt with such matters as the right of sanctuary in temples and the peace of the great roads, and were translated from the original British into Latin by Gildas and by King Alfred from Latin into English (*Hist. Reg.* ii. 17; iii. 5). It is surely a mistake to find in these particulars any echo of an old tradition current among the Welsh as to Dyfnwal, which handed down his name as the primeval British legislator; the "Molmutine" laws of Geoffrey are in repute, not in Wales, but in England, and are extant in the English tongue. A much more natural explanation presents itself; Geoffrey, who undoubtedly used the old Welsh pedigrees as a quarry for proper names, found there his "Dunwallo Molmutius" and was subsequently led, by some haphazard similarity of names, to ascribe to him certain old English laws of the same general character as those embodied in "Leges Henrici Primi" and similar compilations. Such a course would have been quite consistent with his literary methods, as witness his assignment of the Mercian law ("Merchenelage" in the Berne MS.), also said to have been translated into English by Alfred, to an early British queen of the name of Marcia (iii. 13).

In the Codes there is no mention of Dyfnwal, save in one passage (Ven. II. xvii.) of the Venedotian Code, where he appears as the author of the institutions, and, in particular, of the measures of length and of area in force in the island until the age of Hywel Dda. It is pretty certain that this Code was compiled about the beginning of the thirteenth century, in an age when the narrative of Geoffrey had become the common literary property of Western Europe, and when one finds Dyfnwal described in it as "mab iarll Cernyw," the conclusion

[160] The teulu left the king and went on progress after Christmas (Ven. I. vii. 22).

[161] Gir. Camb. vi. 136 (*Itin.* ii. 9).

is inevitable that the lawyer's ideas on this subject were derived, not from native tradition, but from the pages of romance. Genuine Welsh tradition knows, in fact, nothing of this shadowy figure but his name (*cf. Mab.* 109); he is not mentioned in the older triads and first makes his appearance in the untrustworthy third series (Nos. 4, 11, 36, 57, 58).

In 1807 the editors of the *Myvyrian Archaiology* printed in their third volume (pp. 283-318) "Triodd Dyvnwal Moelmud, a elwir Triodd y Cludau a Thriodd y Cargludau," to the number of thirty-four, followed by a much more bulky collection of "Triodd Gwladoldeb a Chywladoldeb," numbering 248. The MS. was a transcript made in 1685 by Thomas ab Ifan of Tre Bryn, near Coychurch in Glamorgan, "o hen lyfrau Syr Edward Mawnsel o Vargam" (1634-1706). Its originals are not now known to exist, and can in no case have been much older than the sixteenth century. In language and spirit the triads are thoroughly modern, and everything goes to show that they are the work of some Glamorganshire antiquary who at the close of the Middle Ages adopted this vehicle for the expression of his political aspirations, delineating the Wales that he desired to see under the guise of a description of a golden age in the prehistoric past. The writer had obviously a considerable knowledge of the old Welsh system, but in his day it was largely obsolete and accordingly he often goes astray in a manner which would not have been possible for a genuine Welsh lawyer. A conspicuous instance is the way in which he confounds the "alltud" and the "aillt," *e.g.*, in No. 66, "aillt neu estron a wladycho yng Nghymru". The statements made as to certain persons having a "spear allowance" for their support (Nos. 166, 199, 200, 239, 240) receive no warrant from any other authority and seem to rest on a misunderstanding of the "ceiniog baladr" or "spear penny" which could be claimed in certain cases by those who were making up the amount of a "galanas" fine. A similar mistake is probably at the root of the theory advanced that every Cymro was entitled to five free erws (Nos. 61, 65, 68, 70, etc.); No. 83 adds "cyfar gobaith" or "co-tillage of the waste," but neither the erws nor the co-tillage find any place in the genuine old documents and it is probable that the former, ample as is the space they occupy in the compiler's ideal reconstruction, have been evolved out of the four erws of the home croft which went with each homestead when a proprietor's land was divided on his death.

It will thus be seen that the Triads of Dyfnwal Moelmud (= book xiii. in *LL.* ii.) are not only valueless as records of the age before Hywel Dda, but do not even furnish good evidence as to ordinary questions of Welsh law and custom in a later age. One cannot but feel that to use them, in however guarded a fashion, is to introduce an element of unreality into the discussion of the history of Welsh institutions, and in the foregoing pages they have been left entirely out of account.

CHAPTER X.

THE AGE OF THE SEA-ROVERS.

(Asser and the various editions and versions (*B.T.* and B. *Saes.*) of the *Annales Cambriae* have supplied most of the material for this chapter. Mr. Stevenson's edition of the *Vita Ælfredi*, Green's *Conquest of England*, and Todd's *War of the Gaedhil with the Gaill*, among modern books I have used with great profit.)

I. The Coming of the Northmen.

CHAP. X.

WITH the opening of the ninth century a new element entered into the history of Western Europe, which profoundly affected the course of events in every country between the Baltic and the Mediterranean. The Western Seas, undisturbed since the Low German marauders had made their home in Britain by the shadow of war or piracy, and fearlessly used as a peaceful highway by monastic pilgrims without number, suddenly swarmed with fierce and intrepid buccaneers, whose vessels sailed from Scandinavian creeks to the uttermost parts of Europe, and whose piratical impulses were not tempered by the least tincture of respect for the Christian religion. The advent of the Northman everywhere marked a new era, checked the growth of the nascent civilisation which was slowly rising out of the ruins of the old, gave the reins of power to prowess and physical force, and created the feudal system. No region was more thoroughly shaken by the Norse inroads than the British Isles; in few countries did they leave a more lasting impression, and it becomes important, therefore, to consider in what manner they affected Wales.

The fact soon becomes evident that, much as the country was exposed to the attacks of the Northmen, and long as it continued to be in danger from them, their total effect was comparatively slight. Further research may yet establish points

CHAP. X.

of contact between the Welsh and the old Norse language[1] and literature, and even between the institutions of the two races, but the salient fact remains that nowhere on Welsh soil was there any permanent Scandinavian settlement. History records no sustained attempt at anything of the kind, and, if it be replied that the contemporary annals are meagre, it may be added that the evidence of Welsh place names does but confirm the negative conclusion drawn from the silence of the chroniclers. There is, it need hardly be said, abundant evidence of the familiarity of the sea-rovers with the features of the Welsh coast; headland, islet and harbour still bear the names which were given them by the bold navigators who cruised around them on their adventurous quests, and the Norse names, through the medium of English, are now more widely known than the original Celtic ones. Thus the ancient Môn became "Anglesey,"[2] the "island of the strait"; "Gwales," far out in the Western Sea, became "Grasholm," the "grassy islet";[3] "Abergwaun" became "Fishguard," the "place of fish".[4] Holms, like Priestholm and Flatholm, fiords like Milford and Haverford, wicks like Goodwick and Oxwich, eys like Ramsey, Caldy and Swansea tell their tale of Scandinavian flitting to and fro among the rocks and inlets of the Welsh seaboard.[5] But all traces of the Northmen disappear as one leaves high-water mark and strikes inland. Even in Pembrokeshire, where the undoubted evidences of Teutonic settlement on a large scale have been connected by some writers with the viking movement, it is clear on examination of the place names in point that they are much

[1] Prof. Kuno Meyer informs me that there are but two loan-words of undoubted Norse origin in Welsh, *viz.*, "iarll" and "tarian".

[2] See note 99 to chap. vi. Angle, on Milford Haven, also takes its name from the strait (old Norse ōngull) at the mouth of the Haven (Owen, *Pemb.* i. 322).

[3] *Mab.* 40, 41; Owen, *Pemb.* i. 112; *Lit. Eng.* p. 72. The thirteenth-century MS. of the *De Excidio* of Gildas known as Camb. Ff. I. 27 has a marginal note stating that the work was written in "Guales insula marina" (ed. Mommsen, 11), so that this lonely islet, like many another of its kind, was traditionally associated with the early anchorites of Wales.

[4] Owen, *Pemb.* i. 225 (note by Sir John Rhys).

[5] A list (which, however, requires some revision) is given of the Welsh names of this class in Taylor, *Words and Places*, pp. 117-8 (1888 ed.). The early forms of Swansea, *viz.*, Sweinesie (Gir. Camb. vi. 73, reading of MSS. R. B.), Sweynesia (*ibid.* 172), Sweinesham (*Ann. Marg. s.a.* 1212), Sweynese (*Ann. C.* p. 109), and "Sweynesse" (*Tax. Nich.* 272), show that it is unconnected with "swan" or "sea" and is really the "ey" of some piratical Sweyn.

CHAP. X.

more likely to be of Anglo-Norman than of Scandinavian origin.[6] The prevailing element is the English "-ton"; no instance is to be found of the Northern "-by".[7] Williamston and Johnston and Jeffreyston are intermingled with Gumfridston and Herbrandston and Haroldston in such a manner as to forbid the assumption that we have to do with a heathen settlement of the viking age, and the historian is relieved from the necessity of finding a place for an encroachment upon the kingdom of Dyfed of which no hint is to be found in the ancient chronicle of St. David's or in the laws of Hywel the Good.

But, if there was no colonisation, such as took place in East Anglia, in the Hebrides, around Dublin and York, there were marauding expeditions without number; in this respect Wales had no immunity. The attacks probably began as soon as the viking boats had learnt to range over the seas which divide Ireland from Great Britain, that is to say, in the closing years of the eighth century. If, as seems most probable, the Isle of Man was visited in 798,[8] Anglesey cannot have had a long respite and the monastic communities of Ynys Seiriol, Caer Gybi, and Bangor must have early borne the brunt of an attack which was specially directed against the defenceless sanctuaries of the Celtic coast. The "gentiles," or heathen folk, as they are termed in the Welsh annals, are first definitely recorded as having relations with Wales in an annal of the year 850, when they are said to have slain a certain Cyngen;[9] three years later Anglesey was ravaged by the "black gentiles".[10] Isolated notices like these merely afford a glimpse of what must have been going on

[6] Taylor (*loc. cit.*) and Laws (*Lit. Eng.* pp. 70-3) argue in favour of a Norse settlement, but Rhys and Jones (*W. People*, p. 27) will allow nothing substantial, and the Rev. J. Sephton, in a letter from which I am kindly permitted to quote, says that he "can see nothing very distinctively Norse" in the -ton names of Pembrokeshire and therefore is "compelled to regard the wicking settlement as doubtful".

[7] Tenby is not an instance, since it is merely a corruption of the Welsh Dinbych, well attested as the ancient name of the place. See chap. viii. note 213.

[8] Todd, *War of G. and G.* Introd. xxxv.

[9] Harl. MS. 3859 (*Cymr.* ix. 165) has "cinnen," for which "cincen" should no doubt be read, in harmony with *Ann.* C. MS. B., *B.T.* and B. *Saes.*

[10] Harl. MS. 3859 (*ibid.*). The "gentiles nigri" are the Dubhgaill or "dark foreigners" of the Irish Chronicles, who appear upon the scene in 851 and contest with the Finngall or "white foreigners" the possession of Ireland. The two sets of invaders are believed to have been Danes and Norsemen respectively (Todd, *War of G. and G.* Introd. lxii).

in Wales throughout the ninth century; they suggest, without describing, an era of general devastation and insecurity, the detailed history of which can never be written. No doubt there were parts of the country which offered little temptation to the invader; the rocks of Eryri and Meirionydd, the uplands of Ceredigion and Ystrad Tywi gave scanty scope for plunder or profitable settlement, and the viking ships seem rarely to have visited the broad expanse of Cardigan Bay.[11] But the corn lands of Anglesey, so open to attack by sea, the pleasant creeks and anchorages of Dyfed, and the fertile regions to which the Severn estuary gave easy access were beyond a doubt exposed to continual inroads, a few of which have been recorded, while scar and holm and wick tell vaguely of the rest.

In Wales, as in other parts of Western Europe, the attacks of the Northmen shook society to its foundations and in particular did fatal injury to the work of culture carried on at the religious centres, but, as the crisis produced in Wessex a deliverer in the person of Alfred, so among the Welsh it brought to the front a new dynasty, which henceforth sways the destinies alike of the North and of the South until the extinction of native rule.

II. THE HOUSE OF KHODRI THE GREAT.

Upon the death of Hywel ap Rhodri Molwynog in 825, the direct male line of Maelgwn Gwynedd appears to have come to an end. A stranger possessed himself of the throne of Gwynedd and the royal seat of Aberffraw. Merfyn Frych (the Freckled) was descended from Llywarch Hên; his father, Gwriad, had married a daughter of Cynan ap Khodri, so that he was not altogether without a hereditary claim to the crown, but it was a claim which would probably have been of little account had it not been backed by personal force and distinction.[12] Merfyn came, according to bardic tradition, "from the land of Manaw,"[13]

[11] No place name of Scandinavian origin is to be found between Bardsey and Fishguard, with the doubtful exception of Harlech (*W. People*, p. 27).

[12] Merfyn is the "Mermini regis" of *Hist. Britt.* c. 16; see note 145 to chap. vii. above. His paternal ancestry is given in *Buch. Gr. ap* C. 30 (721) and Jesus Coll. MS. 20 (*Cymr.* viii. 87); for his mother Etthil or Ethyllt see Harl. MS. 3859 (*Cymr.* ix. 169); *Celt. Folklore*, p. 480.

[13] "Meruin vrych o dir manaw" ("Synchronisms of Merlin" in *IV. Anc. Bks.* ii. p. 222; *Myv. Arch.* I. 141 (110)).

CHAP. X.

and may thus be supposed to have appeared on the scene to put an end to the confusion which ensued on the death of Hywel, though whether his starting-point was the Isle of Man or that other Manaw on the banks of the Forth where it is more natural to look for a scion of Llywarch Hên, must remain an open question.[14] He established himself firmly in Gwynedd and allied himself to the royal house of Powys by marrying Nest, daughter of Cadell ap Brochwel.[15] For nineteen years he maintained his power against all rivals and against the Danish irruptions, and on his death in 844 he was able to hand it on to his son Rhodri, surnamed the Great.[16]

No one will contest the right of Rhodri to a title which he earned, not only by strenuous and gallant resistance to the northern marauders, but even more by his success in uniting the greater part of Wales, so long divided into petty states, in a single realm. The kingdom he founded, though it did not retain its unity for any length of time, afforded future ages an instance of what could be achieved in this direction and set before ambitious princes a goal towards which their efforts might be directed. How deeply his countrymen were impressed by his achievements may be seen from the hold which his dynasty acquired upon Wales; to be of the blood of Khodri Mawr was henceforth the first qualification for rule, alike in Gwynedd and in Deheubarth. The story of Rhodri's rise to supreme power has not been preserved for us by any chronicler, but the two principal steps may be dated within a year or two and partially explained. The first was the acquisition of Powys; it was in 855 that Cyngen, the last of the ancient dynasty of that region, died a pilgrim at Rome, whither he had

[14] Skene (*IV. Anc. Bks.* i. p. 94) favoured Manaw Gododin, as did the present writer in the *Dict. Nat. Biog.* (1894). But the discovery in 1896 in the Isle of Man of an inscription of about the ninth century which runs "Crux Guriat" (The Cross of Gwriad) undoubtedly strengthens the case for the insular origin of Merfyn (*Zeit. Celt. Ph.* i. 48-53).

[15] Jesus Coll. MS. 20 (*Cymr.* viii. 87). This account, harmonising as it does with Harl. MS. 3859, is to be preferred to the common one, which reverses matters, making Nest the mother of Merfyn and Ethyllt or Esyllt his wife.

[16] "Annus cccc. mermin moritur. gueith cetill" (Harl. MS. 3859 in *Cymr.* ix. 165). The attempt of *Gw. Brut* (*s.a.* 838) to connect these two notices ("Gwaith Cyfeiliawc, lle bu ymladd tra thost rhwng y Cymry a Berthwryd (*i.e.*, Burhred) brenin Mers, ac yno y lladdwyd Merfyn Prych") is a good instance of the way in which the compiler of this version of the *Brut* supplied the lack of material by pure invention.

been driven by old age and misfortune;[17] if he left sons, which seems unlikely, they were forthwith ousted by Rhodri, who through his mother Nest was the old king's nephew.[18] Defeat had perhaps abated somewhat the high spirit of the men of Powys and prepared them to accept a deliverer from the fastnesses of Snowdon; for of late it had gone hardly with them in the perennial conflict with Mercia. Mercian greatness was, indeed, at an end, but with the rise of a new power in the South a new danger had arisen; the Mercians, no longer standing in their own strength, had begun to invoke the aid of their West Saxon overlords, and in 830 Egbert, in 853 Æthelwulf had led armies against the Welsh whose victories were no doubt chiefly gained at the expense of the border realm of Powys.[19] The second acquisition of importance made by Rhodri was that of Seisyllwg, the state formed rather more than a century earlier by the union of Ceredigion and Ystrad Tywi. This addition to his realm must have been made soon after 872, when Gwgon, the last of the kings of Ceredigion, met his death by drowning;[20] Rhodri's marriage to Angharad, the dead king's sister, while it gave him no sort of legal claim to the province, made it easy for him to intervene and invested his sons with rights there which would be more generally recognised.[21] At his death Rhodri held in his grasp the whole of North Wales and such portion of the South as was not included in the kingdoms of Dyfed, Brycheiniog, Gwent and Glywysing.

Despite these successes, Khodri was at no period of his long reign free from the menace of Danish invasion. Refer-

[17] "Cinnen (read Cincen) rex pouis in roma obiit" (Harl. MS. 3859 in *Cymr.* ix. 165—for the pedigree see *ibid.* 181). The year implied is 854, but there is reason to think that from about 850 this chronicle is one year behind the true reckoning. See especially the entry under 866, instead of 867, of the fall of York and the assignment to 878 of the death of Aedh Finnliath, an event known from the precise chronological data in *Chron. Scot.* to have occurred in 879. *Chron. Scot.* is believed to be correct from 805 to 904 (Introd. xlvi).

[18] Three sons of Cyngen are mentioned in Harl. MS. 3859, pedigree No. xxxi. (*Cymr.* ix. 182), but they do not appear in the chronicle as kings of Powys and probably did not survive their father.

[19] *A.S. Chr.*, 828 (for the true date see Plummer, ii. 73); *ibid.* 853 (*cf.* Asser, c. 7). It will be observed that Green (*Conq. Eng.* (2), p. 80) has hastily credited Æthelwulf with a conquest of Anglesey which was really a Danish achievement (see note 10 above).

[20] Harl. MS. 3859, *s.a.* 871 (*Cymr.* ix. 166).

[21] Jesus Coll. MS. 20 in *Cymr.* viii. 87 (No. xxi.).

CHAP. X.

ence has already been made to the ravaging of Anglesey in 853 (or 854) by the Dubhgaill or "black" Danes who had newly appeared in Irish waters and attacked the earlier settlers of Norse origin. In 856 Rhodri avenged himself by killing their leader Horm.[22] Nevertheless, he is still found fighting the "black gentiles" at the close of his life; the "gwaith dyw Sul" or "Sunday's fight" fought in Anglesey in 877[23] must have been an encounter with a heathen foe, and its issue is shown by the statement in the Irish Chronicles that Khodri, king of the Welsh, in this year sought safety in Ireland from the attacks of the "black gentiles".[24] In the following year he was back in Wales, to fall a victim, along with his son (or brother) Gwriad, to English enmity.[25] The manner of his death is unknown, but that the loss was fiercely resented may be gathered from the fact that a rout of the English some years later was triumphantly hailed as "God's vengeance for the slaughter of Khodri".

Six sons were left by Khodri to carry on his line, and, after a fashion which, to the injury of the country, widely prevailed in mediæval Wales, his broad realm, so laboriously built up, was divided between them. Little is known of the distribution of the various provinces,—indeed, only three of the sons, Anarawd, Cadell and Merfyn, are mentioned by name in contemporary records.[26] But it is clear that Anarawd, as the eldest, took possession of Anglesey and the adjacent parts of Gwynedd, and most probable that Cadell received as his share a substantial domain in South Wales, where his descendants ruled for many generations. What portion fell to Merfyn can only be conjectured, for he founded no house and nothing is recorded of him in authentic sources save the bare fact of his death.[27] This is nevertheless known of the sons of Rhodri, on

[22] *Ann. Ult. s.a.* 855; *Chron. Scot. s.a.* 856.

[23] "Gueith diu sul in mon" (Harl. MS. 3859 in *Cymr.* ix. 166).

[24] *Ann. Ult. s.a.* 876; *Chron. Scot. s.a.* 877.

[25] "Rotri et filius eius guriat (MS. B., *B.T.* and B. *Saes.* have "frater" and "brawd") a saxonibus iugulatur" (Harl. MS. 3859). *Ann. Ult. s.a.* 877 (=878) also says that Rhodri was slain by the English.

[26] Jesus Coll. MS. 20 (*Cymr.* viii. 87, No. xx.) gives the names of the other three as "Aidan, Meuruc, Morgant".

[27] Anarawd is described by an editor of Nennius who wrote in 912 as "regis Moniae, id est mon, qui regit modo regnum Wenedotiae regionis, id est Guernet" (*Hist. Britt.* ed. Mommsen, p. 146). That he was the eldest son may be inferred

the testimony of their contemporary, Asser of St. David's,[28] that they were a vigorous brood, working strenuously together for the overthrow of the remaining dynasties of the south. In Dyfed, Hyfaidd ap Bledri, himself the terror of the wealthy "clas" of St. David's, dreaded the violence of the new lords of Seisyllwg; in Brycheiniog, Elise ap Tewdwr, of the line of old Brychan, also feared for his crown; and, though for the moment Hywel ap Rhys of Glywysing[29] and Brochwel and Ffernfael ap Meurig of Gwent were chiefly perturbed by the activity of the Mercians, they too had much to apprehend from any revolution which might establish the house of Rhodri in Brycheiniog. Thus arose the political situation which is described by Asser as having existed for a good many years at the date of his composition of the life of Alfred in 893.

That great king's famous victory over the Danes in 878 had given him a commanding position in Southern Britain. Not only did he gain undisputed authority over the whole of Wessex, but, on the death about this time of Ceolwulf, the last king of Mercia, he assumed the control of as much of the ancient province as remained in English hands, while entrusting its actual rule to an ealdorman named Æthelred, with the hand of his daughter Æthelflæd. It was but natural that the minor Welsh kings should seek from Alfred the protection which his known love of justice would dispose him to give, and thus it came about that Hyfaidd, Elise, Hywel, Brochwel and Ffernfael all placed themselves under his patronage and became

from the prominence assigned to him by Asser and from the fact that he held his father's paternal inheritance. Late authorities furnish full details, which grow more precise as time goes on, as to the division of Wales between the sons of Rhodri Mawr; see Gir. Camb. vi. 166-7 (*Descr.* i. 2, 3); Powel, 29; *Gw. Brut. s.a.* 873; *Iolo MSS.* 30-1. Even the earliest of these accounts is full of errors; the statement of Giraldus that Cadell survived his brothers and thus obtained for himself and his descendants the monarchy of all Wales is in flat opposition to the testimony of the chronicles and was no doubt concocted to support certain South Welsh claims; he has further complicated matters by transposing Merfyn and Anarawd and making the former's daughter Afandreg a son.

28 In c. 80 of the life of Alfred (ed. Wise, pp. 49-50; *Mon. Hist. Br.* 488; Stev. 66-7) there is a most valuable account of Welsh politics in the period 880-93, and the ease with which the author moves in a field in which a later forger would have infallibly shown his ignorance is a weighty argument in favour of the authenticity of the work (Stev. lxxv.).

29 I think it very unlikely that this is the Hywel whose death at Rome is recorded in Harl. MS. 3859, *s.a.* 885, since Hywel ap Rhys is associated in *Lib. Land.* 236, with Bishop Cyfeiliog of Llandaff, who belongs to the tenth century.

CHAP. X.

the vassals of a monarch who could succour them by land and by sea. Asser explains, in his apology for his desertion of his native St. David's, how the situation thus created enabled him to serve his beloved monastery even better at Alfred's court than he could have done at home; the friend and companion of Hyfaidd's overlord was in a position to set limits to Hyfaidd's tyranny in a way impossible for the simple bishop of St. David's.

It was now the turn of Anarawd and his brothers to find their power fettered and their triumphant progress brought to a stand. With Mercia they had contended not unequally; a raid upon Eryri conducted by Æthelred in 881 had been arrested by Anarawd at the mouth of the Conway, and the victory of Cymryd—the day of divine vengeance for Khodri—had been won with great slaughter of the foe.[30] In order to secure himself against further attacks from Mercia, Anarawd had then entered into an alliance with the Danish king of York, whose realm, embracing as it did the ancient Deira, extended to the Mersey and possibly took in also the peninsula of Wirral. But the Danes proved indifferent allies, and gradually Anarawd came to the conclusion that it was his interest also, no less than that of the minor chieftains of the country, to make his peace with the strong ruler of Wessex. He found Alfred in no wise loth to respond to his advances; paying him a ceremonious visit at his court—the first of the kind on record paid by a Welsh to an English king—he was received as befitted his rank and treated with marked generosity. It was a part of Alfred's statesmanship to lead the other Christian princes of the island to regard him as their natural lord and protector against heathen attack, and thus it was that Wales came formally under the supremacy of Wessex; Gwynedd under Anarawd was recognised as standing in the same relation to the West-Saxon king as did Mercia under Æthelred, and the basis was laid of the homage which in later ages was regularly demanded from all Welsh princes by the English crown.

[30] Harl. MS. 3859 (*s.a.* 880; it is still a year in arrear—*cf.* the annal 887 with the Irish notices of the death of King Cerbhall of Dublin) has the simple entry: "Gueit conguoy digal rotri adeo" (the battle of the Conway: Rhodri avenged by God). In Wynne, 37-9, there is a detailed narrative, possibly derived from records of the see of Bangor (*cf.* B. Willis, *Bangor*, p. 184), which, while it contains some legendary features, appears nevertheless to embody a genuine tradition.

At the moment when Asser was placing these events on record, English overlord and Welsh king were alike preoccupied with a new danger in the renewal of the Scandinavian attacks on an extensive scale. For some years the peril had seemed to be over, and Asser's pages show no sense of its urgency. But the pirate bands had merely transferred their operations to the Continent, and, upon undergoing a crushing defeat at Louvain in 891, had laid their plans for fresh incursions into England, where they appeared at the end of 892.[31] The army led by Hæsten included not only warriors from over sea, but also Danes of Deira and East Anglia, who looked upon the hostings as agreeable breaks in the monotony of farm life; it swept Southern Britain during the four years 892-6 from sea to sea, ravaging without mercy in summer and passing the winter in some fastness specially chosen and prepared for the purpose. In the chronicle of its movements Wales and the Welsh border occupy a prominent place; some impulse, possibly the desire to get into touch with the Danish settlements in Ireland, constantly drew it west. In 893 it is found at Buttington, close to the confluence of the Severn and the Wye,[32] where it was beset by a joint army of English and Welsh; Mercians and West Saxons on the one hand, men of Gwent and Glywysing on the other,[33] reduced it to sore straits, and, after great slaughter, drove what remained of it back to Essex. Before the close of the year it had repaired its broken ranks, had become again formidable, and, after a long march which was not suspended by night or by day, had taken possession for the winter of the ruined walls of Chester. The Mercians followed hard upon its heels and cleared the country round of all supplies of food; hence it was forced early in 894 to replenish its stores by a raid on North Wales. It may be conjectured that Anarawd received some English

[31] *A.S. Chron.* MSS. A. B. C. D. *s.a.* 893-7 tell the story in detail. Plummer shows (ii. 108, 110) that the dating must be set back a year in the case of each of these annals.

[32] See Plummer, ii. 109-10. Buttington by Chepstow tallies much better with the data of the Chronicle—especially with the composition of the English army and its leaders—than does Buttington by Welshpool.

[33] So I interpret the "sum dæl thæs Norð Weal cynnes" of *A.S. Chr.* The idea of Green (*Conq. Eng.* (2), pp. 172, 173, 183) that other Welsh, under the leadership of Anarawd, were in alliance with Hæsten is plainly inconsistent with the evidence, and seems to have arisen out of a baseless impression that Anarawd did not submit to Alfred until 897.

CHAP. X.

help to repel this invasion; he had at any rate English troops at his command when in the following year he plundered Ceredigion and Ystrad Tywi, a blow directed most probably at his brother Cadell.[34] During most of 894 and 895 the Danes were busy in the neighbourhood of London; at the end of the latter year they were once more in the Severn valley, encamped for the winter at Quatbridge, which cannot have been far from the modern Bridgenorth. This became the starting-point for the last great raid, in the spring of 896, which devastated not only the adjacent parts of Mercia, but also the Welsh districts of Brycheiniog, Gwent and Gwynllwg.[35] In the summer of this year the great confederacy was dissolved; the men of Deira and East Anglia returned to their homes, while the wandering pirates turned their attention once more to the banks of the Seine.

The closing years of Alfred's reign were comparatively peaceful, but his death, in or about 901,[36] was followed by another period of struggle and unrest. The Welsh now found themselves between two fires, for, while the danger of invasion from the Scandinavian settlements in Ireland and the North was no less a matter of apprehension than before, attention had to be paid to the doings of Mercia also, since Edward the Elder was too much occupied with schemes of his own to control its aggressive spirit as had been done by his peace-loving father. In 902 the Celtic element won a temporary triumph over the Scandinavian in Ireland; Dublin was cleared of its heathen folk[37] and very many of them, under the leadership of one Ingimund, made their way to Anglesey, intending, no doubt, to found a new settlement in the island.[38] They were stoutly resisted by the inhabitants and forced to look elsewhere for

[34] "Anaraut cum anglis uenit uastare cereticiaun et strat tui" (Harl. MS. 3859, *s.a.* 894 (= 895)).

[35] "(N)ordmani uenerunt et uastauerunt loycr et bricheniauc et guent et guinnliguiauc" (*ibid. s.a.* 895 (= 896)).

[36] Harl. MS. 3859 records the death of "Albrit rex giuoys" (*i.e.*, of the Gewissae) *s.a.* 900, and thus tends to support the ordinary dating in 901.

[37] *Ann. Ult. s.a.* 901; *Chron. Scot. s.a.* 902.

[38] Harl. MS. 3859 has *s.a.* 902 (= 903) "Igmunt in insula mon uenit. et tenuit maes osmeliavn" (a place not yet identified). A more detailed account of the adventures of "Hingamund" (= Ingimundr) is to be found in a fragment of an Irish Chronicle printed by J. O'Donovan in 1860 for the Irish Archæological and Celtic Society (pp. 225-37). Though the MS. is a late transcript, it seems to embody some genuinely historical material.

a foothold, which they ultimately found, if an Irish account is to be trusted, in the neighbourhood of Chester. This was a concession due, it would appear, to the famous "lady of the Mercians," Æthelflæd, daughter of Alfred and wife of the Mercian ealdorman, who during her husband's lifetime and for seven years after his death led and governed the Mercian folk with such intrepid energy that one accepts without surprise the Welsh and Irish designation of her as a queen.[39] She had already repaired the fallen ramparts of the ancient stronghold on the Dee, rightly estimating its great importance as the key to North-Western Mercia, and realising that in Danish hands it would be a perpetual menace to her power.[40] She maintained her position there, the Irish chronicler tells us, against fierce onslaughts on the part of Ingimund and his men, and then proceeded to buttress the Mercian state by building other forts along the borders specially open to attack. Scarcely anything is known of Æthelflæd's relations with the Welsh; the one event recorded in this connection can have been but an incident. In the early summer of 916 she invaded the realm of Brycheiniog, stormed a royal stronghold near Llyn Safaddon, and captured the queen and a number of followers of the court.[41] The reigning chief was probably Tewdwr ab Elise, the son of the contemporary of Asser,[42] and, whatever may have been his offence against his powerful neighbour, his attitude affords no clue to the solution of the much more important question as to the relations between Æthelflæd and the house of Rhodri. But a little light is thrown upon this matter by the disposition of the great lady's fortresses; though the sites of all have not been identified, it seems likely that some were built on the eastern frontier of Mercia, for instance at Chirbury,[43] and in

CHAP. X.

[39] "Ælfled regina obiit" (Harl. MS. 3859, *s.a.* 917); "Eithilfleith, famosissima regina Saxonum, moritur" (*Ann. Ult. s.a.* 917).

[40] *A.S. Chr.* MSS. B. C. *s.a.* 907.

[41] *Ibid. s.a.* 916. Camden saw that "Brecenan mere" must be Llangorse Lake (*Britannia*, p. 562), but the exact position of the "llys" is not easily determined.

[42] In *Lib. Land.* 237-9, "teudur filius elised," king of Brycheiniog, has dealings with Bishop Llibio of Llandaff, who succeeded Cyfeiliog in 927 and died in 929.

[43] "Cyric byrig" (*A.S. Chr.* MSS. B. C. *s.a.* 915) appears to be Chirbury, which had an ancient church and was head of a hundred before the Norman Conquest ("Cireberie" in Domesd. i. 253*b* 1), rather than Chirk, which takes its name from the river Ceiriog (old Welsh Ceriauc) and had no importance in Anglo-Saxon times.

CHAP. X.

this case she and the leaders of the Welsh can scarcely have been upon entirely friendly and easy terms. It is most probable that her death in 918,[44] in the midst of her career of conquest, came as a relief to men who knew not whither she might next turn her victorious arms.

Edward the Elder at once seized upon the opportunity which was now afforded him of becoming direct ruler of the whole of Mercia and was thus brought into immediate relations with the princes of Wales. His policy was that of his father, one of friendship and protection in return for submission and homage. He had already given proof of kindly sentiments towards the Welsh people. In 915 a viking host had sailed from Brittany into the estuary of the Severn, and, landing on the southern coast of Wales, had spread ruin over Gwent and Glywysing; their daring onslaught carried them as far as Erging, and here, not many miles from Hereford, they captured Bishop Cyfeiliog of Llandaff, and, rejoicing in their good fortune, led him a prisoner to their ships.[45] Edward at once came to the relief of the hapless prelate, and, on payment of a ransom of forty pounds, obtained his release from the clutches of his heathen captors, nor was it until this transaction was complete that vigorous measures were taken for the expulsion of the Danes, who ultimately withdrew by way of Dyfed to their kinsmen in Ireland. Thus it was only to be expected that on Æthelflæd's death the Welsh princes should readily acknowledge the sway of the West-Saxon king; "Hywel and Clydog and Idwal," according to the official chronicle kept at Winchester, "with all the North Welsh (*i.e.*, Welsh) race, sought him as their lord".[46] A new generation of chiefs had arisen since the days of Asser; of the sons of Rhodri, Merfyn had died in 904, Cadell in 909 (or 910), Anarawd in 916.[47] Idwal

[44] Harl. MS. 3859 gives the year as 917 and would seem to be still a year behind; see the entry under 907 of the death of "Guorchiguil," placed by B. *Saes.* in the same year as the death of King Cormac of Munster, *i.e.*, 908.

[45] *A.S. Chr.* MSS. A. B. C. D. The date is no doubt rightly given by B. C. D. as 915. *Lib. Land.* (231-7) makes "Cimeilliauc" a contemporary of Brochwel ap Meurig of Gwent and Hywel ap Rhys of Glywysing and gives 927 as the year of his death. There is fairly good evidence that the early bishops of Llandaff exercised authority in Erging.

[46] *A.S. Chr.* MS. A. *s.a.* 922, the year being actually 918.

[47] Harl. MS. 3859 *s.a.* 909, 915; *Chron. Scot.* (after 904 a year in arrear) *s.a.* 908, 915; B. *Saes.* *s.a.* 901, *B.T.* p. 18 (for Merfyn).

the Bald, son of Anarawd, now ruled over Gwynedd, Hywel and Clydog, the sons of Cadell, in the south. CHAP. X.

III. Hywel the Good.

One prince only, among the many who bore rule in Wales in the Middle Ages, was honoured by posterity with the title of "Good"—a circumstance which in itself imparts a peculiar interest to the reign of Hywel Dda.[48] Yet history has hardly anything to tell of the personal traits of one who gained for himself so secure a place in the affections of his fellow-countrymen; the facts of his life, as handed down by the ancient sources, are extremely meagre, and, though they reveal in some measure the greatness and distinction of the man, leave much unexplained, so that even in the briefest outline of his career the historian must not seldom invoke the aid of conjecture.

He was the son of Cadell ap Rhodri, and when he and his brother Clydog—a younger brother, it may be inferred from the order of the names—offered submission to Edward the Elder in 918, it is safe to conclude that they were rulers of Seisyllwg, which they had divided between them in accordance with Welsh custom. But it is most probable that Hywel had also by this time come into possession of Dyfed. No king of that region appears after the death in 904 of Llywarch ap Hyfaidd, who was doubtless the last of the old line,[49] and, as Hywel is known to have married his daughter Elen,[50] it seems clear that, either then or shortly afterwards, the realm came into the hands of Cadell's eldest son as the result of the marriage alliance. Clydog did not long survive the submission of 918; two years later he died,[51] when it may be presumed that Hywel obtained the whole of Seisyllwg; united to Dyfed, it formed the kingdom of Deheubarth, a compact area which covered the whole of the South-west of Wales from the Dovey to the Tawe. The foundation of this kingdom, which was that of

[48] The title does not appear in Harl. MS. 3859 or any other contemporary source, but obtained an early currency from the prefaces to the editions of the Laws.

[49] "Loumarch filius hiemid moritur" (Harl. MS. 3859 *s.a.* 903).

[50] Pedigrees Nos. i. and ii. (Owain ap Hywel) in Harl. MS. 3859.

[51] "Clitauc rex occisus est" (Harl. MS. 3859, *s.a.* 919).

CHAP. X.

Rhys ap Tewdwr and, save for Norman acquisitions, of Rhys ap Gruffydd, is the first notable event in the history of Hywel.

The next was his visit to Rome in 928, an undertaking which finds no true parallel in the life of any other Welsh prince.[52] Two earlier instances are no doubt recorded of pilgrimage on the part of Welsh chieftains to the Holy City,[53] but of both Cyngen of Powys and the unknown Hywel of 886 it is said that they died at Rome, so that it is clear that the journey was a penitential effort at the close of a busy and not too scrupulous reign, intended to smooth the pathway to a better world. Hywel's visit does not at all suggest the repentance of a dying man; he returned to Wales to wield the sceptre with vigour and marked intelligence for twenty years, and must have been in this year of pilgrimage a man in the full prime of his career. What took him so far out of the common-place round of princely life in Wales in his day must have been, one cannot doubt, that breadth of sympathy, that enlightened interest in the life of other nations than his own which come to light in other parts of his history. There is good reason to think that he made Alfred, in whose reign he was doubtless born, his model and exemplar; Alfred had twice visited Rome as a boy and had maintained the connection by frequent gifts to the holy see, and it was thus to be expected that, when Hywel found himself free to undertake this journey, he should adventure upon it. Rome itself was in this age scarcely worthy of the veneration lavished upon it by the Church of the West; whether the pope to whom Hywel made his obeisance was Leo VI. (928-9) or Stephen VII. (929-31), he was probably in either case a creature of the notorious Marozia.[54] But, though there may have been little in the atmosphere of the city to sustain the fires of a high spiritual enthusiasm, the historic memories of the spot must have cast their spell over the wanderer from distant Dyfed, and each league of the long and

[52] "Higuel rex perrexit ad romam" (Harl. MS. 3859, *s.a.* 928). The date may be correct, as the chronicle seems hereabouts to right itself and soon afterwards to get a year in advance of the true dating. The battle of Brunanburh, the death of Athelstan, that of Olaf Godfreyson (Abloyc rex), the devastation of Strathclyde and the murder of Edmund are all post-dated a year.

[53] See note 44 to chap. vii.

[54] Gregorovius, *History of the City of Rome in the Middle Ages*, Eng. trans. iii. pp. 282-3.

perilous journey must have left its impress upon the mind of one so observant and so ready to learn.[55] CHAP. X.

The remarkable feature of the years which followed Hywel's return is his close association with the English court. Edward the Elder had died in 924 or 925 at Farndon on the Dee, having been summoned to this region by a revolt of the city of Chester, in which the neighbouring Welsh were concerned.[56] He was succeeded by Athelstan, who showed the utmost energy and resolution in maintaining and extending the power which of late had fallen to the king of Wessex. It would appear that about 926 or 927 he summoned the leading Welsh princes to Hereford, imposed a tribute upon them of gold, silver, cattle, hunting dogs and hawks, and fixed the Wye as the boundary between the two races in that part of the country.[57] Hywel of West Wales and Owain of Gwent (son of Hywel ap Rhys) are expressly mentioned in a MS. of the English Chronicle as having submitted to Athelstan;[58] of Idwal Foel there was a story current that the English king for a time deprived him of his realm,[59] so that his position at this juncture is not quite cer-

[55] According to an early editor of Ven. (*LL.* i. 216), whose statements were copied into certain South Welsh MSS. (*LL.* i. 342, MSS. S. and Z.), Hywel when at Rome sought the approval of the pope for his laws and obtained it. Not only is it highly improbable that papal authority was ever given to laws which so frequently run counter to those of the Church, but there are also chronological objections. The compilation of the code belongs to Hywel's later years, not to the early period of his reign, for he was not in a position to undertake the task until 942.

[56] Wm. Malm. *G.R.* i. 144 (i. 210). The authority used by William for this part of his account of Athelstan's reign was an ancient metrical life, written most probably during the king's lifetime (Stev. Asser, 184, n. 4). The mention of Chester shows that Farndon by Holt is intended, not Faringdon (suggested by Plummer, ii. 380-1). "Fearndun" was literally translated into Welsh as "Rhedyn-fre" in the name "Siat Rhadynfre" found for St. Chad in *Myv. Arch.* II. 52 (429).

[57] Wm. Malm. *G.R.* i. 148 (i. 214).

[58] *A.S. Chr.* MS. D. *s.a.* 926. The names are introduced parenthetically ("Huwal West Wala cyning . . . Uwen Wenta cyning") into an account of Athelstan's dealings with the Danes of Deira on the death of their king Sitric in 927, and it is not really intended to state that the Welsh and other kings mentioned met at "Ea mot" on the 12th of July (Plummer, ii. 136). Plummer (ii. *addenda viii.*) thinks that "West Wala" must be Cornwall, and that the reference is not to Hywel the Good, but to an otherwise unknown Cornish ruler. This is not, of course, impossible, but it is surely a simpler supposition that West Wales is used in this passage in an unusual sense. "Yuein," son of Hywel ap Rhys, appears in a notice in *Lib. Land.* 236 of the time of Bishop Cyfeiliog.

[59] Wm. Malm. *G.R.* i. 142 (i. 206). This story does not come, it would seem, from the metrical life, and has the suspicious feature of making Idwal king of *all* the Welsh.

CHAP. X.

tain. It will be seen that Athelstan was bent upon turning into a real subordination the formal submission demanded from the Welsh by Alfred and Edward, and what is notable is the manner in which Hywel accepted the situation and did his best to turn it to account. Valuable evidence is furnished on this head by the English land-charters.[60] These documents are usually attested by a large number of witnesses, members of the assembly of "witan" or "wise men" which approved the grant, and, as Athelstan adopted the policy of summoning his "subreguli" or under-kings to occasional meetings of this body, the names of Welsh princes are often found among those of the attesting counsellors, taking precedence of those of earls and thegns, and sometimes even of those of bishops. Some of these charters rest under considerable suspicion, since their text has only been preserved in cartularies or charter-books compiled at a much later date by monastic houses which were very jealous of their rights and not unwilling to forge documentary evidence in support of them in case of need. Nevertheless, though it is not possible to accept the testimony of every charter for the facts which it professes to record, some are undoubtedly genuine, and even in the forged charters the names of the witnesses are probably drawn from authentic documents. It is, therefore, a significant fact that Hywel is of all the Welsh princes the most prominent in this connection; from 928 to 949 his name is appended to every charter which has Welsh signatures and is among them placed first; in three cases he is the only under-king who joins in the grant. He is often supported by Idwal Foel and Morgan ab Owain of Morgannwg, and once by Tewdwr ab Elisedd of Brycheiniog, but no prince seems to have entered so heartily into Athelstan's design of linking Wales with England by this system of attendance at the English court. All that is known of Hywel points him out as a warm admirer, not only of Alfred, but also of English civilisation; he led no expedition across the border, but instead secured to Athelstan the faithful allegiance of his brother chiefs, even in that year of rebellion, 937, when the league against Wessex included the Scots, the Danes and the Strathclyde Britons, and only the Southern Britons held aloof English influence is manifest in the law of Hywel and betrays itself even in the naming of his

[60] See note A appended to this chapter.

sons, for Edwin ap Hywel Dda bore an English name,[61] which was possibly given him out of compliment to the young son of Edward the Elder who perished in 933.

Hywel was now about to reach the zenith of his career and to become, as he is termed in the codes, " by the grace of God ruler of all Wales ".[62] This was a position he certainly did not hold during the life of Idwal Foel ab Anarawd, for the evidence makes it clear that Idwal and Hywel ruled North and South Wales respectively under the overlordship of Athelstan.[63] But in 942 Idwal, never quite easy under the English supremacy, seems to have broken into revolt against the power of the new king Edmund ; he and his brother Elisedd met the Saxon in battle and were both slain.[64] In the natural course the sovereignty of Gwynedd should have passed to the sons of Idwal, Iago and Idwal, the latter often called Ieuaf (or " Junior ") to distinguish him from his father. Hywel, however, now appeared upon the scene, and, driving out the young heirs,[65] made himself master of Gwynedd and, most probably, of Powys also. It is quite impossible to say whether there were good grounds, recognised as valid by Welsh public opinion, for this act of aggression ; one may nevertheless conjecture that the revolution was favourably viewed by the English, and no attempt to reverse it was made while Hywel lived. Whether

[61] He died in 954 (*Ann. C.*; *B.T. s.a.* 952). The form " Guin," found in *Ann.* C. MS. B., is due to a misunderstanding of "*Et*guin ".

[62] " O rat Duw . . . brenhin Kymry oll " (Dim. i. 338). *Cf.* Lat. B. ii. 814 : " Dei gratia atque providentia rex Howel . . . totius Wallie principatu praesidebat pacifice ". All the texts of the laws emphasise in their prefaces the extent of his rule.

[63] See the charters mentioned in the note at the end of this chapter and note 58 above.

[64] " Iudgual et filius eius elized a saxonibus occiduntur " (Harl. MS. 3859, *s.a.* 943). The year was that which followed the death of Olaf Godfreyson, shown by Irish records to have happened in 941. The MS. followed by *Ann.* C. MS. B., and *B.T.* makes Idwal son of Rhodri, but the ordinary account, contained in Jesus Coll. MS. 20, No. xxvi. (*Cymr.* vii. 88), is to be preferred as better suiting the chronological data. As to Elisedd, " filius " would seem to be an early error of transcription for " frater," corrected in the older texts of *B.T.* (but not in B. *Saes.*), which have "urawt" (B*ruts*, 261 ; *B.T.* p. 20); see Dwnn, ii. 10, 16; Harl. MS. 3859, *s.a.* 946 (=945)—" Cincenn filius elized ueneno periit" ; Carlisle, *s.v.* Hawarden (" Cynan ap Elis ap Anarawd ").

[65] " Iago et Ieuaf, quos Howel e regno expulerat " (*Ann.* C. MS. C. p. 18, n. 20). It was at this period of his life, no doubt, that Hywel issued the coin, the only one known to have been struck for a Welsh prince, which is described by Mr. Carlyon-Britton in *Trans. Cymr.* 1905-6, 1-13.

CHAP. X.

justified or not, it united Wales almost as completely as any recorded movement in its history. Morgannwg and Gwent still retained their independence under the sons of Owain, Cadwgan and Morgan the Aged,[66] but this was a part of Wales which never, save for a few years under Gruffydd ap Llywelyn, entered into any wide-embracing Welsh realm.

The events of 942 prepared the way for the crowning and distinctive achievement of Hywel's life, namely, the reduction of the varying royal and tribal usages of Wales to a uniform and consistent system, accepted by the whole country and permanently embodied in a written code. No direct evidence exists that this work was actually done by Hywel save the statements made in the various copies of the code itself, and none of these copies are of older date than the end of the twelfth century. But the unanimity with which they ascribe this great legal reform to the "good" king, and the unchallenged assumption throughout Welsh literature that the work was his, without suggestion of a rival for the honour, constitute as strong a proof as tradition can well supply; if Hywel was not the author of the code which bears his name, how came he to be singled out from among his fellows and invested by later generations of Welshmen with this unique distinction? It may well be believed that the task was the principal object he set before himself in his career; the union of Dyfed and Seisyllwg under his rule would bring him in early life face to face with the inconveniences of conflicting tribal custom, the example of Alfred, always his guiding star and embodiment of the princely ideal, would invite him to the beneficent path of legislative reform, and his foreign experience would teach him how much the Welsh had still to learn ere social institutions among them could rest on a firm foundation.

[66] Morgan Hên succeeded his father Owain ap Hywel (the "Uwen Wenta cyning" of *A.S. Chr.* MS. D. *s.a.* 926) about 930 and long survived Hywel, dying at a patriarchal age in 974. His brother Gruffydd, who was king of Gower in 928 (*Lib. Land.* 239-40), was killed in 935 (or 934) by the men of Ceredigion (*Ann.* C. MSS. B. C.; *B.T.*; B. *Saes.*). The third brother, Cadwgan, appears in *Lib. Land.* 224-5 as "Catguocaun rex filius Ouein" and lord of the region of Margan about 940; his death in battle against the English is recorded about 950 (Harl. MS. 3859; *Ann.* C. MS. B.; *B.T.*). "Caducon" may be the correct reading, instead of "Cadmon," in *Cart. Sax.* iii. 39, in which case Cadwgan, with his brother Morgan and Hywel Dda, was at the court of Edred in 949.

He was obliged to wait for many years for the realisation of his hopes, but at last the whole of Wales lay at his feet and the hour was ripe for his enterprise. CHAP. X.

According to the unanimous testimony of the prefaces to the various versions of the code,[67] Hywel's first step was to summon a representative assembly, in which each cantref[68] was represented by six men, to his hunting lodge of Y Ty Gwyn ar Daf (The White House on the Taff), now marked by the village of Whitland in Carmarthenshire.[69] No other national gathering of the kind is recorded in Welsh history until the fifteenth century, but the occasion, it should be remembered, called for very exceptional measures. The laws of the Welsh were not the creation of any legislator, owing their origin to the royal fiat and capable of being altered by the same authority. They were the ancient customs of the race, handed on in each tribe as a precious heirloom from generation to generation, preserved by the tradition of the elders, and having the sanction of immemorial antiquity. In order to annul or modify them, nothing short of the assent of a national conclave was sufficient, and an editor of the Venedotian code lays down the principle that no part of the law of Hywel itself can be abrogated save by leave of a body as large as that which met at Hywel's behest.[70]

The prefaces state that the conference was held in Lent[71] and occupied the whole six weeks of that season, so that the deliberations must have been long and the revision of the laws entered into with great thoroughness. They give discrepant accounts of the way in which the final text of the revision was arrived at, the Dimetian and the Gwentian prefaces ascribing

[67] *LL.* i. 2, 214-6 (Ven.), 338-42 (Dim.), 620-2 (Gw.); ii. 749 (Lat. A.), 814 (Lat. B.), 893 (Lat. C.).

[68] Only MSS. B. D. of Ven. have "cantref" (*cf.* however, C. D. K. in pref. to bk. iii. p. 214), the other MSS. and codes reading "cymwd". But the substitution of the cymwd, the actual, for the cantref, the archaic area in MSS. of the twelfth and thirteenth centuries is more easy to explain than would be the reverse process. Reasons have already been given (p. 301) for thinking that the cymwd had not come into existence in the age of Hywel Dda.

[69] For Whitland see chap. v. note 129.

[70] Ven. i. 216 (MSS. C. D. K.). Other passages which illustrate the doctrine of the necessity of national assent for all new laws are to be found in Dim. i. 594 (heading of III. ii.); *LL.* ii. 394 (§ 43); *De Nugis*, ii. 22 (antequam in contrarium *decreta* ducent *publica*, nihil novum proferamus).

[71] Gw. and Lat. B. omit this detail.

CHAP. X.

the actual compilation of the new code to a commission of twelve laymen and one cleric, while the other MSS. seem to assign the task to the whole assembly.[72] It is most probable that some small body of men practised in the law was charged at the end of the conference or during its sessions with the business of embodying its decisions in writing, but one can hardly go further and believe with the author of the Dimetian code that the commission did everything and that the Lenten assembly was solely occupied with fasting and prayer. Many hostile interests had to be reconciled, many discordant usages brought into harmony and the general will enforced against local peculiarities—all of it work, not for a drafting committee, but for a genuine popular assembly. It was, no doubt, ere the assembly broke up that the formal proclamation of the new laws was carried out and a solemn malediction laid upon all evil-disposed men who should infringe the dooms thus set forth by national assent.

Many lawyers of repute must have lent their aid to Hywel in his great undertaking, but nothing is known of any of them save Blegywryd ab Einon. In the various copies of the Dimetian Code, Blegywryd is made to play a leading part in the proceedings at Whitland; he is the "master" or "scholar" who acts as clerk to the twelve lay commissioners, and later texts dub him Archdeacon of Llandaff and send him to Rome with the deputation which, it is alleged, went thither to obtain for the new code the benison of the holy see.[73] It is clear that from this source no trustworthy information about him is to be gleaned, but there are other references to him of a less doubtful complexion. Some rudely formed Latin hexameters found in two or three late copies of the laws would seem to have been originally written at the end of a copy of the code transcribed by Blegywryd for the use of the court of Hywel and its judge, Gwrnerth Lwyd of Is Cennen.[74] In these he is

[72] MSS. S. Z. name the commissioners, but the list is merely one of famous lawyers, without regard to chronology. Morgeneu and Cyfnerth were the compilers of the Gwentian Code (Gw. i. 622, MSS. *U*. X.), Goronwy ap Moreiddig was a lawyer one of whose dicta is quoted in Dim. II. xviii. 37, and both he and Gwair ap Rhufon were authors of editions of the laws said to have been used by Iorwerth ap Madog in the compilation of Ven. (i. 218).

[73] MSS. S. Z. For the supposed visit to Rome on this special business see note 55 above.

[74] Pref. to *LL*. i. xxxiv. (Bodl. MS.) and MSS. S. *Z*. (i. 342). Sir J. Rhys, in

described as teacher of law to the household of Hywel, and it is implied that his knowledge of the law and his power of exposition were of an exceptional kind. In agreement with this the *Liber Landavensis* speaks of "that most famous man, Blegywryd son of Einon," as intervening in 955 in a quarrel between the see of Llandaff and the king of Gwent and forbidding a breach of the law of sanctuary.[75] Another reference in the same authority suggests that his home lay in Gwent and, in direct opposition to the statements in the codes, sets him down, with his brother Rhydderch, as a layman.[76] It would seem likely, on the whole, that Blegywryd was not a churchman (Welsh lawyers, in point of fact, were not drawn from the ranks of the clergy),[77] and that while he gave his services, so highly prized in his generation, to the king of Deheubarth in the great enterprise of his reign, he returned after Hywel's death to his native hamlet in the plains of Gwent.[78]

No copy of the original code of Hywel has survived in any form,[79] for not only are all extant MSS. of the laws of later date that 1150, but they represent improved and enlarged editions of the law book of Whitland, compiled from time to time by distinguished lawyers for the use of particular districts or communities. Three of these recensions, written in Welsh, the original language of the code, have, by reason, no doubt,

Cymr. xviii. 115-7, discusses these verses and supplies a corrected text from the Oxford MS. They are clearly ancient, having been torn from their true place as a colophon, and are the source of many of the statements made in late MSS., such as that of Dim. i. 340 as to the writing of three law books and the assertion of MSS. S. Z. (i. 342) that Blegywryd was doctor of civil and canon law! The "iudex cotidianus" is the "ynad llys," who dispenses justice from day to day in the "llys peunyddiol" of Dim. i. 344.

[75] *Lib. Land.* 219. The mention of "houel britannicum regem" is, of course, an anachronism, but it is possible that the name read originally *Owain ap* Hywel.

[76] *Ibid.* 222. The "Bledcuurit" who appears among the clergy on p. 230 can hardly be identified with the lawyer of Hywel's day, for the grant he witnesses was made by the Hywel ap Rhys of Asser.

[77] See especially Dim. II. viii. 124 for the disability which excluded a cleric from the office of judge in a secular court.

[78] That Blegywryd was of this region is suggested by his appearance in 955 at the church of SS. Iarmen and Febric, probably St. Arvan's (*Lib. Land.* 219, 405), and by his witnessing with his brother (*ibid.* 222) the grant of "Cair Nonou," which was not far from Caerwent and Llanfihangel (by Roggiet?).

[79] For a discussion of the history and relationship of the chief MSS. of the laws see note B. appended to this chapter.

CHAP. X.

of their excellence of form and substance, long ago onsted all others, so that all the existing MSS. in Welsh are copies of the Venedotian, the Dimetian, or the Gwentian Code, or have been compiled out of these three sources. The Venedotian Code has the advantage of the other two in respect of the age of its oldest MS., for the Black Book of Chirk dates from about 1200, while no extant copy of either of the other two can be ascribed to an earlier date than the fall of Llywelyn ap Gruffydd. Nevertheless, there is good reason to suppose that it is in substance comparatively recent, having been compiled about or not long before 1200 by one Iorwerth ap Madog as a special law book for North-west Wales. The Gwentian Code (to give it the title by which it has of late become generally known, though no evidence for its connection with Gwent or with Morgannwg has been adduced) appears to be also a compilation, to be ascribed, perhaps, to Morgeneu and his son Cyfnerth, who are mentioned as the authors in two or three of the MSS. The Dimetian Code seems to have best preserved, both in substance and in arrangement, the original Law of Hywel, but it is obviously a greatly amplified edition of that law and contains a reference to an enactment made by the Lord Rhys ap Gruffydd, who died in 1197. Of greater antiquity, probably, than any of the Welsh texts are the Latin versions, of which three are printed in the Record edition of the laws. Their divergence is too marked to allow it to be supposed that they represent an original Latin draft by one of Hywel's clerks, from which the earliest Welsh editions were translated; they were clearly themselves translated at different times from different Welsh originals, in order to enable foreign ecclesiastics to understand and administer the national customs. But they appear to be based on older Welsh texts than any which have come down to modern times, and the matter which is common to them may be taken as the nearest approximation we are ever likely to attain to the code which was promulgated by Hywel.

Hywel died in 949 or 950,[80] having done something for Welsh unity by his career of conquest, but far more by his work as a legislator. The realm he founded died with him, but the

[80] Harl. MS. 3859 has "Higuel rex brittonum (a title only previously bestowed in this MS. upon Rhodri Molwynog) obiit" under the year corresponding to 950.

code he gave to Wales was the beginning of Welsh jurisprudence; it was the solid foundation upon which the lawyers of later ages built at their leisure in the practice of a noble and peaceful profession. Though local customs still continued and were embodied in local documents, the conception of one law, valid for the whole of Wales, took its rise from the measures of Hywel and was developed by the activity of the legal commentators—in this domain the Welsh people early arrived at national self-consciousness. CHAP. X.

IV. Civil Strife and Foreign Alarms.

Hywel the Good was not able to hand over to his descendants the authority he had acquired in North Wales, and accordingly the realms of Gwynedd and Deheubarth once more owned different rulers and waged war upon each other. The ninety years which followed the death of the legislator are filled with barren strife, with provincial feuds and family quarrels, seeming to lead to no result; in spite of a multitude of claims, the man had not yet arisen who could gather the whole nation around his banner and breathe life and force into the national aspirations. In the background, meanwhile, was the double menace of the sea-rovers and the English, which the Welsh might only forget at their peril; ever and anon they were roughly reminded, by piratical raid or border foray, that their ancient enemies were at their gates, in readiness for the hour of weakness or disunion.

It will perhaps be best to take the dynastic history of Gwynedd, Deheubarth and Morgannwg separately and thereafter to discuss briefly the relations of these states with the English and with the "gentiles" of the opposite coast of Ireland.[81] On the death of Hywel, the men of Gwynedd at

[81] The last entry in Harl. MS. 3859 belongs to the year 954, and henceforth the historian has to rely upon the two later editions of the Menevian annals, known as MSS. B. and C. of *Ann. C.* *B.T.* and B. *Saes.* often supply valuable additions. The notices are meagre at this point and it is often difficult to distinguish the various princes named Idwal, Rhodri, etc. As to chronology, it should be observed that B. *Saes.* antedates by two years the killing of Congalach, king of Ireland, in 956 (*Ann. Ult.* and *Chron. Scot. s.a.* 955; *War of G. and G.* xcvii. 44) and the visit of Edgar to Chester in 973 (for the year see Plummer ii. 160), but only by one year the death of Edgar in 975 and the expedition of Godfrey Haroldson (see note 120 below) in 987. One adds, therefore, two years to its dates until 972 (= 974) and one year afterwards.

CHAP. X.

once threw off the southern yoke and marched to meet the sons of the dead king under the leadership of their own princes, Iago or Jacob and Idwal or Ieuaf, the sons of Idwal the Bald. The battle was fought at Nant Carno, in the region of Arwystli, on the borders of North and South Wales, and was a victory for the sons of Idwal, who were thereby secured in the possession of Gwynedd, and, it may be, of Powys also. Peace and good neighbourhood, nevertheless, were not at once established between the two houses. In 952 Iago and Idwal led their men as far south as Dyfed on an errand of fire and slaughter; the sons of Hywel in 954 retaliated by a march into the Conway valley, where their progress was checked not far from Llanrwst and a defeat inflicted upon them which emboldened the men of Gwynedd to pursue them into Ceredigion. After these reverses, the southern folk forbore for a time to harass the house of Idwal and devoted their energies to other enterprises. Left to themselves, the rulers of Gwynedd spent their strength in civil war; in 969 Ieuaf was taken prisoner by his brother Iago and henceforth plays no part in the affairs of the kingdom, though he seems to have languished in captivity until 988. It was Iago's turn next to feel the edge of misfortune; after a temporary defeat in 974, from which he seems to have recovered, he was taken captive in 979 by the son of his dispossessed brother, and Hywel ab Ieuaf thereupon became king of Gwynedd. Hywel retained this position for six years, and on his death in 985 was succeeded by his brother Cadwallon. The line of Idwal the Bald then lost for some years its royal rights in Gwynedd, for in 986 Maredudd ab Owain of Deheubarth invaded the realm, slew the new king and annexed the northern to the southern state.

Of the three sons of Hywel the Good who fought with the sons of Idwal, Khodri died in 953 and Edwin in 954,[82] leaving Owain undisputed ruler of Deheubarth, a dignity which he held until his death in 988. The dynastic position of Owain was a strong one; his brothers had left no heirs, and thus he was the sole representative of Cadell ap Rhodri, as well as of the native line of Dyfed, which had ended with his mother Elen. It is not surprising, therefore, that he should have taken special pains

[82] See note 61 above.

to get together a permanent record of his claims. Both the chronicle and the genealogies contained in Harleian MS. 3859 were unmistakably compiled in the reign of Owain ap Hywel Dda, though the actual copy in which they are preserved is of later date.[83] The chronicle is based upon the annals kept throughout this period at St. David's; its purpose is to record particulars of the persons mentioned in the genealogies, and it was originally intended to bring it as far as the year 977—an intention not quite fulfilled. The pedigrees immediately follow; the first is that of Owain, tracing his descent from Cunedda and Maelgwn and Rhodri the Great; the second is that of his mother, going back to Voteporix of Dyfed and that prince's father, Agricola of the Long Hand. A number of other pedigrees are then inserted, giving the lineage of the ancient princes of Powys, Strathclyde, Morgannwg, Ceredigion, Meirionydd, and other districts, but it is remarkable that in not a single instance are these lists brought down to Owain's own day;[84] there is no mention of Idwal and his sons or of Morgan of Morgannwg—it must be supposed that Owain desired to represent himself as the one lawful heir of the ancient dynasties, alike in North and South Wales. Nevertheless, as was noted above, he took no active steps after the battle of Llanrwst to enforce his pretensions to the throne of Gwynedd; he and his son Einon, who now appears upon the stage, turned their arms instead upon Morgannwg: in 960 Owain crossed the Tawe and ravaged the border cantref of Gorfynydd;[85] in 970 and again in 977 Einon laid waste the plains of Gower, of which the chiefs of Morgannwg had perhaps got temporary possession. It was on an enterprise of this kind that Einon met his death; in 984 the "uchelwyr" of Gwent fell upon him and slew him, in vindication, no doubt, of provincial liberties which he was seeking to destroy. Owain was now growing too old for the labours which were imposed by tribal ideas upon a Welsh prince, and his place was taken by his son Maredudd, who proved his mettle at the outset of his career by his conquest of Gwynedd from Cadwallon ab Ieuaf.

[83] See note on this MS. appended to chap. v.

[84] No. xvii. (line of Dunoding) is the only one which is brought down to the tenth century, ending about 930.

[85] B. *Saes. s.a.* 958 has "goryuyd" (for "goruynyd"), of which I take the "Goher" of *Ann.* C. MS. C. and the "Gorwyd" of *B.T.*, MS. C. to be corrupt forms.

CHAP. X.

The thirteen years of the rule of Maredudd (986-999[86]) form something of a contrast to the time of confusion just described, in that this prince maintained a hold over both North and South Wales and opposed a bold front both to the English and to the Norse buccaneers. He is recorded to have led a raid into Maes Hyfaidd, or the plain of Radnor, where he no doubt sacked the Mercian villages of the neighbourhood;[87] in his dealings with the sea-rovers, too, he showed an alert and resourceful spirit, redeeming their captives by the payment of a large ransom. For the times he was a man of mark, not undeserving of the title bestowed upon him by the Bruts of "most famous king of the Britons".[88] Yet his reign was a troublous one, disturbed by foreign attacks and by movements in favour of his nephew, Edwin ab Einon, and the sons of Meurig ab Idwal, who sought to win back Gwynedd for the old line. On his death his work was entirely undone; Gwynedd was regained by a scion of Idwal the Bald in the person of Cynan ap Hywel ab Ieuaf, who ruled for six years (999-1005),[89] while a veil falls over the history of Deheubarth which suggests the beginning of a period of anarchy unexampled even in that turbulent age.

What is most noteworthy in the period now reached is the success of men who were out of the direct line of succession from Rhodri the Great in seizing royal authority in Gwynedd and Deheubarth. Such a successful pretender was Aeddan ap

[86] The chronology of this reign is tolerably certain, the true date being found by adding one year to the date of B. *Saes.* Observe the following correspondences:—

B. Saes. 986—"marwolaeth ar yr ysgrybyl" = the murrain of *Ann. Ult.* 986 (= 987), *A.S. Chr.* MSS. C. D. E. F. 986, and *Fl. Wig.* 987.

B. *Saes.* 988—D. of "glumayn vab abloyc" = the killing of Gluniarainn, son of Olaf Cuaran, in *Ann. Ult.* 988 (= 989) and *Chron. Scot.* 987 (= 989).

B. *Saes.* 995—Burning of "Arthmatha" = destruction of Armagh in *Ann. Ult.* 995 (= 996), *Chron. Scot.* 994 (= 996) and Tighernach (*Rev. Celt.* xvii. p. 350).

[87] "Maes Hyfaidd" means, of course, the vill, and not, as Woodward supposed (i. 203), the county of Radnor. See *Trans. Cymr.* 1899-1900, p. 125.

[88] "Clotuorussaf vrenhin y brytanyeit" (*Bruts*, 264). So B. *Saes. s.a.* 998.

[89] About the year 1000 there appears to be confusion in the dating of *B.Saes.* The "Ivor porthalarchi" of 1001 is Ivar of Port Lairge or Waterford, who died in 1000 (*Ann. Ult. s.a.* 999; *Chron. Scot.* 998). With the annal 1005 we return, however, to the system of adding two years, for the first year "decemnouenalis cicli" was, of course, 1007 (Giry, *Manuel de Diplomatique*, p.193).

Blegywryd, who, after a reign of uncertain length, was killed, with his four sons, by Llywelyn ap Seisyll in 1018. Another was Rhydderch ab Iestyn, king of South Wales from 1023 to 1033, and founder of a house which, though it failed to retain its hold upon the crown of Deheubarth, nevertheless played a prominent part in Welsh history during the eleventh and twelfth centuries. Of wider fame than either was the Llywelyn mentioned above. Nothing is known of the origin of his father Seisyll; he had, however, if the pedigrees are to be trusted, some royal blood in his veins through his mother Prawst, daughter of Elise ab Anarawd [90] and he further strengthened his position by marrying Angharad, daughter of King Maredudd.[91] His own energy and force of character did the rest: by his overthrow of Aeddan and his defeat at Abergwili (1022) of the Irish pretender Rhain, who claimed to be a son of Maredudd, he attained a commanding position in Wales, which, despite his brief enjoyment of it (he died in 1023),[92] was long remembered by his fellow-countrymen [93] and not only stimulated the ambition of his son Gruffydd but gave him a great initial advantage in the struggle for supreme power.

During these vicissitudes the region of Morgannwg remained under its own princes and for the most part escaped the revolutions which distracted the rest of Wales. Glywysing, to which the name of Morgannwg was now frequently restricted, and Gwent still formed separate realms, but the kings of Gwent of Asser's day had, apparently, left no descendants, and both kingdoms fell into the hands of the posterity of Hywel ap Rhys of Glywysing. Arthfael ap Hywel was king of Gwent in the time of Bishop Cyfeiliog of Llandaff, who died in 927; [94] he was

[90] Dwnn ii. 10, 16 (Prawst is the right spelling—Owen, *Pemb.* i. 294). See note 64 above and *Trans. Cymr.* 1899-1900, p. 125, to which it may be added that Hawarden was probably in English hands and not at all likely to have been the home of a Welsh chief.

[91] *Bruts*, 296-7; Jesus Coll. MS. 20 in *Cymr.* viii. 88.

[92] The date, given by B. *Saes.* as 1021, is fixed by the Irish evidence, for the death of "Leobelin," king of the Britons, is entered in *Chron. Scot.* *s.a.* 1021 = 1023), *Ann. Ult.* *s.a.* 1023, and in Tighernach (*Rev. Celt.* xvii. p. 363).

[93] *B.T.* (p. 36) and B. *Saes.* (*s.a.* 1020) tell a wonderful tale of the prosperity enjoyed by the Welsh in Llywelyn's time, with which should be compared what is said in *Lib. Land.* 253 of his successor, Rhydderch ab Iestyn, and in *War of G. and G.* pp. 136-40, of Brian Boru.

[94] *Lib. Land.* 236 (h[illegible]gel rex filius ris . . . filiorum suorum yuein et arthuail), 237.

CHAP. X.

succeeded by his son Cadell, who died in 942.[95] A new dynasty then came into possession, represented in 955 by Noe ap Gwriad[96] and carried on by his son Arthfael, whose murder of his brother Elise and solemn atonement by the gift of land to Bishop Gwgon (d. 982) are recorded in the *Liber Landavensis*.[97] The sons of Elise, named Khodri and Gruffydd, next ruled over Gwent,[98] but about 1020 gave place to one Edwin ap Gwriad,[99] of unknown origin, who was the last independent king of this region, holding it until he was dispossessed, blinded and imprisoned by Meurig ab Hywel of Morgannwg.[100] Meanwhile, the house of Hywel ap Rhys had retained a firm hold of the country west of the Usk. The three sons of Owain ap Hywel had each some authority in this region, but the death of Gruffydd in 934 (or 935) and of Cadwgan in 949 (or 950) finally left the whole land under the sway of Morgan the Aged,[101] whose long reign did not close until 974. The next in succession was Owain ap Morgan, whose sons Rhys and Hywel carried on the line into the eleventh century.[102]

The close connection between the Welsh princes and the court of Wessex which marked the reign of Hywel the Good continued for some years after his death. It would appear that Edred and the advisers of Edwy were anxious to maintain the policy of Athelstan and to encourage the attendance of the Welsh at meetings of West Saxon magnates. Accordingly there is evidence of the presence in 955 of three leading chiefs at the court of Edred, *viz.*, Morgan the Aged, Owen ap Hywel Dda and Iago ab Idwal. But, when Edgar came to the throne, there was a reversal of this line of action, and henceforth no Welsh attestations are to be found in the charters of English kings. What occasioned the change it is not easy to discover; possibly it was held that the attempt at conciliation had been a failure, and with no Hywel to advocate peace and friendship with the English, it was in fact little likely to succeed. Of one

[95] *Lib. Land.* 223, 224; *Ann. C.*, *B.T.*, B. *Saes.* (*s.a.* 941). Harl. MS. 3859 has (*s.a.* 943) "Catell filius artmail ueneno moritur". For the true date see note 64 above.

[96] *Lib. Land.* 218.

[97] *Ibid.* 244-6.

[98] *Ibid.* 251, 252.

[99] *Ibid.* 249-51.

[100] *Ibid.* 255-7.

[101] See note 66.

[102] *Lib. Land.* 246, 252, 246-7. Hywel ab Owain died in 1043 (*Ann. C.*, *B.T.* and B. *Saes.*).

thing one may feel certain, namely, that the return to the old relations of mutual suspicion betokened no real weakening of the English hold upon Wales.[103] Edgar, as is well known, was an active and strenuous monarch, and his possession of a fleet would make him specially formidable to the Welsh. The story that he imposed upon Ieuaf an annual tribute of three hundred wolves may be mere legend,[104] but the account of the submission to him at Chester in 973 of all the chief kings of these islands, including those of the Welsh, is not to be disposed of so readily.[105] Both the Welsh and the English contemporary chronicles speak of a great gathering of vessels at the "city of the legion," presided over by Edgar himself; the English narrative is further supported by independent evidence when it states in addition that six kings there met the overlord of Britain and swore to be faithful to him and to act with him by sea and by land. That the six (or the eight, if the latter account be accepted) included Welsh princes is highly probable, even though it may not be possible to identify more Welsh names than that of Iago ab Idwal in the list handed down by tradition. It is, of course, a good deal more difficult to accept the picturesque detail that Edgar sat at the helm while the eight kings rowed him in his barge from the castle to St. John's Church and back again—surely a romantic embellishment of the plain, unvarnished fact of the submission. Edgar the Peaceable, the statesman and wise administrator, was not the man to hazard the substance of his power by a theatrical dis-

[103] Green (*Conq. Eng.* (2), pp. 323-4) seems to misinterpret the situation.

[104] Wm. Malm. *G.R.* i. 177 (i. 251). "Iudval(us)" is Idwal, the true name of Ieuaf.

[105] For the naval gathering see *Ann.* C. MS. C., *Bruts*, 262 (where "edwart" is a slip), and B. *Saes. s.a.* 971. The two Welsh chronicles wrongly translate "urbe legionum" as "kaer llion ar wysc," instead of Caerlleon ar Ddyfrdwy; in the *Gw. Brut* (p. 691), the inconsistency of this with the English account is solved by bringing Edgar to Caerleon in 967 and to Chester in 968! For the submission see *A.S. Chr.* MSS. D. E. F. *s.a.* 972 (= 973—see note above); Stevenson has shown (*Eng. Hist. Rev.* xiii. pp. 505-7) that there is good evidence, dating from about 996, of the trustworthy character not only of this entry, but also of the fuller account in Fl. Wig. i. 142-3, so far as it names eight kings, and among them, those of the Cumbrians and the Scots. Florence's "Jacob" is, no doubt, Iago ab Idwal; "Huwal" and "Juchil" offer some difficulty, for Hywel ab Ieuaf did not obtain power until 979, while Ieuaf (or Idwal) lost it in 969. Wm. Malm. *G.R.* i. 165 (i. 236) probably borrowed his account from Fl. Wig. (Asser, ed. Stev. lxii).

CHAP. X.

play of it, to the humiliation and mortification of his royal vassals. His hold upon the coasts of Wales was patent to all and needed no such advertisement.[106]

The English king did not long survive his great triumph at Chester, and after his death in 975 the forces of dissolution began to make themselves felt in the West Saxon realm, so that, with England parcelled out among great ealdormen, the crown ceased to be much concerned with the doings of the princes of Wales. As in the days before Alfred, it was the ruler of Mercia who now kept an eye upon the movements of the Welsh and directed punitive expeditions against them. Already, in 956, Ælfhere had been invested with the Mercian earldom,[107] and in 967 had ravaged the lands of Iago and Ieuaf;[108] in 983, at the end of his long tenure of office, he is found acting with Hywel ab Ieuaf of Gwynedd in an attack upon Einon ab Owain of Deheubarth, which the latter repelled with much slaughter.[109] After the banishment of Ælfhere's son Ælfric in 985, there was for many years a vacancy in the earldom of Mercia, and it is not easy to say who the Æthelsige was of the expedition of 992, when Edwin ab Einon obtained the help of an English force to harry the dominions of his uncle Maredudd.[110] But in 1007 Mercia received an earl once more in the person of the notorious Eadric Streona; hence it is Eadric who in 1012 leads the English attack upon Mynyw, an attack which may well have been made by sea, with the aid of some of the Danish ships taken this year by King Ethelred into his service.[111] The Eilaf who in 1022 repeated this raid upon the ancient seat of St. David[112] was not Earl of Mercia

[106] According to the records of the cathedral church of Bangor, Edgar founded the neighbouring church of St. Mary, or Llanfair Garth Brannan (B. Willis, *Bangor*, p. 183—*cf.* 72).

[107] *Crawford Charters*, 84.

[108] *B.T.* alone introduces Ælfhere (MS. C. Alfre) into this annal, and it may be the case that its compiler has inadvertently doubled the notice of 983.

[109] *Ann.* C. (Alfre), *B.T.* (Aluryt), B. *Saes. s.a.* 982 (Alfred).

[110] *Ann.* C. MS. B. supplies the form "Edelisi" from which Æthelsige is inferred (*e.g.*, by Freeman, *Norm. Conq.* i. (3) 285).

[111] *Ann.* C. MS. B. has "Edris," MS. C. "Edrich," pointing clearly to Eadric Streona (*Norm. Conq.* i. (3), p. 351). His companion "Ubis" has not been traced.

[112] "Eilaph venit in Britanniam (*i.e.*, Wales) et vastavit Dyvet et Meneviam" (*Ann.* C. MS. C.). This was Eglaf or Eilifr, a Dane in the service of Cnut (*Norm. Conq.* i. (3), p. 447).

(a position held under Cnut by Leofwine), but he clearly filled some post of authority on the border, for the life of St. Cadog calls him "an English sheriff" and tells how he invaded Morgannwg with a mixed force of Englishmen and Danes and so alarmed the clergy of Llancarfan that they carried off the shrine of their saint to the mountain retreat of Mamheilad.[113] Moreover, if there is no record of any Welsh invasion conducted by Earl Leofwine, it was his son Edwin who led the English on the fatal day of Rhyd y Groes.[114]

Throughout the whole of this period the hapless inhabitants of Wales had to bear the brunt of the piratical onslaughts of the sea-rovers, which were more frequent and more difficult to foresee and ward off than invasions from over the English border. It was unusual during the half-century between 950 and 1000 for more than five years to pass without a Danish attack upon some quarter of Wales important enough to be recorded in some chronicle of the time.[115] Anglesey, Lleyn, Dyfed and the shores of the Severn especially suffered from this scourge, but no part of the coast was wholly secure. As in the ninth century, the raiders were chiefly attracted by the plunder of the monasteries; the sack of Aberffraw, the royal seat of Gwynedd, in 968 stands alone, for the other places said to have been raided by the foreigners were all the sites of important churches. Holyhead was despoiled in 961, Towyn in 963, Penmon in 971, Clynnog in 978,[116] Mynyw (St. David's) in 982, 988 and 999, and in 988 a whole series of sanctuaries, including Llanbadarn Fawr, Llandudoch (St. Dogmael's), Llanilltud and Llancarfan. It need scarcely be said that much of the plunder took the form of saleable captives, for the Danes were traders as well as pirates and the slave trade was one of the most flourishing branches of their commerce.[117] Two thousand captives are said to have been carried off by Godfrey son of Harold from Anglesey in 987, and in 989 Maredudd

[113] *Cambro-Br. SS.* 77.

[114] See p. 360.

[115] *Ann.* C. records the attacks of 971, 982, 987, 988, 999 and 1002, *B.T.* and *B. Saes.* in addition those of 961, 963, 968, 972, 978, 980 and 993. *A.S. Chr.* MSS. C. D. E. *s.a.* 997 mention a raid on the coast of Morgannwg ("on Norðwalum") not noticed in the Welsh annals.

[116] *B. Saes.* (*s.a.* 977) has here the right reading—"y diffeithwyt *lleyn* a chelynnauc vaur". As *Ann.* C. MS. C. says that Hywel won his victory of the following year with "gentile" aid, it is probable that "saeson" in this annal is a mistake of the original of *B.T.* and B. *Saes.*

[117] *Conq. Eng.* (2), p. 118.

CHAP. X.

redeemed very many of his subjects from thraldom at a cost of one penny a head. The centre of Danish power in the western seas was the city of Dublin, where Anlaf Cuaran ruled from about 945 until his abdication in 980 and was succeeded by his sons Gluniarainn (*i.e.*, Iron-knee) and Sitric of the Silken Beard.[118] But, though the "sons of Abloec" (Anlaf) in 961 ravaged Holyhead and Lleyn, this house is less prominent in the tale of ruin and slaughter than that of Limerick, where a Danish dynasty had been established in the ninth century which also became master of the Hebrides and the Isle of Man.[119] Magnus or Maccus son of Harold, of this line, in 971 made a descent upon Penmon, while his brother Godfrey, who succeeded him about 977, appears on four occasions as the leader of a flotilla bound for Wales in pursuit of booty. In 972 he ravaged Anglesey; in 980 he helped Cystennin ab Iago in an attack upon the same island which was directed against Hywel ab Ieuaf; in 982 he invaded Dyfed; in 987 he and his Danish host, in a third irruption into Anglesey, won a victory over the Welsh, the fame of which—for a thousand of the enemy were left dead on the field and two thousand carried into captivity—penetrated to Ireland and was thought worthy to be preserved in the annals of that country.[120] The Welsh of the age of Maredudd ab Owain had no more persistent or pitiless foe than Godfrey Haroldson.

At the very end of the tenth century the Danish peril was still as instant and real as at any time during the previous two hundred years. In 999 St. David's was pillaged and its Bishop Morgeneu was slain. The evil day was long remembered, not only by reason of its tragic history, but also because the bishop's death was deemed to have been of the nature of a judgment. He had been the first of all the long line of successors of Dewi to break the custom of the see and to eat meat; no one, therefore, was surprised to hear that on the night of his death a bishop in Ireland had encountered his ghost, wailing and showing his wounds, with the pitiful cry—"I ate flesh and am become carrion".[121]

[118] *War of G. and G.* pp. 280-7, 288.

[119] *Ibid.* pp. 271-2.

[120] The "Cath Manand" of *Ann. Ult. s.a.* 986 (= 987), won by "mac Aralt" and the Danes, with the slaughter of a thousand men, must be the same as that recorded in *Ann. C.*, *B.T.* and B. *Saes.*

[121] Gir. Camb. vi. 104 (*Itin.* ii. 1).

NOTE A. TO CHAPTER X. *We sh Attestations to Old English* [illegible].

Some [illegible] old English Charters are attested by [illegible] princes, and the evidence [illegible] [illegible] [illegible] be disposed in [illegible] form as follows:—

[illegible]	Cart. Sax.			[illegible]			Da e.	[illegible]	King.	Under-kings [illegible] [illegible].	Authority for the [illegible].
	[illegible]	Vol.	P.	[illegible]	[illegible]	P.					
1	663	II.	342	1101	V.	190	[illegible] 16, 928.	[illegible]	[illegible].	[illegible], [illegible], Wurgeat.	Winchester [illegible] (Ad. MS. 15,350). Marked as [illegible] by [illegible].
2	675	,,	361	1103	,,				,,	[illegible], uðwa [illegible], Eugenius.	MS. [illegible] B. vi.
3	677	,,	364	353	II.	171	12,		,,	Howael, [illegible].	Cot [illegible] viii. 16—an original charter n B [illegible].
4	689	,,	380	1107	V.				,,	[illegible], [illegible], [illegible], Wurgeat.	The sam as N
5	697	,,	397	363	II.			[illegible]	,,	Huwol.	MS. Vitellius A. [illegible].
6	702	,,	404	364	,,			[illegible].	,,	[illegible] t	[illegible] Aug. ii. 65.
7	703	,,	406	352	,,			Nottingham.	,,	[illegible], t, I	[illegible] by
8	705	,,	410	1110	V.			[illegible].	,,	[illegible].	. I
9	716	,,	424	367	II.		21 937	Dorchester.	,,	Eugenius, [illegible], Morcant, [illegible].	ked
10	721	,,	429	369	,,	204	[illegible]	—	,,	[illegible].	.
11	882	III.	38	426	,,	296	[illegible]	—	[illegible].	Howael, Marcant.	fac-
12	883	,,	39	424	,,	292	[illegible]	—	,,	[illegible], ;,	1.
13	909	,,	71	433	,,	303	[illegible]	—	,,	Morcant, Jacob.	. ti-
14	937	,,	115	451	,,	325	[illegible]	[illegible].	Edwy.	Ast, Eadgar, t.	iii.

CHA X.

NOTE B. TO CHAPTER X. *MSS. and Editions of the Welsh Laws.*

The history of the various texts of the law of Hywel in Welsh and Latin is far too large a subject to be discussed within the limits of a note, but an attempt may perhaps be made to indicate the principal features of the problem and to furnish some evidence on behalf of the statements made in the body of this work.

No progress can be made with the study of the subject until it is recognised that the Welsh MSS. fall into three distinct groups, representing three recensions of the original law of Hywel. The Venedotian, the Dimetian, and the Gwentian Codes, to use the names commonly applied, must be separately dealt with in any edition of the laws which is to be of service to the historical student. Ignorance of this fundamental fact very largely destroyed the value of the *editio princeps* of the laws, prepared by Dr. William Wotton (1666-1726), with the assistance of Moses Williams (1686-1742), and issued after Dr. Wotton's death by William Clarke, his son-in-law, under the title, *Cyfreithjeu Hywel Dda ac Eraill seu Leges Wallicae*, etc. (London, 1730). Moses Williams was a good Welsh scholar, but by selecting as the main text to be printed Titus D. II., a MS. of the Venedotian Code (= Aneurin Owen's B.), and representing all departures from it in the form of various readings, he introduced a confusion upon which learning spent itself in vain. *Leges Wallicae* preserves for us some readings not elsewhere to be found in print, notably from the lost Wynnstay MS. which Wotton styles Ll., and the translation and glossary were valuable pioneer work. But fruitful study of the laws only became possible on the appearance of the edition undertaken by Aneurin Owen (1792-1851) for the Record Commission, which was published in 1841. In this the three codes are separately printed, each with the various readings of the MSS. of its class; the supplemental matter found in many MSS. forms a second volume; each of the Latin MSS. is printed *in extenso*. Another advantage possessed by this edition over that of 1730 is that adequate use is made in it of the great Hengwrt (now the Peniarth) collection of MSS., which is rich in copies of the laws, but was little used by Wotton and Williams. Exception may be taken to the editor's choice of MSS. in some cases (for the strange neglect of Peniarth MS. 30 (= Hengwrt MS. 12), see Evans, *Rep*. i. pp. 361, 367), but in the main the Record edition is of such a character as to place the student under very great obligations to it, and, short of printing each MS. as a separate text, it is difficult to see how, in the main, it could have been more usefully arranged.

The oldest extant Welsh MS. is a Venedotian text, *viz.*, Owen's A. (Pen. MS. 29 = Heng. 26), known as the "Black Book of Chirk". Old as it is, its ascription by Owen (i. Pref. xxvi.) to "the early part of the *twelfth* century" is a mistake; the date suggested by Dr. Gwenogvryn Evans (*Rep*. i. p. 359) is about 1200, and reasons will be given below for thinking an earlier one to be unlikely on other than palæographical grounds. Other important Venedotian MSS. are B. (Cott. MS. Titus D. II.), which dates from the end of the thirteenth century and records the customs of Gwynedd below Conway (*e.g.*, as to the amount of the amobyr payable by a king's aillt; *cf. LL*. i. 94, note 38, with the sum said in *Rec. Carn.* to be due under this head from the villein trefs of Creuddyn); C. (Caligula A. III.), written between 1225 and 1250 (Evans, *Rep*. i. Pref. to Pt. 2, p. viii); Pen. MS. 30, which is of the thirteenth century, and G. (Pen. MS. 35), which is of the last quarter of that century (*Rep*. i. p. 367). In spite of the age of the oldest MS., the Venedotian Code appears to embody a late recension of the law of Hywel. The passage in C. (*LL*. i. 218 "Ar llevyr hvn") in which this is expressly asserted and the name of the compiler given as Iorwerth ap Madog would, no doubt, carry little weight if unsupported by other evidence (see Evans,

Rep. i. Pt. 2, Introd. viii), but the name of Iorwerth occurs in other passages of undoubted authority (i. 104, 292; ii. 20) as the editor of the code, dealing freely with older material, and the whole structure of the work, departing as it does widely from all other arrangements of the laws (note, for instance, its treatment of the protections, sarhads and lodgings of the king's officers in bk. i), supports the view that it is an independent compilation. Moreover, a reference to the *Historia Regum* of Geoffrey of Monmouth (i. 184: "Dywynwal moel mud . . . mab . . . yarll kernyw"—*cf. Hist. Reg.* ii. 17) and another to the order of Knights Hospitallers (i. 170: "Teyr gorsetua . . . abat ac escop ac hyspyty"), both occurring in the original text, as evidenced by E. (a transcript supplying the lacunæ of A.), show that this compilation cannot have been made before the middle of the twelfth century. Indeed, if C. is right in giving the full name of Iorwerth as Iorwerth ap Madog "vap Rahawt" (i. 292), the work can hardly have been put together before the first years of the thirteenth (to which A. is ascribed), for his brother, Einion ap Madog "ab Rahawd" (in the case of so rare a name as Rhahawd, a mere coincidence is not to be thought of), was the contemporary of Gruffydd, the eldest son of Llywelyn ab Iorwerth (*Myv. Arch.* I. 391 (266)). It may well be the case that the code was compiled at the bidding of Llywelyn, who desired to emphasise the supremacy of Gwynedd by the issue of the laws in a distinctively Venedotian form.

The oldest extant MSS. of the Dimetian Code belong to the end of the thirteenth and the beginning of the fourteenth century, that is, to the period immediately following the loss of independence. O. (Pen. MS. 36A) is deemed by Dr. Evans (*Rep.* i. p. 369) to be the oldest of all, preceding by some years L. (Titus D. IX.), which was adopted by Owen as the main text of his edition of the code and is assigned to the neighbourhood of the year 1300. This version of the laws embodies legislation by Rhys ap Gruffydd of South Wales (II. xxxi. 9) and its compilation must therefore be ascribed to the period 1150-1250. In its structure it conforms pretty closely to what one may suppose the original code of Hywel to have been, but the material has been amplified and supplemented. The special references to South-West Wales (I. ii. 6; II. xxiv.; II. xxxi. 9) quite justify the title which has been bestowed upon it of the Dimetian Code.

The so-called "Gwentian" Code is found in a group of MSS. of which the oldest are *U.* (Pen. MS. 37) and V. (Harl. MS. 4353), assigned by Dr. Evans to the end of the thirteenth century. It may be inferred from *U.* that the compilers of the code were one Morgeneu and his son Cyfnerth, who wrought the old law of Hywel into a version resembling the Dimetian Code, but shorter and more concise. According to i. 218, Iorwerth ap Madog used, among other sources, "the book of Cyfnerth ap Morgeneu," and this is confirmed by the reference in Ven. I. xvi. 8 (end), introduced by "rey adeueyt" (some maintain), to a rule which is peculiar to the Gwentian Code (see Gw. I. xvi. 21). The code is therefore older than 1200, but cannot, notwithstanding what is said in the late MS. S. (i. 340) of "Morgeneu ynat" and his son "Kyfnerth," be pushed back as far as the age of Hywel himself, for "yn oes Hywel Dda" was already, when it was drawn up, a distant past (I. xxxv. 19). As to its local connections, there is nothing to connect it with Gwent, where indeed Welsh rule came to an end before 1100; I. ii. 3 points rather to Deheubarth.

Three Latin versions of the laws are printed in the second volume of Aneurin Owen's edition. The first (Lat. A.) is taken from Pen. MS. 28, which is assigned by Dr. Evans to 1175-1200, and is, therefore, older than any Welsh text. If one may judge from the inclusion in it of the section (II. xviii.) on the "Bishop-houses" of Dyfed (with the unauthorised addition to the list of Llawhaden), it is a Dimetian MS. and perhaps belonged to a bishop of St. David's. The second Lat. B.) is from Br. Mus. MS. Vespasian E. XI. of the beginning of the four

CHAP. X.

teenth century; it is also distinctly Dimetian (*cf.* II. xlii. lv. lvi.), but contains material drawn from various sources. The third (Lat. C.) is also from a British Museum MS., Harl. 1796, and is ascribed to the thirteenth century. Though in no way connected with the Venedotian Code, it is a Venedotian MS., as shown by the reference to the supremacy of the king of Aberffraw (I. v.), while the distinction drawn (p. 906) between the cattle of "Mon" and those from "vltra Menei" is evidence of an Anglesey origin.

It has been maintained that the law of Hywel was originally written in Latin and that the Welsh codes are therefore translations, in so far as they draw upon a common stock. In the absence of direct evidence, it is difficult to say what happened at Ty Gwyn ar Daf, but, so far as the extant Latin texts are concerned, they may safely be ranked as adaptations for a special purpose from Welsh originals. Not only single words, but whole clauses and sentences are left untranslated (see Lat. A. II. ii. 22; xi. 9; Lat. B. I. xxvi. 2; II. xx. 10; Lat. C. xiii. 9); technical terms are differently rendered in the three texts—thus, for penteulu we have "penteylu" in the first, "princeps militie" in the second, and "paterfamilias" in the third; while such various renderings as the following are inconsistent with the notion that there was current in Wales a primitive Latin text as old as the time of Hywel:—

Lat. A. II. i. 1. Animalium que usui hominum sunt necessaria.
Lat. B. I. ix. 29. Animalium que necessaria sunt ad opus hominum.
Lat. C. xiv. 7. Animalium quae necessaria sunt ad usus humanos.

The versions would appear to have been made for the benefit of ecclesiastical landowners and judges who did not know Welsh. Lat. B. II. lv. 1, for instance, explains ("solent enim Wallenses") the Welsh system of counting "galanas" scores; Lat. C. i. 1 adds to the usual statement that the laws of the court have the first place the pious qualification, "secundum seculum". Lat. B. II. xlix. (De Variis Iniuriis) embodies a number of ecclesiastical canons, ancient but having no reference to the forms of Welsh law (H. and St. i. 127).

It thus becomes clear that no MS. in Welsh or Latin preserves for us the original code of Hywel. The Latin, no less than the Welsh, MSS. speak of the time of the great legislator as a bygone age (Lat. A. II. xxiv. 32; xlii. 2; Lat. B. I. xiii. 31; II. xi. 4). The nearest approach to evidence of what was contained in the first law-book is the consensus of all codes and versions, and there is, in point of fact, so much in common between them as to make this criterion not unserviceable.

END OF VOL. I.

ABERDEEN THE UNIVERSITY PRESS